DATE DUE

In the
Public Domain

In the Public Domain

Presidents and the
Challenges of Public Leadership

Edited by

Lori Cox Han
and
Diane J. Heith

State University of New York Press

Published by
State University of New York Press, Albany

© 2005 State University of New York

All rights reserved

Printed in the United States of America

No part of this book may be used or reproduced in any manner whatsoever without written permission. No part of this book may be stored in a retrieval system or transmitted in any form or by any means including electronic, electrostatic, magnetic tape, mechanical, photocopying, recording, or otherwise without the prior permission in writing of the publisher.

For information, address State University of New York Press,
194 Washington Avenue, Suite 305, Albany, NY 12210-2384

Production by Michael Haggett
Marketing by Michael Campochiaro

Library of Congress Cataloging-in-Publication Data

In the public domain : presidents and the challenges of public leadership / edited by Lori Cox Han and Diane J. Heith.
 p. cm. — (SUNY series on the presidency)
 Includes bibliographical references and index.
 ISBN 0-7914-6575-6 (hardcover : alk. paper)
 1. Presidents—United States—Public opinion. 2. Political leadership—United States. 3. Political planning—United States. 4. Executive power—United States. I. Han, Lori Cox. II. Heith, Diane J. III. Title. IV. Series: SUNY series in the presidency.

JK516.I485 2006
973.92—dc22

2005009491

To our husbands,
Tom Han
and
Steve Kline

Contents

Preface	ix
1 Introduction: The President and the Public Revisited *Doris A. Graber*	1

PART I
THE CHALLENGE OF PERCEPTION

2 Celebrity in Chief: The President As a Pop Culture Icon *Michael A. Genovese*	13
3 Party Labels in Presidential Acceptance Addresses: 1948–2000 *Sharon E. Jarvis and Emily Balanoff Jones*	29
4 What Gets Covered? How Media Coverage of Elite Debate Drives the Rally-'Round-the-Flag Phenomenon: 1979–1998 *Matthew A. Baum and Tim Groeling*	49

PART II
THE CHALLENGE OF POLICY MANAGEMENT

5 The White House Public Opinion Apparatus Meets the Anti-Polling President *Diane J. Heith*	75

6 Presidential Leverage and the Presidential Agenda: 1967–1996   89
   Daniel E. Ponder

7 Second-Term Presidents: Free Birds or Lame Ducks?   113
   William Cunion

PART III
THE CHALLENGE OF PRESENTATION

8 Presidential Ideology and the Public Mood: 1956–1994   141
   Jeffrey E. Cohen and John A. Hamman

9 The Rose Garden Strategy Revisited: How Presidents Use Public Activities   163
   Lori Cox Han

10 Doing Diversity across the Partisan Divide: George H. W. Bush, Bill Clinton, and the American National Identity   179
   Mary E. Stuckey

11 A President Transformed: Bush's Pre- and Post-September 11 Rhetoric and Image   207
   Jeremy D. Mayer and Mark J. Rozell

PART IV
THE CHALLENGE AFTER THE WHITE HOUSE

12 Life after the White House: The Public Post-Presidency and the Development of Presidential Legacies   227
   Lori Cox Han and Matthew J. Krov

13 Not Going Public: George W. Bush and the Presidential Records Act   255
   Nancy Kassop

Contributors   279

Index   283

Preface

The publication of *The President and the Public* in 1982, a volume edited by Doris A. Graber, sought to examine the linkages between the president and the American public. This book represented an important change that was occurring in the study of the American presidency, as the volume marked one of the earliest attempts among both presidency and political communication scholars to better understand the impact of the mass media and public opinion polling on presidential governance and leadership. According to Graber's preface, the idea behind the book began in the fall of 1980 as the nation prepared for the presidential election when American voters would choose between Jimmy Carter and Ronald Reagan. With an "election hinging on factors of confidence rather than specific issues or party allegiance . . . many professional president-watchers put a spotlight on various aspects of that relationship." The major issues covered within the chapters of the book included the presidential image, media portrayals of the president, the electoral connection, and appraisals of presidential performance. As Graber stated, the topics were interrelated, since "relations between the president and the public are much like a seamless web. One area merges into the other, and there is substantial overlap."[1]

Prior to the early 1980s, few scholars seemed interested in either a systematic or theoretical understanding of the public aspects of the American presidency. With the exception of Elmer Cornwell's *Presidential Leadership of Public Opinion* (1965), few studies existed that looked explicitly at the relationship between the president and the public—this during a time of expanding and changing technological capabilities that seemed to greatly impact both the governing and electoral processes. Whether the election of Ronald "The Great Communicator" Reagan in 1980 was a catalyst for creating scholarly interest in the public aspects of presidential leadership or simply a coincidence may never be known. Nevertheless, the Reagan years witnessed the publication of several groundbreaking and seminal works on presidents and the press, presidents and public opinion, the rhetorical aspects of the presidency, and how those areas were impacting presidential leadership and performance. Most notably, those works included Michael Grossman's and Martha Joynt Kumar's *Portraying the President: The White House and the News Media* (1981), David L. Paletz's and Robert Entman's *Media Power Politics* (1981), George C. Edwards's *The Public Presidency* (1983), Theodore Lowi's *The Personal President* (1985), Sam Kernell's *Going Public* (1986), and Jeffrey Tulis's *The Rhetorical Presidency* (1987).

Graber's *The President and the Public* also belongs on the aforementioned list, as it represented the coming together of various presidential scholars interested in asking timely questions about the changing relationship between presidents and the public due to the growing influence of television and the increased reliance on public opinion (both inside and outside the White House). In reviews of the book, other scholars agreed that the subject matter dealing with the linkage between presidents and the public was necessary to further advance the understanding of presidential leadership in the latter years of the twentieth century and recognized the value of not only the substantive findings that the essays provided but the many important questions that were raised on the topic for further study. According to Thomas Cronin, "Teachers and researchers will learn from these research essays. They will especially learn how much remains to be studied if we are more rigorously to comprehend the interaction of presidential leadership and American citizens."[2] Similarly, Alana Northrop commended the book for addressing the issues of public perceptions of presidents as portrayed in public opinion polls, as well as the issue of media influence in elections and presidential governance. She concluded by recommending the book for anyone interested in understanding important issues "raised by recent research on the president and the public."[3]

For several years, we have considered putting together an edited volume that would serve as an update to the Graber book. The idea was born soon after we first met as graduate students at a conference honoring Richard Neustadt at Columbia University in 1996. The purpose of such an endeavor would be to once again bring together several essays by scholars who have focused their research on these same linkages between the president and the public to examine how much progress has been made in our understanding of these key issues in the past two decades. This edited volume does just that, and it includes timely research by some colleagues who share our intellectual curiosity about the many aspects of the public presidency. We also are honored to include the introductory essay by Doris Graber that links the issues within her edited volume, published more than two decades ago, to the current state of scholarship on the relationship between the president and the public.

Following Graber's introduction, the book is broken into four distinct categories that consider the presidential challenges of public leadership. Part I,

The Challenge of Perception, considers external factors that challenge public leadership in the areas of presidential image, party politics, and news media coverage. Because of fictional portrayals in the mass media, American presidents are now viewed as cultural icons—an image with which real-life presidents must compete in the media-saturated political environment (Genovese). Presidents must also respond to partisan pressures once elected—a candidate-centered approach during the presidential primaries must be replaced by a party-centered approach for the nominee and eventual victor of the presidential campaign, as these roles dictate representing the party as a whole (Jarvis and Jones). Presidents also must be mindful of news media coverage, as the tone of coverage of a particular policy can shift public opinion on a White House initiative, particularly during wartime (Baum and Groeling). Part II, *The Challenge of Policy Management*, addresses how presidents use public leadership to pursue their policy goals and objectives. They rely on public opinion polling but do not want to appear overreliant, regarding policy decisions (Heith). Presidents also must rely on informal powers of the public presidency as leverage in achieving their policy goals (Ponder), and second-term, lame duck presidents face unique challenges in pushing their legislative agendas, despite recent electoral success (Cunion).

Part III, *The Challenge of Presentation*, considers the importance of public opinion, rhetorical strategies, and public activities. Presidents do not want to stray too far from established public opinion on certain policy issues (Cohen and Hamman). And due to the television age, presidents are now expected to keep up a regular schedule of public activities (Han) and must rely on the news media, particularly television, to aid in their public leadership efforts (Mayer and Rozell). Presidents also face many challenges in recognizing and acknowledging the diversity of the American public, whether on a national level or within specific groups, through their rhetorical efforts, and many recent presidents have failed at this task (Stuckey). Mastering these areas of public leadership, however, has proved difficult for many recent occupants of the White House. Part IV, *The Challenge after the White House*, looks at the public concerns of former presidents—how news media coverage impacts the development of presidential legacies (Han and Krov) and recent developments involving the Presidential Records Act and access to documents in presidential libraries (Kassop).

We would like to thank all of the contributors to this volume for their willingness to share their time and expertise in the creation of this book. We also would like to thank John Kenneth White and Michael Rinella for their interest and enthusiasm for this project when it was merely a list of potential contributors and chapters. A special thank you as well goes to Mark Rozell and Robert Spitzer for their suggestions and advice along the way. And finally, we offer our deepest gratitude to our families for their never-ending support and encouragement.

NOTES

1. Doris A. Graber, Preface to *The President and the Public* (Philadelphia: Institute for the Study of Human Issues, 1982), v–vii.

2. Thomas E. Cronin, Review of "The President and the Public," ed. Doris A. Graber, *The Journal of Politics* 46:2 (May 1984): 605–607.

3. Alana Northrop, Review of "The President and the Public," ed. Doris A. Graber, *The American Political Science Review* 78:1 (March 1984): 224–25.

1

Introduction

The President and the Public Revisited

Doris A. Graber

The outcome of presidential election campaigns often depends on the rapport that candidates can establish between themselves and their publics. Electoral success may hinge on the winner's ability to convince prospective voters that he or she is the best choice to solve the country's major problems. Accordingly, scholars of presidential elections and practicing politicians often focus their attention on the strategies that candidates use to persuade the public that they are politically astute, trustworthy, empathetic, and "presidential," and that they espouse solid political programs that they will and can execute. Analysts scrutinize what candidates told their audiences and how they framed their appeals. They want to know what channels they used to communicate their messages to the public and how the public responded. Such matters have always intrigued students of American government, although they have not been the main focus of scholarly attention.

The desire to provide richer insights into the interactions between Americans and their presidents during elections but also during other phases of the president's term led to the 1982 publication of a volume of essays titled *The President and the Public*.[1] The rationale for the book was the inadequacy of readily available scholarly information about a broad array of issues relating to communication between the chief executive and average Americans, despite general acknowledgment that the issues deserved attention. Accordingly, the volume thrust the limelight on the public's expectations about the presidency, people's perceptions about the president's style and performance in office, and media portrayals of the presidency, along with neglected aspects of the electoral connection.

Why is linkage between the president and the public sufficiently important to devote an entire book to it? There are many reasons. Foremost is the fact that this linkage is a crucial element of democratic governance. Democracy, by definition, means government by the people. In large societies, where the duties of governing have to be delegated to representatives of the electorate, communication is necessary between the principals and their agents. Within the modern American system, that means the president at the national level.

Most Americans consider the president the public's chief national representative. He or she is the only public official elected to serve the entire nation rather than territorially limited constituencies. The framers of the Constitution had planned otherwise. They thought that legislators would be viewed as the chief representatives of the public. They did not expect that the president would become the single most powerful actor in the government, taking a leading role in generating and executing domestic and foreign policies. The president's prominence in these governmental activities now makes him the key official to whom publics turn when they are concerned about political developments and public policies.

Indications that the leader of the country keeps in touch with the nation are important to make people feel that the government belongs to them, even when linkage amounts to little more than sporadic, often purely symbolic, contacts. Signs that the president enjoys public approval for his actions lend them the aura of procedural correctness that makes them acceptable. They are the tokens that signify legitimacy.

This is why presidents often "go public" to pass their legislative agenda. They appeal for demonstrations of public support to show that large constituencies throughout the nation support their plans. Congress often yields to such demonstrations of popular support, partly because defiance of the people's will creates unfavorable images that Congress members prefer to avoid, and partly out of fear that constituents will deny their votes to legislators who oppose and obstruct a president backed by the public.[2] Like members of Congress, journalists are loath to anger their audiences. Going public may therefore have the additional benefit of short-circuiting adverse media criticism of the president's proposals.

Even if presidents are disinclined to continuously stay in touch with the public, political necessities tend to force them to communicate with their national constituencies. The news media cover the presidency far more amply than other branches of government. That focuses public attention on the president, forcing him to communicate with the public to create and maintain an image that reassures people that the government is in capable hands.

Presidential scholar Richard Neustadt calls the president's ability to use the White House as a bully pulpit to address and persuade nationwide audiences his main political weapon.[3] Presidents need popular support to govern. They must be able to rally the public when major policies, such as conserving energy or going to war, require willing cooperation from large numbers of people. The symbolic significance of public support makes it important even when policies do not require direct public action. If presidential programs face major congressional opposition, then public speeches allow the chief executive to focus public attention on the issues in question and gather public support for his stands. Presidential appeals for support are likely to be effective, especially if the president is popular. It also helps that the public pays more attention to news by and about the president than to news about other politicians.

Of course, the most pressing reason for linkage is the fact that presidents depend on the vote of the national electorate for their initial election to office and for reelection to a second term. Campaigning for office necessitates communicating effectively with the publics whose votes the president seeks. Winning election to a first term requires presidential candidates to persuade voters that they are a good choice; for reelection, they must convince their constituents that they have performed well.

Is it useful to revisit issues pertaining to the interactions of presidents and their publics and to put together a sequel to the earlier volume? I believe it is. These linkages remain extraordinarily important and are an ever-present challenge for the president as well as the public. I am therefore delighted that two keen analysts of the presidency—Lori Cox Han and Diane J. Heith—have assembled a collection of essays that sheds fresh light on linkage issues and problems as they present themselves at the start of the twenty-first century.

Specifically, it is important to cover changes in the linkage relationship brought about by the passage of time. The political climate has changed substantially in the intervening decades, and major new information technologies have transformed political communication. Fireside radio chats by Franklin D. Roosevelt differ in impact from John F. Kennedy's more casually scripted televised news conferences that bear no resemblance to George W. Bush's blogs. It also is important to broaden and deepen the study of the interface between presidents and their publics. Topics absent from the first volume need to be added, issues analyzed need to be explored in greater depth and with more sophisticated methods, and entirely new developments need to be acknowledged.

Furthermore, to systematically study the political behavior of American presidents and their publics requires time to allow for comparisons of an array of presidents. Presidential studies have always been plagued by the fact that there were only a few presidents available for comparison in a particular era. If one takes 1960 as the start of the television era of political communication, then only five presidents were available for comparison in 1980, including John F. Kennedy and Gerald Ford, whose terms were abbreviated. By 2004, that meager number had nearly doubled.

The current volume makes major contributions to filling gaps in the story about the president's image and the public's reactions. Like the earlier volume's authors, the current contributors devote considerable time to discussing why and in what ways linkage is important. But they devote more attention to developing and testing specific hypotheses, and they use a broader array of quantitative and qualitative methods. These more intensive approaches produce more precise findings than before, though much room remains for further refinement.

Michael Genovese's chapter on the president as a pop culture icon is one of many excellent examples of the focus on recent developments. The mere fact of honing in on entertainment offerings as an important form of political communication is innovative and still unduly rare. Depicting the president as a pop culture icon is even rarer because it documents a sea change in the treatment of presidents in films. Fawning hero worship, as in films about former presidents Abraham Lincoln, Franklin D. Roosevelt, and John F. Kennedy, has given way to often sneering cynicism, as in films about Richard Nixon. Former presidents who appear in films and videos are no longer the revered leaders of the nation, blessed with super-human virtues and devoid of most major human failings. They have been transformed into ordinary human beings, warts and all, and some of the warts, such as corruption, dishonesty, and shamelessly self-seeking behaviors, are large, inviting scathing condemnation or merciless ridicule.

Changing the character of presidential images may have profound consequences. In this case, the new images may have contributed to the precipitous decline in trust in government that surfaced during the Nixon administration's Watergate scandal. The decline has persisted since then, although trust has increased periodically, as during the Reagan administration and the country's involvement in hostilities with Iraq.

Genovese's study also is novel in employing an exceptionally broad comparative approach that ranges across the entire history of presidential portrayals in films. In the process, Genovese raises important questions about the likely impact of films and video presentations on images of the person occupying the presidential office. There seems to be close correspondence between the character qualities and the skills attributed to nonfictional and fictional presidents. The favorability of their images rises and falls together as art imitates life, and vice versa.

Persistent Past Problems

Political life is a seamless web in which patterns of the past persist side by side with patterns of the present and harbingers of the future. Clean breaks are rare. So it is with relations between presidents and their publics. They are a blend of perennial and new issues that embeds the seeds of the future. Many of the situations that defied accurate measurement in 1980 still do so. For example, contributors to the earlier volume used public opinion polls and surveys to discern how Americans view their president and what they like or dislike about him. Although polling methods have improved since the 1980s, poll results remain problematic as accurate measures of the views of various publics.

Most detrimentally, in polls and surveys researchers still decide which questions to ask and how to frame them. Their choices determine the subject matter around which respondents' answers revolve and the criteria by which the issues in question will be appraised. For instance, when pollsters assess the public's confidence in the president by asking how certain they are that the president can lower health care costs or ensure air travel safety, it matters that these two problems were raised. Reported confidence levels might be higher or lower if the poll questions revolved around unemployment or global warming. It also matters which word choices the poll offers. Respondents may be willing to call the president's achievements "very good" if that is the highest rating used in the poll but may balk at choosing the top spot if it is labeled "outstanding" or "excellent."

It remains difficult to judge the dimensions of the opinions reported by polls. Pollsters rarely ask how strongly people feel about the matters at hand, or why they feel the way they do. They hardly ever inquire about changes in contingencies that might alter opinions. When pollsters ask for evaluations of a president's job performance, it is generally unclear which criteria the respondents used to make their judgments. In fact, there are indications that responses may be largely tied to overall political conditions. When times are good, or when presidents are involved in major, seemingly successful foreign ventures, they often receive favorable evaluations, irrespective of the contributions they have made to these conditions. When situations turn sour, presidents frequently suffer the blame, even when the turn of events was completely beyond their control. A disastrous, worldwide economic downturn became "Hoover's depression," while a spectacular economic boom was credited to lucky incumbent Bill Clinton. If ratings of presidential performance are largely context dependent, then comparisons among presidents continue to be problematic.

The concluding section of the earlier book raises as yet unresolved perennial questions about the capacity of average Americans to judge presidential performance accurately, given the complexity of modern American politics. It remains unclear and debatable whether they get enough sound political information from the news media to meld it into meaningful images about what the president is doing or might be doing under the prevailing circumstances. If the information base for judgments is seriously flawed or underused, then are the heuristics that people use to facilitate judgments sufficient to reach sound conclusions? For example, is there enough information so that citizens can judge the quality of the president's performance by monitoring the views of trusted leaders or brief reports about unemployment fluctuations?

Good communication channels between presidents and their publics remain a prerequisite for satisfactory linkage. In the twenty-first century, as in the waning years of the twentieth century, adequacy of communication channels remains a major problem, particularly for upward message flows from various publics to the president. Presidents attempt to gauge public opinions through watching general public opinion polls and special polls run by the executive branch. But the information extracted from polls is marred by the weaknesses outlined earlier. Direct messages from various publics via petitions and letters and now e-mail and other Web-based messages are tools used almost exclusively by elites. Even then, most messages intended for the president miss their target because the human capacity to listen and absorb is out of synch with the overabundance of information seeking a hearing. When millions of e-mails arrive at the White House each year, it is not surprising that only a tiny proportion will ever come to the president's attention.

While downward messages fare better than upward ones, data remain sparse about the quality and truthfulness of presidential messages and their effects on average people and various elites. The problem is confounded by the fact that journalists paraphrase most presidential pronouncements rather than allowing people to hear what the president said and extract their own meanings. Frames used in news reports often distort or destroy what the president meant to convey. Withdrawal from a humanitarian intervention that the president depicts as a courageous decision to serve American interests, for instance, may be transformed by hostile news media accounts into an act of cowardice and national shame. Depending on the framing, the action redounds to the president's credit or discredit.

Media framing tends to prime media consumers' memories so that they judge presidential messages against the backdrop of the primed situation. For example, when news consumers were primed with visions of the disastrous Vietnam War by stories that compared it to Operation Iraqi Freedom, they were likely to associate the operation with failures in Vietnam, counteracting the president's optimistic predictions. In fact, peoples' images of the president depend less on what he says or actually does and more on how media elites judge him in news stories transmitted to members of the public. Matthew Baum and Tim Groeling provide excellent illustrations of the impact of framing in this volume by demonstrating that the tenor of media coverage shaped the rally phenomenon in the two recent wars that pitted the United States against Iraq.

The New Ball Game

Reading the earlier work and its current sequel makes it clear that many fresh winds are blowing when it comes to communications between presidents and their publics. Again, as with problems carried over from the past, I shall sample only a few. One major change since the Nixon years concerns the mood of the country. Political elites, including journalists as well as the public, have become far more negative in their evaluations of government, including the presidency. Interactive talk shows, cable television, and the Internet provide many new outlets for voicing opposition to the president. Of course, these venues also provide presidents with many more opportunities to win supporters. But supportive messages have always carried less weight than attacks.

The public's increased skepticism about political life has had important consequences. On the good side, public servants now are viewed in a more realistic light as human beings with flaws as well as virtues. That realization clears the air for fruitful communication, because it whittles down expectations to levels that are achievable. Increased skepticism is bad if the pendulum swings too far and all public officials become suspect. That seems to be happening as more and more people take Lord Acton's dictum that power corrupts as an infallible prediction rather than as a statement of possibilities. Skepticism turned into cynicism becomes an insurmountable barrier to good communication between presidents and their publics. Disillusionment with public officials, especially presidents, also is harmful because it may keep the president from serving as a symbol of reassurance in times of crisis. As Murray Edelman has pointed out, a frightened public takes comfort in times of crisis in the thought that the person at the helm of state is fully capable of coping with looming calamities.[4] That reassurance keeps political life on a more even keel.

Interestingly, while there has been an increase in partisanship and a decrease in civility in the current climate of combative politics, there has actually been a decline in emphasizing partisan alignments during elections. Presidents now try to appeal to publics across party lines, as Sharon Jarvis and Emily Balanoff Jones document in this volume by examining party labels used in presidential acceptance speeches from 1948 to 2000. Acceptance speeches may not be the best barometer of reduction of partisan mentions because presidents want to be seen as unifiers at the start of their term. However, numerous other developments suggest that the phenomenon may indeed be pervasive because it reflects changing political conditions. The growing numbers of television stations along with Web sites allow candidates to reach out to the public and to raise money for their campaigns without help from their party. Minimal assistance from the party leaves presidents less beholden to it and free to ignore their party in their public discourse.

Technological developments have produced some of the greatest changes in the interrelation between presidents and their publics. The swiftness and ease of air travel allows presidents to personally visit widely scattered locations at home and abroad without major disruptions of their normal schedule. Cable television and the Internet have markedly changed election and reelection strategies. Continuous campaigns have become a permanent feature of the political scene. The president appears on television screens in the nation's living rooms on a daily basis, often morning, noon, and night. In fact, presidents almost seem to govern more by appearance than by accomplishment. In the image game, adept use of photo opportunities may count more than words, and censoring disturbing pictures may avoid a crisis.

Web sites give presidents opportunities for exposure on their own terms rather than being at the mercy of journalists beyond their control. On the negative side, Web sites carrying messages hostile to the president have multiplied as well. Presidential messages have benefited from employing well-trained communication and public relations experts. Since the 1980s, the art of spinning the news has progressed greatly, largely due to advanced social science research. There is more emphasis on political symbolism and on a quick rebuttal of negative publicity.

New technologies, especially the Internet and cable television, like CNN 'round-the-clock news programs, also have shrunk the time available for presidents to analyze situations, assess public opinions, and develop responses accordingly. When hasty decision making abounds, often based on incomplete information, public deliberations about the wisdom of policies are reduced to Monday morning quarterbacking laments.

Overall, relationships with the press have become more routine. However, the professionalization of message construction and dissemination has not abated critics' complaints that too much of the news is primarily infotainment and that too many presidential messages are intentionally vague or even deceptive to protect the president's image. Nonetheless, most people claim to feel moderately well informed and able to perform essential civic functions such as voting intelligently and participating in political discussions.[5] Continuous campaigns have raised the problem of overexposure of the president, which may breed inattention, boredom, and even contempt. The fears of scholars such as Neil Postman, that overexposure and humanization of the president will trivialize the presidency, may be well grounded.[6]

SOME UNFINISHED BUSINESS

The linkage problem that concerns me most is the inequality of access to linkage. It is often mentioned only in passing, and little has been done to assess its full impact. Communicating with top officials and gaining a hearing is primarily a right enjoyed by socioeconomically privileged members of society. The least privileged are largely left out. This inequality defies eradication, because it springs from a system where most opportunities are open to everyone, but the ability and motivation to seize them is greatly enhanced by upper-class status. The lack of socioeconomic advantages during childhood and adolescence becomes a major handicap to success in life.

Election systems, including primaries and the Electoral College procedure, further increase inequalities. Single-district election arrangements that are almost universal in the United States drown out the voices of millions of members of losing parties. Low voter turnouts, especially by socioeconomically disadvantaged groups, explain why most presidents usually are the choice of only one-fourth to one-third of the electorate. To make matters worse, the Electoral College procedure allows a candidate to become president despite losing the popular vote. That raises serious questions about whether citizens' voices are receiving equal consideration so that majority rule prevails in the end. The Electoral College procedure gives populations in smaller states more political influence than their fellow citizens in larger states, increasing the advantaged positions they already enjoy because the Senate represents states equally, irrespective of population size.

Another form of distortion of communication between presidents and their publics comes from presidential secrecy. As perennial leaks and periodic investigations make clear, presidents conceal much information or spin it to the point of distortion for political reasons unrelated to national security concerns. The executive branch strives mightily to control information by limiting the release of political data. That leaves the public in the dark about many important matters that it needs to know to reach sound political judgments.

Assessments of the president's success in leading public opinion are plagued by unrealistic expectations and faulty assumptions. Pundits and even scholars routinely characterize presidents as weak, unpopular persuaders if they fail to gain approval from large majorities of Americans. That ignores the fact that people have well-formed opinions on many issues that run counter to those of the president. Once people have made up their minds, it is difficult to change them. Success in persuasion should therefore be assessed in terms of the numbers of people who were still receptive to the president's arguments. Except for totally new issues about which the public knows little and partisan divides that have not yet emerged, the numbers of people open to persuasion usually are quite small.

The ability of political leaders to persuade their constituents is limited, at best. Presidents live within the nexus of their historical periods, which may or may not provide opportunities for opinion leadership. Moreover, leaders cannot be too far ahead of the public. It may require a substantial period of time to overcome culturally ingrained attitudes, such as race and gender prejudices or the reluctance to become embroiled in military activities in distant parts of the world. Even a superb orator such as President Franklin D. Roosevelt knew that he could not easily overcome the American public's reluctance to enter the Second World War. Therefore, he proceeded gradually from small breaches of American neutrality to increasingly massive interventions in the conflict.

Finally, it remains an unresolved philosophical question whether linkage encourages pandering. According to the dictionary, pandering involves seeking benefits for oneself by catering to the weaknesses and vanities of others.

Phrased in political terms, should leaders take their cues from the public and try to accommodate public wishes? Should they shun policies that are likely to be unpopular, even when they are convinced that the policies are sound, though unlikely to win public approval? Such questions deserve more attention, because pandering is common and new communication technologies make pandering increasingly easy and effective.

In sum, establishing sound relationships between presidents and average Americans remains as challenging as ever. *In the Public Domain: Presidents and the Challenges of Public Leadership* presents important analyses of the dynamics of linkage interactions. It updates many of the findings in the earlier volume and adds much that is new and important. But it definitely is not the last word. It still leaves many important areas, such as linkage inequalities, untouched, and many of its final findings will become merely interim statements as time marches on. The ultimate satisfaction for its talented contributors will be to see their work spark yet another volume a few decades hence. If that volume lives up to the quality of the current one, then it will be an important contribution to understanding crucial facets of the American presidency.

NOTES

1. Doris A. Graber, *The President and the Public* (Philadelphia: Institute for the Study of Human Issues, 1982).

2. Samuel Kernell, *Going Public: New Strategies of Presidential Leadership*, 3rd ed. (Washington, D.C.: CQ Press, 1997).

3. Richard Neustadt, *Presidential Power and Modern Presidents: The Politics of Leadership from Roosevelt to Reagan* (New York: Macmillan, 1990).

4. Murray Edelman, *The Symbolic Uses of Politics* (Urbana: University of Illinois Press, 1964).

5. Pew Research Center for the People and the Press, "Attitudes toward the News: Internet Sapping Broadcast News Audience," http://people-press.org (accessed June 11, 2000).

6 Neil Postman, *Amusing Ourselves to Death* (New York: Viking Penguin, 1984).

I

The Challenge of Perception

For all modern presidents during the television age of politics, image matters. Presidents must not only be aware of their image as a leader but must also pay attention to public opinion and partisan concerns as the head of their party. The three chapters in Part I address some of the specific challenges that presidents face in connecting with the American public and the presidential image as portrayed through the mass media.

As presidents face the challenge of appearing in public, the importance of their image as a leader among the American public cannot be ignored. Moreover, due to the mass media's influence over the political environment, both the news and entertainment spheres influence the president's image. While in office, the president must transmit his image and message via the mass media, which are outside of his range of influence through news coverage, books, movies, and television programs. As Michael A. Genovese shows in "Celebrity in Chief: The President As a Pop Culture Icon," the portrayal of the president can range from one extreme (an adored father figure) to the other (an evil and unscrupulous politician). The combination of attention in both the news media and popular culture results in a loss of control over the presidential image. The president's rise to the status of an icon in popular culture adds another dimension to the office and to presidential leadership. Genovese argues that the challenge for the actual, rather than virtual, president is how to use the current image rather than be used by it. The current iconic presidency emerges out of the realities of Vietnam and Watergate, as well as the dramatic portrayals of those cataclysmic political events. The result is a significant challenge to any effort at public leadership, as the president must always confront both realities.

Even before they are elected to the White House, presidential candidates learn quickly the importance of connecting with the public. Prior to achieving their party's nomination, candidates are attentive and respond to public opinion polls and trips to the voting booth during the frenzied primary season. Candidates who do not personally appeal or stake out individually identifiable issue positions do not survive long in the race for the nomination. Thus by the time of the nomination, candidates are well schooled in using the rhetoric of personal public appeals—in other words, in producing candidate-centered behavior. However, with the nomination comes the attachment of the party label, and party identification remains the strongest influence on voting behavior, regardless of its decline in recent years. The challenge for the presidential nominee is one that continues for the victor: how to incorporate the party rhetoric with candidate (or presidency-) -centered behavior. In "Party Labels in Presidential Acceptance Addresses: 1948–2000," Sharon E. Jarvis and Emily Balanoff Jones find that candidates tend to use party labels positively, with negative party critiques reserved for adversaries. The party label, however, appears more empowering for elites than for the public at large, due likely to the reluctance of candidates to pepper their rhetoric with references to the party and party ideology.

Finally, any presidential effort to garner public support for a person, program, or policy requires that the public receive knowledge of the preferred presidential option or outcome. Since the media serve as the means for transmission, the mode of presidential coverage matters for presidential outcomes. The usual challenge then is for the president to deal with the quality of the news coverage and how it influences attitudes and opinions. During wartime, public opinion generally supports the president in what scholars call a "rally 'round the flag." The phenomenon, a rise in support for the president and military efforts abroad, is significant, because it often mitigates criticism of presidential military efforts. Matthew A. Baum and Tim Groeling find in "What Gets Covered? How Media Coverage of Elite Debate Drives the Rally-'Round-the Flag Phenomenon: 1979–1998" that the magnitude of a presidential rally is contingent upon media presentation of elite criticism, in particular, a wave of negative media coverage is increasingly shortening rallies. Baum and Groeling find a potentially devastating challenge to presidential leadership, as congressional criticism combines with media preference for conflict to eliminate or limit the power of public support for the president.

2

Celebrity in Chief

The President As a Pop Culture Icon

Michael A. Genovese

Take One: The president's plane has been hijacked with the president aboard, but our heroic president (played by Harrison Ford), super-macho hero that he is, uses brains and brawn to single-handedly foil the bad guys and save the day in *Air Force One*.

Take Two: Aliens have invaded, but our president (Bill Pullman) as star fighter takes to the skies and pilots a plane that takes on these evil invaders and saves the day in *Independence Day*.

Take Three: Just prior to the election, the president has been caught in a sex scandal with an underage girl. What to do? Create a phony war, of course, a war pageant to distract the public—and so it goes in *Wag the Dog*.

Take Four: The president is utterly mad! He walks around the White House talking to the portraits of former presidents. Even the secretary of defense, wary of the mental state of the president (played by Anthony Hopkins), orders the military not to obey orders from the commander in chief in *Nixon*.

The president as hero and villain—ah, but it was not always so. Initially, presidents were portrayed in commercial films with reverence. Until the fallout from Vietnam, Watergate, the Iran-Contra scandal, and the Clinton sex scandal, Hollywood tended toward fawning hero worship in its cinematic treatment of presidents—real or fictional. But in the past quarter century, the presidential film image has gone through a roller coaster ride of high worship and object scorn. What a ride![1]

PORTRAYING THE PRESIDENT ON FILM

Among the changes in film coverage in the past two decades is the increased use of the American president as a symbol, character, and key component in a wide variety of films. The presidency is a potent symbol of American politics and nationhood and has become an attractive focal point in countless movies. The president, once treated in popular art with reverence, has been transformed from a national icon to a pop idol, with all of the negatives of familiarity that come with pop star status.[2]

In a nation with no official religion or sacred text and few unifying national symbols, the president has been converted into a high priest and symbolic representative. Our monuments to presidents tower over the Washington, D.C., landscape. We have Mount Rushmore to honor our presidents, and we erect grand palaces in their names in the form of presidential libraries, the modern cathedrals of presidential worship. If one goes to Disney World in Orlando, Florida, one can visit the Hall of Presidents. We have constructed the paraphernalia of quasireligious worship to the men who serve as presidents. The presidency has become more than a political or constitutional institution. It is the focus of emotions, hopes, and aspirations.[3] Since the Vietnam conflict, the presidency has been the focal point for complex and contradictory attachments and emotions. As such, the good, the bad, and the ugly of the American presidency have become the focus of numerous films.

In some ways, technology has rewritten the U.S. Constitution. Television has refocused public attention away from the separation of powers and has given the presidency center stage. This also is true with commercial films. As the focal point of our attention, the impression created is one in which the presidency appears more powerful and important than the Constitution intended. The president gets so much more television coverage than Congress that the electorate begins to believe that the president is the center of the political universe. Yet constitutionally, the president must share power with a Congress that visually is more obscured but politically more powerful than is at first obvious.

The creation of this electronic throne raises public expectations of the president's powers; the resulting demands placed upon the president become unrealistic. When the president fails to meet these high expectations, disappointment sets in: the president often finds himself in a no-win situation, often resorting to "impression management" rather than an exercise of power.

Presidents devise sophisticated strategies to use the media, lest they get *used* by the media. Television has enlarged the presidency by focusing so much attention on that institution, but it also has shrunk the presidency by overexposing and therefore trivializing the office. How have movies and television dealt with this complex and sometimes contradictory office?

The Evolution of Presidential Image

In the early days of moving pictures, the presidency drew little attention. Rarely was the president portrayed as a fictional character in films, and while some historical portrayals made it to the screen (especially of Abraham Lincoln), the presidency was infrequently a part of films.

Prior to the disillusionment of Vietnam, Watergate, the Iran-Contra scandal, and the Clinton sex scandal, presidents—when portrayed in films—were presented primarily as political giants, saints who oozed goodness. No president received a greater cinematic boost than Abraham Lincoln. With such films as *Abraham Lincoln's Clemency* (1910), *Lincoln's Gettysburg Address* (1912), *Lincoln the Lover* (1913), *Lincoln's Thanksgiving Story* (1914), *The Life of Abraham Lincoln* (1915), *The Lincoln Cycle* (1917), *The Highest Law* (1921), *The Heart of Lincoln* (1922), *The Dramatic Life of Abraham Lincoln* (1924), *Abraham Lincoln* (1930), *Of Human Hearts* (1938), *Lincoln in the White House* (1939), *Young Mr. Lincoln* (1939), and *Abe Lincoln in Illinois* (1940), a type of blind hero worship was created around Lincoln.

This began to change during the Great Depression, when the search for hope led some filmmakers to turn their attention to politics and the creation of a presidential hero, amid all of the squalor and misery. During periods of crisis (the depression) and war (World War II), it is not unusual to see the president portrayed as a hero or savior. In times of stress, the public looks to the president for reassurance, comfort, and rescue. Films such as *Gabriel over the White House* (1933) presented an activist, quasiauthoritarian president who (after the spirit of the angel Gabriel enters his body) accomplishes miraculous deeds of reform and political regeneration, albeit in violation of constitutional restraints. This wishful thinking and hero worship presented the president as a popular hero and savior.[4]

In *The President Vanishes* (1934), an honest president, beset by a corrupt Congress, fakes his own kidnapping. In *The Phantom President* (1932), George M. Cohan plays the dual role of T. K. Blair, a cold, colorless presidential candidate, and a Blair look-alike, song-and-dance man Doc Varney. The political bosses have Varney run for president as Blair. Varney wins and stays on as president, "to run the country for the people's benefit."

Presidential cinematic hero worship continued into World War II as a patriotic fervor swept the nation and the film industry. Movies featuring pro-American and pro-presidential themes proliferated as Hollywood was enlisted to boost morale and support the war effort. It did so enthusiastically.

After the hot war, a cold war developed between the United States and the Soviet Union. This ideological and geopolitical war led to the Red Scare in the United States (1947–1955), and the result was the McCarthy era. This period had a chilling effect on Hollywood, and most filmmakers shied away from overt political messages. The occasional cinematic representation of a fictional president can be found, such as in Frank Capra's *State of the Union* (1948), but the McCarthy era is best known in Hollywood as the time of the blacklist and the retreat from social problems.

State of the Union, starring the popular duo Spencer Tracy and Katherine Hepburn, has Tracy playing successful industrialist Grant Matthews, who goes after the Republican presidential nomination. But the well-meaning Matthews is manipulated. Finally, seduced by the political bosses, he goes from a man of integrity to a political pawn. He becomes "one of them," but at his wife's urging, Matthews has a change of heart, and in true Capra fashion, he once again becomes a man of integrity, speaking truth to power.

For roughly the next dozen years, political or social problem films declined, falling victim to the oppressive forces of McCarthyism and the Hollywood blacklist. By the 1960s, presidential films such as *Sunrise at Campobello* (1960), dealing with FDR's response to paralysis in his pre-presidential years, and *PT 109* (1963), about John F. Kennedy's bravery during World War II, presented a reverential, hero-worshipping portrayal of individual courage. It was politics at a distance: the personal was the political, and the president was the hero.

Complex presidential images also were evident in films such as *Advice and Consent* (1962), *The Manchurian Candidate* (1962), *The Best Man* (1964), and *Fail-Safe* (1964), but in general, the reverential depiction was the order of the day. For the most part, presidents were portrayed as "forceful, wise, and selfless; they were stolid embodiments of republican virtue."[5]

This changed rather dramatically in the post-Vietnam, post-Watergate era.[6] The age of the heroic presidency gave way to the demonization of the presidency and the decline of public trust in government. An age of cynicism enveloped the political landscape, and the cinematic portrayal of presidents reflected this shift.[7]

Before Vietnam and Watergate, it was all but unthinkable to cinematically portray a real life president in anything but the most flattering light. All presidential rogues were fictional characters. But the fallout from Vietnam and Watergate changed everything.

All the President's Men (1976), starring Robert Redford and Dustin Hoffman as *Washington Post* reporters Bob Woodward and Carl Bernstein, dealt with the lies and corruption of Richard Nixon. There followed a spate of Nixon-bashing films, from *Secret Honor* (1984) to Oliver Stone's biopic *Nixon* (1995) to *Dick* (1999).

Even when the president was not a central character, it was not unusual to present a president in a less-than-flattering light. In *The Right Stuff* (1983), for example, Lyndon Johnson comes off as a buffoon and George and Barbara Bush as comic characters in *Naked Gun 2 1/2: The Smell of Fear* (1991). It is the era of the post-heroic presidency, brought painfully to scale.

In the 1960s, as a result of the cultural rebellion of the period, we saw the rise of the "anti-hero." This trend filtered its way into the presidential image as well. Commercial films are designed, first and foremost, to make a profit. Therefore, filmmakers are less likely to shape views than they are to reflect the ideas, biases, tastes, needs, and desires of their audience. Filmmakers give the audience "what it wants," and with the counter-culture movement of the

1960s, Vietnam, and then Watergate, the public grew cynical, and films played to, fed, and exploited the dissatisfaction and disaffection of the American movie-going audience, and thus the American voter. Slowly, portraits of presidents as venal, corrupt, and self-serving began to appear. *Being There* (1979), a film about an amiable dunce becoming presidential timber, began to deflate the presidential image. Instead of simplistic adulation, a paradigm shift took place: it was now simplistic condemnation. Instead of Hailing the Chief, we were Railing the Chief. In *Wild in the Streets* (1968), when fourteen-year-olds get the right to vote and age minimums for holding office are eliminated, one of the new president's first acts is to forcibly place everyone over thirty-five in "retirement" camp. In *Putney Swope* (1969), we see President Mimeo, a marijuana-smoking midget, more interested in fooling around with the First Lady than in governing. In *The Virgin President* (1968), fictionalized President Fillard Millmore, a thirty-five-year-old idiot, cannot even figure out that his cabinet is going to bomb China. And in *Hail to the Chief* (1972), a megalomaniac president orders his private police force to massacre hippies.

During the 1980s, life began to imitate art when an actor, Ronald Reagan, actually became president. And as memories of the turbulent 1960s, Vietnam, and Watergate began to fade, we saw a revival of a more hopeful, even heroic (some would say imperial) presidency. Reagan, the star of such movies as *The Knute Rockne Story* (where he played George Gipp, "the Gipper") and *Bedtime for Bonzo* (where Reagan costarred with a chimp), began to mix up life and art.

Reagan told the Israeli prime minister that he would never let Israel down because he was there when the Americans liberated the Jews from Nazi concentration camps, and that he would never, could never, forget. Of course, this never occurred. Reagan was not there when the allies liberated the Jews, but he had *seen it* in a movie! Reagan even drew ideas and inspiration from popular films, as when he announced that he would build a protective bubble (the strategic defense initiative) over the United States and name it after the movie *Star Wars*. Reagan even challenged Congress in cinematic language, telling it, "Go ahead, make my day!," another popular movie line.

By the 1990s and the end of the cold war, the public's confusion regarding what it wanted and expected of the presidency worked its way into the movies. Conspiratorial or critical depictions of presidents such as *JFK* (1991) and *Nixon* (1995) mixed with lighthearted, hopeful portrayals such as *Dave* (1993) and *The American President* (1995). If the images were mixed and mixed up, then one thing was perfectly clear: the American president had become a star of Hollywood movies.

Even a partial list of presidency-oriented films reveals just how popular and marketable the presidential image and office have become. From Oliver Stone's conspiracy homage in *JFK* (1991), to the president as a liberal icon in *The American President*, to the president as a *star wars* hero in *Independence*

Day (1996), to the president as comic relief in *Mars Attack* (1998), to the president as super-macho man in *Air Force One* (1997), to the president as—well, as Clinton—in *Wag the Dog* (1997), and to Clinton as Clinton in *Primary Colors* (1998), presidential images cluttered the silver screen, and many of these films drew large audiences. Even *Beavis and Butthead Do America* (1997) had a not-so-lifelike president.

I LIKE JED!

Art imitates life in the hugely popular NBC series *The West Wing*. Created in 1999 by Aaron Sorkin, *West Wing* won nine Emmy awards in its first season.[8] A fictionalized insider's account of life in the White House where the brilliant, liberal Democrat, Josiah Bartlet (Martin Sheen), wages a battle within himself between high-minded idealism and the demands of practical politics, *West Wing* has filled a void in our politics and in entertainment. Smart, witty, and topical, it has, in effect, replaced the Democratic Party as the "loyal opposition."

The Democrats, weak, confused, and leaderless after Clinton, have been both unwilling and unable to put up credible opposition to President George W. Bush in the aftermath of the September 11 tragedy. Thus the fictional Bartlet is the president (nearly) everyone wishes existed. He is the intelligent alternate to the failures of the Bush administration. In post-September 11 America, the role of the "loyal opposition" party is filled by a fictional TV character, Jed Bartlet, the president on *The West Wing*.

Centering on the lives (and sometimes loves) of several key White House staffers, *West Wing* feeds the public hunger for matters of substance in an otherwise superficial television wasteland. Not without its flaws, the show nonetheless presents the president as a smart and good man who must compromise, cut corners, and sometimes accept defeat. And it leaves viewers with the gnawing question, why can't we get a real-life Jed Bartlet in the real White House?[9]

FIRST FAMILY FOLLIES

Not only is the president subject to cinematic examination (if not exploitation), but the president's spouse and children also have become fodder for filmmakers. Prior to the 1980s, you could count on one hand the number of substantive portrayals of presidential family members. Today, it is commonplace.

In *First Lady* (1937), a light-hearted fictional saga of political catfighting between Washington wives, a former president's granddaughter, played by Kay Francis, campaigns to have her husband (Preston Foster) elected president. *Magnificent Doll* (1946) is the cinematic story of Dolly Madison. The *President's Lady* (1953) deals with Andrew Jackson's wife, Rachel. And *Guarding Tess* (1994) finds a fictional former first lady, played by Shirley MacLaine, causing comedic headaches for the Secret Service agents assigned to protect her. Even the president's (fictional) children have found their way onto the screen in *First Kid* (1996) and *First Daughter* (1999).

First Family (1980), directed by Buck Henry and starring Bob Newhart as a fumbling, bumbling president burdened with an alcoholic wife and a sexually overactive daughter is a lame, if good-hearted, comedy. And *Kisses for My President* (1964) is a gender-bender effort to reverse roles when the president (Polly Bergen) faces the problems her husband has as "First Husband" (Fred McMurray). And how does the first "First Husband" deal with this? By asserting his male authority, impregnating his wife, and coaxing her to resign from office to assume her "proper" role as a woman and mother![10]

PRESIDENTIAL IMAGE: DOES IT MATTER?

What are the consequences of this presidential familiarity? And does familiarity breed contempt (or boredom)? What is one to make of the president as a pop cultural icon? Does it demean and diminish the presidential office or make it more accessible and democratic? Certainly it feeds into both the cynicism of our culture and also the illusion that the president is (nearly) all-powerful. In short, we are told that (1) the president is the government; the presidency is more powerful and central to governing than it is in reality, thereby creating a false impression; (2) many presidents are venal and corrupt; and (3) individuals, not institutions, popular movements, or the system, matter.

When one adds the cinematic presidency to the televised presidency, we see how the proliferation of the presidential image penetrates to the very core of our political and pop cultures. It is the president as celebrity in chief, pop cultural icon. And while the cinematic representation of presidents (both real and fictional) has an impact, it is the day-to-day television coverage of presidents that has a more immediate effect.[11]

The explosion of media outlets has dramatically altered our political world. With the rise of cable television, the time frame for presidential action has shrunk, and the response time of presidential initiatives has accelerated. Issues that decades ago could be allowed to "ripen," issues that could at one time be ignored, now take center stage. (As pictures of starving children or exploding bombs intrude into our dinner table viewing, public demands for action grow. As images of ethnic cleansing confront us on the evening news, demands for action increase.)

We expect, even demand, that the president as a superhero become our Superman, able to leap tall separations of power in a single bound to solve our problems and satisfy our demands. But woe to the president if the problem is not solved "right away" or if the war is not won with few casualties. Fueled by cartoonlike caricatures of presidents as superheroes (e.g., *Independence Day* or *Air Force One*) in a world of cartoonlike heroes (e.g., Sylvester Stallone and Arnold Schwarzenegger), we develop unrealistic expectations, and when our president proves to be merely human, we are disappointed. Since presidents cannot meet the unrealistic expectations of pop culture icons or heroes, they must either accept inevitable defeat or attempt to govern via blue smoke and mirrors, as in *The Wizard of Oz*.[12]

Politically the president is the nation's center of attention. But rarely can a president reach out and touch "real people." The media serve as the president's conduit for reaching the public. Through the media, especially television, the public sees the president, hears about his ideas, and interprets how well or how poorly he is doing his job. Another way of putting it is that "Presidents cannot succeed without the media, but they have difficulty surviving because of the media."[13]

Because the president is the nation's center of political attention, public expectations are fueled, and the impression is created that the president is more powerful than he is. The media's fascination with presidents, their families, and even their pets has led to increased attention lavished upon the president, who serves as the nation's "celebrity in chief." Not imperial, not imperiled, but the "intimate presidency." The gravitational pull of the presidency gives the president a ready-made bully pulpit, but it also has a downside. In an era of hypercritical investigative reporting, everything and anything a president does is fodder for tabloid journalists. With TV talk shows such as *Hard Copy* and *Larry King Live* and radio call-in shows with slash-and-burn DJs, we have an abundance of information but a shortage of knowledge. The micro coverage of the president trivializes the office, the man, and politics itself. Washington has become Hollywood on the Potomac, and the president becomes just one more pop culture icon.

Presidents are too politically attractive to ignore. John Orman's study of periodical literature shows that Franklin D. Roosevelt averaged 109.5 stories per year about the presidency, John F. Kennedy averaged about 200, Jimmy Carter averaged 407, and Ronald Reagan averaged over 500.[14] By contrast, network news coverage of Congress declined by roughly 50 percent between 1975 and 1985.[15]

This trend has both positive and negative consequences, but one thing is clear: it places the president at the center of media attention and elevates him in the minds of the public. As Hedrick Smith writes:

> As a nation, we focus obsessively on the president, out of proportion with other power centers. This happens largely because the president is one person whom it is easy for television to portray and whom the public feels it can come to know. Other power centers are harder to

depict: The Supreme Court is an aloof and anonymous body; Congress is a confusing gaggle of 535 people; the bureaucracy is vast and faceless. It is almost as if the president, most politicians, and the press, especially television, have fallen into an unconscious conspiracy to create a cartoon caricature of the real system of power. There is a strong urge for simplicity in the American psyche, a compulsion to focus on the single dramatic figure at the summit, to reduce the intricacy of a hundred power-plays to the simple equation of whether the president is up or down, winning or losing on any given day or week.[16]

Since the media serve as the president's conduit to the public, and because so much is riding on good press coverage, no president can afford to ignore, or even leave to chance, his relations with the media. Presidents must devise and implement strategies for attaining good press, and efforts at media manipulations are quite common.

This has led to the creation of what Thomas E. Cronin has called the "theatrical presidency,"[17] in which public relations specialists take precedence over policy people, and style rules over substance. Reagan handler Michael Deaver (dubbed the "Vicar of Visuals") went so far as to admit that "image is sometimes as useful as substance."[18] With the rise of the theatrical presidency has come an increase in efforts at presidential self-dramatization, at using public relations techniques and image management as a replacement for policy, at staging media events and framing the president in "pretty pictures" for the evening news. (During the 1988 presidential race, it seemed impossible to turn on a television set and not see George Bush wrapped—literally and figuratively—in an American flag.)

Given that presidents are limited in what they can accomplish, and given that the public expects presidents to deliver the goods, sometimes, when faced with an inability to achieve policy results, presidents will resort to political grandstanding to create the impression that they are doing something. No administration used image management more often or better than the Reagan team. It is no overstatement to say that they were obsessed with image, and that style was often used as a replacement for substance.[19]

In a perverse example of the tail wagging the dog, policy often is used for the public relations advantage that it might deliver, and presidents can use selected pictures and images to erase political reality. At the time Reagan proposed a cut in funds to assist the handicapped, the president went to a Special Olympics event and the pictures on the evening news showed a caring, concerned president, while the reality was that the president wanted to cut funding. And when polls revealed that the public disapproved of Reagan's civil rights policies, the president paid a very public (and media-filled) visit to a black family that had had a cross burned on their front lawn. (The cross burning occurred five years before Reagan's visit, but when one needs good visuals, what is a few years?) Reagan *appeared* to be concerned and caring. If his policies revealed an attempted reversal in civil rights enforcement, then his pictures had to supplant reality. It was the Wizard of Oz *before* Toto pulled back the curtain. If carefully managed, one picture truly can be worth a thousand words (or facts).

This obsession with image has forced presidents, in effect, to campaign 365 days a year. The permanent campaign has forced presidents to attempt to govern in a campaign mode. This means that one must constantly paint pretty pictures for public consumption. As Hedrick Smith notes,

> In the image game, the essence is not words, but pictures. The Reagan image-makers followed the rule framed by Bob Haldeman, the advertising man who was Nixon's chief of staff, the governing principle for politics in the television era: The visual wins over the verbal; the eye predominates over the ear; sight beats sound. As one Reagan official laughingly said to me, "What are you going to believe, the facts or your eyes?"[20]

Going Public

The image-management strategy of presidential power in the media age is called "going public." Samuel Kernell sees an unending political campaign in which presidents go public in an effort to increase political clout within the Washington community.[21]

In this, the United States has come a long way from what the creators of the presidency envisioned. The inventors of the presidency, as Jeffrey Tulis reminds us, feared a president who was too closely linked to the public, because it might "manifest demagoguery, impede deliberation, and subvert the routines of republican government."[22] Such fears reflected the opposition to democracy shared by many of the Founding Fathers. Over time, such concerns gave way to the unstoppable logic of the electronic media and the need to use whatever levers a president could find to increase power.

Today, presidents go public because they have few other options. In a political landscape cluttered with the carcasses of failed presidents, an incumbent must use whatever resources are available, and governing by appearance—when governing by accomplishment fails—is something to which presidents often resort.

Does the Camera Distort?

Television has both *enlarged* and *shrunk* the presidency. It has enlarged the presidency by focusing a disproportionately large amount of attention on the presidency at the expense of Congress (if there is a balance of power, it rarely shows on television). It has shrunk the presidency by an overexposure that has led to the trivialization and/or the intrusion of the press into the most personal and private of presidential activities. Before the 1992 election, Bill and Hillary Clinton were asked by Mike Wallace of *60 Minutes*, "Are you prepared to say you never had extramarital affairs?" And after the election, a young woman, with TV cameras running, asked Clinton, "Mr. President, the world's dying to know, is it boxers or briefs?"

The media are a two-edged sword that cuts both ways. Some presidents use the media, while others are used by it. Kennedy and Reagan, poised, witty, and self-assured, were able to use television to their advantage. Nixon, Ford, Carter, and Bush, stiff, nervous, and awkward, did not fare as well. Clinton was sometimes able to win good media coverage, largely due to his superior interpersonal skills.

Generally, presidents get somewhat favorable press coverage.[23] But in the aftermath of Vietnam and Watergate, reportage has become much more critical. In an age of cynicism, the media have seen their role as more adversarial and, with the proliferation of cable television, as more personal and intrusive.[24]

Before Vietnam and Watergate, the press was more deferential to presidents. Certain private peccadilloes, while known, were deemed unfit to report. Even an obvious handicap such as FDR's paralysis was not mentioned, nor were pictures plastered on the front page showing a handicapped president confined to his wheelchair or being lifted to a podium. Today, TV programs such as *Hard Copy* would flood the public with images of a "weak and struggling" FDR, and it is unclear whether such a person would be elected.

We generally want to know about the personal foibles, in detail, of our celebrities and public officials. With the increased number of media outlets comes greater competition for a limited viewing audience. Thus sensationalism increases, responsible reporting is pushed to the side, and the personal and private become targets for investigative reporting and the White House press corps.[25]

As political scientist Larry Sabato noted:

> It has become a spectacle without equal in modern American politics: the news media, print and broadcast, go after a wounded politician like sharks in a feeding frenzy. The wound may have been self-inflicted, and the politician may richly deserve his or her fate, but the journalists now take center stage in the process, creating the news as much as reporting it, changing both the shape of election-year politics and the contours of government.[26]

Even the more responsible media outlets have been affected. Both print and electronic journalists have had to respond to market demands, with print imitating the *USA Today* "light news" format and television adopting the fast-cut, short, quick shots of MTV. Style wins out over substance. The average "sound bite," the time devoted to a candidate's statements, has shrunk from forty-two seconds in 1968 to seven seconds in the 1990s.[27]

Today, presidents must do what they can to manage the news. They attempt to elicit positive stories and favorable coverage and can leave little to chance. They must have a clear strategy for dealing with the media. The strategy attempts to generate stories that add to the mystique of the president's *image* (strength, knowledge, political skill), *personality* (intelligence, family involvement, reassuring style), and *leadership* (in command, decisive, in control of events).

It was hard enough for presidents to manage the news when there were only three major TV networks and a handful of newspaper reporters to worry about. Today, everywhere presidents turn cameras and microphones are thrust into their faces in the new twenty-four-hour news cycle. News coverage has altered presidential politics. The impact of the Cable News Network (CNN), with twenty-four hours of coverage, instant information, and live, on-the-spot reporting from every corner of the globe, forces presidents to face some issues they otherwise might wish to (or perhaps need to) avoid. Because it was on TV, in the living rooms of the public, presidents often feel pressured to act in remote areas on issues not vital to the national interest. Issues may not be able to ripen, and presidents may feel compelled to make quick decisions. Speed is valued over deliberation.

How would the presence of CNN have altered the Cuban missile crisis? If President Kennedy had been forced to show his hand earlier, when more aggressive military options seemed likely, then the crisis could have ended in a nuclear war. As it was, Kennedy could consult with advisors away from the glare of television, the issue could ripen, and wiser heads could prevail. Is this less likely in an age of instant communications?

As television images show hunger, oppression, famine, and war around the world, the president may face great pressure to intervene. Disturbing pictures can create a crisis atmosphere in which a president must act lest both his leadership and humanity be called into question: inaction may be wise, but it also may appear as weakness.

When the public sees pictures of a dead U.S. soldier dragged through the streets of Mogadishu, Somalia, the cries for action can be deafening. But would action be wise? Once largely hidden from view, now every issue becomes closer, more proximate, and larger than it may be. And the pressure to act—even when action may not bring a remedy—may be irresistible.

The impact of talk radio, a medium that in the 1990s became popular for people to vent their spleen, has been astonishing. Called "hate radio" by some, this raw form of media democracy has fanned the embers of America's fears. Talk radio has, in part, taken up the role of the mediating institution that the parties have forfeited, and it has given the general public a sense of connection to politics. Generally conservative and male oriented,[28] these programs offer an outlet and a vehicle for the government-bashing antipolitics, politics that began in the 1990s.

CONCLUSION

Unlike the world of movies, presidents are neither Jedi-type star fighters *(Independence Day)* nor megalomaniacal madmen *(Hail to the Chief)*. They are living, breathing beings with strengths and weaknesses—men (and soon women) embedded in a frustrating and complicated Madisonian system of checks, balances, powers, and roadblocks.

To a great extent, films paint a wildly unrealistic image of the president, his job, and his power, as well as the systemic checks he must face. In film, all politics is personal and individual, not systemic or institutional. We get a distorted image of our presidents, which feeds into the illusions of presidential government and presidential power that most Americans hold. We do ourselves, and our presidents, a disservice in embracing these false notions.

Must a president lead by cultivating popular imagery?[29] While one may be tempted toward cynicism regarding this question, there is another way to look at it that is far less discouraging. In part, presidents do lead by the creative use of symbols.[30] But such leadership need not be cynical in motivation. Abraham Lincoln, for example, evoked cherished myths of the founding of America to lend meaning to his words both at Gettysburg and in his second inaugural address.

Lincoln relied heavily on images of the American past, especially the founding era, in giving meaning and direction to the tragic events of the Civil War.[31] By evoking the American past, Lincoln connected symbol to reality and demonstrated a continuity between the honored past, the painful present, and a possible future. Such uses of symbolism are at the very core of creative leadership.

The double-edged sword of presidential imagery reminds one of George Bernard Shaw's warning: mother's milk nourishes the saint as well as the sinner. The president as the nation's celebrity in chief is both empowered and emasculated, enlarged and diminished by the level and scope of media and cinematic attention drawn to the institution. Some presidents use the media, while others are used by it. Presidents both gain from and pay a price for the proliferation of the presidential image—Hollywood is neither the cause nor the culprit here but merely a coconspirator.

NOTES

1. See Michael A. Genovese, *The Political Film: An Introduction* (Needham, Mass.: Simon & Schuster, 1998).

2. See Gary Crowdus, ed., *The Political Companion to American Film* (Chicago: Lakeview Press, 1994).

3. See Thomas E. Cronin and Michael A. Genovese, *The Paradoxes of the American Presidency* (New York: Oxford University Press, 1998).

4. Lawrence W. Levine, "Film Images during the Great Depression," in *Unpredictable Past: Explorations in American Cultural History*, ed. Lawrence W. Levine (New York: Oxford University Press, 1993), 235–39.

5. "Nuke the Wife," *The Economist* 344:8030 (August 16, 1997): 66.

6. Michael A. Genovese, *The Watergate Crisis* (Westport, Conn.: Greenwood Press, 1999).

7. Ann-Marie Bicaud,"Les présidents américains au cinéma," *Cinéma* 263 (1980): 60–2; and "Réflexions sur l'iconograhie présidentielle américaine," in *Cinéma* 263 (1980): 50–59.

8. Keith Topping, *Inside Bartlet's White House: An Unofficial and Unauthorized Guide to the West Wing* (London: Virgin Books, 2002).

9. Chris Leham, "The Feel-Good Presidency: The Pseudo-Politics of the West Wing," *Atlantic Monthly* (March 2001): 93; Fred McKissack, "The West Wing Is Not a Wet Dream," *Progressive* (May 2000): 39; Michael Wolff, "Our Remote-Control President," *New York Magazine* (December 4, 2000): 25–29.

10. As another role-shattering film, *The Man* (1972) deals with the first African American to become president.

11. Bruce Miroff, "The Presidency and the Public: Leadership as Spectacle," in *The Presidency and the Political System*, 4th ed., ed. Michael Nelson (Washington, D.C.: CQ Press, 1995,) 273–96.

12. For a fuller examination of the political allegory of "Oz," see Michael A. Genovese, "Political Allegory in the *Wizard of Oz*," *Los Angeles Times*, March 19, 1988, p. 8.

13. Harold Barger, *The Impossible Presidency* (Glenview, Ill.: Scott, Foresman, 1984), 357.

14. John Orman, "Covering the American Presidency: Balanced Reporting in the Presidential Press," *Presidential Studies Quarterly* 14 (1984): 381–82.

15. Norman Ornstein and Michael Robinson, "The Case of Our Disappearing Congress," *TV Guide*, January 11, 1986, pp. 4–10.

16. Hedrick Smith, *The Power Game* (New York: Random House, 1996), 10.

17. Thomas E. Cronin, *The State of the Presidency* (Boston: Little Brown, 1980), 140–51.

18. Michael Deaver, *Behind the Scenes* (New York: William Morrow, 1987), 73.

19. John Maltese, *Spin Control: The White House Office of Communications and the Management of Presidential News* (Chapel Hill: University of North Carolina Press, 1992).

20. Smith, *The Power Game*, 407.

21. Samuel Kernell, *Going Public: New Strategies of Presidential Leadership* (Washington, D.C.: Congressional Quarterly, 1986).

22. Jeffrey K. Tulis, *The Rhetorical Presidency* (Princeton: Princeton University Press, 1987), 95.

23. Michael B. Grossman and Martha Joynt Kumar, *Portraying the President* (Baltimore: Johns Hopkins University Press, 1981), 255–63.

24. Michael J. Robinson et al., "With Friends Like These . . . ," *Public Opinion* (June–July 1983): 2–3.

25. Kenneth T. Walsh, *Feeding the Beast, the White House vs. Press* (New York: Random House, 1996).

26. Larry Sabato, *Feeding Frenzy* (New York: Free Press, 1993), 1.

27. Daniel Hallin, "Sound Bite News: Television Coverage of Elections," *Journal of Communication* (Spring 1992): 5–24.

28. Howard Kurtz, "There's Anger in the Air," *The Washington Post National Weekly Edition*, October 31–November 6, 1994, pp. 8–10.

29. See Arthur Miller, *On Politics and the Art of Acting* (New York: Viking, 2001).

30. Murray Edelman, *The Symbolic Uses of Politics* (Champaign, Ill.: University of Illinois Press, 1990).

31. Garry Wills, *Lincoln at Gettysburg: The Words That Remade America* (New York: New Star Media, 1992).

3

Party Labels in Presidential Acceptance Addresses: 1948–2000

Sharon E. Jarvis and Emily Balanoff Jones

> To achieve these aims we must have total victory; we must have more Republicans in our state and local offices; more Republican governments in our states; a Republican majority in the United States House of Representatives and in the United States Senate; and, of course, a Republican in the White House. Today is the first day of this great battle. The road that leads to November 4 is a fighting road. In that fight I will keep nothing in reserve.[1]

In 1952, President Dwight Eisenhower delivered an acceptance speech to the Republican Nominating Convention that left little room for doubt—he wanted to win, and he wanted his fellow Republicans to win as well. Before describing the "total victory," he told his audience that "the aims of this Republican crusade are clear: to sweep from office an administration which has fastened on every one of us the wastefulness, the arrogance and corruption in high places, the heavy burdens and anxieties which are the bitter fruit of a party too long in power."[2]

Thirty-eight years later, another Republican presidential candidate accepted his party's nomination by taking a different rhetorical approach—by positioning himself as a "uniter, not a divider." George W. Bush shared that he had "worked with Republicans and Democrats to get things done" while governor in Texas, and that his was a "bittersweet party" because someone was missing "the late Lt. Governor of Texas Bob Bullock. Bob was a Democrat, a crusty veteran of Texas politics, and my great friend."[3] Bush credited Democrats in Texas as being central to his success in the past, and he believed that Republicans and Democrats should work together in the future, specifically "to end the politics of fear and save Social Security together."

The shift in political priorities from Eisenhower to Bush might not surprise political scientists familiar with the contention that presidential campaigns are becoming increasingly candidate centered. Many might interpret

Eisenhower's relative comfort in discussing Republicanism as a throwback to a stronger party era, one in which candidates could promote their party labels and voters would reward them by selecting straight-party tickets. Bush's candidacy, in contrast, appeared at a time in which individuals are believed to engage in strategies that foreground their personal characteristics and background their party allegiances. While there is evidence that presidential candidates have become less likely to market themselves as Democrats and Republicans over the past fifty years, and that voters have been less loyal over this time period, two key political realities have nevertheless remained constant: the major political parties still organize and facilitate American elections, and party identification continues to be the prime predictor of the vote.

These campaign certainties create a tension for presidential hopefuls, particularly with regard to their convention addresses: How do these candidates rhetorically negotiate (1) their roles as the parties' nominees, and (2) an increasingly prevalent temptation to wage a "candidate-centered" campaign? Although some research has noted that candidates are increasingly at the center of convention planning,[4] and reluctant to feature party labels in their acceptance addresses,[5] scholars have yet to conduct a systematic analysis to assess how candidates juggle these roles in their campaign discourse. Accordingly, little is known about the following concerns: How do candidates rhetorically position themselves at their conventions? Do they attempt to inspire identification by emphasizing their labels? Do they attempt to galvanize their followers by highlighting division with the opposition's labels? When they are used, are party labels depicted as partisan or agreeable? As positive or problematic? As stable or unsteady? As powerful or impotent? In other words, how have the linguistic choices of presidential candidates encouraged audiences to understand the place and potency of parties in modern campaigns?

While these questions may appear modest, inquiring into the sentence-level details of convention addresses is vital to a rich understanding of the role of parties in the American system. As Murray Edelman maintains, people are more likely to experience the "language about political events rather than the events themselves."[6] His statement is particularly relevant to parties in the United States; that is, Americans are more likely to be subject to the discourse of partisanship via candidate statements and media reports than to participate in actual partisan meetings or fund-raisers. The way in which parties are constructed in discourse is influential, for political events often are understood through the language used to describe them, and people's understandings of political institutions rest on their beliefs or perceptions of them, whether or not those cognitions are accurate.[7]

Observers from a variety of disciplines have pointed to the power of naming and the impact of label use for political life. Michael Schudson goes so far as to argue that "little is more important than naming, marking, and reminding."[8] In his mind, individuals learn culture by observing how things are named, and people learn the importance of things given how often they are reminded to think about such things. Kathleen Hall Jamieson illustrates how these processes can be used for political gain.[9] In her analysis of the 1988 presidential campaign, she details how the George H. W. Bush team was able to rename a criminal (from "William Horton" to "Willie Horton"), to label his actions (from rape and murder to "torture" and "terrorize"), to define a political policy (a furlough program became "weekend passes" and a "revolving door"), and to entice the media to include such phrasings in their news reports. The Bush campaign's proactivity in these rhetorical matters shifted the ways in which Americans came to know an issue (the furlough program), and the Bush team's discipline in sticking to this language increased the likelihood that citizens heard these terms again and again.

In his work on poverty, Edelman shows how "naming" can aid or prevent the creation of public policy by giving choices to politicians and the public.[10] Specifically, Edelman discusses how when a phrase such as "the deserving poor" is introduced into a policy debate, new choices emerge. Should the government help the "deserving" poor? What should be done with the "undeserving" poor (a rhetorical by-product of the deserving poor)? Do both groups deserve help? The very creation of a symbol for the deserving poor, concludes Edelman, encourages (1) government to do nothing for millions of poor people (after verbally categorizing them as "undeserving"), and (2) impoverished citizens to regard other poor people as "undeserving" (siding with governmental elites rather than identifying with those who share their economic condition).

Inspired by the function of names and labels in political life, and the rhetorical situation facing presidential nominees at their conventions, this chapter examines how candidates have used party labels in their acceptance addresses, from 1948 to 2000. We do so armed with a set of assumptions of words in the polity: language changes with time, and the meanings of words can expand, contract, or shift from original meanings;[11] language aids politicians and citizens in shaping their thoughts;[12] and language helps individuals understand their social and political situations.[13] Our goal is to explore these acceptance addresses to see how candidates have juggled the roles of "party nominee" and "candidate-centered campaigner" in these strategic and scripted moments. In so doing, we also hope to gain insight into how candidates have used labels over the past fourteen elections as well as to learn more about how they have encouraged citizens and the media to imagine and understand political parties in presidential contests.

CANDIDATE-CENTERED CAMPAIGNS

The contention that high-profile campaigns have become candidate centered has received considerable support. Martin Wattenberg offers perhaps the most detailed assessment of a movement away from party-brokered electioneering, and his argument can be summed up as follows: a contest for the electorate's attention has taken place since 1952, which has led to a gradual shift in the focus of American politics from parties to candidates;[14] Americans have begun to "see both of these groups [as] less relevant in solving the most important domestic and foreign policy issues of the day," as "the parties are losing their association with the candidates and the issues that the candidates claim to stand for;"[15] and, the increase in alienation toward the parties has been minimal, for the key shift has been toward a neutral attitude rather than a negative evaluation of the parties. As Wattenberg puts it, "the shift to candidate-centered campaigns can be seen as a change that had been developing over time ... the parties' ability to polarize opinion into rival camps weakened, creating a vacuum in the structure of electoral attitudes ... like nature, politics abhors a vacuum, and candidates are the most logical force to take the place of parties in this respect."[16]

Other scholars have attended to the conceptual properties and theoretical utility of this argument. With regard to the former, Mathew McCubbins believes that three conditions are required for candidate-centered campaigning. In his mind, candidates must gain widespread recognition at a low cost; they must create a coalition of voters that will support their reputation rather than a party, and this coalition must be potentially decisive.[17] John Aldrich weaves candidate-centered politics into the theoretical rationale of his influential book *Why Parties?* In his words, "The theory of the contemporary party is a theory about a party facing a candidate-centered electoral arena and an individualized, incumbent-centered government."[18]

Still others have factored this shift into political analyses. They observe that candidate-centered campaigns may have short- and long-term effects on individual-level party identification,[19] can contribute to party responsiveness and change,[20] and may be linked to future governing activities.[21] Studies have examined the intersection of candidate-centered campaigns and public communication, as is witnessed in L. Sandy Maisel's investigation of party platforms in a candidate-centered era,[22] in Thomas Patterson's discussion of how candidates have become entrepreneurial in an electoral system in which party labels are less powerful than in the recent past,[23] and in the first author's analysis of partisan markers and personal cues in acceptance addresses.[24] To date, however, attention has yet to focus on the language that candidates use to help their audiences make sense of their dual roles as party nominee and individual candidate.

These rhetorical tensions are not unlike the strategic ones between parties and political consultants, a subject that has been explored by Robin Kolodny and that may be helpful in developing expectations for the rhetorical patterns in the acceptance addresses.[25] As she describes, early research presumed that there was an "adversarial" relationship between these two sets of actors, largely because consultants were believed to adhere to the "Madison Avenue" values of advertising and marketing (of crafting compelling messages and working for candidates who could afford their salaries), which were regarded as clashing with traditional party values (of providing a consistent party message, working to get a slate of party candidates elected, and supporting experienced candidates who would represent the group well). In a survey administered in 1997, however, Kolodony discovered that 88.6 percent of consultants said that their clientele belonged predominantly to one party, about half of the consultants had previously worked for a political party, the majority of political consultants claimed that political parties were clients of theirs, and most consultants suggested that they worked with political parties often, and that such work improved their effectiveness.[26] These data violate the "adversarial view" and lend support to the contention that consultants and parties experience an interdependent relationship, both benefiting from "long-term electoral partnerships."[27]

PARTISAN, RHETORICAL, AND ORGANIZATIONAL IDENTIFICATION

The concept of identification is central to the tensions facing candidate-centered campaigners at their party conventions. While political scientists are certainly familiar with the importance of partisan identification in electoral politics, Stacey Connaughton's work indicates how attending also to the rhetorical and organizational aspects of identification can enrich one's understanding of modern campaigns.[28]

To begin, party identification is observed by many as the most important development in modern electoral behavior research. Traditionalists in this area regard party identification as an individual-level psychological attachment that is acquired early in life, is likely to grow stronger with age, is ideally resistant to change, provides a sense of electoral stability, serves as a type of perceptual screen (affecting one's selection of information about politics and perception of the candidates), and strongly influences an individual's vote choice over time and across different offices. In *The American Voter*, Angus Campbell and colleagues submit that "few factors are of greater importance for our national elections than the lasting attachments of tens of millions of Americans to one of the parties. These loyalties establish a basic division of electoral strength within which the competition of particular campaigns takes place."[29]

Since *The American Voter*, the concept of party identification has been examined as a stabilizing force in politics, regarded as a cognitive shortcut, associated with higher levels of popular support of one's candidates and presidential job approval, considered to provide a sense of self-esteem and sense of belonging, and regarded to stay with a voter over a life cycle.[30] Some scholars have amended the "traditional" conceptualization of party identification, suggesting that while identification may begin through socialization at a young age, voters keep a running tally of party performance, and a mature party identification results from that tally (and thus can fluctuate a bit over time).[31] In Morris Fiorina's retrospective model, for instance, identification is the result of a voter's net recollection of past political experiences, a by-product of weighing the costs and benefits of the political parties.[32] While the traditionalist and revisionist approaches differ a bit (largely because they reflect the political realities of their eras, the late 1950s to early 1960s and the 1980s, respectively), both view identification as being key to understanding the dynamics of American politics.

Although he approaches the concept from a different vantage point, rhetorical critic Kenneth Burke also considers identification central to human attitudes and behaviors, so much so that it serves as a key tenet to his theory of persuasion. Specifically, Burke believes that people are divided due to their numerous identities and affiliations, and that communication helps people transcend these differences to find similarities or shared substance (by "identifying your way" with that of another person).[33] While many cues could be used to do so (language, gesture, tonality, order, image, idea, attitude), Burke advances three key means of this process: explicit identification, identification through antithesis, and implicit identification.[34] The construct of identification has been widely extended in communication research, most notably for this chapter to analyses of political advertising and organizational groups.[35]

On this latter point, those who study organizing contend that identification is essential to understanding group membership. Studies show that individuals who identify with their group are more likely to be committed to it, more likely to behave consistently with its identity, interests, and beliefs, and less likely to leave it.[36] For organizational communication scholars, identification is a communicative and reciprocal process. While individuals may seek out groups or organizations to fill their needs, it is often the case that organizations must make a case that they merit initial and continued attachment from members.[37] Consistent with their colleagues in political science, these researchers believe that there are many organizational benefits to cultivating strong identifiers, and that it is increasingly difficult to inspire identification in a postindustrial era.[38]

Attending to the political, rhetorical, and organizational aspects of identification, this encourages the consideration of at least two sets of possibilities for these addresses. At the macro level, if campaigns (or other forces) do not prime party labels, then voters may become agnostic about such terms, or they may fail to see them as salient (leading to the types of patterns discussed by Wattenberg[39]). At a more micro level, if the individual parties engage in divergent discursive activities, then the American public may be encouraged to understand parties and partisanship in distinct ways. For instance, if one party abandons its language (as Democrats began to do in the 1980s with the term *liberal*), while the other party continues to use it (as Republicans did by continually casting the term in a negative light), then the meanings of party labels may shift.[40] Such semantic movements, of course, may affect the political and cultural attractiveness of the specific terms and may influence citizens' willingness to identify with them. In an over-communicated media age, it is entirely possible that the ways in which party labels are discussed may contribute to the likelihood that individuals will come to "realize" partisanship and possibly act consistent with this identification,[41] and that parties can control the meanings of their labels (as opposed to watching other political forces add or subtract meanings from their brands). For these reasons, the quantitative and qualitative uses of party labels merit our attention.

CONVENTION RHETORIC

Party nominating conventions continue to be some of the most visible events of modern campaigns. These conventions date back to the 1830s and have been televised since 1948. Conventions were aired in their entirety from 1956 through 1976, and at that time they were regarded as the most important event covered by news departments. The networks have cut back on their coverage since 1980, however, and tend to allocate airtime in direct proportion to the perceived competitiveness of the race as well as the potential conflict within a party's nomination.

A common assumption of analyses of acceptance speeches is that these addresses are public, staged, and strategic, and that they are increasingly managed by candidates as opposed to parties.[42] In this chapter we pay special attention to how candidates deploy two party labels (Democrat, Republican) and the term party. While tracing the quantity and quality of these words in convention addresses cannot tell us all that needs to be known about how candidates negotiate their roles as party nominees and candidate-centered campaigners, it can offer insight into how Americans have been encouraged to think of the dual roles that these candidates have played. Accordingly, we advance the following questions: How have presidential nominees discussed party labels at their conventions? Have the discussions changed across time, label, speaker, and circumstance?

METHOD

To answer our research questions, we conducted a quantitative and qualitative content analysis of twenty-eight acceptance addresses delivered by Democratic and Republican nominees between 1948 and 2000. This time period was selected to observe how candidates delivering televised addresses have navigated the tensions of being the party's nominee and organizing a candidate-centered campaign. Admittedly, the earlier campaigns in this sample predate the candidate-centered campaign argument; they are included here, however, so that a richer understanding of potential shifts over time can be gained.

These texts were read in their entirety by the first author. Then they were scanned and introduced to a Keyword-in-Context program. The Keywords program located all instances of the three key terms (Democrat, Republican, party—and their derivatives—Democrats, Republicans, parties, etc.). These words were chosen because they are the most obvious ways to refer to the parties.

After locating these terms, the Keywords program reproduced them, preceding and following each one with twenty words of verbal context. These forty-one word clusters serve as the coding units for this study.[43] In total, we located 158 instances of Democrat, Democrats, and Democratic, 168 instances of Republican and Republicans, and 251 instances of party, parties, and partisan. All terms were read for suitability for this project, and twenty-seven were rejected because they did not fit the analysis ("democratic republic," "party this evening"). Five hundred and fifty terms were analyzed (140 Democrat and derivatives, 160 Republican and derivatives, and 250 party and derivatives).

The content-analytic scheme used in this chapter was inspired by the research questions advanced earlier and was designed to measure the rhetorical and political nuances of party labels. There were two parts to the following coding scheme. First, it included a series of descriptive measures, including year of label, specific label, era of label, and speaker.[44] Next, it featured a set of variables derived from the literature on political parties (including role, potency, time, context, and position) and rhetorical identification (identification strategy).[45] All coding decisions were designed to be mutually exclusive for each variable.

Similar to other recent works in quantitative and qualitative content analysis, we analyzed each text independently and then came together to discuss and reach agreement on coding decisions.[46] Descriptive and nonparametric statistics were run on the data, with textual examples from the speeches used to illuminate the quantitative patterns.

How Have Presidential Nominees Discussed Party Labels at Their Conventions?

Descriptive statistics appear in Table 3.1, and in the first column we see that labels were most commonly deployed to establish identification, to depict elite activities, to be placed in a positive context and in the present moment, and to

TABLE 3.1
Rhetorical Features of Party Tokens

		Total		Democrat		Republican		Challenger		Incumbent		Winner		Loser	
		%	(n)	%	(n)	%	(n)	%	(n)	%	(n)	%	(n)	%	(n)
Token	Party	45.5	(250)	44.6	(129)	46.4	(121)	39.3	(84)	49.4	(166)	49.3	(133)	41.8	(117)
	Democrat	25.5	(140)	33.2	(96)	16.9	(44)	25.2	(54)	25.6	(86)	24.8	(67)	26.1	(73)
	Republican	29.1	(160)	22.1	(64)	36.8	(96)	35.5	(76)	25.0	(84)	259	(70)	32.1	(90)
Strategy	Identification	59.4	(327)	51.2	(148)	68.6	(179)	70.1	(150)	52.7	(177)	60.7	(164)	58.2	(163)
	Division	26.7	(147)	33.6	(97)	19.2	(50)	16.4	(35)	33.3	(112)	25.9	(70)	27.5	(77)
	Unclear	13.8	(76)	15.2	(44)	12.3	(32)	13.6	(29)	14.0	(47)	13.3	(36)	14.3	(40)
Position	Elite	64.2	(353)	64.7	(187)	63.6	(166)	54.2	(116)	70.5	(237)	70.4	(190)	58.2	(163)
	Mass	12.5	(69)	11.8	(34)	13.4	(35)	9.8	(21)	14.3	(48)	11.9	(32)	13.2	(37)
	Global	23.3	(128)	23.5	(68)	23.0	(60)	36.0	(77)	15.2	(51)	17.8	(48)	28.6	(80)
Context	Identity	23.6	(130)	22.5	(65)	24.9	(65)	25.7	(55)	22.5	(75)	21.9	(59)	25.4	(71)
	Positive	43.1	(237)	39.1	(113)	47.5	(124)	51.9	(111)	37.5	(126)	45.9	(124)	40.4	(113)
	Negative	24.4	(134)	27.0	(78)	21.5	(56)	17.3	(37)	28.9	(97)	23.3	(63)	25.4	(71)
	Unclear	8.7	(48)	11.4	(33)	6.1	(16)	5.1	(11)	11.3	(38)	8.9	(24)	8.9	(25)
Time	Present	72.5	(399)	74.7	(216)	70.1	(183)	70.1	(150)	74.1	(249)	71.1	(192)	73.9	(207)
	Past	18.4	(101)	18.3	(53)	18.4	(48)	18.7	(40)	18.2	(61)	20.7	(56)	16.1	(45)
	Future	9.1	(50)	6.9	(20)	11.5	(30)	11.2	(24)	7.1	(26)	8.1	(22)	10.0	(28)
Potency	Unclear	8.4	(46)	8.0	(23)	8.8	(23)	9.3	(20)	7.7	(26)	7.0	(19)	9.6	(27)
	As actor	61.6	(339)	58.1	(168)	65.9	(172)	60.7	(130)	62.5	(210)	66.7	(180)	57.1	(160)
	As recipient	26.7	(147)	30.8	(89)	22.2	(58)	26.2	(56)	27.1	(91)	23.7	(64)	29.6	(83)
	Balanced	3.1	(17)	3.1	(9)	3.1	(8)	3.7	(8)	2.7	(9)	2.6	(7)	3.6	(10)
		550		289		261		214		336		270		280	

Source: Collected by the authors from analysis of National Party Convention Acceptance Addresses, 1948–2000.

portray parties as actors as opposed to recipients of action. In the main, these rhetorical patterns support an "allied view" between candidate-centered campaigns and parties.

Consider these textual examples. First, candidates linked themselves to their labels, as evident in the following phrases: "we of the Democratic Party," "as Democrats we are heirs," "we Democrats believe," "we Republicans know," and "our Republican cause." In these instances, candidates used Burke's implicit identification to associate themselves and their audiences with the party label. Next, candidates referred to parties as powerful through these types of statements: "strong, creative Democratic leadership," "party that trusts in the people," and "we Republicans are pledged to restore." Candidates also suggested that parties were contributing to a positive political order. Notice how these phrases called attention to the positive nature of parties: "to be a Republican in this hour is to dedicate one's life to freedom," "confidence and security have been brought by the Democratic party," "the hearts and hands of this great Republican party," "a party united, with positive programs," and "the Republican party is broad and inclusive."

Rhetorically, it appears that candidates have not disassembled party labels in building their own candidacies. As Table 3.1 illustrates, these terms have been deployed to do positive, integrative work indeed.

How Have the Discussions Changed over Time, Label, Speaker, and Circumstance?

It also is illustrative to examine the nuances of Table 3.1, particularly with regard to time, speaker, and circumstance to assess whether these factors influence the ways in which candidates discussed party labels.

Regarding time, Figure 3.1 displays the use of party labels between 1948 and 2000, and while these decreasing patterns are not linear, a downward trend is unmistakable. When the data in Figure 3.1 are examined in greater detail, the following patterns appear: Democratic candidates have decreased their use of the terms *Democrat* and *party* (but not *Republican*); Republican candidates have decreased their use of *party* and *Republican* (but not *Democrat*); winners have decreased their use of *party* and *Republican* (but not *Democrat*); and losers have decreased their use of *party* (but not *Democrat* or *Republican*).

These trends expose a subtle divisiveness in the addresses. It appears that candidates (particularly Democrats) in the latter years of the study are more comfortable addressing the party labels of their opponents than in trafficking in their own labels. Even though the overall use of party terms has been largely positive (see Table 3.1), these instances of discussing the opponent's party are expectedly negative.

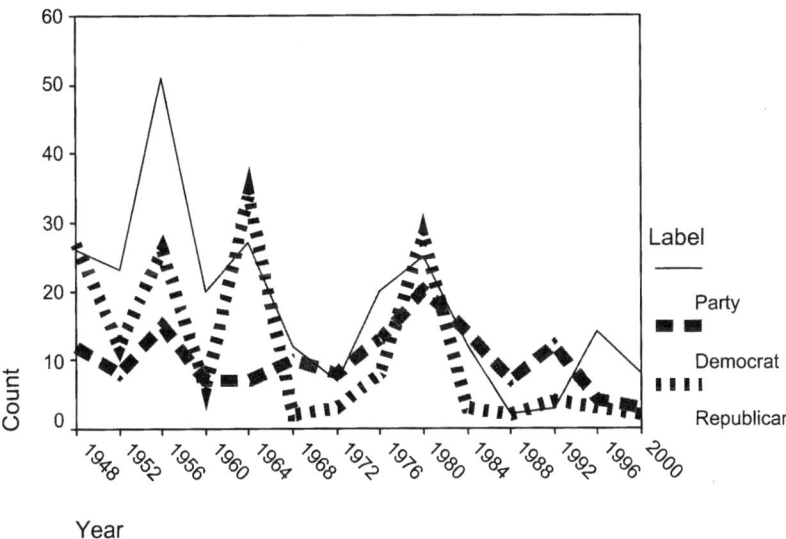

FIGURE 3.1   Labels over Time—All Speeches

Source: Collected by the authors from analysis of National Party Convention Acceptance Addresses, 1948–2000.

A second pattern in the data over time also points to an increased divisiveness in the deployment of party labels (Figure 3.2). These rhetorical patterns seem to roughly match quantitative trends of dealignment in the electorate. That is, between 1948 and 1964, candidates largely used their own party labels to identify with their constituencies; starting in 1968, the candidates used fewer labels and opted for a mixed approach of labels and identification and division. It is notable that the rhetorical cues that may increase commitment to party loyalty have fallen out of these public addresses.

When the speeches are examined by speaker type, two sets of differences emerge. First, Republicans displayed patterns that were distinct from Democrats. Specifically, Republicans were more likely to use Burke's identification strategies than Democrats [$\chi^2(2)$ = 18.43 (p. = 000)]. The differences were most stark for two types of identification: character and individual group. Here Republicans were more likely to discuss their label with certainty, resoluteness, and confidence, as did Thomas Dewey in 1948 when he mentioned "the permanent ideals of the Republican party," or Dwight Eisenhower in 1956 who discussed a "party of long-range principle," or Richard Nixon in 1968 who suggested that "a party that can unite itself will unite America," or George W. Bush in 2000 who spoke of "the party of ideas and innovation."[47] Similarly, Republicans were apt to link their party label to individuals and sets of Republicans. Gerald Ford, Ronald Reagan, and Bob Dole all referred to

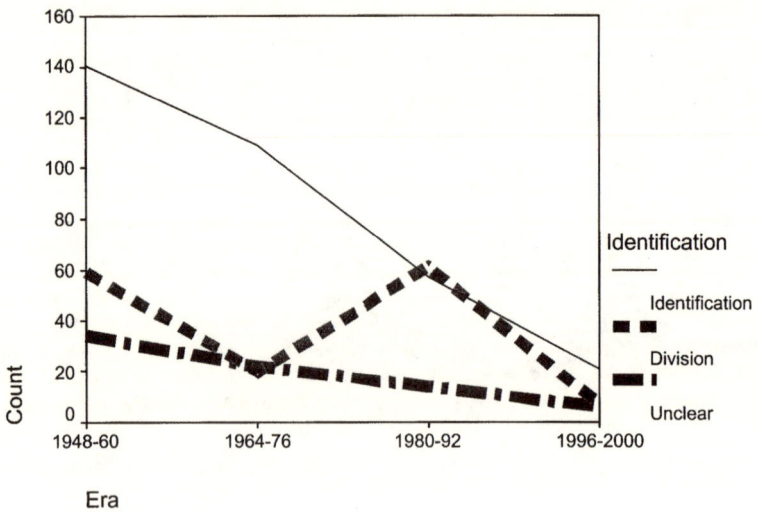

FIGURE 3.2   Identification versus Division—All Speeches

Source: Collected by the authors from analysis of National Party Convention Acceptance Addresses, 1948–2000.

"the party of Lincoln," Barry Goldwater mentioned "my friend and great Republican, Dick Nixon," and George W. Bush reminded his audience that he had "worked with Republicans."[48]

Republicans also were less likely to discuss the Democratic label than Democrats were to discuss the Republican label [$\chi^2(2) = 24.6$, p = .000)]. A result of this pattern was that Republican speeches contained more positive instances of party labels, more inclusive speeches, and more unity. The Grand Old Party (GOP) addresses featured such phrases as "the party that draws people together," "our party's going to win," "proud of our party tonight," and "a party united." Meanwhile, Democrats were likely to use division to galvanize their base, saying such things as "the Republican party is a house divided," "truth is, unhappily, not in the Republican president's words," "contrast with our Republican competitors," "Republican failures," "Republicans have campaigned against big government," and "drowsy harmony of the Republican party." Research from organizational identification might suggest that the Republicans used labels to encourage commitment and attachment and to persuade their base to adopt a long-term identification with their party. The Democrats' strategy, in contrast, appeared less committed to cultivating strong attachment to their labels and more interested in priming the importance of acting against the opponent.

With regard to circumstance, some distinctions between incumbents and challengers emerged. Incumbents were more likely to use the term *party*

$[\chi^2(2) = 7.93\ (p = .019)]$, to regard parties as elites $[\chi^2(2) = 31.8\ (p = .000)]$, and to discuss negative (divisive) attributes of parties $[\chi^2(4) = 21.9\ (p = .000)]$ than were challengers. For their part, challengers were less likely to try to connect with the audience through divisive appeals $[\chi^2(2) = 20.78\ (p = .000)]$. Perhaps because of their station in government, or because of their propinquity to party elites, incumbents seemed more comfortable using party labels. Challengers, in contrast, hesitated to use such terms when introducing themselves to the country as their party's nominee.

IMPLICATIONS

Overall, our rhetorical patterns suggest an interdependent relationship between candidate-centered speeches and party labels that is similar to that located by Kolodony between consultants and the parties. Examining the texts from quantitative and qualitative approaches uncovers several nuances to this relationship, three of which are described next.

Candidate-Centered Campaigns Have Worked to Maintain a Rhetorical Relationship with Party Organizations: Our analysis reveals that candidates appeared most concerned with rhetorically maintaining the relationship with the party in organization. While recent scholarship suggests that the modern party is indeed an outgrowth of elite interests meeting its goals, and may be best conceptualized as located in the "organization,"[49] the practice of protecting the relationship with party elites may, linguistically at least, honor the campaign organization at the expense of the voter.[50] Writing about the breakdown of machine politics, Gerald Pomper claims that "in its stress on coalitional goals, the machine carried the seeds of its own destruction. . . . The greatest defect of the machine was not its corruption; it was most deficient in its training in citizenship . . . it was inherently unable to teach the broader meaning of citizenship, the involvement of self in a larger social enterprise."[51] A similar temptation emerges with label use. Because they have largely constructed parties as groups of elites, candidates may be missing an opportunity to encourage voters to imagine and involve themselves in "the larger party enterprise." These rhetorical patterns—in subtle yet steady ways—may tempt citizens to believe that parties are far away from them.

Organizational communication research reminds us that identity is not static and that groups must constantly persuade members to identify with the organization and value such a commitment. If a specific organization is not actively recruiting and retaining its membership, then chances are its members may begin to regard their attachments as less salient (a point that Wattenberg makes regarding voter assessment of the parties), or another group may try to mobilize these individuals. While there are several predictors of voting behavior, we are intrigued that at a time of low turnout, two types of individuals have been found likely to vote: those who have been contacted, and those who live with another voter.[52] It is possible that human communication may underlie both of these effects; in the former instance, an individual has been asked to participate; in the latter, voting has been made familiar by a proximate other. Our data show that at the close of the twentieth century, candidates have been reluctant to ask "Democratic" or "Republican" voters to support them. Their avoidance of such constructions may make such labels less familiar to the electorate. Although there may be strategic reasons for eschewing labels related to the electorate, such language, theoretically, could have short- and long-term effects. If labels were to be gradually reinserted into campaign speeches that linked voters to the parties (intriguingly, a move of the George W. Bush campaign in 2000), then such language might function to inspire voters to imagine partisanship as familiar to them and to regard it as a salient part of their identity. The work of Schudson and Jamieson and the trajectory of the word "liberal" remind us that meanings of labels can change with time. These shifts can lead to new political understandings that can, and sometimes do, have political effects.

Republicans Appear More Comfortable in Approaching Audiences as Candidate-Centered Nominees: As described in the findings, GOP candidates were more likely than their Democratic peers to communicate identification and unity via their labels, negotiating their roles as party nominees and candidate-centered campaigners in ways that flattered the overall goals of their party. Other scholars have noted that the Republican Party displays a more straightforward cognitive style and favors a more orderly organizational culture.[53] Its use of labels mirrors these trends and may lead to more empowering, consistent, and positive invitations identification to the audiences of their speeches.

Challengers Negotiate the Role Differently Than Incumbents: Finally, challengers were more reluctant to discuss party labels and treated them more gingerly than did incumbents. Perhaps this pattern is related to the dates of these conventions (with the challenger's appearing before the incumbent's), the status of the challenger as the leader of the "out party," a common strategy of challengers to run against government, or a mixture of these factors. In any case, these rhetorical patterns raise the point that there may be considerable diversity in candidate-centered campaigning, and that challengers may be (by choice or necessity) more likely to use candidate-centered tactics.

Questions for the Future: Ultimately, this chapter raises as many questions as it answers. Concerning the use of party labels, future research could examine these terms in other contexts, as uttered by other speakers, as interpreted by audiences, and as related to electoral and policy outcomes. With regard to contemporary politics, studies could investigate the distinctions between

Democratic and Republican label use, particularly to assess whether the patterns located here point to perceptions of greater unity and identification with the Republican label as well as if Republicans negotiate the dual role of party nominee and candidate-centered campaigner more comfortably in other communication venues (speeches, advertisements, Web pages, etc.). And, in thinking about identification as a by-product of organizational communication, it would be heuristic to explore the connection between party labels and "unrealized partisans" as well as party labels and social influence. Theories and methods from organizational identification can be employed to better understand the intersection of communication and group membership, salience, and compliance. To date, party identification has been investigated through traditional measures (survey and turnout data) and largely as a static entity. We believe that attending to the unfolding presence or absence, stability, health, and attractiveness of party labels in campaign discourse also can contribute to what is known about electoral politics.

CONCLUSION

This chapter analyzed the ways in which the twenty-eight nominees prior to 2004 have rhetorically negotiated the temptation to wage candidate-centered campaigns and use party labels during their acceptance addresses. The findings reveal that, overall, party labels are depicted as positive, empowered, a source of identification, and functioning at the elite level; the use of party labels has decreased and has become more divisive over time; and there are notable differences between the ways in which Democrats and Republicans and incumbents and challengers deploy these labels.

The data show that candidate-centered campaigns have not rhetorically disassembled the parties in pursuit of assembling their own candidacies. When candidates chose to employ party labels, they generally were supportive of party institutions and were only critical when they discussed their opponent's label (a pattern that was more common for the Democrats than the Republicans). For their part, Republicans were more positive about their label and connoted greater unity and identification with it. The texts suggest that Republicans may be more comfortable in negotiating their roles as nominees and candidate-centered campaigners and more likely to garner support by encouraging their audience to identify with them. In contrast, the Democrats worked to galvanize their troops by emphasizing the negative aspects of the Republican label.

Much of the work on party decline and resurgence has focused on traditional measures such as survey and turnout data. Attending to how voters are encouraged to come to know parties through language offers an additional means of learning about their role in public life. By blending understandings of identification from political science, rhetoric, and organizational communication, we have attempted to enrich what is known about how presidential candidates have influenced the meanings of party labels and attempted to organize the electorate in their acceptance speeches. Because organizational identification is a communicative and dynamic process, it is important for political observers to note the quantitative and qualitative use of party labels—particularly at a time when some candidates are reluctant to use them. Looking at the overall number of labels in public discourse helps us see whether the electorate is being reminded to consider parties and partisanship as important; tracing the ways in which labels are used provides insight into how some terms stay solid, whereas others shift.

Research on candidate-centered campaigns needs to be sensitive to the centrality of party labels to contemporary elections. Even though candidates may be less likely to use them than they once did, labels provide powerful cues, continue to function as a key variable in voting behavior, and may be noticed by elected officials, party organizations, and voters. How candidates publicly discuss these relationships will influence how citizens understand and make sense of the parties. To call for a "total Republican victory" sends a different message to a party and to the country than to announce that one is a "uniter, not a divider." While these differences may seem modest, residing at the sentence level as they do, they expose perspectives that may create and constrain opportunities for public life.

NOTES

1. Dwight D. Eisenhower, "Nomination Acceptance Address at the Republican National Convention," Chicago, Illinois, July 11, 1952.

2. Ibid.

3. George W. Bush, "Nomination Acceptance Address at the Republican National Convention," Philadelphia, Pennsylvania, August 3, 2000.

4. Judith Trent and Robert Friedenberg, *Political Campaign Communication* (Westport, Conn.: Praeger, 1997).

5. Martin Wattenberg, *The Decline of American Political Parties, 1952–1996* (Cambridge, Mass.: Harvard University Press, 1998).

6. Murray Edelman, *Political Language* (New York: Academic Press, 1977), 142.

7. Murray Edelman, *Politics as Symbolic Action: Mass Arousal and Quiescence* (New York: Academic Press, 1971), 65.

8. Michael Schudson, *Advertising: The Uneasy Persuasion* (New York: Basic Books, 1986). Schudson continues: "But most of the names an adult encounters in a normal day are familiar. *This does not make them unimportant.* Culture works by taking things we already know and *making them actionable*" (xxi–xxii). Emphasis in original.

9. Kathleen Hall Jamieson, "The Subversive Effects of a Focus on Strategy in News Coverage of Campaigns," in *1–800 President, by the Twentieth Century Fund Task Force on Television and the Campaign of 1992* (New York: Twentieth Century Fund Press, 1993), accessible via http://www.tcf.org/task_forces/tv_1992_campaign/Jamieson.html (accessed May 15, 2004).

10. Edelman, *Political Language*, 10.

11. Victoria Fromkin and Robert Rodman, *An Introduction to Language* (New York: Holt, Rinehart, and Winston, 1974).

12. Gunther K. Kress and Robert H. Hodge, *Language as Ideology* (London: Routledge & Kegan Paul, 1981).

13. Peter L. Berger and Thomas Luckman, *The Social Construction of Reality* (Garden City, N.Y.: Doubleday, 1966).

14. Martin Wattenberg, *The Rise of Candidate-Centered Politics: Presidential Elections of the 1980s* (Cambridge, Mass.: Harvard University Press, 1991).

15. Wattenberg, *The Decline of American Political Parties*, 89.

16. Wattenberg, *The Rise of Candidate-Centered Politics*, 2.

17. Mathew McCubbins, "Party Decline and Presidential Campaigns in the Television Age," in *Under the Watchful Eye: Managing Presidential Campaigns in the Television Era*, ed. Mathew McCubbins (Washington, D.C.: Congressional Quarterly, 1992), 30.

18. John Aldrich, *Why Parties? The Origin and Transformation of Party Politics in America* (Chicago: University of Chicago Press, 1995), 161.

19. Ronald B. Rapoport, "Partisanship Change in a Candidate-Centered Era," *Journal of Politics* 59 (1997): 185–99.

20. Gregory S. Pastor, Walter J. Stone, and Ronald B. Rapoport, "Candidate-Centered Sources of Party Change: The Case of Pat Robertson," *Journal of Politics* 61 (1999): 423–44.

21. Kelly D. Patterson, Amy A. Bice, and Elizabeth Pipkin, "Political Parties, Candidates, and Presidential Campaigns: 1952–1996," *Presidential Studies Quarterly* 29 (1999): 26–39.

22. L. Sandy Maisel, "The Platform Writing Process: Candidate-Centered Platforms in 1992," *Political Science Quarterly* 108 (1992): 671–99.

23. Thomas E. Patterson, *Out of Order* (New York: Vintage, 1994).

24. Sharon E. Jarvis, "Campaigning Alone: Partisan versus Personal Language in the Presidential Nominating Convention Acceptance Addresses, 1948–2000," *American Behavioral Scientist* 44 (2000): 2152–71.

25. Robin Kolodony, "Electoral Partnerships: Political Consultants and Political Parties," in *Campaign Warriors: Political Consultants in Elections*, ed. James A. Thurber and Candice J. Nelson (Washington, D.C.: Brookings Institute Press, 2000), 110–32; Robin Kolodony and Angela Logan, "Political Consultants and the Extension of Party Goals," *PS: Political Science and Politics* 31 (1998): 155–59.

26. Kolodony, "Electoral Partnerships," 117.

27. Ibid.

28. A detailed discussion examining these aspects of identification in tandem is shown in Stacey Connaughton, "The Latino Voter" (Ph.D. dissertation, University of Texas at Austin, 2001).

29. Angus Campbell, Philip E. Converse, Warren E. Miller, and Donald E. Stokes, *The American Voter* (New York: Wiley, 1960).

30. Phillip E. Converse and Georges Dupuex, "Politicization of the Electorate in France and the United States," *Public Opinion Quarterly* 26 (1962), 1–23; Samuel Popkin, *The Reasoning Voter* (Chicago: University of Chicago Press, 1994); Wattenberg, *The Rise of Candidate-Centered Politics*; Henri Tajfel, ed., *Social Identity and Intergroup Relations* (Cambridge: Cambridge University Press, 1982); M. Kent Jennings and Richard G. Niemi, *Generations and Politics: A Panel Study of Young Adults and Their Parents* (Princeton: Princeton University Press, 1981).

31. See Norman H. Nie, Sidney Verba, and John Petrocik, *The Changing American Voter* (Cambridge, Mass.: Harvard University Press, 1976).

32. Morris P. Fiorina, "The Decline of Collective Responsibility in American Politics," *Daedalus* 109 (1980): 25–45.

33. Kenneth Burke, *A Rhetoric of Motives* (Berkeley: University of California Press, 1969).

34. Kenneth Burke, *Dramatism and Development* (Barre, Ind.: Clark University Press with Barre Publishers, 1972).

35. Identification is examined from a communication perspective in William L. Benoit, "Comparing the Clinton and Dole Advertising Campaigns: Identification and Division in 1996 Presidential Television Spots," *Communication Research Reports* 17 (2000): 39–48; George Cheney and Phillip K. Tompkins, "Coming to Terms with Organizational Identification and Commitment," *Central States Speech Journal* 38 (1987): 1–15.

36. Blake E. Ashforth and Fred Mael, "Social Identity Theory and the Organization," *Academy of Management Review* 14 (1989): 20–39; Alan M. Saks and Blake E. Ashforth, "A Longitudinal Investigation of the Relationships between Job Information Sources, Application Perceptions of Fit, and Work Outcomes," *Personnel Psychology* 50 (1997): 395–426; Craig R. Scott et al., "The Impacts of Communication and Multiple Identifications on Intent to Leave," *Management Communication Quarterly* 12 (1999): 400–35; George Cheney, "On the Various and Changing Meanings of Organizational Membership: A Field Study of Organizational Identification," *Communication Monographs* 50 (1983): 342–62; Phillip K. Tompkins and George Cheney, "Communication and Unobtrusive Control in Contemporary Organizations," in *Organizational Communication: Traditional Themes and New Directions*, ed. Robert D. McPhee and Phillip K. Tompkins (Thousand Oaks, Calif.: Sage, 1985), 179–210.

37. Kimberly D. Elsbach. "The Process of Social Identification: With What Do We Identify?," in *Identity in Organizations: Building Theory through Conversations*, ed. David A. Whetten and Paul C. Godfrey (Thousand Oaks, Calif.: Sage, 1998), 232–37.

38. Stuart Albert, Blake E. Ashforth, and Jane E. Dutton, "Organizational Identity and Identification: Charting New Waters and Building New Bridges," *Academy of Management Review* 25 (2000): 13–17.

39. Martin Wattenberg, *Where Have All the Voters Gone?* (Cambridge, Mass.: Harvard University Press, 2002).

40. Sharon E. Jarvis, "The Talk of the Party: Political Parties in American Discourse, 1948–1996" (Ph.D. dissertation, University of Texas at Austin, 2000).

41. Edward G. Carmines, John P. McIver, and James A. Stimson, "Unrealized Partisanship: A Theory of Dealignment," *Journal of Politics* 49 (1987): 376–400.

42. Addresses have been studied for their ironic (see Mark P. Moore "From a Government of the People, to a People of the Government: Irony as Rhetorical Strategy in Presidential Campaigns," *Quarterly Journal of Speech* 82 [1996]: 22–37), structural (see Trent and Friedenberg, *Political Campaign Communication*, 186), and mythic (see Henry Z. Scheele, "Ronald Reagan's 1980 Acceptance Address," *Western Journal of Speech Communication* 48 [1984]: 51–61) properties.

43. A discussion of this coding unit can be found in Roderick P. Hart and Sharon E. Jarvis, "The Delegates' Dialogue on the Issues," in *The Poll with a Human Face: The National Issues Convention Experiment in Political Communication*, ed. Maxwell McCombs and Amy Reynolds (Mahwah, N.J.: Lawrence Erlbaum, 1999), 59–84 .

44. A discussion of these descriptive variables can be found in Roderick P. Hart, *Campaign Talk: Why Elections Are Good for Us* (Princeton: Princeton University Press, 2000).

45. For the variables derived from the literature on political parties, see Sharon E. Jarvis, "Imagining Political Parties: A Constructionist Approach," in *Communication in U.S. Elections: New Agendas*, ed. Roderick P. Hart and Daron Shaw (Lanham, Md.: Rowman & Littlefield, 2001); for the variable identification, see Benoit, "Comparing," 48.

46. Michael Burgoon, Michael Pfau, and Thomas S. Birk, "An Inoculation Theory Explanation for the Effects of Corporate Issue/Advocacy Advertising Campaigns," *Communication Research* 22 (1995): 485–505; William L. Benoit and Joseph R. Blaney, "Acclaiming, Attacking, and Defending: A Functional Analysis of U.S. Nominating Convention Keynote Speeches," *Political Communication* 17 (2000): 61–84.

47. Thomas Dewey, "Nomination Acceptance Address at the Republican National Convention," Philadelphia, Pennsylvania, June 24, 1948; Dwight D. Eisenhower, "Nomination Acceptance Address at the Republican National Convention," San Francisco, California, August 23, 1956; Richard Nixon, "Nomination Acceptance Address at the Republican National Convention," Miami Beach, Florida, August 8, 1968.

48. Gerald Ford, "Nomination Acceptance Address at the Republican National Convention," Kansas City, Missouri, August 19, 1976; Ronald Reagan, "Nomination Acceptance Address at the Republican National Convention," Dallas, Texas, August 23, 1984; Barry Goldwater, "Nomination Acceptance Address at the Republican National Convention," San Francisco, California, July 17, 1964.

49. Aldrich, *Why Parties?*, 4.

50. Kolodony, "Electoral Partnerships," 113.

51. Gerald M. Pomper, *Passions and Interests: Political Party Concepts of American Democracy* (Lawrence: University of Kansas Press, 1992), 82, 84.

52. Wattenberg, "Where Have All the Voters Gone?," 73.

53. For research on cognitive consistency, see Phillip Tetlock, Kristen Hannum, and Patrick Micheletti, "Stability and Change in Senatorial Debate: Testing the Cognitive versus Rhetorical Style Hypothesis," *Journal of Personality and Social Psychology* 46 (1984): 979–90; for research on party cultures, see Jo Freeman, "The Political Culture of the Democratic and Republican Parties," *Political Science Quarterly* 101 (1986): 327–56.

4

What Gets Covered?

How Media Coverage of Elite Debate Drives the Rally-'Round-the-Flag Phenomenon: 1979–1998

Matthew A. Baum and Tim Groeling

Immediately following the initiation of the first Persian Gulf War on January 17, 1991, President George H. W. Bush saw his approval ratings spike by 24 percentage points (from 59 percent in a January 3–6 Gallup Poll to 83 percent in a January 17–20 Gallup Poll). Prior to the outbreak of the second Gulf War ("Operation Iraqi Freedom") in March 2003, President George W. Bush's approval rating (58 percent) was nearly identical to that of his father prior to the initiation of Operation Desert Storm. While, following the outbreak of war, the younger Bush's approval ratings also spiked, the rise was only about half as large—13 percentage points (from 58 to 71 percent)—as that enjoyed by the elder Bush.[1]

Why did the elder Bush receive a rally effect nearly twice as large as that of his son prior to the outbreak of war in the Persian Gulf? Brody suggests a possible explanation.[2] He argues that the existence or absence of elite criticism of the president immediately following the initiation of a use of force determines—or at least strongly influences—the magnitude of a post-use of force rally.[3] Perhaps there was greater criticism of the younger President Bush among political elites. If so, this could explain the differential in their rallies. Yet a review of the pre-war debates during the periods 1990–1991 and 2002–2003 suggests that this explanation is, in all likelihood, insufficient. The elder Bush barely managed to gain congressional authorization for using force to evict Iraq from Kuwait (by a 53 to 47 vote in the U.S. Senate), while the younger Bush gained overwhelming congressional support for using force against Iraq (by a 77 to 23 vote in the Senate). And pre-war levels of public support for using force were similar during the run-ups to the two Gulf Wars, with the younger Bush enjoying slightly higher levels of public support for his war policy. In five Gallup Polls conducted in December 1990, for instance, between 48 and 55 percent of respondents favored "going to war with Iraq in order to drive the Iraqis out of Kuwait."[4] In two separate Gallup Polls, conducted on February 28 and March 17, 2003, public support for going to war against Iraq measured 59 percent and 64 percent, respectively. These data suggest that, in all likelihood, greater elite criticism cannot account for the smaller rally received by George W. Bush.

Baum offers an alternative explanation.[5] Building on Brody and Shapiro and Brody, he argues that the extent of elite debate may matter less for the size of rallies than the extent of *media coverage* of any such debate and the partisan makeup of the debaters. Baum's argument differs from Brody's, however, by explicitly recognizing that these factors may not always move in tandem. To explain why this may be the case, Baum builds on a theory developed by Groeling, who argues that the presence of divided or unified control of government can significantly alter elite partisan discourse in the news.[6] In particular, Groeling argues that because the news media generally prefer novel, balanced, and conflict-filled stories featuring important actors, they prefer to devote precious airtime to stories about strife and discord within the president's party, particularly when the president's party controls both branches of government. Conversely, the nonpresidential party in both unified and divided government can either oppose or support the president and be relatively assured of receiving coverage. Unified government, therefore, serves to amplify media coverage of conflict within the presidential party.

Groeling further argues that because they are atypical and represent costly signals, opposition party endorsements of, or presidential party attacks on, the president are extremely credible.[7] More generally, typical individuals will consider statements by elites from their own party as being more credible than statements by opposition elites. Hence, while the day-to-day patterns of press coverage during divided government include large quantities of opposition party attacks on the president, these very patterns, combined with journalists' preference for novel stories, and the greater credibility to party identifiers of statements by their fellow partisans, may actually enhance the size of rallies during divided government. Moreover, because the public expects a president's fellow partisans to support him during an international crisis, the magnified novelty of any continued intra-party discord during rally events should be *even more* newsworthy for journalists, and so even more likely to gain airtime, as well as being especially damaging to the president's standing with the public.

This suggests that at least one factor contributing to the difference in magnitude of the rallies enjoyed by the two Presidents Bush may be the differing degrees of partisan control of government during their administrations. In other words, the elder President Bush went to war during divided government, while the younger Bush did so during a time of unified government. It may simply be the case that for reasons having little to do with the relative merits of the two conflicts, the elder Bush received more favorable coverage in the media. Of course, absent data on the tenor of media coverage, this explanation remains conjectural.

In fact, most theoretical discussions of Brody's and Shapiro's elite indexing hypothesis depend on a critical, yet an unproven, underlying assumption concerning the tenor of media coverage of elite debate surrounding U.S. uses of military force. That is, these arguments assume that the valence and extent of elite debate are accurately reflected in media coverage. In addition, with several exceptions,[8] they also have treated the public as an undifferentiated mass. Indeed, most previous studies of the rally phenomenon have either failed to account for partisan differences in rally effects or have based their arguments largely on the aforementioned unproven assumption, or both.[9]

In the absence of reliable longitudinal data on the nature and extent of elite discussion in the mass media, the latter assumption has never been subjected to rigorous empirical testing.[10] This chapter corrects that deficiency. We explicitly investigate whether, as Groeling and Baum argue, differences in *media coverage* of elite debate in unified versus divided government can help account for variations in the size of post-use-of-force rallies. We also investigate the role of political partisanship as a mediating factor in influencing the likelihood that different types of individuals will rally under differing circumstances. To do so, we have collected data on media coverage of congressional discussion of the president and his policies in periods before and after all major U.S. uses of military force between 1979 and 1998. We find, somewhat surprisingly, that while, as Brody and Shapiro and others have argued, the magnitude of rallies does indeed appear to vary systematically with the tenor of elite discussion in the media, the *actual* tenor of such elite discussion is overwhelmingly negative, even during rally events. Moreover, the end of the cold war appears to have produced virtually no effect on this near-constant drumbeat of negativity. Indeed, we find little evidence of a partisan truce at the water's edge.

The remainder of this chapter proceeds as follows. We begin by presenting our theoretical argument. We then discuss our methods and data and present the results of our empirical investigation. In the final section, we consider the implications of our findings and offer conclusions.

THEORY AND HYPOTHESIS

What Is Newsworthy?

Politicians expend considerable effort in seeking to shape their messages and images in the news media. However, because of their function as "gatekeepers" of political news content, journalists and news organizations maintain ultimate control over the content of their news programs. In deciding which political material is or is not "news," certain characteristics of stories or sources make them more (or less) desirable for journalists. In particular, Groeling argues that journalists are generally more likely to air a story if it is novel, conflictual, and balanced, and if it involves authoritative political actors.[11]

In brief, a preference for *novelty* implies simply that journalists place a premium on stories that are actually new (all else equal, journalists prefer stories that contain new or unexpected information to stories presenting old or expected information).[12] Journalists also prefer to emphasize negativity, or *conflict*, in their coverage, as this adds drama (all else equal, journalists prefer stories in which political figures attack each other to stories in which political figures praise each other).[13] Journalists' preference for *balance*, in turn, follows from their strong incentive to use procedures or strategic "rituals" of objectivity in doing their jobs[14] (all else equal, journalists prefer stories that include both parties' views to stories that only present the views of members of a single party). Finally, the premium placed on *authority* reflects reporters' belief that "the higher up an official's position in government, the more authoritative a source he or she was presumed to be, and the better his or her prospects for making the news"[15] (all else equal, journalists prefer to include sources with greater authority in their stories over less authoritative sources).

Table 4.1 applies these story characteristic preferences to four types of partisan evaluations of the president. This allows us to determine which types of stories are most likely to gain airtime. With such evaluations, Table 4.1 illustrates that praise of the president by his own party is of little interest to journalists, especially during divided government. This is because it is neither novel nor conflictual when a member of the president's party praises the president. In contrast, presidential party criticism of the president is highly attractive to journalists, especially during unified government. After all, criticism is, by defini-

TABLE 4.1
Newsworthiness of Partisan Evaluations of the President

| | *Journalist Payoff from:* | | | | |
| | | | | *Authority* | |
Message Type	*Novelty*	*Conflict*	*Balance*	*Div. Govt.*	*Uni. Govt.*
President praised by his party	low	low	low	low	high
President criticized by his party	high	high	low	low	high
President praised by other party	high	low	high	high	low
President criticized by other party	low	high	high	high	low

Source: Collected by the authors from the Vanderbilt Television Archives, *ABC World News Tonight*.

tion, conflictual. And it is certainly novel—relatively unusual and unexpected—when a president's fellow partisan criticizes him. Evaluations of the president by the nonpresidential party, in contrast, tend to be newsworthy, regardless of which party controls Congress, albeit somewhat more so in divided government. This is because such comments are always either novel—if they consist of praise for the president—or conflictual—if they are critical of the president. Airing comments by the opposition party also helps add balance to stories about the president and his policies. Finally, journalists' preference for authoritative sources leads to a tendency to overrepresent the majority party in Congress. If the majority party happens to share the president's party affiliation, then, for the reasons outlined earlier, this leads to the strongest possible incentive for journalists to air any intra-party criticism of the president, as such criticism is novel, conflictual, and authoritative and also may enhance balance (at least if the story features the president or members of his administration advocating his policies).

"Rally Events" As Special Cases

If Table 4.1 delineates the newsworthiness of "politics as usual," then this raises the question of how newsworthiness in a foreign policy crisis might systematically differ. Implicit in the very notion of a "rally-'round-the-flag" is that international crises will induce each party to increase its support for the president. From a standpoint of newsworthiness, however, the impact is somewhat more complex.

If journalists do, in fact, expect politics to "stop at the water's edge" in times of crisis, then their perception of the novelty of the various types of evaluations of the president might differ from "normal" times as well. In other words, if journalists *expect* partisans from both parties to rally behind the president during a crisis, then criticism of the president by *either* party—but especially the presidential party—becomes even more newsworthy than during noncrisis periods. Table 4.2 illustrates this point. While this table tells us little about each party's intent to support the president in a time of crisis, it does

TABLE 4.2
Novelty of Partisan Evaluations of the President, "Normal" versus "Rally" Periods

Message Type	Normal	Rally
President praised by his party	low	lower
President criticized by his party	high	higher
President praised by other party	high	lower
President criticized by other party	low	higher

Source: Collected by the authors from the Vanderbilt Television Archives, *ABC World News Tonight*.

suggest that should any members of either party choose to criticize the president, then those members will find journalists even more eager to air their comments than during noncrisis times.

What Is Persuasive?

In determining each message type's effect on viewers, it is important to note not just the *content* of the message itself but also its *credibility* and that of the speaker. Party messages are not "injected" into a passive public but rather are processed by individuals who will accept or reject such messages, depending in part on their credibility.[16]

One source of credibility for a message is the belief that the speaker and listener have common interests.[17] Restated in partisan terms, this suggests that statements by a listener's own party will be regarded as more credible than those of the opposing party, all else equal. We call this our "partisan credibility conjecture."[18]

Another important source of credibility derives from the interaction of source and message: whether the message being spoken is costly to the speaker.[19] Messages viewed as harming the interests of the speaker are regarded as being more credible than those that impose no costs (so-called "cheap talk").[20] In the context of partisan messages, it follows that messages by partisan speakers that appear to damage their own party or help the other party are regarded as more credible than messages that help their own party or damage the other party. We call this our "costly credibility conjecture." Such costly messages should be at least somewhat credible regardless of the party affiliation of the listener. Table 4.3 summarizes the relative credibility of different partisan messages about the president based on their partisan and costly credibility.

Table 4.3 demonstrates the relatively weak persuasive power of "politics as usual" statements (i.e., nonpresidential party attacks on the president and presidential party praise). Such statements serve only to rally their own followers, who in all likelihood *already* approved of the president *prior* to any rally event and, hence, are unable to reevaluate the president upward following a use of military force.[21] In contrast, nonpresidential party praise should be exceptionally persuasive and beneficial to the president, especially among citizens belonging to the nonpresidential party. If rally events really do produce bipartisan elite support for the president, then this suggests that such support should be highly effective at moving public opinion—especially among opposition identifiers—in support of the president. Similarly, if members of the president's own party attack him, then the effects on public opinion should be similarly dramatic (but negative), especially among the president's fellow partisans. In both cases, media demand for such stories virtually ensures that they will receive coverage if offered.

TABLE 4.3
Party and Costly Credibility By Party of Speaker and Viewer

	Non-Presidential Party (NPP) Attacks Presdident			Presidential Party (PP) Attacks President		
	NPP viewer	Ind. viewer	PP viewer	NPP viewer	Ind. viewer	PP viewer
Party Credibility	+	−	−	−	−	+
Costly Credibility	−	−	−	+	+	+

	Non-Presidential Party (NPP) Praises Presdident			Presidential Party (PP) Praises President		
	NPP viewer	Ind. viewer	PP viewer	NPP viewer	Ind. viewer	PP viewer
Party Credibility	+	−	−	−	−	+
Costly Credibility	+	+	+	−	−	−

Source: Collected by the authors from the Vanderbilt Television Archives, *ABC World News Tonight.*

HYPOTHESES

A large number of hypotheses concerning the nature, extent, and consequences of partisan rhetoric in the media follow from the theory summarized earlier. For this chapter, however, we focus our empirical tests on seven hypotheses pertaining, directly or indirectly, to the implications of the theory for the rally phenomenon.[22]

1. *The Elite Indexing Hypothesis: The more supportive the elite commentary presented in the media during rally events, the larger the rally effect among the general public.* This hypothesis tests the indexing hypothesis advanced by Brody and Shapiro[23] and others.
2. *The Negativity Hypothesis: Overall, a majority of all elite comments concerning the president featured in the media will be critical of the president and his policies, even during rally events.* This hypothesis tests one of the assumptions of our model.
3. *The Credible Cue Hypothesis: Presidential evaluations by members of a given party will have a stronger effect on the propensity to rally of that party's identifiers than will comments by party elites of the other party.* This hypothesis specifically tests the impact of *partisan credibility* on public opinion.
4. *Corollary 1 to the Credible Cue Hypothesis: As praise by the nonpresidential party increases, relative to criticism by the presidential party, rallies*

will increase in magnitude. This corollary predicts a strong, persuasive impact from partisan statements with a high level of *costly credibility.*

5. **Corollary 2 to the Credible Cue Hypothesis:** *Variations in the ratio of criticism by the nonpresidential party to praise by the presidential party will have a weaker effect on rallies.* In contrast to Corollary 1, this hypothesis predicts a weaker impact of partisan statements with the lowest level of *costly credibility.*

6. **The Unified Government Hypothesis:** *Presidential party criticism of the president will be featured more frequently in the media during unified government than during divided government. Nonpresidential party criticism of the president will be similarly featured in the media during both unified and divided government.* This hypothesis predicts that unified government will increase media coverage of internal disputes within the presidential party.[24]

7. **The Unified Rally Hypothesis:** *Due to the exceptional novelty of rally events, presidential party criticism of the president will be featured even more prominently during this time than in other periods. The praise-to-criticism ratio for the nonpresidential party will vary less across unified and divided government, or across rally and nonrally periods.* As illustrated in Table 4.2, the special case of rallies increases the novelty value of internal disputes within the presidential party, particularly in unified government.

Data and Methodology

Mueller lists six categories of rally events: (1) sudden military interventions, (2) major military developments in ongoing wars, (3) major diplomatic developments, (4) dramatic technological developments, (5) meetings between the U.S. president and leaders of other major powers, and (6) the start of each presidential term.[25] He argues that for an event to be classified as a potential rally event, it should satisfy three criteria: (1) be international, (2) directly involve the United States in general and the president in particular, and (3) be "specific, dramatic, and sharply focused."[26] Oneal and others further restrict their definition of rally events to "major uses of force during a crisis."[27] This, they argue, ensures that they are "considering only cases that were truly consequential for the U.S. and salient to the public, necessary conditions for a rally." Following Oneal and others, we restrict our analysis to major uses of force during foreign policy crises.

For our data set, we rely on Baum, whose data encompass the period 1953–1998.[28] Baum's data are derived from an updated version of Blechman's and Kaplan's data set on political uses of force.[29] We code all uses of force measuring levels 1–3 on Blechman's and Kaplan's scale as "major uses of force." Of these, also following Baum, we exclude several events that appeared inconsistent with the aforementioned definitions, either because they represented long-scheduled military exercises (e.g., "Team Spirit" in Korea in March 1990) or a cancellation of a previously scheduled withdrawal of forces rather than a proactive and an unscheduled force deployment (e.g., November 1991 in Korea), or because they clearly did not constitute major uses of force during a U.S. foreign policy crisis (e.g., U.S. support for withdrawal of UN forces from Somalia during the period January–March 1995, which took place long after the United States withdrew its forces from that nation). Our data include a total of thirty-seven rally events, representing "major uses of force" by the United States between 1979 and 1998.

With the aid of a small army of research assistants, we collected data on congressional comments on the president and the executive branch of government during the periods immediately preceding and following each candidate rally event.[30] Because American uses of military force typically do not emerge overnight as bolts from the blue, we collected data for a sixty-day window surrounding each rally event, from thirty days prior to thirty days after the start date. Given our primary interest in explaining short-term media and public responses to foreign policy rallies, for our primary analysis we designate rally periods beginning ten days prior to the start date of each event until twenty days following the event. Figure 4.1 illustrates the preponderance of congressional commentary in the media regarding foreign policy within this window.

For each event, we first searched the Vanderbilt Television News Abstracts to locate every instance on the evening news broadcasts of a representative broadcast network (ABC's *World News Tonight*) in which a senator or representative appeared in stories related to the president or the executive branch of government. Next, our research assistants watched videotaped recordings or read verbatim transcripts of all of the stories, coding the valence (positive, negative, or neutral) of each member of Congress's comments, as well as their subject matters (foreign or domestic policy issues) and the characteristics of the speaker (party affiliation, leadership position in Congress, etc.). In order to be included in our analysis, the member's statements had to be presented in the broadcast as a direct quote of an identifiable member, and the statement had to pertain directly to the president or executive branch of government. (The content analysis coding form is presented in the Appendix at the end of this chapter.) We identified a total of 625 comments on *World News Tonight* appropriate for coding during the 2,220 days falling within ±thirty-day windows surrounding our thirty-seven rally events.[31] The magnitude of the coding project prevented us from assigning multiple coders to all of our observations. As a "second-best" alternative, we performed intercoder reliability tests on a randomly selected subset of approximately 20 percent of our data. The results from these tests indicated that our coders agreed on

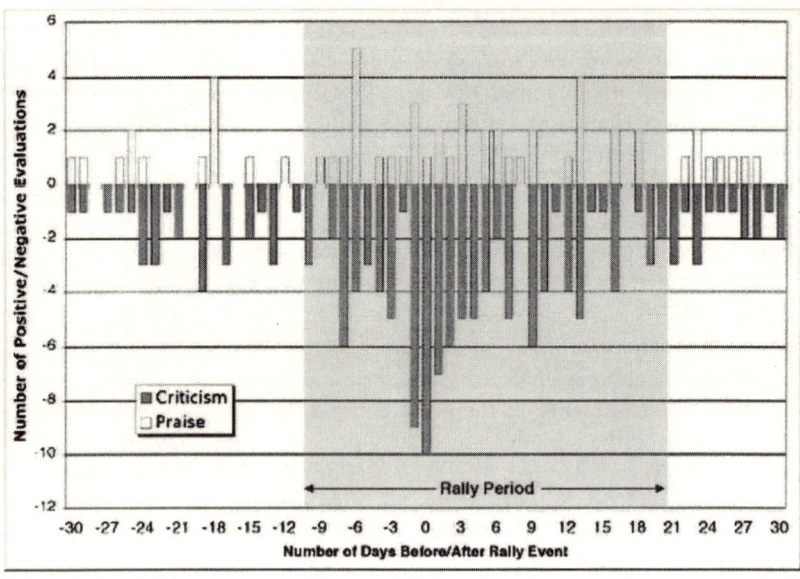

FIGURE 4.1 Trend in Positive and Negative Foreign Policy Evaluations Preceding and Following Rally Events

Source: Collected by the authors from the Vanderbilt Television Archives, *ABC World News Tonight*.

approximately 80 percent of all coding decisions. Though certainly not ideal, we consider this an acceptable level of intercoder agreement for this initial stage of our research. We turn next to our findings.

STATISTICAL RESULTS

We begin by testing the Elite Indexing and Credible Cue Hypotheses.[32] Figures 4.2–4.4 illustrate the relationship between changes in the valence of partisan discussion in the media and the size of post-use of force rallies. The curve in Figure 4.2 appears to confirm the Elite Indexing Hypothesis; in these data, each 1 percent increase in positive elite discussion on *World News Tonight* is associated with about a 1.4 percent increase in the magnitude of a post-use of force rally. The R^2 indicates that the valence of media coverage of elite discussion alone accounts for nearly 18 percent of the variation in rally magnitude in our data.[33]

Figures 4.3 and 4.4, in turn, test the Credible Cue Hypothesis, along with its two corollaries. Once again, the results are consistent with all three hypotheses. In Figure 4.3, the dashed gray curve tracks the relationship

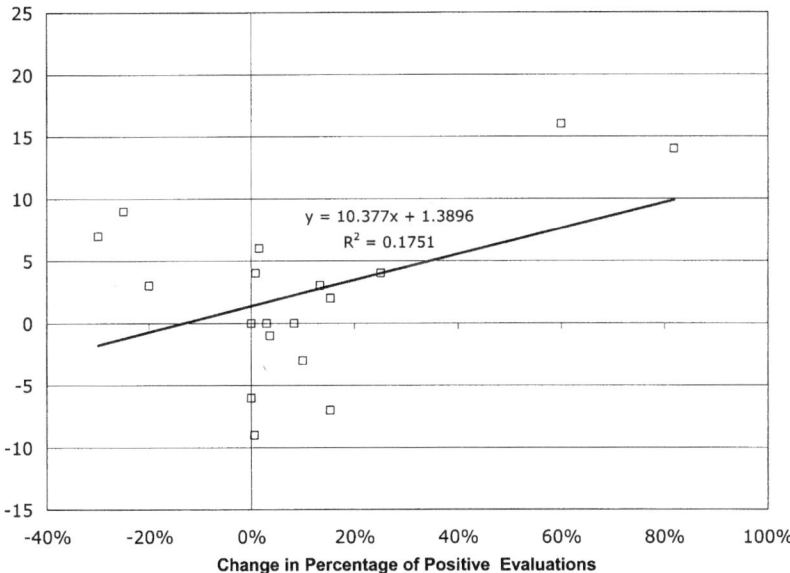

FIGURE 4.2 Overall Rally Size as a Function of Changes in the Valence of Evaluations from All Sources

Source: Collected by the authors from the Vanderbilt Television Archives, *ABC World News Tonight.*

between the valence of presidential party comments about the president during rally events and the size of rallies among the president's fellow partisans. The solid dark curve then does the same for the nonpresidential party. In both cases, the curves are substantially steeper than in Figure 4.2 and the R^2 values are much larger (.30 and .27, respectively). This indicates that, presumably due to their relatively greater credibility, rallies among members of a given party are much more strongly influenced by elites from the same party than by elites from the opposition party.

Figure 4.4 tests our two corollaries to the Credible Cue Hypotheses. The credible evaluations data, shown in gray, offer strong support for the first corollary. In these data, increases in credible praise, and/or decreases in credible criticism—from either party—are clearly associated with increases in the overall size of post-use of force rallies. In contrast, increases in noncredible praise or decreases in noncredible criticism (shown as solid black) have virtually no effect on rally magnitude. This represents clear support for the second corollary.

We turn next to the Negativity Hypothesis. Table 4.4 summarizes the valence of partisan evaluations in our data. The most noteworthy pattern in Table 4.4 is the consistent, overwhelming predominance of negative evaluations

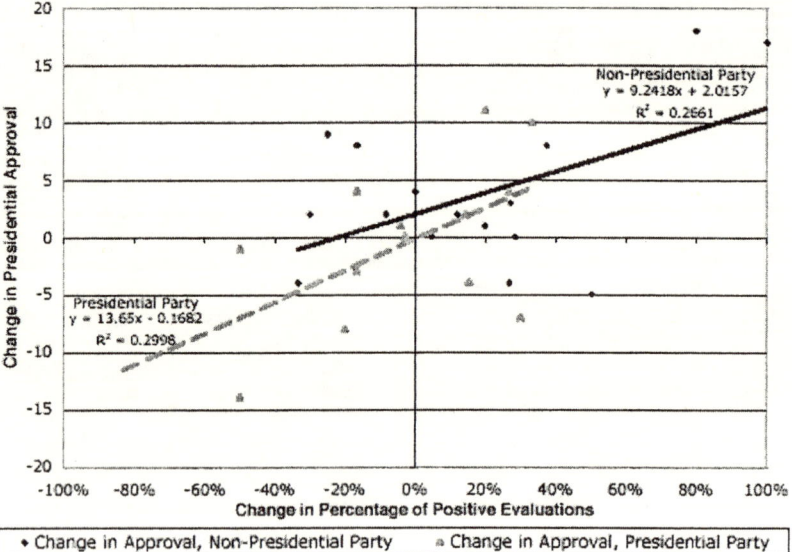

FIGURE 4.3 Partisan Rally Size as a Function of Changes in the Valence of Evaluations from Fellow Partisans

Source: Collected by the authors from the Vanderbilt Television Archives, *ABC World News Tonight*.

of the president and his administration, both with foreign and domestic politics. Regardless of how the data are parsed, roughly three-quarters of all evaluations featured on *World News Tonight* during the sixty-day window surrounding rally events was *negative*.

Somewhat more surprisingly, as Table 4.5 indicates, the overwhelming predominance of negativity ebbs hardly at all during rally events. Indeed, when we focus only on foreign policy evaluations, criticism of the president and his administration actually *increases* modestly following the initiation of a rally event.

One possible explanation for these patterns may be the disproportionate weight our data places on the post-cold war era, which accounts for fully half of the years included in our investigation. Some scholars have conjectured that absent the unifying threat to national survival posed by the Soviet Union, domestic politics may wield a stronger influence on American foreign policy in the post-cold war era.[34] If so, we would expect to see a shift in our data in the level of negativity between the cold war (1979–1988 in our data) and post-cold war (1989–1998) periods. Yet, as shown in Table 4.6, our results offer, at most, limited support for this conjecture. While the level of negativity in congressional evaluations did rise in the post-cold war period, the differences are

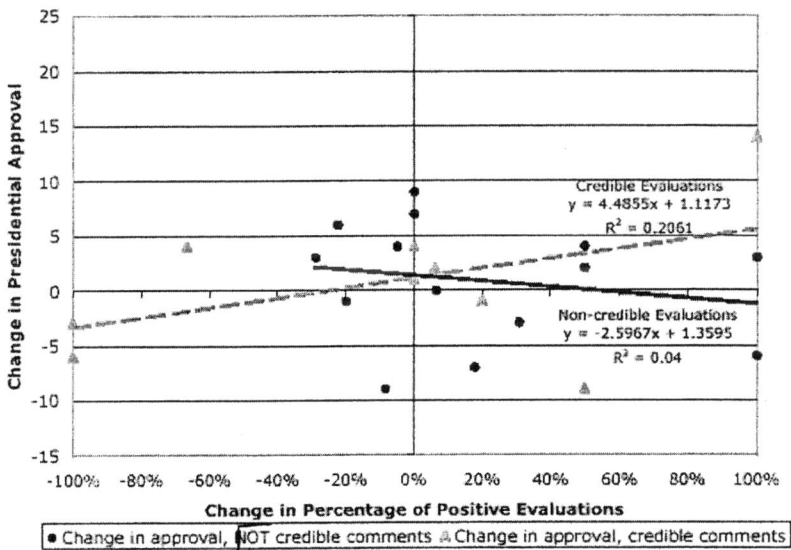

FIGURE 4.4 Partisan Rally Size as a Function of Changes in the Ratio of Credible/Not Credible Positive and Negative Evaluations
Source: Collected by the authors from the Vanderbilt Television Archives, *ABC World News Tonight*.

small and statistically insignificant for comments by members of both the presidential and nonpresidential parties.

Taken together, the results from Tables 4.4–4.6 offer strong support for the Negativity Hypothesis. On both foreign and domestic policy issues, during rally and non-rally periods, as well as during and after the cold war, the patterns of elite discussion of the president and his policies featured in the media remain consistently and overwhelmingly negative and critical.

The final two hypotheses we investigate are the Unified Government and Unified Rally Hypotheses. Table 4.7 offers support for the former hypothesis. As predicted, presidential party criticism of the president and his policies increases by 13 percentage points during unified government, from 64 to 77 percent of all presidential party evaluations featured on *World News Tonight* ($p \leq .05$). As also predicted, the praise-to-criticism ratio for the nonpresidential party, as featured in the media, changes hardly at all from unified to divided government.

Finally, Figure 4.5 presents the results of our test of the Unified Rally Hypothesis. The first two bars in Figure 4.5 show the flows of elite discussion during unified government. As predicted, due to their exceptional novelty—and, once again, contrary to the conventional wisdom regarding the

TABLE 4.4
Valence of Congressional Evaluations of the President or Government

	Valance of Message		
	Negative	Positive	n
President and/or Government	78%	22%	490
President Only	74%	26%	291
Foreign Policy Only	78%	22%	197
President Foreign Policy Only	74%	26%	119

Source: Collected by the authors from the Vanderbilt Television Archives, *ABC World News Tonight*.

TABLE 4.5
Valence of Congressional Evaluations of the
President or Government, Rally and Non-Rally Periods

Target	Valance of Messages (Non-Rally)			Valance of Messages (Rally)		
	Negative	Positive	n	Negative	Positive	n
President and/or Government	79%	21%	182	78%	22%	308
President Only	79%	21%	90	76%	24%	201
President and/or Government Foreign Policy Only	75%	25%	55	77%	23%	141
President, Foreign Policy Only	72%	28%	29	76%	24%	90

Source: Collected by the authors from the Vanderbilt Television Archives, *ABC World News Tonight*.

TABLE 4.6
Valence of Congressional Evaluations of the
President or Government, during and after the Cold War

	Valance of Messages (Cold War)			Valance of Messages (Post-Cold War)		
	Negative	Positive	n	Negative	Positive	n
Presidential Party	68%	32%	96	69%	31%	91
Nonpresidential Party	81%	19%	140	87%	23%	163

Source: Collected by the authors from the Vanderbilt Television Archives, *ABC World News Tonight*.

Matthew A. Baum and Tim Groeling 63

TABLE 4.7
Valence of Congressional Evaluations of the
President or Government, Unified and Divided Government

	Valance of Messages (Unified Government)			Valence of Messages (Divided Government)		
	Negative	Positive	n	Negative	Positive	n
Presidential Party	77%	23%	62	64%	36%	125
Nonpresidential Party	86%	14%	51	84%	16%	252

Source: Collected by the authors from the Vanderbilt Television Archives, *ABC World News Tonight*.

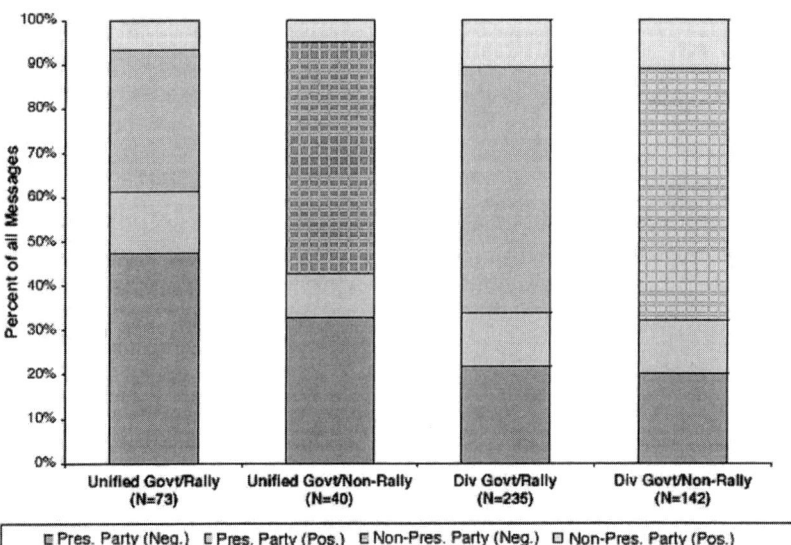

FIGURE 4.5 Valence of Evaluations from Presidential and Non-Presidential Party during Unified and Divided Government, Rally and Non-Rally Periods

Source: Collected by the authors from the Vanderbilt Television Archives, *ABC World News Tonight*.

rally phenomenon—criticism of the president by the presidential party actually *increases* during rally events. In contrast, the existence or absence of a rally event makes virtually no difference in the tenor of elite discussion in the media during divided government.

Several other interesting patterns are apparent in Figure 4.5. First, during unified government, at least in terms of media coverage, nonpresidential party criticism of the president appears muted during rally periods. At the same time, media coverage of nonpresidential party praise of the president rises during rallies in unified government, both absolutely and relative to nonpresidential party criticism. These results, though not directly predicted by our hypotheses, may help explain Baum's finding that the bulk of post-use of force rallies occurs among opposition party identifiers rather than among the president's fellow partisans. Baum attributes this to the greater number of opposition disapprovers potentially available to rally. (After all, if one *already* approves of the president's job performance, then there is no room to reevaluate upward.) Our findings suggest that a second, complementary causal factor also may be at play. That is, even as criticism by the president's fellow partisans becomes increasingly prevalent in the media following rally events, such criticism by the nonpresidential party drops off dramatically, while nonpresidential party praise increases considerably (particularly as a proportion of all nonpresidential party comments). Hence, not only are more opposition party identifiers *available* to rally, but they also are more likely than the president's fellow partisans to receive highly credible signals of support for the president (i.e., supportive comments from their own party's elites appearing in the media).[35]

Perhaps mitigating this tendency, at least to some extent, is an additional interesting pattern apparent in Figure 4.5. That is, during unified government, but not during divided government, the nonpresidential party appears in the media far less frequently during rally periods than during nonrally periods. This may help account for the pattern highlighted earlier. It may be the case that nonpresidential party elites are continuing to criticize the president, but that journalists are simply more likely to ignore such criticism during rally periods, instead focusing on the relatively small number of supportive comments by opposition party elites.[36] The net effect would be a predominance of positive commentary in the media by nonpresidential party elites, albeit in the context of a substantially reduced overall volume of opposition party rhetoric in the media.

CONCLUSION

We now briefly return to the anecdote with which we began this chapter. Our theory suggests that a likely explanation, at least in part, for the difference in the magnitude of the rallies enjoyed by the two Presidents Bush may be the differences in elite rhetoric presented by the media. We have found evidence that attacks on the president will tend to be more prevalent in the media during times of unified government, as prevailed during the 2003 war in Iraq, than during periods of divided government, as prevailed during the 1991 Persian Gulf War. And, in fact, a review of media content during the sixty-day window surrounding the start dates for the two wars reveals that the younger president Bush does appear to have endured greater criticism of his war policy from congressional elites than did his father.

In the month prior to the first Persian Gulf War, partisan rhetoric in the media followed predictable patterns: Democratic members of Congress appearing on *World News Tonight* were three times as likely to criticize as to praise the president, while Republicans were five times as likely to praise him. Yet once the war started, *World News Tonight* featured *not one* criticism of the president by a member of Congress.[37] In sharp contrast, during the entire sixty-day window we investigated surrounding the 2003 war in Iraq, *World News Tonight* presented not a single supportive comment toward the president from a member of Congress. Indeed, as we anticipated, the younger President Bush appears to have received uniformly more critical coverage than his father in at least this one prominent media outlet. Of course, there are many possible explanations for this pattern—such as the far more extensive criticism of U.S. policy from some of America's traditional allies and hence for the difference in rally magnitudes enjoyed by the two presidents.[38] These results should, therefore, be interpreted as being merely suggestive.

More generally, our findings, though preliminary, hold potentially important implications for future presidents. With the possible exception of full-scale wars, we find little evidence that future presidents can expect to consistently enjoy meaningful rallies following uses of force abroad, at least to the extent that rally magnitude does indeed follow from the nature and extent of elite debate presented in the media. (We found evidence in support of this hypothesis, yet further testing is clearly necessary.) Indeed, the most striking pattern in our findings is the seemingly unyielding wave of negativity in media coverage of elite discussion concerning the president and his policies. The emergence of rally events appears to hardly matter to the tone of elite discussion featured in the media. Regardless of how we parse the data, roughly three-quarters of all comments concerning the president or his administration by members of Congress was critical.

In addition to offering support for our theory concerning the effects of individual and institutional factors in shaping the nature and extent of post-use of force rallies, our findings also hold an important implication for diversionary war theory.[39] If presidents cannot be confident of receiving favorable treatment by the media when they employ military force abroad—at least short of a full-scale war such as Operation Iraqi Freedom—then it seems highly unlikely that they would do so for purely domestic political purposes. Our data suggest that attempting to divert public attention from domestic difficulties through a use of force abroad is a highly risky strategy.

Our findings in this initial inquiry suggest that while Brody's hypothesis[40] concerning the link between elite debate and the magnitude of rallies appears to be borne out by the data, one central implication of this hypothesis—given the apparent predominance of critical congressional comments in the media—is that politically consequential rallies are likely to be relatively few and far between, particularly in times of unified government. To more thoroughly test our hypotheses, however, as well as a variety of additional hypotheses that follow from our theory, we intend to expand our content analyses to include additional media outlets, additional sources of elite rhetoric, and additional years. By expanding our investigation, we hope, in part, to determine whether, perhaps, supportive comments from other sources, such as policy experts or administration officials themselves, may in at least some instances counterbalance the effects of incessant congressional criticism. If so, perhaps the rally phenomenon may yet prove to be of some political consequence.

Appendix

What is your student ID number?

To ensure accuracy, please re-type your student ID number here:

Story Identifier Code:

Was at least one member of Congress (MC) or Senator QUOTED or did they SPEAK in their own voice in the story? ● Yes
[If no, stop here. If yes, please fill out the information below for EACH Senator or MC speaking in the story] ○ No

1. Is the person a Senator or a member of the House of Representatives?
   ○ Senator
   ○ Representative
   ● Unidentified

2. What is their name?

3. What is their state? (If you don't know a state's two-letter Postal abbreviation, you can look it up here. If their state is not given in the story at all, please code their state as ZZ)

4. What is their party?
   ○ Democrat
   ○ Republican
   ○ Independent
   ○ Not Given in Story/Unknown

(Note: Only code their party if it is explicitly cited in the story... don't look it up or guess or rely on your existing knowledge)

5. What is their position within the legislature?
[In other words, do they have a title such as a leadership position or committee chairmanship noted in the story other than Rep or Senator? Things like "Majority Whip", "Commerce Committee Ranking Member" etc. Leave blank if they're only identified as a senator or rep]

6. For each of the issue areas below, please indicate if the member quoted above praises or criticizes the *president* in their quoted comment or statement, or imparts neutral information/talks about the subject without taking a position (note that a single member might do both in the same statement):

☐ Praise ☐ Criticize ☐ Neutral	Management of the U.S. Economy
☐ Praise ☐ Criticize ☐ Neutral	International Trade/Finance
☐ Praise ☐ Criticize ☐ Neutral	Government Budget/Deficit/Spending/Taxation
☐ Praise ☐ Criticize ☐ Neutral	Foreign Policy/Military
☐ Praise ☐ Criticize ☐ Neutral	Domestic Policy (including Welfare, Social Security/Medicare, Crime, Education, Abortion)
☐ Praise ☐ Criticize ☐ Neutral	Scandal/Personal Behavior
☐ Praise ☐ Criticize ☐ Neutral	Personal characteristics/Leadership
Other Praise? Please specify:	
Other Criticism? Please specify:	

7. For each of the issue areas below, please indicate if the member quoted above praises or criticizes a *member/agency/department of the executive branch or the policy of the government in general* in their comment/statement their quoted comment or statement, or imparts neutral information/talks about the subject without taking a position(note that a single member might do both in the same statement):

☐ Praise ☐ Criticize ☐ Neutral	Management of the U.S. Economy
☐ Praise ☐ Criticize ☐ Neutral	International Trade/Finance
☐ Praise ☐ Criticize ☐ Neutral	Government Budget/Deficit/Spending/Taxation
☐ Praise ☐ Criticize ☐ Neutral	Foreign Policy/Military
☐ Praise ☐ Criticize ☐ Neutral	Domestic Policy (including Welfare, Social Security/Medicare, Crime, Education, Abortion)
☐ Praise ☐ Criticize ☐ Neutral	Scandal/Personal Behavior

NOTES

1. Source: Gallup Polls, March 14–15, 2003, and March 22–23, 2003.

2. Richard A. Brody, *Assessing Presidential Character: The Media, Elite Opinion, and Public Support* (Stanford, Calif.: Stanford University Press, 1991).

3. Richard A. Brody and Catherine R. Shapiro, "A Reconsideration of the Rally Phenomenon in Public Opinion," in *Political Behavior Annual*, vol. 2, ed. Samuel Long (Boulder, Colo.: Westview Press, 1991), 77–102; John R. Oneal, Brad Lian, and James H. Joyner Jr., "Are the American People 'Pretty Prudent?' Public Responses to U.S. Uses of Force, 1950–1988," *International Studies Quarterly* 40 (1996): 261–80.

4. John E. Mueller, *Policy and Opinion in the Gulf War* (Chicago: University of Chicago Press, 1994), 219.

5. Matthew A. Baum, "The Constituent Foundations of the Rally-'Round-the-Flag Phenomenon," *International Studies Quarterly* 46 (June 2002): 263–98.

6. Tim Groeling, "When Politicians Attack: The Causes, Contours, and Consequences of Partisan Political Communication" (Ph.D. dissertation, University of California, San Diego, 2001).

7. See Gary F. Koeske and William D. Crano, "The Effect of Congruous and Incongruous Source-Statement Combinations upon the Judged Credibility of a Communication," *Journal of Experimental Social Psychology* 4 (1968): 384–99; Donald Dutton, "The Maverick Effect: Increased Communicator Credibility as a Result of Abandoning a Career," *Canadian Journal of Behavioral Science* 5 (1973): 145–51; Alice H. Eagly, Wendy Wood, and Shelly Chaiken, "Causal Inferences about Communicators and Their Effect on Opinion Change," *Journal of Personality and Social Psychology* 36 (1978): 424–35; Alice H. Eagly, "Recipient Characteristics as Determinants of Responses to Persuasion," in *Cognitive Responses and Persuasion*, ed. Richard E. Petty, Thomas M. Ostrom, and Timothy C. Brock (Mahwah, N.J.: Erlbaum, 1981), 173–95; Arthur Lupia and Mathew D. McCubbins, *The Democratic Dilemma: Can Citizens Learn What They Need to Know?* (Cambridge: Cambridge University Press, 1998); Groeling, "When Politicians Attack."

8. For example, see Clifton T. Morgan and Kenneth N. Bickers, "Domestic Discontent and the External Use of Force," *Journal of Conflict Resolution* 36:1 (1992): 25–52; Matthew Baum, "The Constituent Foundations of the Rally-'Round-the-Flag Phenomenon," *International Studies Quarterly* 46 (June 2002): 263–98.

9. See John E. Mueller, *War, Presidents and Public Opinion* (New York: John Wiley & Sons, 1973); "Presidential Popularity from Truman to Johnson," *American Political Science Review* 64 (1970): 18–34; Suzanne L. Parker, "Toward Understanding of 'Rally' Effects: Public Opinion in the Persian Gulf War," *Public Opinion Quarterly* 59 (1995): 526–46; Sam Kernell, "Presidential Popularity and Electoral Preference: A Model of Short Term Political Change" (Ph.D. dissertation, University of California, Berkeley, 1975); Richard A. Brody and Catherine R. Shapiro, "Policy Failure and Public Support: The Iran-Contra Affair and Public Assessment of President Reagan," *Political Behavior* 11:4 (1989): 353–69; Oneal et al., "Are the American People Pretty Prudent?, 261–79; Donald L. Jordan and Benjamin I. Page, "Shaping Foreign Policy

Opinions: The Role of TV News," *Journal of Conflict Resolution* 36 (1992): 227–41; Lian, Bradley, and John R. Oneal, "Presidents, the Use of Force, and Public Opinion Journal of Conflict Resolution" 37 (June 1993): 277–300; Brody, *Assessing Presidential Character*, 1991.

10. One partial exception is Brody, in *Assessing Presidential Character*, which analyzes the content of media coverage surrounding several specific rally events. His data do not, however, investigate *all* potential rally events during the period he investigates. He also does not consider the effects of the partisan makeup of elites appearing in the media on different partisan subgroups in the population. Baum, in "The Constituent Foundations," in contrast, undertakes the latter two investigations, but not the first.

11. See chapter 2 of Groeling, "When Politicians Attack," for a more complete presentation of this argument.

12. As ABC's John Cochran observed, "We do try to find places where we can surprise people.... If you can find a surprise, you've got to find a way to get them in the tent," in Howard Kurtz and Bernard Kalb, moderators of "Press Tunes Out Do-Nothing Congress; Did NBC Strike Out with Its Pete Rose on CNN's *Reliable Sources*," October 30, 1999, transcript downloaded on November 1, 1999, http://www.cnn.com/TRANSCRIPTS/9910/30/rs.00.html. See also Tim Groeling and Sam Kernell, "Is Network News Coverage of the President Biased?," *Journal of Politics* 60 (1998): 1063–87, for empirical evidence of the media's sensitivity to changes in presidential support in their decisions to air such stories.

13. Authors such as Thomas E. Patterson, "Bad News, Period," *PS: Political Science and Politics* 29 (1996): 17–20, Larry J. Sabato, *Feeding Frenzy: How Attack Journalism Has Transformed American Politics* (New York: Free Press, 1991), and Joseph N. Cappella and Kathleen Hall Jamieson, *Spiral of Cynicism: The Press and the Public Good* (New York: Oxford University Press, 1997) have observed that while negativity and conflict have long been staples of American journalism, the news media have increasingly embraced "attack journalism" and cynicism since the 1960s. Regardless of whether one attributes the shift to underlying changes in cynicism, competition, standards of performance, or other causes, there seems to be consensus within the scholarly literature that negativity is dominant in modern news coverage.

14. See Gaye Tuchman, "Objectivity as Strategic Ritual," *American Journal of Sociology* 77 (1972): 660–79.

15. Leon V. Sigal, "Sources Make the News," in *Reading the News: A Pantheon Guide to Popular Culture*, ed. Robert Karl Manoff and Michael Schudson (New York: Pantheon Books, 1986), 20.

16. For some examples about how the source of a message can affect its credibility, see Soloman Asch, *Social Psychology* (New York: Prentice Hall, 1952); Paul M. Sniderman, Richard A. Brody, and Philip E. Tetlock, *Reasoning and Choice: Explorations in Political Psychology* (New York: Cambridge University Press, 1991); John Zaller, *The Nature and Origins of Mass Opinion* (New York: Cambridge University Press, 1992); James H. Kuklinski and Norman L. Hurley, "On Hearing and Interpreting Political Messages: A Cautionary Tale of Citizen Cue-Taking," *Journal of Politics* 56

(1994):729–51; James N. Druckman, "The Limits of Political Manipulation: Psychological and Strategic Determinants of Framing" (Ph.D. dissertation, University of California, San Diego, 1999).

17. Vincent P. Crawford and Joel Sobel, "Strategic Information Transmission," *Econometrica* 50 (1982): 1431–51.

18. Note that this does not imply that a voter will regard her or his own party's statements as unvarnished truth, but rather she or he would be less willing to believe the same statement coming from a member of the opposite party. This assumption also is consistent with observations of partisan perceptual screens, such as those discussed by John Zaller, "The Diffusion of Political Attitudes," *Journal of Personality and Social Psychology* 58 (1987): 821–37.

19. See A. Michael Spence, *Market Signaling* (Cambridge, Mass.: Harvard University Press, 1973).

20. A related line of inquiry is research in the social psychological literature into the influence of "incongruous" stances, or ones that appear inconsistent with a speaker's best interests. See Elaine Walster, Elliot Aronson, and Darcy Abrahams, "On Increasing the Persuasiveness of a Low Prestige Communicator," *Journal of Experimental Social Psychology* 2 (1966): 325–42; Kocskc and Crano, "The Effect of Congruous," 384–99. This perspective also is reinforced by further findings that "disconfirming" messages (i.e., messages in which a speaker takes an unexpected position) are more persuasive than "confirming" messages. See Eagly, Wood, and Chaiken, "Causal Inferences," 246–59; Eagly, "Recipient Characteristics," 173–95.

21. See Baum, "The Constituent Foundations," 263–98.

22. For tests of a broader range of hypotheses derived from the theory, see Groeling, "When Politicians Attack."

23. Brody and Shapiro, "Policy Failure," 77–102.

24. See Groeling, "When Politicians Attack."

25. See Mueller, "Presidential Popularity," and *War, Presidents, and Public Opinion*.

26. Mueller, *War*, 209.

27. Oneal, et al., "Are the American People," 265.

28. See Baum, "The Constituent Foundations," 263–98.

29. See Stephen S. Kaplan and Barry M. Blechman, *Political Uses of the United States Armed Forces, 1946–1976*, Computer File Compiled by Stephen S. Kaplan and Barry M. Blechman, Brookings Institution, ed. ICPSR (Ann Arbor, Mich.: Inter-university Consortium for Political and Social Research, 1978). See also Barry M. Blechman and Stephen S. Kaplan, *Force without War: U.S. Armed Forces as a Political Instrument* (Washington, D.C.: Brookings Institution, 1978); Oneal et al., "Are the American People," 261–79.

30. We are indebted to the tireless efforts of Jeff Barry, Connie Choe, Jenny Cocco, Jennifer Dekel, Betty Fang, Brette Fishman, Rita Ghuloum, Daniel Gordon, Kazue Harima, Julia Heiser, Marchela Iahdjian, Sangeeta Kalsi, Robert Kelly, Jihyun Kim, Alain Kinaly, Priya Koundinya, Jennifer Lee, Andrea Peterson, Brittney Reuter,

David Rigsby, Brooke Riley, Dean Sage, Paula Simon, Erin Skaalen, Katherine Steele, Julia Tozlian, Alyson Tufts, Phuong Vu, William Whitehorn, and Jordan Yurica, and especially to Michael Sefanov, Maya Oren, Alexandra Brandt, and Elizabeth Cummings.

31. Note that several of the rally events occurred at relatively close intervals, so their "windows" overlapped. About 10 percent of our coded evaluations (63 out of 625) occurred fewer than thirty days before one rally *and* fewer than thirty days after another rally.

32. The former hypothesis simply restates Brody's argument (see *Assessing Presidential Character*) with the exception that we focus more explicitly on the presentation of elite discussion in the media rather than on the *true* extent of elite support or criticism.

33. Note that Figures 4.2–4.4 do not use the rally/non-rally period division discussed earlier (e.g., ten days prior/twenty days after the event). Rather, because we are interested in changes in valence and approval, we simply divide our data into thirty-day periods before or after rallies. To avoid double counting observations when rally periods overlapped, if an evaluation occurred within thirty days before one rally event and thirty days after another, then we would only include that evaluation as *after* the prior rally event. We also had to exclude rally observations that did not include evaluations before *and* after the event.

34. For example, see Ole R. Holsti, *Public Opinion and American Foreign Policy* (Ann Arbor: University of Michigan Press, 1996).

35. Matthew Baum, *Soft News Goes to War: Public Opinion and American Foreign Policy in the New Media Age* (Princeton: Princeton University Press, 2003), reports evidence of a trend between 1953 and 1998 toward *larger* rallies among the least-educated members of the public, but *not* among their highly educated counterparts. At first glance, this seems inconsistent with our findings of (1) an overwhelmingly critical elite discussion of the president during rally events since 1979, and (2) a strong relationship between such coverage and rally magnitude. Yet in addition to increased nonpresidential party support for presidents during unified government, these results are not necessarily contradictory, for at least three reasons. First, education levels in America have risen so that the least-educated group has constricted as a proportion of the overall public since the 1950s. It may simply be the case that smaller rallies among highly educated Americans outweigh the effects of larger rallies among the least-educated segments of the public. Second, Baum's time series extends far longer than our data, making it difficult to draw direct comparisons between our findings and his. And third, there may be other factors not included in our present analysis—such as support for the president from noncongressional sources—working against the rally-suppressing effects of congressional criticism.

36. An alternative explanation for the prevalence of supportive comments from the nonpresidential party in the media during rallies might be that journalists are fearful of appearing unpatriotic when the United States is at war, lest they alienate their audience, and thus lose ratings. Of course, absent systematic evidence that news outlets do in fact suffer lower ratings when they present critical coverage of the president in times of crisis, this possibility remains conjectural.

37. Note that ABC and other networks provided considerable news coverage outside of their normal half-hour news programs during both Gulf Wars. However, ABC continued to present and archive its flagship evening news broadcast as a separate entity throughout both war periods.

38. There also may have been a substitution effect in the 2003 case: unlike in 1991, when leaders of the Democratic majority in Congress were the most prominent representatives of the opposition Democratic Party, in 2003, a veritable army of Democratic presidential candidates aggressively competed for media attention.

39. See Jack S. Levy, "The Diversionary Theory of War: A Critique," in *Handbook of War Studies*, ed. M. I. Midlarsky (New York: Unwin-Hyman, 1989), 259–88.

40. See Brody, *Assessing Presidential Character*.

II

The Challenge of Policy Management

Tending to the national policy agenda is perhaps the president's greatest priority as well as one of his greatest challenges. The three chapters in Part II address specific public challenges that presidents face in pursuing their policy agendas.

Modern presidents appear to have solved a particular challenge of public leadership—how to incorporate the public's opinion into presidential decision making. Since the days of Richard Nixon's administration, the White House has employed a public opinion polling apparatus designed informally around existing staff arrangements. This apparatus funnels public opinion data to user designees. Increased attention to the public, via public opinion polling and other campaignlike public activities, led to charges of a leaderless presidency and a "permanent campaign" for public support. As Diane J. Heith shows in "The White House Public Opinion Apparatus Meets the Anti-Polling President," George W. Bush, in his campaign for the presidency, was particularly condemning of the polling apparatus. However, an exploration of Bush's first two years in office suggests that despite his denials to the contrary, a polling apparatus is indeed present and in fact more fully imbedded in the White House than previously witnessed.

Similarly, the president's constitutional weakness in terms of formal powers leads to the development of his informal powers, most notably in the ability to call upon the American people. To succeed, many scholars and officials have argued, requires maximization of these informal powers; in short, maximizing the use of the public. Typically, when scholars and elites discuss capitalizing on public support, they turn to approval ratings. In "Presidential Leverage and the Presidential Agenda: 1967–1996," Daniel E. Ponder contends that the approval rating does not reveal enough about the relationship between the president and other governmental actors. Ponder argues that the challenge for the president is not simply achieving high approval ratings but acting with leverage, which he describes as the interplay between presidential popularity and other indicators of governmental confidence. For the president to act with success, he needs an advantage; with leverage, he achieves more actions and more policy proposals. Thus he needs to be popular with the public, but that popularity also must be relative to other actors and other institutions.

Finally, the notion of a second-term, "lame duck" president became formalized with passage of the Twenty-second Amendment and its prohibition of more than two consecutive terms in office for a single individual. A second-term president seemingly has it easy as the demands of electoral politics disappear: no reelection fund-raising, no Electoral College concerns, and no group and constituency demands directly linked to remaining in office. However, public leadership demands do not disappear. Thus the amendment's limitation on the presidency creates an uncomfortable challenge for the second-term president: how to exercise public leadership for legacy-building legislative efforts in the absence of an electoral connection via the voting booth. In "Second-Term Presidents: Free Birds or Lame Ducks?," William Cunion finds that the lack of electoral connection in fact poses a considerable hurdle for success with Congress, because both the institutional and political constraints on the president remain.

5

The White House Public Opinion Apparatus Meets the Anti-Polling President

Diane J. Heith

In 1965, Elmer Cornwell noted that, "Since little is likely to be done constitutionally to strengthen the President's hand, his ability to lead and mold public opinion, for all its inherent limitations, must remain his prime reliance.... More than ever before in the history of the Republic, the strong president will be the skillful leader of public opinion."[1] For Cornwell, public opinion polls and other collections of public sentiment bulwark the presidency and provide a source of influence, a source of power. Cornwell considered the position of opinion leader an untapped resource, as the president alone can "generate publicity and command public attention." Thus the public represented a tool ripe for utilization, but the question of how to connect the public to the institutionalized White House remained underdeveloped, for scholars and for the president.

As Han notes, presidential appeals to, and their relationship with, the public came of age during the Kennedy administration.[2] Over time, institutional components were added to the White House organizational structure to relate to the public: the Press Secretary, the Office of Communication, and the Office of the Public Liaison.[3] The Nixon administration first developed the mechanism to distribute public opinion polling throughout the White House, although scholars document the presence of a polling apparatus as early as the Franklin Roosevelt administration.[4] Subsequent administrations continued the practice but did not add a formal office to the White House organizational chart.[5] Increased attention to the public, via public opinion polling alongside other campaignlike activities, led to charges of a leaderless presidency amid charges of a "permanent campaign" for public support. The permanent campaign does exist but did not dominate White House decision making as it remained a haphazard influence.[6] The polling apparatus and the permanent campaign remained in check as long as it remained awkwardly arranged around traditional approaches to decision making and policy making.[7] However, the George W. Bush administration challenged past administrations' haphazard incorporation and institutionalization of public opinion. With the George W. Bush White House, public opinion and public leadership were fully integrated into decision making, and public management became the primary function of the president's top advisors.

Previous Administrations and the Polling Apparatus

Between the Nixon administration and the Clinton administration, the polling apparatus grew in significance. The top staff, former campaign workers, and the president were all very attentive to public opinion, although the cabinet and other purely policy-driven offices were not.[8] The polling apparatus was predominantly present for agenda building and mapping the president's legislative battles with Congress during its first two years in office, suggesting a strong connection between public opinion and the president's agenda.[9] The poll apparatus moved the White House beyond mere evaluations of performance via the popularity rating. Using a continuous supply of differentiated data from their pollsters, all White Houses since Nixon identified, tracked, and used the public's opinion across agendas, issues, and popularity ratings.[10] Presidential staffers put to use the increase in knowledge about the public, primarily in communication strategy (i.e., message design via phrasing, speeches, and event evaluation).[11] Jacobs and Shapiro designate the application of public opinion knowledge to rhetorical design, or "crafted talk."[12] Crafted talk is the art of employing public opinion polls and focus groups to choose words and phrases that resonate with the public, even when the policy does not. Jacobs and Shapiro explore the use of polls in two cases: the 1993–1994 health care reform campaign and the 1994–1995 tumultuousness of Newt Gingrich's elevation to House Speaker. Significantly, Jacobs and Shapiro argue that the use of the public does not necessarily produce responsiveness to that public. Instead, the decision to "craft" is largely a product of the desire to ignore the public rather than respond to it.[13]

Moving beyond two cases in the Clinton administration, however, suggests that the poll apparatus influences more than rhetorical design; it also effects constituency relations and presidential leadership. The poll apparatus also enables a president to separate himself from the party and design presidency-centered and not party-centered rhetorical and constituency strategies.[14] The White House uses, evaluates, and monitors its presidential constituency by isolating what drives support for the president, originating with the campaign and continuing through the issues of the presidency. Ideally, presidents need and want to maintain and expand their electoral coalitions in order to win a second term.[15] Thus by 2000, the polling apparatus was a significant component of the White House communication efforts and electoral strategic design. No president, Democrat or Republican, appeared able, or indeed wanted, to function independent of the public opinion apparatus.

GEORGE W. BUSH AND PUBLIC OPINION

Despite its presence in previous Republican White Houses, the polling apparatus represented a source of evil for George W. Bush, in essence as a reminder of the excesses of the previous administration. During his acceptance speech at the 2000 Republican National Convention, Bush claimed: "I believe great decisions are made with care, made with conviction, not made with polls.... I do not need to take your pulse before I know my own mind." However, the oddity of winning the presidency in the Electoral College but losing the popular vote trumped President Bush's attitudes in practice for his staff. The difference of opinion between the president and his staff and the dramatic nature of the period 2001–2004 yield a complicated relationship between the White House, public, and public opinion apparatus. In terms of public opinion attitudes, there were three stages to the Bush tenure: the preterrorist attacks divisions; the post-September 11 conviviality; and Iraq and its aftermath. In terms of public opinion usage, there was one attitude: use the polls extensively, but hide the usage from outsiders in order to retain the mantle of leadership.

The Problem

All previous White Houses devoted a significant portion of their polling apparatus to maintaining and expanding their electoral coalitions.[16] George W. Bush, problematically, entered the White House without a popular victory. Thus he lacked an effective electoral coalition from which to build governing coalitions. Gerald Ford also served as president without an electoral coalition, having been appointed to his term as vice president and then succeeding to the presidency. The lack of electoral coalition forced Ford and his pollsters to work from a "base line ... employing a standard, almost stereotypical, measure for comparison."[17]

The Bush team had a coalition; it unfortunately was numerically and demographically challenged for the future. The voting in the 2000 presidential election fell neatly along party lines, reflecting the distribution of Republicans, Democrats, and Independents across the country. White men and married white women supported Bush, while African Americans, Jews, most Hispanics, Asians, union members, and unmarried women voted for Gore.[18] More striking than the demographic disparities was the dramatic geographic disparity. To produce the infamous blue-edged and red-middled United States electoral map, Bush dominated among the smaller, less populous "heartland" but lost the larger urban areas. Thus "both parties attempted to reach beyond their traditional bases, and both pretty much failed."[19] With the controversial election behind him, George W. Bush entered the White House in January 2001 lacking a mandate, a cohesive base of support, and the apparent will to use the polling apparatus to reach an audience.

The Conflict

Early in his administration, Bush frequently went out of his way to disparage poll usage, claiming, "We set out a set of principles and stand by them. . . . We don't use polls and focus groups to figure out where to head."[20] As his public comments indicate, Bush clearly found polling usage distasteful and lacking in leadership, in great contrast to the attitudes of his top staff. Bush's White House leadership found value in the polling apparatus, producing a remarkable and dangerous dichotomy.

Despite the negative assertions from the top,[21] the Bush White House followed typical polling apparatus patterns: the most active users of public opinion are former members of the president's campaign staff.[22] Moreover, those individuals are likely to employ public opinion in a campaignlike approach. To that end, these staffers use public opinion to identify resonate themes, to shape rhetorical appeals, and to create and monitor winning coalitions.[23] The Bush White House, despite the public assertions to the contrary, followed and in some cases enhanced these identified patterns of public opinion usage.

The Bush White House staff arrived primarily through three routes: the campaign for the presidency, Texas, and Bush family loyalists. Former campaign workers are the most likely to rely on public opinion polling, as typically they are the most comfortable with the data. After all, most candidates vet their campaign strategy and tactics through pollsters and their polling data. The top three aides to George W. Bush were involved in the campaign, had connections to Texas, and were family friends. The intimate connections and the power-sharing arrangements between Senior Advisor Karl Rove, Counselor Karen Hughes, and Chief of Staff Andrew Card represented a new "troika of advisors that . . . dominate decision making in the Bush White House."[24] This troika rather neatly divided and overlapped its responsibilities. "Mr. Rove is the master of the political universe, Andrew H. Card Jr. is the organized and discipline chief of staff," and Ms. Hughes represented the trusted inner-confidant with authority over communications and speechwriting, until she left in July 2002.[25]

Rove, as the president's key political strategist, represents the origination for public opinion data into this White House. Rove runs the Office of Political Affairs, the Office of Public Liaison, and the new Office of Strategic Initiatives (OSI). The OSI exists to expand Bush's electoral coalition and monitor the Republican base.[26] It oversees the work of "an elaborate and integrated strategic planning effort."[27] In previous administrations, Office of Political Affairs and Public Liaison were heavily involved in the polling apparatus. Like previous administrations, the top staff was actively involved in planning, which included public opinion usage. The high-level involvement during the first years of the administration included Domestic Policy Advisor Margaret LaMontagne, Economic Adviser Lawrence B. Lindsey, National Security Adviser Condoleezza Rice, Chief of Staff Andrew Card, and Communications Specialists Karen Hughes, Margaret Tutwiler, and Mary Matalin.[28]

Rove's position in this White House represents the evolution of public opinion polling and staffing arrangements. Traditionally, the outside pollsters work for the National Committee and funnel the poll data to particular staffers who translate the information for usage. The Bush White House retained that arrangement as outside pollsters, like Jan van Lohuizen, reported to Matthew Dowd at the Republican National Committee (RNC). In order for public opinion polling to flourish in the White House, knowledgeable staffers desiring the data need to exist on the inside and the outside polling consultant needs to be trusted. From the Nixon administration to the Clinton administration, these functions were not combined. Patrick Caddell, Richard Wirthlin, Lee Atwater, and Richard Morris were presidential strategists, pollsters, and all-around advisors, but none officially worked inside of the White House.

Rove changes this pattern and more closely connects polling to decision making than in the previous White Houses. In fact, the Bush White House spent more than previous administrations, if, as Tenpas argues, one includes the polling the White House pollsters did for the National Committee in the calculus.[29] Tenpas finds that including the work of the presidential pollsters for the committee bumps the anti-polling President Bush to spending similar to Reagan and Clinton.[30]

Moreover, with Rove on staff, the information gleaned from the polls is, in a sense, laundered. "Politics seeps silently into policy," as Rove and others do not mention poll data explicitly to the president, preferring instead to work the information into their arguments obliquely.[31] "Bush maintains several degrees of separation from his pollsters."[32] The political patterns were so entrenched that one disgruntled professor and the former staffer in charge of the highly touted and short-lived Faith-Based Initiative, John DiIulio Jr., claimed, "There is no precedent in any modern White House for what is going on in this one: a complete lack of a policy apparatus. What you've got is everything, and I mean everything, being run by the political arm. It's the reign of the Mayberry Machiavellis."[33]

Using Public Opinion in the Bush White House

Below the level of president, the Bush White House was very attentive to public opinion, all the while supporting the boss's contention that polling was not a component in this White House. As noted earlier, circumstances presented this White House with three distinct patterns of public opinion: pre-September 11 contentiousness, post-September 11 cordiality, and the Iraq firestorm. However, the changing public opinion did not produce a significant change in the employment of polls. The apparatus remained trained on rhetorical design and constituency-building efforts in all three periods. Moreover, Jacobs's and Shapiro's "crafting" for manipulative purposes was quite evident.

Rhetorical Design

In previous administrations, an important component of the public opinion polling apparatus fell under the auspices of public relations, efforts to sell the president's agenda at home and abroad, as well as to sell the individual occupying the office. Public opinion polling is exceptionally effective when designing language, as it can reveal the words and phrases that resonate with the public. Moreover, public opinion polls are useful for evaluating the success of rhetorical efforts.

The Bush team spent much of its first nine months employing public opinion and simultaneously distancing itself from the Clinton poll-driven presidency. "Before rolling out Bush's energy plan in the summer of 2001, the White House hired pollster Jan van Lohuizen to test public reaction to the proposal."[34] Despite the test run, Andrew Card, Bush's chief of staff, informed reporters that the Bush White House was not concerned with polls but rather with *marketing*. Therefore, "if a policy goes amok, it may not be the policy that is at fault, Card suggested, but flawed marketing."[35]

In a classic example of "crafted talk," Green finds that the Bush team prefers to define its policies and mold only the talking points in response to public desires. For example, on Social Security, Bush focused on privatizing retirement not privatizing the Social Security Fund. In a brief speech, Bush "repeated the words 'choice' (three times), 'compound interest' (four times), 'opportunity' (nine times), and 'savings' (eighteen times)."[36] The repetition stems from phrases tested and supported by polls and focus groups from the campaign. Green argues that because Bush's policies are not popular with a majority of voters, the pollsters must find the language to make the unpalatable palatable. As Jacobs notes, the Bush White House does not "poll to find out issues that the public supports so that he can respond to their substantive interests. He's polling on presentation. To those of us who study it, most of his major policy statements come off as completely poll concocted."[37]

The clearest example of rhetorical polling efforts and attempts at crafted talk appears to arise from Bush's strongest example of issue leadership: foreign policy and war. The Bush administration consistently received high marks from the public regarding its efforts to vanquish terrorism and to respond to September 11, and so it tried to use that support for the Iraqi war effort. The president and his advisors' language in the "full court press" to sell the decision to go to war in Iraq to the American people rested upon the dangers of weapons of mass destruction and linking Iraq to Al Queda and terrorism. Initially, 50 to 60 percent of the public supported the decision. The crafting and rhetorical design for the rationale behind the decision were effective among a majority of Americans. Although there was a high level of public skepticism, it divided primarily along partisan lines. However, by the June 2004 handoff of Iraq to the provisional government, 60 percent of the American people disapproved of Bush's Iraq policy, and "60 percent, including a majority of independents, said the war has not been worth the cost."[38]

What happened? First and foremost, rhetorical efforts do not occur in a vacuum, and the White House dealt with a series of setbacks, including the lack of weapons of mass destruction and the prisoner abuse scandal. In addition, however, "poll-tested messages are often easy to parry,"[39] particularly in a period of relentless media attention. Carefully crafted speeches can rarely counter war images and body counts. Moreover, the dearth of weapons of mass destruction, and the resulting public firestorm over their lack, reveals the flaw in careful crafting. The administration effectively sold the decision to go to war as a nondecision, a "no-brainer," given the threat of weapons of mass destruction and the potential link between those weapons and terrorists. Having convinced Americans that the presence of weapons of mass destruction was a sufficient rationale for war, the lack of weapons presented a real public relations challenge for the Bush administration. As the White House repackaged the war as a humanitarian effort to free the people of Iraq from a terrible dictator, Bush lost support. Humanitarianism as a rationale for war did not resonate with the public prior to the war and most definitely not after it began. No amount of language tinkering or any presidential rhetorical efforts ever altered that public opinion.

Constituency Relations

In his first months in office, Bush and his advisors were very aware of the need to "enlarge his fragile political base."[40] As noted earlier, Bush entered the White House with an Electoral College victory and not a popular one. Moreover, Bush's electoral coalition was relatively narrow. To expand the coalition, Bush desperately needed independents. Like Clinton, Bush was sharply polarizing;

he was immensely popular with his own party and despised by Democrats. Karl Rove and the OSI planned a Fall 2001 offensive, "aimed at carving out a different kind of orthodoxy for the party."[41] Rove's aborted plans were similar to Patrick Caddell's and Dick Morris's efforts to assemble a presidency-centered coalition for Jimmy Carter and Bill Clinton, respectively.[42]

According to Ornstein, the Bush White House "from the beginning, had begun to think through the lessons of the 2000 election in terms of electoral building blocks—not just the states and Electoral College votes, but groups in the electorate, Catholics, Southerners, Hispanics, African Americans, suburbanites, and so on."[43] The polling apparatus is superb at this kind of sophisticated tracking and monitoring.

A chief goal of the administration, particularly the OSI, was minority voting in 2004, particularly Hispanics.[44] The interest in minority blocs and specialty blocs, such as Catholics, stems from the realization that "if the same percentage of minorities backed the Democratic candidate in 2004 as in 2000, Bush would lose by 3.5 million votes."[45]

Under Rove's and the OSI's leadership, the Bush White House targeted both traditional groups as well as those only discerned by the poll data. For example, Rove, in a presentation to Republicans, argued that "coal and steel" were "top priorities" of the administration, in preparation for 2004.[46] In March 2002, Bush issued broad tariffs designed to protect Big Steel although ultimately had to rescind and scale back as the free traders rebelled.[47]

The catering to key groups sat in striking contrast to the "above politics" approach that the administration advertised. Bush's reversal on the closing of the Vieques bombing range in Puerto Rico, the tap-dancing around the controversies over fetal tissue research, and the energy crisis in California highlight the constituency monitoring via the poll apparatus. John Harris suggests that "like his predecessor, Bush found it easier as a candidate than he has as president to satisfy multiple constituencies—capturing the political center while keeping his ideological base content."[48] The tacking back and forth between the conservative base, the political center, and vulnerable Democratic constituencies such as Catholics continued to spotlight the difference between the administration's behavior under Rove and the president's messages about leadership without polling.

Ultimately, however, the terrorist acts and the subsequent war efforts in Afghanistan and Iraq allowed the highly focused polling for constituency purposes to remain hidden. The aura of the wartime president and the reality of the terror attacks served to unite the country behind the president in an unprecedented fashion, particularly for such a polarizing figure. A year and a half prior to the president's reelection bid, Rove made the Bush campaign strategy clear to political science students at St. Anselm College: "It's the terror, not the economy."[49] The thinking of the pollsters and the White House staff was obvious: place the focus on the one issue, and respond to the issue that trumps divisive constituencies. However, the Bush team did not account for the separation and divisiveness achieved by the war in Iraq. Just six months after Rove articulated the importance of terrorism and the war in Iraq for the 2004 campaign, "public confidence in President Bush's ability to deal wisely with an international crisis . . . slid sharply."[50] In the year counting down to the election, Bush's monstrous support, evident across several levels of public opinion, deteriorated, despite "winning" the war in Iraq quickly, killing Hussein's sons, and capturing Saddam Hussein. Over 2003 and into 2004, the Bush White House dealt with the continued turmoil in Iraq, the scandal stemming from the torture of the Abu Gharid prisoners, and the growing consensus that there were no weapons of mass destruction. In short, by the time of the handover of Iraq to the provisional government on June 28, 2004, five months before the presidential election, almost all of the "rally-'round-the-flag" positive polling results due to terrorism and war had dissipated.

A central rationale for using the polling apparatus is the effort to maintain and expand the presidential electoral coalition. The terrorist attacks of September 11, 2001, and the wars in Afghanistan and Iraq initially appeared to lessen the need for constituency maintenance, as a unifying cause seemed to exist. After September 11, George W. Bush did not need to rely on his shaky electoral coalition as the basis for a governing coalition—terrorism and war made those connections. However, the connection between the electoral coalition and reelection remained. George W. Bush entered office with a problematic coalition, as he did not win the 2000 popular vote. His coalition was not necessarily viable for 2004. By June 2004, it became clear that war and terrorism may not necessarily solve the problems that make a polling apparatus so critical for the presidency.

Discussion

George W. Bush entered the 2000 presidential race promising to be a different type of president. He denounced the permanent campaign and promised to not "stick our finger in the air trying to figure out which way the wind is blowing . . . I do what I think is right for the American people."[51] Bush's White House found a way to sell these principles while not putting them into practice. In short, the Bush staff polls as frequently as previous administrations, uses the information in much the same manner as previous administrations, and yet has successfully sold the premise that this administration is different.

Bush's approach to public opinion does not adhere to the behavior of the two presidents he most admires. Ronald Reagan was not directly involved in the polling apparatus of his administration, yet he was aware of and supported the use of public opinion polling. Reagan received color-coded presentations designed to mediate the complexities of deciphering constituency support for policies. Like Reagan, George W. Bush is not a "details man"; he leaves that to others. However, Bush's presentations and decision-making sessions are notably devoid of polling numbers. Of greater contrast, George H. W. Bush was more involved in the polling apparatus than most of his staff.[52] The senior Bush received raw polling information and myriad memos filled with public opinion data. According to most reports, George W. Bush internalized the failures of his father's administration to attend to domestic policy after the Gulf War and promised to avoid the same mistakes. Nevertheless, George H. W. Bush was comparatively more accepting of polling data than his son has been as president.[53]

What makes George W. Bush's contempt for, and inattention to, public opinion polling so intriguing is that he has surrounded himself with staffers who *do not* share his belief. Moreover, the Bush White House is purchasing the data, although "this White House polls once every two or three weeks, while ... [the Clinton White House] polled weekly even during noncampaign years."[54] Rove effortlessly inserts the political calculation, gleaned from the poll data, into Bush's policy decisions—just not in data format. Bush's senior staff is quite skilled in using public opinion and has successfully incorporated this information into presidential decision making without directly involving the president. It is a striking form of deniability; as long as the president's choices include subsumed public opinion data rather than explicit forms, the president can continue to claim his separation from the permanent campaign during the Clinton years.

Conclusion

Despite all of the protestations to the contrary, which began with George W. Bush's run for office and continues into his presidency, the Bush administration is attentive to public opinion. Moreover, the staff created a mechanism for incorporating public opinion data into decision making. Thus the institutionalization of presidential use of public opinion continues, *even as the president deplores the practice.* Public opinion polling is now necessary to the practices of the modern president. The president requires information in order to maintain, track, and potentially expand his electoral coalition, for governing as well as for reelection efforts. The challenge for presidents has always been to incorporate and utilize public opinion polling for more than merely tracking presidential approval ratings. The Bush administration takes the evolution of the polling apparatus to the next level. The Bush White House fully integrated public opinion data into their daily decision-making and public leadership efforts.

NOTES

1. Elmer E. Cornwell Jr., *Presidential Leadership of Public Opinion* (Bloomington: Indiana University Press, 1965), 303.

2. Lori Cox Han, *Governing from Center Stage: White House Communication Strategies during the Television Age of Politics* (Cresskill, N.J.: Hampton Press, 2001).

3. Diane J. Heith, "Staffing the White House Public Opinion Apparatus: 1969–1988," *Public Opinion Quarterly* 63 (Summer 1998): 165–89.

4. Lawrence Jacobs, "The Recoil Effect: Public Opinion and Policymaking in the U.S. and Britain," *Comparative Politics* (January 1992): 199–217; Robert M. Eisinger, *The Evolution of Presidential Polling* (New York: Cambridge University Press, 2003).

5. Diane J. Heith, *Polling to Govern: Public Opinion and Presidential Leadership* (Stanford, Calif.: Stanford University Press, 2004).

6. Ibid.

7. Ibid.

8. Heith, "Staffing the White House,"

9. See Heith, *Polling to Govern.*

10. Ibid.

11. Ibid.

12. Lawrence Jacobs and Robert Shapiro, *Politicians Don't Pander: Political Manipulation and the Loss of Democratic Responsiveness* (Chicago: University of Chicago Press, 2000).

13. Ibid.

14. See Eisinger, *The Evolution of Presidential Polling*; Heith, *Polling to Govern.*

15. Heith, *Polling to Govern.*

16. Ibid.

17. Ibid, 62.

18. Wilson Carey McWilliams, "The Meaning of the Election," in *The Election of 2000*, ed. Gerald M. Pomper (New York: Chatham House, 2001), 184.

19. Ibid., 184–85.

20. Alexis Simendinger, "In His Own (Mixed) Words," *National Journal* (April 28, 2001): 1249.

21. The denial of interest and attention to public opinion was commonplace among presidents and their staffs, until Bill Clinton. See Heith, *Polling to Govern.*

22. Heith, "Staffing the White House"; *Polling to Govern.*

23. See Heith, *Polling to Govern*; Jacobs and Shapiro, *Politicians Don't Pander.*

24. Dana Milbank, "Bush Names Rove Political Strategist; Choice Completes Troika of White House Advisors," *Washington Post*, January 5, 2001, p. A1.

25. Elisabeth Bumiller, "White House Memo: Minus One, Bush Inner Circle Is Now Open for Sharp Angling," *New York Times*, July 14, 2002, p. A12:1.

26. Kathryn Tenpas and Stephen Hess, "Bush's A Team: Just Like Clinton's, But More So," *Washington Post*, January 27, 2002.

27. Dana Milbank, "Serious 'Strategery' As Rove Launches Elaborate Political Effort, Some See a Nascent Clintonian 'War Room,'" *Washington Post*, April 22, 2001, p. A1.

28. Ibid.

29. Kathryn Dunn Tenpas, "Words vs Deeds: President George W. Bush and Polling," *The Brookings Review* (Summer 2003) 21:3: 32–35.

30. Ibid.

31. Matt Bai, "Rove's Way," *New York Times*, October 20, 2002.

32. Joshua Green, "The Other War Room," *Washington Monthly* (April 2002): 2.

33. "Ex-Aide Insists White House Puts Politics Ahead of Policy," *New York Times*, December 2, 2002, p. A16.

34. Anne Kornblut, "For Bush Team, Getting Reelected Is Constant Theme," *Boston Globe*, December 29, 2002, p. A1.

35. Bill McAllister, "Bush Polls Apart from Clinton in Use of Marketing," *Denver Post*, June 17, 2001, p. A14.

36. Green, "The Other War Room."

37. Quoted in Green, "The Other War Room," 7.

38. Adam Nagourney and Janet Elder, "Bush's Rating Falls to Its Lowest Point, New Survey Finds," *New York Times*, June 29, 2004, p. A1.

39. Green, "The Other War Room," 7.

40. Dan Balz, "Partisan Divisions Bedevil Bush: Advisors Seek Ways to Redefine Presidency, *Washington Post*, July 1, 2001, p. A1.

41. Ibid.

42. See Heith, *Polling to Govern*, pp. 63–65, 105–108 for a discussion of Caddell's plans.

43. Kornblut, "For Bush Team," p. A1.

44. Milbank, "Serious 'Strategery,'" p. A1.

45. Mimi Hall, "New White House, New 'War Room' for Strategizing," *USA Today*, July 5, 2001.

46. Bai, "Rove's Way."

47. Ibid.

48. John Harris, "Clintonesque Balancing of Issues, Polls; Role of Politics Evident in Bush White House," *Washington Post*, June 24, 2001, p. A1.

49. Francis Clines, "Karl Rove's Campaign Strategy Seems Evident: It's the Terror, Stupid," *New York Times*, May 10, 003, p. A1:20.

50. Todd Purdum and Janet Elder, "Poll Shows Drop in Confidence on Bush Skill in Handling Crises," *New York Times*, October 3, 2003, p. A2:1.

51. Harris, "Clintonesque," p. A1; Maureen Dowd, "By The Numbers; Bush Has Not Shunned the Pollsters As He Said He Would," *New York Times*, April 4, 2002, p. A15.

52. See Heith, *Polling to Govern*.

53. Ibid.

54. Harris, "Clintonesque," p. A1.

6

Presidential Leverage and the Presidential Agenda: 1967–1996

Daniel E. Ponder

One of the paradoxes of modern American politics is that while presidents are afforded enormous attention, both foreign and domestic, they operate from a position of weakness.[1] Not only are presidents institutionally weak, at least on paper, but they also are constrained by the time within which they govern. This is the case not only in terms of a relationship with the public but in the alternative governing institutions themselves that seek purposive action.[2] Thus the president's place in the system can serve as a resource for conveying to him his relative institutional strength and can perhaps influence decisions about the pursuit of presidential activity.

My purpose in this chapter is to take a step backward to try to measure the degree to which a president's "place" (by which I mean the political context within which he governs and his relationship to that context) in the American political system influences his role in the formulation of public policy. A natural corollary is to ask what consequences, if any, flow from this activity. Put differently, I try to determine the degree to which a president's situation, both institutionally and publicly, causes him to be strategic in setting the public agenda. I also seek to trace the extent to which the president is advantaged, if at all, in securing congressional concurrence with his agenda. The same set of expectations that hinders his progress also can be used as leverage in the policy process. How the public views the president as an individual leader in relation to the government as a whole is only one part of this dynamic, but I will argue that it is an important one. In order to try and capture one dimension of his "place" in the American system, I develop a measure of presidential leverage, which focuses attention on the president in relation to the rest of the national government. I then test the theory on data from presidents Johnson to Clinton to see if this "feeling" has any discernable impact on decisions to load the agenda, innovate, or employ an administrative presidency strategy in pursuit of policy goals.

In the rest of this chapter, I develop and apply a theoretical perspective accounting for presidential leverage and devise a battery of measures that considers where the president "is" at any one time, given personal, institutional, and economic circumstances. The problem with calling leverage a theory as it presently stands is that it is difficult to determine a priori a directional component to the measure. I discuss this matter later. I also determine whether it has a significant impact on two aspects of agenda activity: the total number of first-time policy requests the president proposes in the State of the Union address, and the total number of legislative requests made by the president in a given year (what I call the "front end" of agenda activity). The chapter ends with a discussion of presidential theory and where the research process should venture next.

DEVELOPING A THEORETICAL PERSPECTIVE: THE CONCEPT OF PRESIDENTIAL LEVERAGE

There is a substantial literature concerning presidents and agendas.[3] Indeed, it is not a stretch to say that most of the work on the presidency touches on what presidents do and how they do it. This strand takes many forms, but can be termed, however loosely, as agenda setting and/or advertising of that agenda. Presidents can influence public agendas as well as those of competing institutions. Cohen's analysis of State of the Union addresses reports that presidents influence public opinion on what the public deems is the "most important problem," but that this influence is mostly gone by the end of a year after the address.[4] But presidents are influenced as well. The notion of a presidency constrained by the president's place in the broader context of the American system, especially if this is partially determined by public perceptions of the president relative to the whole of government, implies some semblance of strategic behavior on the part of the president. In other words, do presidents tailor their actions to how they fare in the American polity at a given time? And, do they use their leverage in the system? If so, how?

The degree to which the public distinguishes between the president, the presidency, and the government as a whole, and determining any individual president's position in this relationship, is one way of understanding how presidents can strategically act so as to maximize their power potential. Indeed, the president as an individual is almost always held in greater esteem than is the institution of the presidency. Striking evidence of this trend is presented in Figure 6.1, which shows the relationship between presidential approval, public confidence in the presidency, and public confidence in governing institutions between 1967 and 1996. I explain the operationalization of each of these measures later, but for now I note that with the exception of George H. W. Bush's unprecedented approval readings in the aftermath of the Gulf War, presidential approval has always far outdistanced levels of public confidence in the presidency. And with the exception of the immediate post-

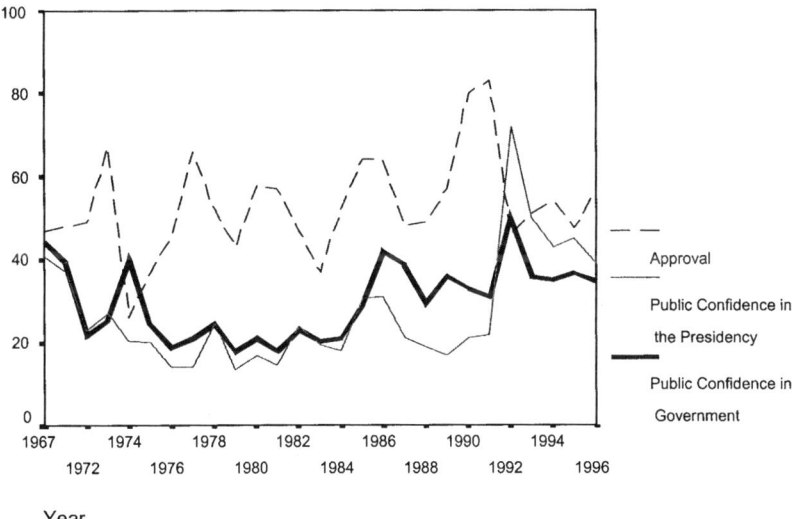

FIGURE 6.1   Presidential Approval and Government Confidence, Selected Measures
Source: Gallup Polling Organization, 1967–1996.

Watergate era, presidential approval has generally remained much higher than public confidence in the government.

Separate dynamics seem to be at work here in public evaluations of the individual as president, public confidence in government, and confidence in the institution of the presidency. Though eyeballing the measures might lead one to the conclusion that they are linearly related, such is not the case. For example, the relationship between public confidence in the presidency and presidential approval is slightly negative and does not come close to realizing conventional levels of statistical significance (r = –.08, p = .71, 2–tailed test). Similarly, the relationship between public confidence in government and the president's approval is again negative, and even further from significance (r = –.03, p = .87). The lack of a relationship between these variables lends credence to the argument that the public sees these institutions as separate entities and can sort out the difference between the president and the institution. Not surprisingly, only the relationship between public confidence in the presidency and confidence in government achieves significance, and this because confidence in the presidency is included in the measure of confidence in government (r = .78, p = .000). This analysis is only one part (albeit an important part) of determining how a president is situated in the American system.

Opportunities for presidential action are fleeting, and presidents need to act when their "warrants for action" are most potent. Skowronek puts it most succinctly when he writes, "[P]residents stand paramount in American politics when government has been most thoroughly discredited, and when political resistance to the presidency is weakest, presidents tend to remake the government wholesale."[5] In other words, president's actions are most powerful when their stature exceeds governmental capability writ large, when public trust in government is low. One way to get at elements of this notion is to measure the degree to which the president as an individual is advantaged in the public's eye vis-à-vis its assessment of the government as a whole. I explore this question by creating a summary measure of what I call "presidential leverage" over other institutions in the American polity by combining indicators of public perceptions of governmental institutions and placing the president squarely in that institutional context.[6]

Trying to measure the president's "place" in the system is tricky, especially when considering methodological questions such as face validity. Nonetheless, I argue that the index of presidential leverage provides one theoretical tool with which to systematically explore the recurring notion of a president's "place" in American politics at any one time in a systematic way.[7]

Since 1966, various polling agencies have intermittently asked survey respondents how much they trust various institutions to "do the right thing."[8] Unfortunately, no polling organization asks respondents how they view the government as a whole. To correct this, I simply sum the percentage of respondents reporting that they had a high degree of confidence in the Supreme Court, Congress, and executive branch, respectively, and then take the average. This average yields a summary measure indicating how much confidence the American people have in their government and is incorporated into the index as the denominator.[9] The numerator is simply the president's average approval as measured in the Gallup Polls in the closest measurement period prior to the State of the Union address, or in the case of the total size of the president's agenda, in the year in which the agenda was presented. The measure is a ratio of presidential approval to the average confidence of Americans in their government. The transformation is straightforward and takes the following form:

$$IPL = \frac{Presidential\ Approval}{([E_c + Cng_c + Crt_c])/3}$$

Where IPL is the Index of Presidential Leverage, Presidential Approval is the average annual approval in the year previous to measurement of the dependent variables; E_c is the average annual public confidence in the executive branch; Cng_c is the average annual public confidence in Congress; and Crt_c is the average annual public confidence in the Supreme Court. In reflecting these dynamics, the measure captures some of what Skowronek and others have elaborated, namely, the relationship in the public eye of the president to his institutional counterparts. By utilizing presidential approval, it captures essential features of the interaction between the public and the president; by utilizing the average of confidence measures, it considers global institutional assessments, whether crude or sophisticated.[10] This ratio thus captures one (though certainly not the only) element of the *individual* in relation to the *institution*, especially the institutional context of the public, the president, and the rest of government.[11]

To make things a bit more concrete, Figure 6.2 displays a schematic representation of presidential leverage. The higher the value of the index as measured on the continuum, the more "leverage" the president has relative to government. Since as a matter of both theoretical and empirical reality, neither the numerator nor the denominator will ever assume negative values (though they may be asymptotic to zero), the lower bound of the index is zero. Of course, this can only be observed if the president is absolutely unpopular, a theoretical possibility that has never been realized empirically. However, as the value moves higher (i.e., farther and farther to the right of zero), other possibilities take shape. An index value of less than 1 indicates that public confidence in governmental capability outsteps that of the president. Since he is in quite a weak position relative to the rest of the national institutional apparatus, the president has no leverage; indeed, competing institutions (Congress especially) have leverage over him. For example, in 1974, Richard Nixon had an average approval of 26 percent, which is inserted as the numerator of the index formula. Average confidence in institutions (the denominator) was 39.94. Since Nixon's approval was lower than institutional confidence, his leverage index was .65.

A president at 1.0 on the schematic depiction has leverage exactly equal to competing institutions. This would rarely occur, but it is useful to think not in terms of a president falling at exactly 1.0 but right around this leverage point, either just above or below. In such a circumstance, the president is not without leverage, but he does not, as Skowronek noted, "stand paramount" in

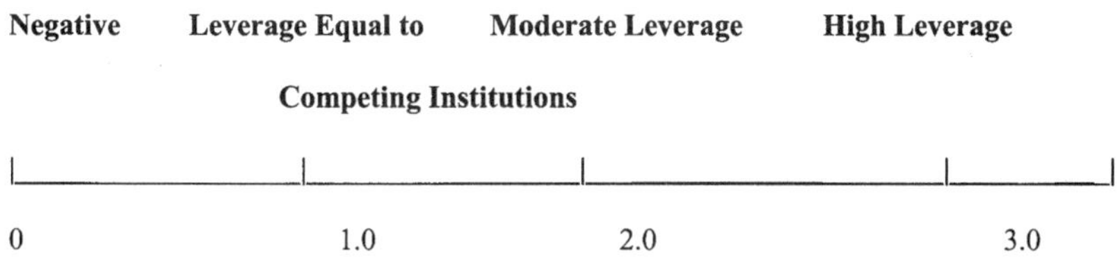

Negative	Leverage Equal to Competing Institutions	Moderate Leverage	High Leverage

|_____|_____|_____|_____|

0   1.0   2.0   3.0

FIGURE 6.2   Schematic Depiction of Presidential Leverage

Source: Collected by the author from the Gallup Polling Organization and the State of the Union addresses, 1967–1996.

relation to other institutions. This would occur when a president had average approval about equal to public confidence.[12] Finally, as we move outward toward positive infinity, presidents have more and more leverage. Of course, positive infinity is a theoretical construct and is never approached empirically. But as we cross various thresholds, it does indicate that presidents enjoy varying degrees of leverage. For example, a president with an index of 2.0 has an approval base twice the size of the confidence levels of governmental institutions in general, so 2.5 means that his approval base is two-and-one-half the size, and so on.

One advantage of this conceptualization of leverage is that it is couched in relativistic terms. In other words, it does not rely merely on presidential approval or institutional assessments but considers them in relation to one another. I do not argue that presidents use this measure as they might a more tangible resource, such as approval. Rather, the ratio allows a more specific, concrete specification of what might be called a "feeling." This feeling would be a contextually based one, based on how the president is situated vis-à-vis the rest of the system. A popular president, for example, may not enjoy high levels of leverage if public confidence in government is similarly high. Conversely, a relatively unpopular president may have a rather high degree of leverage if government trust is extremely low. So an unpopular president may still have some warrant for action if his stature is above that of the rest of the institutions, that is, if public confidence in institutions is particularly low.[13] This is what I mean by the word "leverage." When the president stands paramount in the system, his leverage is great. When he does not, his leverage shrinks. It follows, then, that high levels of approval might, but need not, accompany high leverage.[14] It is this relativistic feature that allows for a more direct interpretation of the place of the president in the context of other governmental institutions.

In order to inspect variation in leverage over time, Figure 6.3 displays the trend of the index from the last part of Lyndon Johnson's administration to halfway through Bill Clinton's first term. The measure has face validity. As might be expected, the lowest value is observed in the last year of Nixon's presidency, undoubtedly reflective of the Watergate crisis. Somewhat surprisingly, presidential leverage is at its peak both in the middle of Carter's administration and in the beginning of Reagan's first term. Carter's is likely explained by the fact that he was the first post-Watergate president, was of the opposite party, and pledged openness about government and governing. For Reagan, it is most likely a function of a broad perception that Carter had utterly failed, and thus the public responded to Reagan's more optimistic message and the fact that the hostages had been released on his watch. The index fluctuates throughout the rest of the Reagan years, dipping into troughs about the time of the Iran-Contra scandal and at the beginning of the Bush administration. It rises again in 1991, most likely in response to the Gulf War, but it plum-

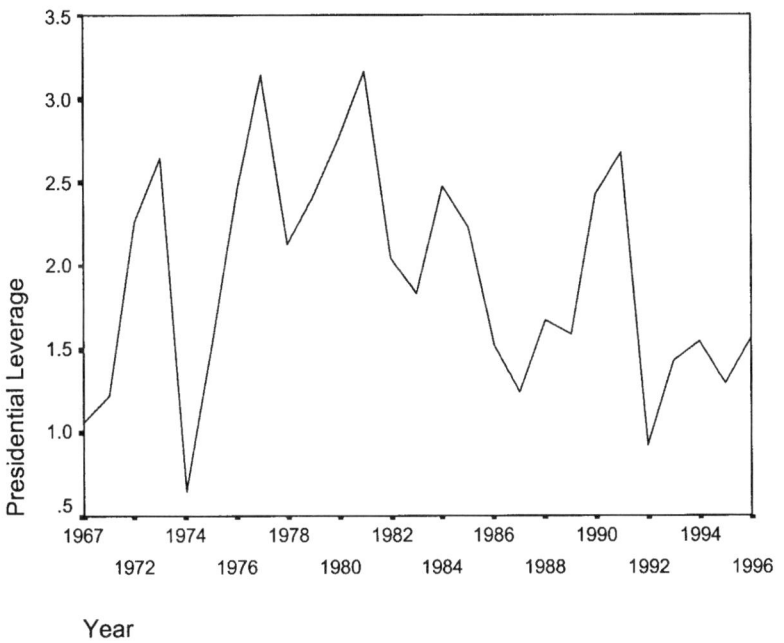

FIGURE 6.3 Presidential Leverage
Source: Collected by the author from the Gallup Polling Organization.

mets soon afterward, making possible Bill Clinton's ascension to the presidency. It stays low through the rest of the time series, probably as a consequence of continued public disaffection with government as a whole. The important question is not whether presidents *have* leverage; empirically, they do. The theoretically interesting question is instead, what do they do with it? Indeed, it is possible that presidents are not aware of or, if they are aware of it, mute the context of leverage for a number of reasons.

Theoretical Linkage

Presidential success comes in many different forms. In a separated system of institutions with overlapping powers and responsibilities, presidents will use whatever they can get. Presidents are thus "one among many," and they will likely exploit whatever advantage they can to assert their agenda. This is most likely true at the beginning of a president's term. But as the crush of politics takes its toll, it is reasonable to expect presidents to temper their agenda activity in line with various considerations of legitimacy, such as that represented by the concept of leverage. Presidents are not likely to be oblivious to structures or conditions that bode well or ill (or perhaps neutral) for the size and strategies of agenda building.

What is lacking, however, is a sound theoretical basis for expecting directionality should the concept of leverage prove a significant predictor of agenda activity. Indeed, perhaps the primary purpose of this chapter is to determine the utility, if any, of the concept of leverage, and to propose directions for theoretical development, some of which I have already begun. For now, and temporarily setting aside the null result, at least two theoretical possibilities present themselves. I sketch these now, leaving for future work a more fully specified theory for each.

Scenario One: Leverage as Positive Impact

If presidents take into account their place in the American system, then they might use whatever leverage they have in the pursuit of doing "more," given the codification of a feeling that more is expected. With a greater degree of leverage, a president may appropriately feel that he has more leeway or legitimacy to do more than would normally be the case. Recall that leverage is a ratio that essentially places the president inside the context of competing institutions. Times of high leverage, then, leave the president more or less free to put forth a greater number of proposals, given that public pressure works against Congress (or the government in general) rather than the president, leaving a strategic president free to adjust as the nature of the times warrants. Of course, there is an outer bound to what presidents will want to put forth.

Scenario Two: Leverage as Negative Impact

Ironically, it may be the case that presidents temper their activity in times of high leverage. Mueller offers a "coalitions of minorities" explanation of presidential action, part of which argues that presidential policy proposals alienate various factions of their support.[15] Such an effect is likely to be cumulative, with public support falling as the number of initiatives increases.[16] If presidents lose public support for each policy or cluster of policies they propose (given that each policy represents giving to some and taking away from others), then a leveraged president might very well do less in total numbers but feel empowered to concentrate on large-scale policy change.[17] Thus while the leverage framework suggests activity, it is bounded at some point such that they will try and avoid losing a comparative advantage. In times of low leverage, presidents cannot legitimately sustain a "mandate" for high levels of activity and will likely wish to minimize their already low levels of popular legitimacy. This state of affairs, in concert with other factors such as ideological compatibility with Congress, a rational staff with limited attention resources, and other exogenous factors such as the state of the economy, places realistic limits on what the president can do.

Obviously more could be done to flesh out the expectations of each, but for this chapter suffice it to say that each is, at this point in the conceptualization process, a plausible motive for presidents, and theory development has not progressed far enough to allow me to make positive predictions. Time and space constraints leave this for future work, but I come back to some of the implications of this in the conclusion.

If it is indeed the case that leverage influences agendas, does Congress take account of this leverage as well? What are the consequences of politics at the "back end"? More specifically, does it defer to (or, put another way, is it more likely to agree with) the president in times of high leverage and reject him more often in times of low leverage? Congressional response to presidential agendas is likely to be conditional,[18] but it is reasonable to suppose that Congress might take account of the increased leverage the president enjoys over Congress and increase the likelihood of concurrence in times of high leverage. Of course, if leverage does influence aggregate levels of concurrence, then there is likely to be an upper bound. Mark Peterson has shown that high levels of presidential approval increase legislative conflict.[19] Applying this logic, leverage might play a part in congressional concurrence with presidential initiatives, but any net effect is likely to be far less than the influence of leverage on the more proactive, president-controlled decisions as to how much to put forth. Other factors that put the president in a direct relationship with Congress are likely to explain as much or more of the rate of congressional concurrence than is leverage, though leverage theory suggests that there should be a relationship, even when inter-institutional features are controlled for.

The statistical analysis presented next explores the question of whether and how presidents respond to and exploit this leverage. The rest of this chapter examines only presidential activity as measured by the number of programmatic requests in the State of the Union address and the total number of legislative requests issued, treating all events as more or less equal. What I hope to accomplish is a determination of the usefulness of leverage theory for explaining agenda activity and how presidents distribute their activity levels accordingly in concert with other institutional and situational features of American politics.

Data, Methods, and Operationalization of the Theory

In this section, I specify in some detail the elements of the model that will be tested against competing explanations for agenda activity.

Operationalization of Agenda Components

Presidents need success, however they can get it. That often means that symbolic elements are employed in pursuing success with Congress, interest groups, the public, and the bureaucracy.[20] Presidents are constrained from or compelled to action on a number of fronts. In study after study, it is assumed that the president's place in American government is conditional upon purposive political action, whether symbolic or substantive.[21] I examine presidential use of public and somewhat less public efforts to shape the American political and policy landscape. In doing so, I focus on two measures of agenda activity for the period 1967–1996, both of which take place at what I have called the "front end" of agenda setting. The first is *public volume*, alternately operationalized as the total number of policy proposals in the annual State of the Union address; and the total number of requests made by the president annually. These are reasonably straightforward, but their linkage to theory needs some consideration.

In formulating their agendas, presidents make decisions about how much or how little to pursue, how much to publicly commit themselves to, and how much and in what areas to engage in unilateral action via the administrative presidency strategy.[22] With the exception of crisis messages, State of the Union addresses epitomize the president on the public stage.[23] Presidents decide to "go public" with policy proposals, whether symbol or substance.[24] At least part of that activity concerns agenda setting.[25] Presidents use the State of the Union address as a public platform from which they publicize their agenda and begin to make their case for its implementation. The justification for studying the State of the Union address as an indicator of presidential activity is well documented.[26] Unlike others, though, I examine the volume of policy activity embodied in the message rather than its content. Presidents are constrained in this decision only by their commitment to deliver at least symbolic legislation or action and the time in which to do it. These are constraints, to be sure, but it might be more costly for presidents to put forth a large number of requests, only to fall short of achieving their goals as publicly stated in the address. Putting forth proposals in the State of the Union address establishes a public record that later can be subjected to careful (and not so careful) scrutiny by journalists, political adversaries and allies, and the general public.

Finally, though it is not a direct test of the leverage theory of agenda activity, I test to see whether there is support for the hypothesis that competing institutions defer to the president in times of high presidential leverage (the "back end" of presidential agenda activity). Thus I regress the rate of congressional concurrence with stated presidential positions on the vector of explanatory variables. The theoretical framework elaborated earlier suggests that this is a reasonable assumption, but that the imperatives of institutional independence would tend to moderate any expected relationship. Nonetheless, the hypothesis is that, in the presence of other explanatory variables, leverage will be positively related to concurrence rates. The rate of concurrence is not directly related to the application of agenda activity, in that Congress votes not just on the president's agenda but on its own as well. Additionally, many of the votes taken in Congress will not be on those items put forth in the president's State of the Union address, nor explicitly proposed by the president (i.e., those on which the president takes a stand), so the linkage is not direct. Nonetheless, it is a reasonable approximation of presidential success in Congress, and as such, it is included to round out the analysis by testing for the existence of a relationship between leverage and presidential success in Congress.[27]

Operationalization of Independent Variables

So far the concept of presidential leverage has made reference to institutional and situational features of the American system but has not labored to identify these in a concrete way. This subsection is meant to link independent variables more succinctly to the leverage concept. The projected impact of leverage on the dependent variables needs to be assessed in a contextually richer environment that allows for a more direct understanding of the role, if any, that leverage plays in agenda decisions while simultaneously testing various alternative hypotheses. I argue that presidential agenda activity is further influenced by at least three classes of variables: those that embed the presidency in an institutional environment; those that are more or less time contextual; and the nature of economic constraints.[28] I state my expectations for directionality at the end of the description of variable operationalizations.

Institutional

The main institutional variable of interest is presidential *leverage*. At least one other institutional variable is relevant to my analysis. Any theoretical framework seeking to explain strategy in presidential agenda setting needs to take into account some measure of presidential relationship with Congress. Usually this is done simply by conceptualizing presidential strength in Congress as a function of the number of copartisans in each chamber. However, as much recent research has shown, a relatively large number of presidential copartisans in Congress is neither a necessary nor a sufficient condition for presidential success.[29] Thus if partisan strength is not linked to success, then there is no robust theoretical expectation that it should play a part in strategic calculations as to the front end of agenda activity. Since presidents cannot necessarily count on partisan support, even when they have a majority (witness the case of Jimmy Carter), I employ an alternative measure of presidential "strength," namely, ideological compatibility with Congress. A president who is ideologically compatible with Congress may propose more agenda items in anticipation of success and thus avoid being overturned by hostile legislation.[30] To measure this concept, I construct a measure of presidential partisanship using inflation-adjusted ideology scores of both the president and Congress.[31] *Ideological compatibility* is operationalized as the absolute value of the difference between the president's ideological score and that of the median member of Congress. The greater this distance (i.e., the larger the number), the less compatible the president is with Congress. I expect the compatibility coefficient to be negatively related to the number of agenda items proposed, and negatively related to congressional concurrence rates.

Incidentally, one other methodological issue is worth exploring. I had anticipated exploring chamber-specific measures to measure the degree to which a strategic president might make differing decisions based on bicameral differences. However, I was forced to construct a measure of the congressional median, given the fact that chamber ideology scores correlate quite highly with one another. The inclusion of both distance measures subjected the model to multicollinearity problems and thus created complicated matters of interpretation. Thus since removing one of the chamber variables was not consistent with any part of the leverage theory, I opted for the substantively less satisfying but methodologically more appropriate congressional measure, which accounts for both chambers simultaneously.[32]

Time Contextual
Some theories of presidential action hold that a president needs to be cognizant of the historical circumstances in which he serves and must accurately perceive the nature of the times within which he governs and act accordingly.[33] An explication of the leverage framework needs to take these potent insights into account. The problem is, of course, that any systematic understanding of presidential time or circumstance is likely to be ad hoc. In this section, I argue that proxy measures, though far from perfect, offer some measure of the environment that can be conceptualized as at least partly measuring the "nature of the times" that is so important in historically based theories. Though other variables in the analysis (e.g., leverage and, to some extent, economic variables) can be thought of as part of a time-contextual dimension, the operationalization of the variables in this section assumes that form most directly.

First, one obvious mark of the time within which a president governs is whether or not the nation is engaged in war. Previous studies have shown war to be a significant predictor of presidential resources, such as public opinion.[34] The variable *war deaths* captures the cumulative effect of ongoing war. Some studies that seek to model presidential approval employ a measure of cumulative Vietnam deaths,[35] which is included to capture and isolate the effect of Lyndon Johnson's exceptional decline in approval. Though I am not modeling approval, or even leverage, I include a similar measure to these other studies on the assumption that the effect of war deaths on the nation's psyche might be reflected in increased levels of presidential activity. Whether or not this is the case, accounting for the historical circumstance in which a president acts must reflect the "war-peace" dimension. I expect war to be positively related to agenda components and concurrence rates, given the increased capacities for presidential action in times of high tension abroad.

Next I employ Stimson's concept and measure of public mood.[36] The inclusion of this variable highlights the idea that the context of American government in a representational capacity waxes and wanes over time. Accounting for this is one major component of time and historical context. The variable is updated from Stimson's study to include the period to 1996. Recently, the concept has enjoyed wide currency as a general measure of the public's revealed preferences. Krehbiel, for example, uses it as a proxy for governmental preferences given the electoral mechanism.[37] Additionally, he argues that it reflects much of what Mayhew calls "creedal passion" and "public purpose."[38] Stimson and his colleagues employ it as a global measure of public opinion and argue that "Mood is the major dimension underlying expressed preferences over policy alternatives in the survey research record . . . [the] measure represents the public's sense of whether the political temperature is too hot or too cold, whether government is too active or not active enough."[39] I adopt and extend this reasoning to include mood as one measure of "time."

Finally, though it is not related to historical time per se, I include a measure of presidential time by measuring the point in the presidential term at which activity is undertaken. This is simply the temporal environment roughly corresponding to the president's year in office when the dependent variables were measured. Inclusion of this variable is necessary, as a control for the policy surges at the beginning of a president's term,[40] and variables decrease in number as the term ages.[41] Additionally, a president is most likely to gain congressional concurrence early on.[42] To ensure that any results are not driven by this secular trend, I include a counter variable that tracks the years of a president's term. The variable assumes values ranging from 1 to 4 for one-term presidents and 1 to 8 for two-term presidents. The important test is whether or not presidential leverage achieves statistical significance when the policy and political trends corresponding to a president's term are controlled for. The expectation is that the coefficient for *term* will be negative in all three models.

Economic Conditions
Finally, I include variables measuring the annual budget deficit and the annual misery index. As deficits grow, policy-making possibilities become more constrained. The public often holds the economy as its most important problem, and thus as the deficit rises, politicians may adjust policy strategies accordingly. To understand the economic constraints on presidents, I include a variable reflecting the yearly size of the *deficit* in the year prior to the measurement of

the dependent variables. Similarly, I include a simple measure of the *misery index* (inflation + unemployment). During economic downturns, presidents might feel empowered to engage in more activist policy making than what might be expected in more tranquil times. Thus I expect both coefficients to be positive in the front-end models. As for concurrence, I expect the null result, since there is no reason to expect congressional deference to be influenced by the state of the economy or size of the deficit. The public volume models, which are counts of uncorrelated events, are estimated with exponential Poisson regression (EPR) analysis.[43]

Findings and Discussion
Table 6.1 displays the EPR results for the two models of agenda activity. I concentrate my discussion only on those variables found to be significant in the full model.

The Poisson estimates cannot be interpreted directly as they can in Ordinary Least Squares (OLS) regression, but the sign and impact of the variables can be assessed. The proposition that presidential leverage is an important variable in predicting agenda making finds strong support in both agenda equations. First, the results indicate that as a president enjoys increased leverage, he acts strategically by proposing *less* in the way of requests in the politically charged environment of the State of the Union address, as well as the total number of requests made. These proposals can be thought of as part of a larger effect that increases the president's standing with the public in the period after the address,[44] and thus helps further enhance his leverage. This finding is strong and robust and is consistently significant in the presence of other predictors. Indeed, while perhaps surprising, this finding of a negative relationship is resilient across different models, operationalizations, and conditions. Substituting presidential approval for leverage yields the same negative finding, but the models are weaker (these models are not presented here).[45]

This finding is particularly interesting, given that it says that the *stronger* the president is in relation to the rest of the government, the *less* he puts forward. As noted earlier, this is perhaps indicative of a strategic decision to let well enough alone, to moderate or decrease activity so as to preserve the president's strength. Conversely, as presidential leverage decreases, the president may feel the need to increase his activity in the public arena via the State of the Union address to reclaim some prestige. This appears to be the case in the present situation, with presidents focusing on fewer but possibly more "important" agenda items, thus prospectively preserving their stature with the public. Conversely, the weaker the president is in relation to other institutions, the more likely he is to put forth proposals in a highly publicized context, perhaps to try and compensate for lost prestige. It is possible that the president is more likely to put forth fewer proposals in times of high leverage, but those pro-

TABLE 6.1
Exponential Poisson Regression Estimates for Front-End Agenda Components

	State of the Union Requests	All Requests
INSTITUTIONAL		
Leverage	−.23**	−.38***
	(−2.12)	(−2.29)
Distance	.005	.007
	(1.14)	(1.17)
Democrat	.57***	.53*
	(2.27)	(1.57)
TIME CONTEXTUAL		
Mood	.08***	−.027
	(4.19)	(−.781)
War Deaths	.02***	.006
	(2.29)	(.770)
Term Counter	−.15***	−.112***
	(−4.94)	(−3.22)
ECONOMIC CONDITIONS		
Misery Index	.05***	−.02
	(2.41)	(−.70)
Deficit	−.002***	−.003***
	(−3.36)	(−2.25)
CONSTANT	29.90	441.9
Log Likelihood	29.90	441.89
Significance: p<.10* p<.05** p<.01***		

Note: For considerations of space, results for the concurrence model are not reported here. Only one covariate (Distance) was significant in that estimation. See text for explanation.

Source: Data collected by the author from the State of the Union Addresses, 1967–1996.

posals may be highly salient and/or politically controversial (e.g., health care reform, welfare reform), but of course this will require further theorizing and empirical research.[46]

The results of Table 6.1 indicate strong relationships for most of the other variables as well, but their importance varies across contexts. The measure of ideological distance between the president and the median member of Congress is not significant in the estimation, suggesting that presidents do not take compatibility into account when acting strategically. Indeed, the coefficient is positive (though insignificant). Ideological distance is, however, a major factor in determining a president's success in Congress, which I will explain later. Finally, as expected, Democrats tend to put forth more in both the highly public environment of the State of the Union address as well as in total requests, though the estimation for the latter indicates that the coefficient is significant only at the .10 level.

Turning to the variables measuring the time-contextual aspects of agenda size, public mood is positive and highly significant in determining the State of the Union address requests, but not for all requests. The interpretation for the former is straightforward; as the mood of the public turns to a more activist government, presidents act in a way that comports with public impetus. There is no real effect in terms of the size of the agenda, however. Similarly, as war deaths increase, so does a president's activity in the highly public arena of the State of the Union address, though it does not have much effect on the size of the agenda. As expected, presidents are less active as their terms progress. The deeper a president is into his term, the less likely he is to offer policy requests. This makes sense. As the term progresses (regardless of whether it is the first or second term), the president begins to settle in and focus on completing existing policy initiatives, though this by no means implies that he will offer *no* requests.

Finally, both of the economic conditions variables are significant (though the misery index is not significant in predicting all requests). As the misery index increases, presidents place more before the public, likely reflecting increased economic measures. Structural realities embedded in the deficit are significant predictors and indicate presidential restraint. As the deficit increases, the size of the agenda decreases. Again, this is perfectly reasonable. As the deficit applies greater pressure to budgetary considerations, the president will offer fewer new policy requests, preferring instead to concentrate on the completion of an agenda already in progress. Thus Table 6.1 presents a picture of a contextually based dynamic, with presidents acting in response to their place in the American political system. Presidential and institutional variables explain the majority of decisions to put forth policy proposals. Presidential leverage shows itself to be a significant negative predictor of agenda size in the presence of covariates controlling for various aspects of the American political system at a given time.

All in all, the results present a picture of strong presidents decreasing the absolute numbers of public agenda proposals and supplementing their strength with the administrative presidency strategy. The findings suggest that presidents may be engaging in strategic behavior. When they are strong, they may focus on a few high-ticket items and hammer them home to the public and other institutions. They buttress their strength in other areas by increasing their use of executive orders. When they are weaker, as measured by the leverage index, they increase their public agenda activity, perhaps in an effort to upgrade their condition. They are less likely to pick fights or be seen as usurping "illegitimate" authority by using executive orders too frequently, but they still use the prerogative. For clarification, an analogy can be drawn to market decisions. If a president is rich (i.e., has high leverage), then he may go to the Lexus dealer and use that capital on the purchase of one high-priced commodity. If he is poor (i.e., low leverage), then he may go to Wal-Mart and buy several smaller items that can be more easily purchased. So it is with agenda activity in the public arena. Stronger presidents might focus more on getting large, controversial programs before the public, while weaker ones pursue more, but the nature of those programs might be inherently less contentious. Indeed, Peterson presents evidence that presidents may adopt as their own proposals that had their genesis in Congress and already enjoy broad support there.[47]

Perhaps most notable among the other predictors is that of the term counter which, as expected, is highly significant and negative. Even in the presence of this finding, leverage is a strong predictor of the decision regarding the level of requests made.

The results for the Congressional Concurrence model (not presented here) are similar to what was predicted, with leverage exhibiting no effect on concurrence rates. Recall that my reason for discussing a model of congressional concurrence at all was to determine the extent to which competing institutions took the president's leverage into account when acting on presidential priorities. Recall also that this model was included as a first cut at determining the scope of leverage theory. Thus if leverage had a significant impact on the president's use of agenda strategies (it did), then does it have an impact on the propensity of other institutions to go along? The answer is clearly no. While the sign is in the expected direction, it is highly insignificant. This is not to say that leverage works *against* a president (thus no Peterson-like argument as to the limits of approval can be made with reference to leverage), but it certainly does not seem to help him. Concurrence rates are thus determined by factors outside the boundary of leverage itself. Indeed, the major predictor of concurrence is ideological distance. Not surprisingly, as the president and the median member of Congress move closer to one another, the level of concurrence increases (again, these findings are not presented here).

Taken together, these models indicate that presidents do seem to act in accordance with their "place" in American politics when deciding on various strategies for pursuing their agendas.[48] Further thoughts on this are appropriate at this point. The findings in the model on concurrence indicate where the limits to the scope of leverage theory lie. While it explains much on the front end (a president-side explanation), it does not apply with the same rigor to the back-end (congressional) response to that leverage. Thus while it appears to be true that when presidents stand paramount in the political system they pursue more in the way of their agendas, the institutions competing with them in our separated system of institutions sharing powers do not necessarily defer to this increased prestige. This is not to argue that popular presidents do not have some success in Congress,[49] but that approval in the context of the concept of leverage does not hold greater promise of success than for those with low leverage. This is almost certainly due to the fact that approval is not measured and applied in its "pure" form but rather as a resource relative to that of the standing of governmental institutions.

IMPLICATIONS AND CONCLUSIONS

This chapter began with a development of the connection between public expectations and the place of the presidency in the American political system. I developed and tested a new measure that attempts to capture an important element of this dynamic, which I call the "index of presidential leverage." I supplemented the notion of leverage by simultaneously estimating a battery of variables that strives to measure the essence of the contextual factors possibly influencing presidential activity. The model was estimated via a series of equations explaining agenda activity levels (front end) and the rate of congressional concurrence (back end) of the presidential policy process.

The results indicate that presidents do tend to act in accordance with the "feeling" quantified by the index when deciding what to do and what strategies to pursue but did not extend to congressional concurrence. Strong evidence was presented indicating that covariates implied by the concept of presidential leverage, even in the presence of competing hypotheses, track with the public volume strategy. On the other hand, leverage theory and its derived implications do not hold much promise for understanding congressional concurrence.

The implications of the analysis for furthering theory building are many. Results indicate that public expectations may not be such a burden on presidents and that, to the extent the index captures components of an expectations gap,[50] presidents may be able to use those elements in a positive way. Presidents will always be hindered by an increasing gap between expectations and personal and institutional capacity, but these admittedly preliminary findings seem to indicate that presidents can use these expectations to their advantage in certain circumstances. While the results presented here do not allow for such a conclusion, they certainly are strong enough to warrant continued theorizing and testing. For example, contrary to Lowi,[51] I find that presidents are not entangled in a no-win situation; that is, they are not helpless in the face of circumstances beyond their control (e.g., exaggerated public expectations). Rather, complacency in the face of *potential* power handicaps their capacity.

Two limitations of the current analysis should be noted. The first is that the president depicted here is a decidedly reactive creature. But the president, more than any other actor in American politics, has the opportunity to effect change even in eras of political time not conducive to presidential action.[52] Thus an obvious next step is to examine how presidents might attempt to rally themselves in low leverage periods and shape the environmental context in their favor. The second is that the nature of the dependent variables is limited. While I would certainly argue that the public volume strategy is an important part of agenda setting, and that concurrence rates get at some sort of presidential success in Congress, they obviously are not the only components of the concepts that they represent. Thus future research will explore alternative operationalizations of various parts of presidential activity to further discern the promise and limitations of leverage theory.[53] The challenge for future research is to test the model's explanatory power on a number of other circumstances of presidential activity, such as congressional response to presidential leverage. By applying a number of alternative theoretical and methodological approaches (e.g., formal modeling of strategic behavior), the dynamics of the president's place in the institutional system and his efforts to overcome his position of weakness can be cast in more specific relief. In addition, presidential leverage could be employed as a dependent variable and then modeled as a function of other exogenous factors. The effort made in this chapter to measure one aspect of the place of the president in the system, cast through the eyes of the public, and the success of that measure in explaining agenda activity, provides reason for optimism in pursuing that line of inquiry.

NOTES

1. Richard E. Neustadt, *Presidential Power: The Politics of Leadership from FDR to Carter* (New York: John Wiley & Sons, 1980); Charles O. Jones, *The Presidency in a Separated System* (Washington, D.C.: Brookings, 1994).

2. See Jones, *The Presidency*; Stephen Skowronek, *The Politics Presidents Make: Leadership from John Adams to George Bush* (Cambridge, Mass.: Harvard University Press, 1993); Erwin C. Hargrove and Michael Nelson, *Presidents, Politics, and Policy* (New York: Knopf, 1984).

3. See Paul C. Light, *The President's Agenda: Domestic Policy Choice from Kennedy to Reagan*, rev. ed. (Baltimore: Johns Hopkins University Press, 1991); Jeffrey E. Cohen, "Presidential Rhetoric and the Public Agenda," *American Journal of Political Science* 39 (1995): 87–107; Jones, *The Presidency*; Charles O. Jones, *Separate but Equal Branches: Congress and the Presidency* (Chatham, N.J.: Chatham House, 1995); Dan B. Wood and Jeffrey S. Peake, "The Dynamics of Foreign Policy Agenda Setting," *American Political Science Review* 92 (1998): 173–84; and Kim Quaile Hill, "The Policy Agendas of the President and the Mass Public: A Research Validation and Extension," *American Journal of Political Science* 42 (1998): 1328–34.

4. See Jeffrey E. Cohen, *Presidential Responsiveness and Public Policy Making: The Public and the Policies That Presidents Choose* (Ann Arbor: University of Michigan Press,

1997); Jeffrey E. Cohen and Kenneth Collier, "Reconceptualizing Going Public," paper presented at the Annual Meeting of the American Political Science Association, Chicago, Illinois, 1995. This is the case with civil rights and economic policy, but Cohen and Collier report that public perception of foreign policy stays relatively stable from one year to the next.

5. Skowronek, *The Politics Presidents Make*, 37.

6. It is not hard for the president to stand preeminent over Congress. Congress consistently has extremely low confidence levels. See John R. Hibbing and Elizabeth Theiss-Morse, *Congress as Public Enemy: Public Attitudes toward American Political Institutions* (Cambridge: Cambridge University Press, 1995), for a fascinating account of the problems Congress continually deals with in its relationship with the public and the larger questions of democratic accountability.

7. I do not claim that the measure gets at all of what scholars such as Jones, Skowronek, and Hargrove and Nelson contend places the president in political context. Rather, I argue that it does get at one important part of that notion, namely, how the public views the president in the political system. Other parts, such as the president's place in historical time, must, for now, remain subject to impressionistic assessment.

8. These and other data tremendously useful to presidential scholars have been conveniently collected and presented in Lyn Ragsdale, *Vital Statistics on the Presidency: Washington to Clinton* (Washington, D.C.: CQ Press, 1996). Some of the data for individual institutional confidence from which I constructed the ratio can be found in Table 15-13, pp. 243-44. For the period 1985-1990, none of the reporting polling institutions asked about the presidency. However, Opinion Piece collected similar measures and was used for those years.

9. Some may argue that a better measure is to place the public's confidence in "government" as the denominator rather than simply taking the average of all three federal institutions. While there is a case to be made, my response is twofold: first, no systematic measures of "governmental confidence" exist over the period of this study; and second, the way I conceptualize the denominator actually creates a higher obstacle to overcome in order to lend credence to the idea of presidential leverage as a component of institutional strategy. The fact that confidence levels in the Supreme Court are almost always higher than for Congress or the White House means that using this as part of the measure makes increasing the index harder than would likely be the case if I were able to employ a catchall "government confidence" indicator. Thus if the index employed here achieves statistical significance, then it has done so in a situation that actually makes it more difficult to do so and thus can be viewed as being more robust than other potential measures.

10. Presidential approval and its functional components have been the subject of a deep, rich, and voluminous literature. I will not attempt here to provide a comprehensive set of citations, but see Samuel Kernell, "Explaining Presidential Approval," *American Political Science Review* 72 (1978): 506-22; and Charles W. Ostrom Jr. and Dennis M. Simon, "Promise and Performance: A Dynamic Model of Presidential Approval," *American Political Science Review* 79 (1985): 334-58, for attempts to model the dynamic properties of presidential approval.

11. Like approval, scholars have labored to elaborate presidential action as either the product of institutional constraints, see Terry M. Moe, "The Politicized Presidency," in *The New Direction in American Politics*, ed. John E. Chubb and Paul E. Peterson (Washington, D.C.: Brookings Institution, 1985), pp. 235–71, and "Presidents, Institutions, and Theory," in *Researching the Presidency: Vital Questions, New Approaches*, ed. George C. Edwards III, John H. Kessel, and Bert A. Rockman (Pittsburgh: University of Pittsburgh Press, 1993), pp. 337–56, or of individual characteristics of the incumbent, regardless of the configuration of institutional arrangements. Also see Gregory L. Hager and Terry Sullivan, "President-Centered and Presidency-Centered Explanations of Presidential Public Activity," *American Journal of Political Science* 38 (1994): 1079–1103, for an attempt to integrate the two into one framework.

12. For example, in 1967, Lyndon Johnson had an average approval of 47 percent and institutional confidence was just barely lower, averaging 44.33. This yielded LBJ a leverage index score of 1.06, giving him some theoretical leverage but probably not enough to use as a foundation for a highly activist agenda.

13. One weakness of the measure is that it does not take into account other institutions, such as the group system, the media, and other potentially relevant actors.

14. In fact, in models estimated but not presented here, approval and leverage do not correlate highly with one another. For each model, I calculated the partial correlation between leverage and approval, controlling for variables included in reduced-form estimations. For some models, (presidential requests and executive orders), partial correlations revealed no statistically significant relationships. For the model estimating congressional concurrence, partial r = .62 and was significant at the .002 level. This is, of course, reasonably strong, but perhaps not of much theoretical interest, given that leverage as a variable does not exhibit a systematic relationship with rates of congressional concurrence with presidential legislative positions.

15. John Mueller, "Presidential Approval from Truman to Johnson," *American Political Science Review* 64 (1970): 18–34.

16. See Ostrom and Simon, "Promise and Performance."

17. In future work, I plan to test this empirically using a variety of codifications of large-scale policy change. In Mark A. Peterson, *Legislating Together: The White House and Capitol Hill from Eisenhower to Reagan* (Cambridge, Mass.: Harvard University Press, 1990), Peterson has done the same in his study of legislative-executive relations.

18. See Douglas Rivers and Nancy Rose, "Passing the President's Program: Public Opinion and Presidential Influence in Congress," *American Journal of Political Science* 29 (1985): 183–96.

19. Peterson, *Legislating Together*, 191–94.

20. See Cohen and Collier, "Reconceptualizing Going Public"; Cohen, *Presidential Responsiveness*.

21. See previous citations in this chapter for confirmation of this statement.

22. Richard Nathan, *The Administrative Presidency* (New York: John Wiley, 1983).

23. See Cohen, *Presidential Responsiveness*.

24. See Samuel Kernell, *Going Public: New Strategies of Presidential Leadership*, 2nd ed. (Washington, D.C.: CQ Press, 1993).

25. Cohen and Collier, "Reconceptualizing."

26. See ibid.; Cohen, *Presidential*; Light, *The President's Agenda*; John H. Kessel, "Parameters of Presidential Politics," *Social Science Quarterly* 55 (1974): 8–24.

27. I have consciously avoided using the words "power" or "influence" in describing presidential success in Congress. I follow at least a generation of political scientists that has recognized that presidential success in Congress does not necessarily equate with presidential "power" or "influence." See, among others, George C. Edwards III, *At the Margins* (New Haven, Conn.: Yale University Press, 1989); Peterson, *Legislating Together*; Patrick J. Fett, "Truth in Advertising: The Revelation of Presidential Legislative Priorities," *Western Political Quarterly* 45 (1992): 895–920; Jon R. Bond and Richard Fleisher, *The President in the Legislative Arena* (Chicago: University of Chicago Press, 1990); Jon R. Bond, Richard Fleisher, and Glen S. Krutz, "An Overview of the Empirical Findings on Presidential-Congressional Relations," in *Rivals for Power: Presidential-Congressional Relations*, ed. James A. Thurber, pp. 49–71 (Washington, D.C.: CQ Press, 1996), Kenneth Collier and Terry Sullivan, "New Evidence Undercutting the Linkage of Approval with Presidential Support and Influence," *Journal of Politics* 57 (1995): 197–209; Calvin Mouw and Michael MacKuen, "The Strategic Configuration, Personal Influence, and Presidential Power in Congress," *Western Political Quarterly* 45 (1992): 579–608; Cary R. Covington, J. Mark Wrighton, and Rhonda Kinney, "A 'Presidency-Augmented' Model of Presidential Success on Roll Call Votes," *American Journal of Political Science* 39 (1994): 1001–24.

28. There are, of course, numerous model specifications that can be employed in pursuit of an understanding of agenda setting. It should be clear that I intend not to topple other models that have been used in the literature but rather to suggest a model specification that is consistent with leverage theory. Also, the nature of the analysis is to determine impacts on variation in agenda activity and not in predicting other interesting components of agenda setting, such as full legislative agenda size in Rivers and Rose, "Passing the President's Program," the introduction of small versus large bills in Keith Krehbiel, *Pivotal Politics: A Theory of U.S. Lawmaking* (Chicago: University of Chicago Press, 1998), and Peterson, *Legislating Together*; or policy content in Cohen and Collier, "Reconceptualizing," and Cohen, *Presidential*. As I note later, however, I do apply the model to some of Cohen's data to test whether or not leverage theory holds some promise for explaining the content of the president's State of the Union policy proposals.

29. See Jones, *The Presidency*; Bond and Fleisher, *The President in the Legislative Arena*; David Mayhew, *Divided We Govern: Party Control, Lawmaking, and Investigations 1946–1990* (New Haven: Yale University Press, 1991); and Krehbiel, *Pivotal Politics*.

30. See Krehbiel, *Pivotal Politics*.

31. See the provocative paper by Tim Groseclose, Steven D. Levitt, and James M. Snyder Jr., "Comparing Interest Group Scores across Time and Chambers: Adjusted ADA Scores for the U.S. Congress," *American Political Science Review* 93 (1999):

33–50, which details the need for such a measure and explains a simple, powerful method by which to convert nominal scores to real scores. The scores are adjusted so that they are consistent both across chambers and time, making comparison easier. The D-NOMINATE scores are adapted from Keith Poole and Howard Rosenthal, "Patterns of Congressional Voting," *American Journal of Political Science* 35 (1991): 228–78.

32. Krehbiel, *Pivotal Politics*, 73, makes a similar argument. I did perform a number of diagnostic tests, including measuring variance inflation factors and then removing one variable and then the other from the analysis, with still inconclusive results most likely generated by omitted variable bias when one or the other chamber remains unaccounted for. Thus I constructed the chamber measure. Results from these diagnostic runs are available from the author.

33. See Skowronek, *The Politics*; Erwin C. Hargrove, *The Power of the Modern Presidency* (New York: Alfred A. Knopf, 1974); Hargrove and Nelson, *Presidents, Politics, and Policy*.

34. See John Mueller, *War, Presidents, and Public Opinion* (New York: John Wiley, 1973); Ostrom and Simon, "Promise and Performance."

35. See Kernell, "Explaining Presidential Approval"; Robert S. Erikson, Michael B. MacKuen, and James A. Stimson, *The Macro Polity* (New York: Cambridge University Press, 2002).

36. James A. Stimson, *Public Opinion in America: Moods, Cycles, and Swings* (Boulder, Colo.: Westview Press, 1991).

37. Krehbiel, *Pivotal Politics*, 62, 68.

38. See Mayhew, *Divided We Govern*.

39. See James Stimson, Michael MacKuen, and Robert Erikson, "Dynamic Representation," *American Political Science Review* 89 (1995): 543–65; *The Macro Polity*.

40. See Krehbiel, *Pivotal Politics*; Mayhew, *Divided We Govern*; Light, *The President's Agenda*.

41. Ragsdale, *Vital Statistics*, 359.

42. Ibid., 362.

43. Following King, the Poisson model is represented as follows: $E(\tilde{Y_i})\Box_i = \exp(x_i\Box)$, where Y_i is the number of events (i.e., total requests in the State of the Union address, or number of domestic executive orders issued in a year). The observed events are always positive (i.e., $E(Y_i)0$; $\Box_i 0$); $\Box_i$ is the underlying process from which the observed events are generated and can be represented as an exponential linear function of x_i, a vector of explanatory variables. Finally, are the parameters to be estimated. The log-likelihood function is then maximized, producing the statistical results. This log-likelihood function can be written as follows: $\ln L (\Box y) = \Box [y_i (x_i\Box) - \exp(x_i\Box)]$. For a clear and thorough explanation of this technique, see Gary King, "Statistical Models for Political Science Event Counts: Bias in Conventional Procedures and Evidence for the Exponential Poisson Regression Model," *American Journal of Political Science* 32 (1988): 838–63; Gary King, *Unifying Political Methodology: The Likelihood Theory of Statistical Inference* (Cambridge: Cambridge University Press, 1985). For applications to the presidency, see Paul Brace and Barbara Hinckley, *Follow the Leader:*

Opinion Polls and the Modern Presidents (New York: Basic Books, 1992).

44. See Cohen, *Presidential Responsiveness*.

45. I am in the preliminary stages of extending the data both backward to 1958 and forward to 2000. In preliminary runs, this negative finding again presented itself. I also have used a slightly different operationalization of leverage but again find strong, negative, significant support. These results will be presented in later work.

46. In order to determine whether the model in general and presidential leverage in particular had any impact on policy content, I ran a series of time series regressions in an attempt to determine whether they held any explanatory power. Using data presented in Cohen and Collier, "Reconceptualizing," Appendix, I found that presidential leverage and the president's ideology achieved statistical significance at $p<.10$, with stronger, more conservative presidents more likely to emphasize economics. The time of the president's term was the only significant variable in examining foreign policy emphasis. However, since neither model did well in explaining policy content, I omitted them from the analysis. Results are available from the author.

47. Peterson, *Legislating Together*.

48. Indeed, the predictive strength of the models is quite strong if one compares actual versus predicted values of the dependent variables given actual annual observations. Space considerations preclude presentation of these graphs, but the pattern of observed frequencies closely matches those predicted by the models, especially the "front-end" estimates. This also is the case for the concurrence model, which uses only three explanatory variables and does not include leverage. Its fit is not as good as that observed with the other two models, of which leverage played a large part, but still tracks quite well. These graphical estimations are available from the author.

49. See Rivers and Rose, "Passing the President's Program."

50. See Richard W. Waterman, ed., *The Presidency Reconsidered* (Itasca, Ill.: Peacock, 1993); Cohen, *Presidential Responsiveness*; Michael A. Genovese, *The Presidential Dilemma: Leadership in the American System* (New York: HarperCollins, 1995).

51. Theodore J. Lowi, *The Personal President: Power Invested, Promise Unfulfilled* (Ithaca, N.Y.: Cornell University Press, 1985).

52. See Skowronek, *The Politics*.

53. One of the next steps is to apply leverage to systematic measures of policy content. Preliminary analyses bode well for leverage. As a test, I regressed Cohen's (in *Presidential Responsiveness*) substantive policy content data from Appendix A.2, 251, on the model employed here. I ran three equations measuring foreign, domestic, and economic policy, respectively. While the model did poorly for economic policy (only the time counter was significant), it performed better for the other two. Significant predictors for the foreign policy model include Presidential Leverage ($p<.10$), Mood × Leverage ($p=.05$), and Mood ($p<.10$). It performed best for domestic policy emphasis with Leverage ($p<.05$), Mood × Leverage ($p<.05$), Misery ($p<.10$), and Mood ($p<.02$) accounting for roughly 60 percent of the variance. Future tests will explore other measures of content, but these results bode well for leverage theory.

7

Second-Term Presidents

Free Birds or Lame Ducks?

William Cunion

As the Clinton presidency came to a close in January 2001, pundits offered a full range of comments on his eventful tenure. Many praised his supervision of the economy or lauded his ability to stake out a centrist position on taxes and welfare. Others, though, pointed to his failure to deliver a program of national health care or questioned his foreign policy leadership. Both supporters and critics had much to say about impeachment, an "irrelevancy," by some accounts, and a "stain" in the view of others. Among these standard claims of success or failure, Robert Samuelson's criticism in the *Washington Post* was particularly noteworthy:[1]

> Rarely has a president so dominated the public stage and so little affected the public agenda. His central failure lay not in what he did—which wasn't much—but in what he deliberately avoided. As the first baby boomer president, he had a historic opportunity to prepare for his own generation's retirement. The task was to redraw the compact between workers and retirees by modernizing Social Security and Medicare. Clinton didn't try.[1]

The circumstances for opening a dialogue on these issues, Samuelson claimed, "could not have been more favorable." In addition to the opportunities permitted by economic prosperity, Clinton was both a policy wonk and an effective public speaker—credible and persuasive. Most of all, in his second term, *"he did not have to fear losing reelection"* (emphasis added).[2]

Ratified in 1951, the Twenty-second Amendment prohibits any individual from serving more than two terms as president.[3] Following Dwight Eisenhower and Ronald Reagan, Clinton was just the third president to be subject to its restrictions and to have served a full second term facing a future without elections. From Samuelson's perspective, this electoral freedom should have liberated Clinton to initiate a serious debate on issues such as Social Security and Medicare, which have long been considered the "third rail" of American politics—touch it, and die. This despite the looming crisis: analysts' "best estimates" project that Social Security expenditures will exceed revenues as early as 2018, and that the entire trust fund could be depleted by 2043; for Medicare, the relevant dates are estimated to be 2016 and 2030, respectively.[4] At some point, difficult decisions will have to be made, and the sooner action is taken, the less costly it will be. Without having to fear the electoral reprisals, Clinton could have offered bold proposals to address the impending crises for these two important programs. No third term, no third rail.

Clinton himself alluded to his new electoral freedom in the first State of the Union address of his second term:

> We must agree to a bipartisan process to preserve Social Security and reform Medicare for the long run, so that these fundamental programs will be as strong for our children as they are for our parents. . . . I know this is not going to be easy. But I really believe that one of the reasons the American people gave me a second term was to take the tough decisions in the next four years that will carry our country through the next fifty years. I know it is easier for me than for you to say or do.[5]

From another perspective, though, the situation was far more complex. Even though he was now freed from electoral constraints, Clinton still had to deal with the usual political constraints that all presidents constantly face. After all, Clinton was not elected king; for any of his proposals to become reality, he would need the support of countless others.[6] He might not have had a need to fear the third rail, but nearly everyone else in Washington did.

Although Samuelson largely ignored these other constraints, his criticism is still troubling. Clinton could have begun a national dialogue on these issues. Could his rhetorical skills have created an opportunity for policy makers by reducing the risks associated with being the first to propose difficult solutions? Since he chose not to speak frankly on these issues, the question is hypothetical, but it raises a broader question that is purely empirical: Do presidents engage in more public leadership during their second terms? In other words, do they show more of an effort to move public opinion rather than simply to respond to it?

A variety of expectations—even contradictory ones—can be supported theoretically. We can easily posit reasons that second-term presidents will or will not try to engage in more public leadership. Some might argue that a *lame duck* president will avoid such risks, as fear of being perceived as a failure may inhibit him from addressing problems that other actors in the political system are not eager to confront. Like Samuelson, others may contend that a reelected president is a *free bird*; unconstrained by future electoral concerns, the president may exhibit bold leadership, bringing difficult issues such as Social Security and Medicare to the forefront of the public agenda, particularly if he believes that they may affect his historical legacy. To this point, the evidence has been too thin to provide much support for either theory.

The question requires a more systematic analysis than one pundit's judgment. After all, it is possible that Clinton was leading, but not doing so on the issues that Samuelson believed to have been the most pressing. Among other things, Clinton did champion China's controversial acceptance into the World Trade Organization during his last year in office. Although a more thorough examination of leadership is clearly required, the evidence is necessarily limited, since only three presidents have served a full eight years since the ratification of the Twenty-second Amendment. Conclusions must thus be stated somewhat tentatively. What evidence we have, though, suggests that second-term presidents have not demonstrated bold public leadership; they have behaved more like lame ducks than free birds.

TERM LIMITS

At the heart of this issue is a deeper question about democracy itself, and whether one should expect normatively better policy outcomes to emerge when electoral concerns are muted or even removed. Essentially, the matter can be reduced to a question about the ability or willingness of citizens to make difficult choices that serve their long-term interests. Conventional wisdom suggests that the forces of competitive elections provide disincentives for politicians to promote such costly measures. Walter Mondale's infamous pledge to raise taxes in a debate with Reagan during the 1984 presidential campaign surely quashed whatever dim hopes he had of becoming president. The line also inspired a *Saturday Night Live* skit aptly titled, "What were you thinking?"

The public's aversion to costly solutions is of course the deadly force behind the third rail, and survey evidence would seem to support politicians' fear of this issue. Consider Social Security: though most Americans recognize its impending fiscal problems, they do not seem to favor *any* of the widely discussed proposals for reform. Polls vary, but the pattern is quite consistent: privatization of the system, raising the eligibility age, increasing payroll taxes, reducing cost of living adjustments—*none* of these proposals is widely supported.[7] While Social Security may not be an ordinary political issue, it might be indicative of a shift in the kinds of issues that today's politicians must face, a shift that may have "heightened the conflict between reelection and good policy."[8] It certainly suggests that political pressures can inhibit solutions to our most challenging problems.[9]

Such beliefs have been the main impetus behind the movement to implement term limits on elected officials. There are other arguments both for and against term limits, but the possible effect on independence from public opinion to pursue good policy making is the most relevant here. It is, after all, that independence that presumably provides a second-term president with the necessary latitude to pursue difficult policy decisions. While there are a number of excellent comparative studies and analyses of state legislators assessing the effects of term limits, their findings are largely inapplicable to understanding the behavior of U.S. presidents. Most legislators hope to continue their political careers in other capacities; modern presidents, it seems, do not.[10] Still, the fact that the absence of electoral pressures leads retiring and term-limited legislators to be less responsive to their constituents[11] may raise the expectation of similar behavior for second-term presidents.

THE CONSTITUTIONAL CONVENTION

Contemporary supporters of congressional term limits are typically more skeptical of democracy than their opponents are.[12] But when the framers debated whether their new constitution would permit a president to seek additional terms, these positions were largely reversed.

Given how strongly the framers distrusted executive power, it is initially quite surprising that they rejected limiting the number of terms a president could serve. Their experience with the British monarchy and with British colonial governors had led most of them to equate executive power with tyranny, and as a result, the Articles of Confederation provided for no independent executive. Similarly, most of the early state constitutions invested their governors with limited powers and short terms. But with the many internal and external threats to the country, most of the delegates at the Constitutional Convention recognized the need to create a strong, unitary executive. Still, it is surprising in retrospect that they chose not to limit the president to a single term, especially given the need for political compromises to secure ratification. The document they agreed to was silent on the subject of reeligibility, leaving the number of presidential terms to be limited only by elections and by custom. In fact, a one-term limit was in effect for most of the convention, as the delegates temporarily deferred on the complex questions involving the election of the president. Few of the delegates supported the idea of a popular election, but other proposals seemed to infringe upon executive independence. Thus the initial plan left nearly everyone dissatisfied: the president was to be chosen by Congress for a single, seven-year term. The novel creation of the much-maligned Electoral College provided a solution to the selection problem and to the interrelated concerns of the length of the president's term and the issue of reeligibility. With a completely independent body of electors, the president's independence from Congress would thus be assured without requiring an excessively long tenure. Additionally, the Electoral College satisfied enough delegates to remove the one-term restriction, though the story is more complicated.

It is important to realize that most of the framers conceived of the president as a truly independent, impartial force who would stand as a bulwark against Congress, and against public opinion when necessary. As Alexander Hamilton wrote in *Federalist 71*, the president should not show "an unqualified complaisance to every sudden breeze of passion, or to every transient impulse which the people may receive from the arts of men, who flatter their prejudices to betray their interests. . . . When occasions present themselves in which the interests of the people are at variance with their inclinations, it is the duty of the persons whom they have appointed to be the guardians of those interests, to withstand the temporary delusion, in order to give them time and opportunity for more cool and sedate reflection."[13] Like Hamilton, those delegates who advocated a strong executive were generally those who had the least amount of confidence in the public. Their opposition to term limits was not grounded in the democratic ideal of the electoral process but arose, rather, from the desire to invest the president with sufficient political power to compete with the far more democratic legislative branch. It is no accident that Hamilton, who was probably the *least* democratic of all the framers, also was the most vocal supporter of perpetual presidential reeligibility, at one point even arguing for a *life* tenure.

In the same vein, those who supported limiting presidential terms tended to be more democratically minded. Many of the opponents of the Constitution feared that without such limits the presidency would become an elective monarchy, as perpetual reeligibility would translate into perpetual reelection. Experience in the states provided support for their concerns, as many governors had been in office continuously for years, despite annual elections in most cases. At the Virginia Ratifying Convention, George Mason expressed what was surely a widely held concern: "This president will be elected time after time: he will be continued in office for life."[14] Some of the anti-Federalists contended specifically that term limits would enable the president to better pursue the public good. The *Federal Farmer*, for example, argued that reeligibility would tempt the president to direct his energies toward maintaining his office, and that he would "spare no artifice, no address, and no exertions, to increase the powers and importance of it."[15] But freed from this burden, a president "will be governed by very different considerations. . . . The great object of each president then will be to render his government a glorious period in the annals of his country."[16] It was not until midway through the twentieth century that this claim could be tested.

The Twenty-Second Amendment

Not until Franklin Roosevelt won a third term in office in 1940 did any president successfully violate the two-term tradition.[17] In fact, the political norms of the nineteenth century pushed a number of presidential candidates to pledge to serve only a *single* term, and even some strong presidents (such as James Polk) fulfilled those promises. But even if many presidents served in the knowledge that their current term also would be the end of their political careers, the formal possibility of reelection always remained. The Twenty-second Amendment, however, makes it a certainty that a second term will be a president's last.

Introduced on the first day of the first session of the (heavily Republican) 80th Congress in 1947, this was not the first attempt to limit the number of presidential terms. Constitutional amendments to do so had been proposed on more than 250 previous occasions, though none had obtained the required congressional support to be sent to the states for ratification.[18] Additionally, a number of presidents had expressed support for a constitutional restriction, and the Democratic Party even included it in its official platform in 1912. But Roosevelt's long tenure had changed the dynamics of what had previously been only a hypothetical question.

Most Democrats were opposed to the measure and accused Republicans of being motivated by hostility to Roosevelt's legacy, not the merits of term limits themselves. Senator Scott Lucas of Illinois put it bluntly: "No matter how any Member of the Senate may vote upon the issue now pending before it, truthful men know that the breaking of the two-term precedent by Franklin D. Roosevelt in 1940 and the further shattering of the precedent by his reelection in 1944 are the basic reasons for seeking this constitutional amendment. Partisan inspiration has decreed that it shall not happen again."[19] It is impossible to know whether Republicans were simply being partisan (though their unanimous vote in both chambers raises suspicions), but the congressional debate undoubtedly took place within Roosevelt's shadow. Few mentioned his name explicitly, but Republicans frequently cited the importance of the two-term tradition, claiming that anything longer would jeopardize liberty at the hands of an elected Caesar.

The entire debate—in both chambers, and on both sides—was remarkably thin on the important substantive political questions involved with term limits, with a few exceptions. Democrat Harley Kilgore of West Virginia did raise the matter of a lame duck's political weakness: "The Executive's effectiveness will be seriously impaired, as no one will obey and respect him if he knows that the Executive cannot run again."[20] Though Kilgore provided some evidence from state governors to support his point, his claim was nevertheless open to argument—an argument that never occurred, as no one in either party responded to his concern.

More interestingly, little was said about the potential effects of removing the electoral constraint from the president, and whether the public good would be served or harmed by such a change. Arguing for a substitute amendment that would have limited the president to a single, six-year term, Democrat Emanuel Celler of New York said, "It has always been natural for the incumbent President to have his eyes fixed on reelection, and all the acts of the first term, directly or indirectly, in some measure, are affected by the ambition for a second term. . . . If there is no possibility . . . for reelection, there is no need for the President . . . to suggest legislation that might mean the garnering of additional votes that might be useful at the national convention."[21] Implying that reelection concerns induce such pandering, Celler added, "The attendant political strains and stresses are inconsistent with good government."[22] Also in support of the substitute amendment, Democrat Sam Hobbs of Alabama offered similar arguments, noting especially that cabinet appointments could be made solely on the basis of merit, not political calculations. Kenneth Keating, a Republican from New York, offered the only response, submitting that political pressures force a president to "remain ever mindful of the wishes of a majority of the people of the country" and encourage him to "always weigh carefully the expressed desires and aspirations of the greatest number in arriving at his final conclusion."[23] No one in either chamber ventured to speculate on whether a president ineligible for reelection would attempt to engage in more public leadership—or whether his lame-duck status would inhibit that.

Most of the congressional debate centered on issues of much less importance. Most of the Senate discussion, for example, focused on how to "count" a term that began with a vice president succeeding to office upon the death of a president. Given the lack of serious debate, it seems somehow appropriate that the historic measure passed so rapidly; on a largely partisan vote,[24] the amendment was sent to the states for ratification on March 24—less than three months after its introduction. Rather charitably, Milkis and Nelson describe the debate as "a thin gloss of constitutional philosophy over a highly partisan issue."[25]

WHAT DO SCHOLARS THINK?

Initially, scholarly reaction to the amendment was uniformly negative, sometimes bordering on the apocalyptic. Early political scientists, such as Louis Brownlow, Edward Corwin, and Herman Finer, all objected strenuously to the limitation;[26] Clinton Rossiter in particular found the amendment "ill-considered . . . leaving us naked to our enemies."[27] Most ominously, Louis Koenig thought it was "a tragedy whose full dimensions are yet to be known . . . badly inhibit[ing] the president's power in his second term."[28] But recent scholars have largely ignored the amendment altogether; most of the major contemporary textbooks on the presidency barely mention it at all,[29] and almost none offer any commentary on its effects. Robert DiClerico is an exception, and he notes only that ineligibility "undoubtedly has a significant [weakening] effect upon the president's political leverage as he moves through his second four years," and he leaves the critique at that.[30] Michael Genovese stands out as the most strident opponent of the Twenty-second Amendment, explicitly calling for its repeal on the grounds that it might help "reinvigorate the political leverage of what have become 'lame duck' presidents."[31]

Much of the scholarly assessment of the effects of the amendment is unusually speculative. Since so few presidents have actually faced the restriction, empirical data are not abundant. Paul Light's seminal work on the president's agenda-setting process illustrates the problem. Based on interview data, he concludes that presidents have far less influence in their second terms than in their first, and he offers some plausible explanations (e.g., the lack of a "honeymoon" period) for why this might be so. But his evidence is thin, and the relevant recollections by his subjects are not particularly persuasive. For example, he notes that several of Nixon's aides claimed that the president's lame-duck status was responsible for the failure of a national health insurance program in 1974.[32] Though this could be correct, the alternative explanations—divided government, the Watergate scandal—seem far more plausible as presumptive causes. Light himself acknowledges the lack of "hard data,"[33] though one is struck by his strong claims about the differences between the first and second terms—differences that he contends "have become more important since the Twenty-second Amendment"—given that he does not analyze presidencies that occurred before its existence.[34]

Most of the studies that examine presidential power and behavior in the second term make no distinction between those administrations that came before the Twenty-second Amendment and those that came after. As a result, few offer assessments of its effects, though the general conclusions about second terms have been consistent: "All modern presidents' second terms have been more difficult than their first."[35] It is not clear, however, whether the term limit imposed by the amendment is at all relevant to these difficulties. Nor is it clear whether these difficulties are caused by factors beyond the president's control, as Light contends, or if the president makes decisions that contribute to them.

Looking all the way back to FDR, Grossman, Kumar, and Rourke find that even as incumbent presidents tend to win reelection by very large margins, they experience a "diminished ability to shape the national policy agenda during their second term."[36] In part, the reelection campaigns themselves are largely to blame, since they tend to focus on vague promises of future achievement or vacuous themes intended to secure goodwill for the incumbent; Reagan's 1984 slogans "You ain't seen nothing yet" and "It's morning again in

America" illustrate each of these points. Since presidents do not normally run for reelection by articulating a clear policy agenda, other political actors do not interpret the victory as any sort of a mandate for the president's political goals. Making matters worse, the authors add, reelected presidents *do* tend to interpret their victory that way, and often they pursue highly controversial policies before obtaining the necessary congressional support. The authors cite examples such as Roosevelt's effort to increase the size of the Supreme Court and Truman's decision to enter the Korean War—both of which occurred prior to the Twenty-second Amendment. In their view, the second term is so difficult because reelected presidents, in their overconfidence, make strategic errors. These errors, it should be noted, have nothing at all to do with term limits, thus they offer no thoughts on the amendment's effects.

Brace and Hinckley's analyses of second terms largely mirror their broader thesis, suggesting that the decline in influence is caused primarily by factors beyond the president's control, though his decisions may exacerbate the trend.[37] Before Clinton escaped the pattern, a drop in approval ratings in the second term seemed inevitable, and Brace and Hinckley flatly state that not a single strategic presidential activity can positively affect popularity.[38] Even major addresses, which otherwise tend to increase public support, have no effect during a president's second term. But again, the effects, if any, of the Twenty-second Amendment are not clear, as their studies include Truman (who, since he had served more than half of FDR's final term, would have been subject to the amendment's restriction). Thus the authors generally refrain from speculating about the amendment's effects.

Almost parenthetically, though, Brace and Hinckley do offer one theory for the failure of public addresses to produce improved approval ratings in the second term that may hinge upon the amendment. "Perhaps there is a qualitative difference between terms in these speeches, with presidents more motivated to speak in publicly pleasing ways during their first terms than during their second."[39] While they do not elaborate on this speculation, they seem to imply that the absence of electoral concerns might reduce the inhibitions of presidents, allowing them to speak more candidly to the public.

Clearly we know very little about the effects of the Twenty-second Amendment. Here I propose testable propositions about presidential leadership of the public, and in the following section, I apply a novel approach to examine these two hypotheses.

H1: Since the ratification of the Twenty-second Amendment, presidents engage in more public leadership in their second terms than in their first.

Straightforward as this conjecture is, there may be reasons to have somewhat contradictory expectations as well. After all, the Twenty-second

Amendment was not ratified in a complete vacuum. Even with electoral freedom, the president still faces the usual set of systemic political challenges in a second term. Bold public leadership may be admirable on one level but quite foolish on another, and presidents typically prefer to achieve victories to suffering failures, even if the policies are less consequential. Some scholars have argued that wholly independently of term limits, more recent presidents engage in less public leadership because they have much better access to the state of public opinion and can better maintain high approval ratings by adhering to the polls.[40] Presidents have probably always been interested in public opinion, but at least since the Kennedy administration, the White House has made extensive use of polling data. And during the Nixon administration, a fully institutionalized apparatus for assessing public opinion emerged, which has been maintained ever since.[41] Thus we should observe a decline in public leadership over time, regardless of the cover that term limits provide. With the data analyzed here, we can state this more formally as:

H2: Presidents who have served after 1960 have exhibited less public leadership than those who served previously.

THE METHOD

A proper analysis of presidential leadership requires some careful attention to serious conceptual and methodological problems. Addressing H1 is especially tricky, since only four presidents have faced the restriction of the Twenty-second Amendment. It is tempting merely to offer broad assessments of their second terms, but such commentary is likely to be at least somewhat impressionistic, as such narratives often tend to be. But even if the stories of each presidency could somehow be told perfectly, such an approach would quickly put the focus on the personal styles of individual presidents and the unique historical circumstances during their tenures. While such factors are undoubtedly important (in fact, as I discuss later, Nixon is excluded from this analysis precisely for such reasons), they can inadvertently distract from drawing more general conclusions. Instead of a set of case studies, I propose a rather unorthodox approach to determine the effects of presidential term limits on public leadership more generally.

Jeffrey Tulis has said that public speaking is at the heart of today's presidency and is, in fact, "its essential task."[42] Indeed, modern presidents make countless public appearances, and the speeches they make provide copious data for a robust examination of the aforementioned hypotheses.[43] Specifically, I employ a content analysis of the president's public rhetoric to test these claims in these hypotheses.

The approach here is unusual, but the underlying logic is quite simple: by systematically examining what the president says—or, more specifically, *how* he says it, we can assess how difficult he and his advisors believed it would be to obtain support for a proposal. The coding scheme (described later) captures several fairly abstract types of rhetorical strategies that would tend to indicate that presidents are attempting to lead public opinion. The major assumption is that attempting to change public opinion, against anticipated resistance, will induce presidents to use certain persuasive methods that would be less useful or even counterproductive when the president anticipates immediate support.

To distinguish presidential rhetoric that seeks to lead public opinion from rhetoric that largely exploits or mobilizes existing and readily forthcoming support, it is necessary to identify the features of rhetoric that indicate whether the speech treats the policy as an easy or a hard sell. In other words, we need to determine whether the president is attempting to overcome resistance in the speech or demonstrating his support for a position already attractive to the public. The following list of rhetorical methods or strategies should be more prominent when the president is trying to lead public opinion than when he is following:

1. Mentioning actual opposition to or fears of his policies among ordinary citizens. This dilutes the president's message and will probably be done only when public opposition is sufficiently strong (or potentially so) that to ignore it would make him appear unresponsive or out of touch. This element would presumably be followed by an effort to assuage the fears or concerns behind the opposition. ("I know that many people are worried about how this change will affect them.")
2. Conceding that the policies will actually have some costs to the public. This too dilutes the message and will be done only when there are such obvious costs that to ignore them would cause the president to appear unconcerned or overlooking reality. ("Higher heating oil prices will make it harder to keep our homes as warm as we are used to.")
3. Mentioning objections to his policies. Again, including such points has rhetorical costs and is likely to occur only when an obvious objection needs to be answered. ("Some say that executing a juvenile is too harsh.") Note that mentioning opposition from elites—from members of the other party, or leaders of interest groups, for example—does not count here as mentioning an objection, unless a substantive reason for the opposition is cited. The concept is mentioning a possible or alleged *reason* for not adopting the president's policy.[44]
4. Citing support for a policy, or for some claims on its behalf, by experts or other elites (such as foreign leaders). Typically presidents would rather have the audience agreeing with him on the basis of

their own beliefs or experience. When the president's major claims do not seem self-evident, an appeal to experts plays a larger role. ("The prestigious Brookings Institution has endorsed my plan.")

5. Providing extensive arguments, examples, or evidence to support the main causal claims for the president's policies—that is, to show that they will actually yield the promised benefits. To spell out such arguments at length is not useful if the public habitually takes the causal claim for granted, so it will occur primarily where they need to be convinced. ("Every time we have expanded trade, we have experienced economic growth. Trade barriers may seem like a good idea, but historically, they've led to disastrous outcomes. The barriers created by the Smoot-Hawley tariff, for example, helped cause the Great Depression.")

6. Appealing to the public's sense of obligation or duty to support a policy. We are more likely to appeal to obligation when appeals to interest or inclination are unlikely to work. The president may say that we have "no choice" but to support his policy, given our common values—as if to recognize that if we did have a choice, we might not want to do what he asks. ("It is not right to saddle our children's generation with the task of cleaning up our mistakes.")

For each feature, every instance of a clear mention is given two points, while vague mentions are given one. These points are then added to create a sum total for each individual speech, which will serve as the dependent variable in the analysis that follows. (A complete description of the coding method is available from the author.)

Although it is unorthodox, the method seems to capture the leading one might expect on specific speeches whose political context is well known. For example, Bill Clinton addressed the nation on the North American Free Trade Agreement (NAFTA) on November 6, 1993, only three days before Al Gore's famous televised debate with Ross Perot. Across the political spectrum, many citizens were extremely suspicious of the bill, so Clinton certainly faced a challenge that required leading. Coding indicates that he did attempt to do just that, employing several rhetorical strategies associated here with leading. For example, Clinton issued a preemptive response to Perot by noting the reason for the objection: "The fear that low wages and the lower cost of production in Mexico will lead to a massive flight of jobs down there...." But then arguing why this objection is flawed: "Well, if we don't pass NAFTA, that could still be true. The lower wages and the lower cost of production could still be there. But if we do pass it, it means dramatically increased sales of American products made right here in America." That is not his only defense of the NAFTA; he also exerts substantial effort to demonstrate that the policy will produce the desired effects: "For our country, for every wealthy country, the only way to create new jobs and to raise incomes is to export more products"; "Right now, Mexico's tariffs on our products are two-and-a-half times higher than our tariffs on theirs. NAFTA will remove those barriers, opening up a growing market for our goods and services and creating hundreds of thousands of new jobs for our people." He also invokes a vague call on moral obligations: "So we have to face the choice of facts versus fear. When Americans have faced that choice in the past, they've always chosen honesty and hope." Finally, he closes this speech by mentioning an impressive list of experts who support the NAFTA: "I believe ordinary Americans will agree with every living President, every living Secretary of State, every living Secretary of the Treasury, every living Nobel Prize-winning economist, and over 40 of the 50 governors, that NAFTA means expanding horizons." Judging from this case, when a president is clearly leading, this scoring system picks it up well.[45]

To be sure, the rhetorical features associated here with leading public opinion will all occur occasionally in "following" speeches. Moreover, any public official will typically emphasize the more popular aspects of even the most costly and disliked proposals, if only to the extent of emphasizing the long-term benefits at the end of the difficult road ahead. Nevertheless, these leading elements should all be more frequent in speeches that involve significant leadership of public opinion. A president's use of them reflects a recognition that the people need to be sold on the policy, and their absence would tend to suggest that the public does not need to be convinced of its need or its merit.

It would be much easier, of course, simply to compare a president's policy position with polling data indicating public support (or opposition) on that issue. There are several problems with such an approach, one of which is straightforward: polls are not always available for every issue at the exact time when they are relevant. With the ubiquity of polling data, this is less true today, but this fact severely impedes analyzing the popularity of decisions made during the Roosevelt or Truman years. More importantly, though, there are many conceptual problems with polls that are pertinent in the context of understanding leadership. One such problem is that polls generally do not distinguish between stable opinions and those that are superficial and highly susceptible to change. A savvy politician will always assess the "feel" behind the numbers from any poll. For that reason, Heith has found that analysis of polls in the White House extends far beyond simple reporting of data, as "public opinion is not a tool of the novice user."[46]

The following example will demonstrate this point. On October 7, 2002, George W. Bush gave a well-publicized speech in Cincinnati, Ohio, in which he articulated the reasons for a possible military action against Iraq. According to public opinion polls, Americans seemed to be on the president's side. Typical of several polls from that time, *Newsweek* reported overwhelming approval: by a margin of 69 percent to 26 percent, respondents indicated that they would support military action.[47] A simple comparison of the president's position with public opinion polls might suggest that Bush was merely following public preferences on this issue.

But the question of military action was still in its infancy. The opposition had not yet developed a response to the president, or at least had not communicated its arguments to the mass public. In fact, it was not even clear at that point what the political controversies would involve. Would the Bush administration attempt to obtain a resolution from the United Nations in support of action against Iraq? If one could not be obtained, would the United States act alone, regardless of world opinion? For many Americans, these questions (and others like them) would eventually prove crucial in the formation of their opinions about the matter. Thus even though he enjoyed public support by an almost 3–1 margin that evening, Bush wisely perceived that much of this support was likely "soft," and that keeping it would require effort. Based on this view, it is not surprising that Bush went to great lengths to defend his position that night.

He acknowledged the concerns of the public (even though these concerns were still mostly latent at that point): "Many Americans have raised legitimate questions about the nature of the threat, about the urgency of action"; "Some citizens wonder, after 11 years of living with this problem, why do we need to confront it now?" He recognized (potential?) arguments from the opposition: "Some have argued that confronting the threat from Iraq could detract from the war against terror"; "Some believe we can address this danger by simply resuming the old approach to inspections and applying diplomatic and economic pressure." And he made clear appeals to duty: "We did not ask for this present challenge, but we accept it. Like other generations of Americans, we will meet the responsibility of defending human liberty against violence and aggression. . . . By our courage, we will give hope to others."[48]

This is just a sample of the many leading features from this particular speech, but it illustrates the dangers in associating public opinion with the snapshots provided by polls. The support of even large majorities may not indicate the *kind* of support that will survive a protracted period of debate, and thus a president may recognize the need to "lead" a public that already seems to support him.

The Analyses

Different kinds of speeches are not easily compared to one another, nor are all public speeches intended to advance policies, popular or not. Following Ragsdale, I distinguish major public addresses from minor ones—an admittedly imperfect approach but far preferable to lumping all speeches together.[49] I examine the major addresses from the first and second years only of each term of five presidents (discussed later). Separately, I examine the content of the weekly Saturday morning radio addresses given by Reagan and Clinton during the first year of each of their terms.[50]

Why the first and second years only of each term? The reasons are partly practical, partly theoretical. Practically speaking, including all speeches quickly becomes unwieldy and difficult to interpret, especially as elections draw near and rhetoric becomes oriented toward campaigning, not governing. More importantly, though, as Light has argued, the window of opportunity for policy making declines over time, thus we are likely to find the most relevant and substantive activity early in a term.[51] This somewhat simpler analysis provides results that are both more manageable and more meaningful.

The selection of presidents is straightforward. Eisenhower, Reagan, and Clinton are included because they are three of the four presidents who have faced the term limits of the Twenty-second Amendment; an analysis of their rhetoric will provide a test for H1. Nixon is excluded from the study, as his second term was almost completely consumed with Watergate. Even if his public speeches had not focused on the matter so frequently (though they did), the entire affair clearly deprived Nixon of whatever political freedom is supposed to accompany a president's final term, which makes his decisions theoretically uninteresting for the present purposes. FDR and Truman are included for the purposes of testing H2, as they served multiple terms without constitutional restriction.

Table 7.1 compares first to second (and in Roosevelt's case, third) terms by showing how many major addresses were given by each president in the study, along with the average number of points per major address. From this data, it is immediately evident that there is no simple pattern that might lend

TABLE 7.1
Public Leadership

	N	Points
Roosevelt 1	8	9.4
Roosevelt 2/3	17	16
Truman 1	10	11.7
Truman 2	7	16.9
Eisenhower 1	11	8.5
Eisenhower 2	11	15.8
Reagan 1	13	8.3
Reagan 2	11	6.3
Clinton 1	10	14.8
Clinton 2	6	11

Note: Major addresses only. See text for explanation of values.

Source: Collected by the author from the Presidential Papers of Franklin D. Roosevelt, Harry S. Truman, Dwight D. Eisenhower, Ronald Reagan, and William J. Clinton.

itself to a tidy story about the effects of the Twenty-second Amendment on public leadership. Eisenhower's behavior is clearly consistent with H1, as he engaged in far more leadership during his second term than his first. But so did his predecessors, even in the absence of term limits. In contrast, both Reagan and Clinton exhibited much *less* leadership in their second terms than in their first.

In Table 7.2, the data are collapsed into pre- and post-Twenty-second Amendment categories. The story here provides clear evidence of the *lack* of effects of the amendment: even with the assurance of electoral freedom, presidents apparently do not engage in more public leadership. Ornithologically speaking, they appear more "lame" than "free." At least in their major addresses to the public, second-term presidents have used rhetoric that reflects more of a responsiveness to public opinion than an effort to move it. On this view, H1 is clearly rejected.

A separate analysis reveals an even more interesting finding. Tables 7.3 and 7.3a report the results from coding the weekly radio addresses of Reagan and Clinton, from the first year of each of their terms in which they gave these brief speeches. Not only is there a lack of increased leadership in their second terms, we actually observe a substantial *decrease* in public leadership from the first term to the second. Far beyond merely rejecting H1, it reveals behavior that is the exact opposite of its expectations. It also is evident from these tables that this finding is driven entirely by Clinton, as Reagan's behavior changed only slightly, and the drop in his average leading score is not statistically significant. A quick look at the first few speeches from each of Clinton's terms clearly illustrates a substantial decline in his reach. In 1993, each of his first eight radio addresses focused on the economy, especially his proposals for economic stimulus and deficit reduction. Though he emphasized that most of the

TABLE 7.2
Effects of the Twenty-second Amendment on Leadership

	Pre-Twenty-second Amendment		Post-Twenty-second Amendment	
	First term	Second term	First term	Second term
N	18	24	34	28
Average Points	10.7	16.3	10.3	11.0
t-test for difference of means		2.400 (p = .021)		0.388 (p = .699)

Note: Major addresses only. See text for explanation of values.

Source: Collected by the author from the Presidential Papers of Franklin D. Roosevelt, Harry S. Truman, Dwight D. Eisenhower, Ronald Reagan, and William J. Clinton.

burdens would fall on the wealthy, he was nevertheless candid that his plan also would involve costs to ordinary Americans as well: "We have to ask everyone to contribute something to get the job done."[52] Calls to duty also were common: "Change means asking everyone to pull his or her own weight for the common good. But change is our only choice."[53]

TABLE 7.3
Radio Addresses

	N	Average Points	t-test for difference of means
Reagan (1982)	26	2.9	1.150
Reagan (1985)	44	2.3	(p = .254)
Clinton (1993)	44	4.3	3.135
Clinton (1997)	48	2.7	(p = .002)
All first term	70	3.8	3.347
All second term	92	2.5	(p = .001)

Note: See text for explanation of values.

Source: Collected by the author from the Presidential Papers of Franklin D. Roosevelt, Harry S. Truman, Dwight D. Eisenhower, Ronald Reagan, and William J. Clinton.

TABLE 7.3a
Radio Addresses

	(1) – All	(2) – Reagan only	(3) – Clinton only	(4) – All
Constant	3.771***	2.885***	4.295***	3.266***
	(.281)	(.406)	(.375)	(.363)
Second Term	−1.282**	−.589	−1.629**	−1.196**
	(.373)	(.512)	(.520)	(.371)
Clinton[b]				.804*
				(.371)
N	162	70	92	162
R²	.07	.02	.10	.10

Note: Entries represent OLS regression coefficients, standard errors in parentheses. Dependent variable is the number of points per speech (see text for explanation).

[a] indicates dummy variable (first term = 0; second term = 1)
[b] indicates dummy variable (Reagan = 0; Clinton = 1)
***p<.001; **p<.01; *p<.05

Source: Collected by the author from the Presidential Papers of Franklin D. Roosevelt, Harry S. Truman, Dwight D. Eisenhower, Ronald Reagan, and William J. Clinton.

In contrast, the 1997 version of Bill Clinton played it almost comically safe. As his second term began, he chose to address issues of almost no controversy: reducing teen pregnancy, fighting crime, investigating church fires, increasing food safety regulations, expanding the Family and Medical Leave Act, and improving education. These were the topics of his first six radio addresses in 1997. His seventh began with this not-so-startling proposal: "Today I'm pleased to announce a major new step in our efforts to protect America's children, a universal system for attaching child safety seats in cars."[54] Of course, there is nothing wrong with any of these ideas, and as actual programs, even these would encounter organized opposition, so I am not suggesting that these were completely costless or worthless proposals. What I am suggesting is that they illustrated that Clinton was pursuing a much safer agenda, one that was far less likely to generate a hostile public reaction than his approach to the economy did in 1993. Whereas Clinton in his first term had announced plans to increase taxes, in his second he was asking very little of Americans, focusing instead on things they already wanted—such as reducing teen pregnancy. By 1997, the White House was no longer offering an array of bold, new ideas. That year, *Congressional Quarterly* characterized his State of the Union address as "short on new proposals . . . and long on refashioned, poll-tested campaign initiatives."[55] Elsewhere it added that "many observers chided Clinton for putting forward what they regarded as an excessively timid second-term agenda."[56]

Because the data are so limited, they admit a variety of explanations. Indeed, the contrast between the first and second term for Clinton might stem from his first term—not his second—having been anomalous in its high level of leading activity. One possible explanation for these unexpected results is suggested by H2, that leadership has declined generally, and that Clinton's first term is best understood as the exception in the available observations of post-Twenty-second Amendment terms. The data in Table 7.4 clearly indicate that Reagan and Clinton demonstrated far less leadership than the pre-1960 presidents. Although the data are too limited to make a strong claim

TABLE 7.4
The Decline in Leadership

	N	Average Points	t-test for difference of means
Pre-1960	64	13.3	2.229
Post-1960	40	9.8	(p = .028)

Note: Major addresses only. See text for explanation of values.

Source: Collected by the author from the Presidential Papers of Franklin D. Roosevelt, Harry S. Truman, Dwight D. Eisenhower, Ronald Reagan, and William J. Clinton.

regarding the confirmation of H2, the evidence does suggest why we do not see the hypothesized effects of the Twenty-second Amendment. Because greater reliance on public opinion polls occurred at around the same time, a natural conjecture is that these two changes in presidential incentives, one institutional and the other technological, offset one another. Thus we observe presidents acting rationally in response to better information, choosing the safer route, even in their final terms. Clinton's bold public leadership during his first term is a case in point. Despite remarkable success on a number of difficult issues during 1993, Clinton's approval ratings were low, and voters punished him severely in the midterm elections a year later. It is not surprising that Clinton responded by exhibiting much less leadership in his second term, or as Bert Rockman has characterized it, "cutting *with* the grain" to appeal to the median voter.[57]

Eisenhower stands at the crux of both trends, subject to the term limits of the Twenty-second Amendment, but not as heavily affected by polls as his successors. While one case is not sufficient to make strong conclusions, his behavior does suggest "what might have been" had attentiveness to polling data not intervened. His overall public leadership increased in his second term, as shown in Table 7.1; a brief comparison of two of his speeches illustrates the pattern well. Eisenhower delivered two major addresses on national security, the first on May 19, 1953, the second on November 13, 1957. Both speeches emphasize the challenges in defending the country, but the differences in his rhetoric are striking. In the 1953 address, he identifies the tasks for the nation but focuses mainly on the responsibilities of the government: "Because of the necessary costs of the national security, your government is not just preaching economy but practicing it. Every department of this government has already cut its requests for funds for the next fiscal year. As a result, we have been able to reduce the previous Administration's request for appropriations of new money by some 8 1/2 billion dollars." And rather than asking for sacrifices from citizens, he follows by noting how much this frugality saves them: "This prodigious sum means more than $50 for every man, woman, and child in this country."[58]

Instead of seeking additional tax revenues to support defense costs, Eisenhower states flatly that he believes that "taxes are too high."[59] While he does announce that a tax reduction will be delayed six months due to the crisis, his announcement is almost cryptic:

> I do not believe that the American people think that earlier reduction would be prudent. Your communications to me show that—first of all—you want our nation secure and our dollar sound. This Administration agrees. To advance six months the date of the scheduled reduction would take away 1.5 billion dollars and, to that extent, would risk both of the objectives we seek.[60]

If any radio listeners comprehended this passage, they might have discerned that this plan entailed some cost to them. But it seems safe to say that Eisenhower did his best to obscure that point, so early in his first term. To be sure, the coding scheme reveals that the speech did contain a fair amount of leading: its score of 14 is well above his first-term average, but it pales compared to the score of 31 of the 1957 speech.

To say that Eisenhower was more candid and asked more of citizens in this second speech is to understate the case: "To provide this kind of defense requires tax money—lots of it.... It is clear that production, deployment and installation of missiles over the period ahead ... will be costly.... Our entire citizenry must all do their share.... It takes a lot of hard work and sacrifice to bring about [the triumph of decency and freedom and right.]"[61] No listener had to decipher anything from this speech; the term-limited Eisenhower was direct that securing America's safety would require costs and sacrifice. It is impossible to know whether his freedom from electoral concerns allowed Eisenhower to speak so candidly, and one case—even one full presidency—cannot justify conclusions about the effects of term limits. But it does hint at the possibilities.

Conclusions

Quite obviously, the focus on rhetoric has limitations, and it is not intended to be the only approach to studying public leadership. Nor is it intended to be the last word on the subject. For one thing, these are only speeches, not the decisions themselves. And decisions that are made in a less public fashion could be missed altogether. But to say that these are "only speeches" is to ignore the central role of public rhetoric in the modern presidency.

The criticism also misses the big advantages of analyzing speeches. Since polling data do not provide their own interpretation, simply correlating presidential decisions with the numbers from polls does not tell us whether the White House believed that leadership was warranted. The rhetorical effort works well as a proxy for what the president and his advisors believed about the state of public opinion. To be sure, archival research to analyze specific decisions in detail is far preferable, but this approach requires so much work and detail that it would be inconceivable that general conclusions could be drawn from such a process. For all of its advantages, it cannot possibly be as systematic as the less precise approach employed here.

Another big advantage to studying rhetoric is that it keeps the focus on the concerns about the public. Memoirs of presidents and their staffs often offer assessments of the challenges they faced, but they are sometimes unclear on the nature of those challenges. Consider the claim by Donald Regan, who was chief of staff under Reagan, that the president's tax reform package, which was the legislative highlight of Reagan's second term, was "the most risky."[62] By Regan's own account, crowds went wild over the idea, so he obviously meant that opposition would be strong and well organized—and, in that sense, it *was* risky, and its passage was nearly derailed several times for that very reason. Reagan may have effectively facilitated the public's desire for a simpler, fairer tax code, and his leadership of Congress may have been decisive, but conceptually, the story does not capture the idea of leading the nation to face a difficult problem, such as the insolvency of Social Security or Medicare. Clearly, tax reform was a popular idea—difficult by the measure of the politics of Capitol Hill, but not "risky" in the electoral sense. In other words, the 1986 Tax Reform Amendment (TRA) reflects following, not leading, public opinion.

Along the same lines, presidential advisors sometimes have somewhat faulty memories. One Eisenhower aide boasted to Light that the electoral freedom offered by the Twenty-second Amendment allowed the president to take more risks: "We felt a definite freedom from pressure after 1956, a freedom to take a little more time and a freedom to take on the high rollers. The speech on the military-industrial complex was one example. You can do things in a second term that you could never attempt in the first. I like to think we were a bit more courageous."[63] He might like to think that, and my analysis suggests that he is correct about the president's second term, but his recollection of the military-industrial complex speech omits that this was Eisenhower's *farewell address*. It was certainly a bold move, but the example provides poor support for the general claim about second terms.

The analysis here suggests that Samuelson may have been right about Bill Clinton, that he did not seize his electoral freedom to provide bold leadership on difficult issues. But in the big picture, this probably had less to do with any personal failing on Clinton's part than with the general trend to avoid costly political battles. Even term-limited presidents remain safe by adhering to existing public opinion rather than trying to change it. Because we do face serious public policy problems—such as the solvency of Social Security and Medicare—that require advanced planning, the evidence here is not encouraging. But it does suggest that the term limits of the Twenty-second Amendment do not provide the answer in the current political environment. Thus to the extent that any normative prescriptions are in order, I would hesitate before offering further institutional reforms. The root of the problem may not lie with the presidents, or any other elected officials, but with the people they govern.

Notes

1. Robert J. Samuelson, "President Do-Nothing," *Washington Post*, January 3, 2001, p. A17.

2. Ibid.

3. The amendment permits a successor president—one who succeeds to the presidency in the event of death, for example—to seek reelection to a third term only if he or she has not served more than half of the original term.

4. These are the projections of the Social Security Administration. For the full report, see "Status of the Social Security and Medicare Programs," *Social Security Administration*, March 29, 2002, <http://www.ssa.gov/OACT/TRSUM/trsummary.html> (accessed February 26, 2003). The actual date of insolvency is less relevant than the widespread expectation of it.

5. *Weekly Compilation of Presidential Documents* (Washington, D.C.: U.S. Government Printing Office, 1997), 137.

6. On this point generally, see Richard E. Neustadt, *Presidential Power and the Modern Presidents* (New York: The Free Press, 1990 [1960]).

7. See *The Polling Report*, February 26, 2003, <http://www.pollingreport.com/social.htm> (accessed February 26, 2003), and *Public Agenda Online*, February 26, 2003, <http://www.publicagenda.org/issues/major_proposals_detail.cfm?issue_type=ss&list=2> (accessed February 26, 2003).

8. Paul C. Light, *The President's Agenda: Domestic Policy Choice from Kennedy to Clinton*, 3rd ed. (Baltimore: Johns Hopkins University Press, 1999), 222.

9. This does not necessarily mean that citizens are incapable of making judgments among costly and complicated alternatives. Most notably, James Fishkin has demonstrated that ordinary citizens can reason through even complex policy issues, given the right conditions. See James Fishkin, *Voice of the People* (New Haven, Conn.: Yale University Press, 1995). Moreover, some scholars have argued that citizens do not expect "something for nothing" and do express coherent positions that reflect a recognition of the costs associated with policy benefits (e.g., see Susan Welch, "The 'More for Less' Paradox: Public Attitudes on Taxing and Spending," *Public Opinion Quarterly* 49 [1985]: 310–16; John Mark Hansen, "Individuals, Institutions and Public Preferences over Public Finance," *American Political Science Review* 92 [1998]: 513–32.) A full discussion of the literature is well beyond the scope of this chapter. My point here is merely that politicians, fearing electoral reprisals, generally steer clear of such risks by avoiding difficult proposals.

10. No ex-president has sought a lower elective office since John Quincy Adams served as a representative for seventeen years following his term, which ended in 1829. The last president to have an important post-presidential political career was William Howard Taft, who served as chief justice of the United States from 1921 to 1930. Given Clinton's youth and ambition, many continue to speculate that he may someday return to political office, running for the U.S. Senate perhaps.

11. John M. Carey, *Term Limits and Legislative Representation* (Cambridge: Cambridge University Press, 1996); John M. Carey, Richard G. Niemi, and Lynda W. Powell, *Term Limits in the State Legislatures* (Ann Arbor: University of Michigan Press, 2000); Gary C. Jacobson, "Deficit-Cutting Politics and Congressional Elections," *Political Science Quarterly* 108 (Autumn 1993): 375–402.

12. Supporters of term limits include George F. Will, *Restoration* (New York: The Free Press, 1992); James K. Coyne and John H. Fund, *Cleaning House: America's Campaign for Term Limits* (Washington, D.C.: Regnery Gateway, 1992). Opponents include Victor Kamber, *Giving Up on Democracy: Why Term Limits Are Bad for America* (Washington, D.C.: Regnery Gateway, 1995); Becky Cain, "Term Limits: Not the Answer to What Ails Politics," in *The Politics and Law of Term Limits*, ed. Edward H. Crane and Roger Pilon (Washington, D.C.: Cato Institute, 1994).

13. Alexander Hamilton, James Madison, and John Jay, *The Federalist Papers* (New York: Bantam Books, 1982 [1787–1788]). This passage is found in essay #71, p. 363.

14. Quoted in Richard J. Ellis, *Founding the American Presidency* (Lanham, Md.: Rowman and Littlefield, 1999), 100.

15. Ibid., 102.

16. Ibid.

17. Theodore Roosevelt sought a third, nonconsecutive term in 1912, though his first term was merely a completion of McKinley's presidency. Also, Ulysses S. Grant actively pursued the Republican nomination for a third term in 1876, and especially in 1880, when he led on the first thirty-five ballots at the party's convention. See Earl Spangler, *Presidential Tenure and Constitutional Limitation* (Washington, D.C.: University Press of America, 1977).

18. Paul G. Willis and George L. Willis, "The Politics of the Twenty-second Amendment," *Western Political Quarterly* 5 (September 1952): 469–82.

19. *Congressional Record of the 80th Congress*, vol. 93 (Washington, D.C.: U.S. Government Printing Office, 1947), 1956 (March 12, 1947).

20. *Congressional Record*, 1948 (March 12, 1947).

21. *Congressional Record*, 846 (February 6, 1947).

22. *Congressional Record*, 847 (February 6, 1947).

23. *Congressional Record*, 865 (February 6, 1947).

24. In the House, 285 yea, 121 nay, 26 NV (R 238–0; D 47–121); in the Senate, 59 yea, 23 nay, 13 NV (R 46–0; D 13–23).

25. Sidney M. Milkis and Michael Nelson, *The American Presidency: Origins and Development, 1776–1998*, 3rd ed. (Washington, D.C.: CQ Press, 1999), 287.

26. Louis Brownlow, *The President and the Presidency* (Chicago: University of Chicago Press, 1949); Edward S. Corwin and Louis W. Koenig, *The Presidency Today* (New York: New York University Press, 1956); Herman Finer, *The Presidency: Crisis and Regeneration: An Essay in Possibilities* (Chicago: University of Chicago Press, 1960).

27. Clinton Rossiter, *The American President* (New York: Harcourt Brace, 1956), 159.

28. Louis W. Koenig, *The Chief Executive* (New York: Harcourt, Brace, and World, 1964), 7. Interestingly, Neustadt 1990 [1960] had very little to say about it,

adding only a brief comment that since Eisenhower already faced substantial limitations, he "suffered nothing" (71) from the Twenty-second Amendment.

29. None of the following has any discussion of the Twenty-second Amendment: George C. Edwards III and Stephen J. Wayne, *Presidential Leadership: Politics and Policy Making*, 5th ed. (New York: St. Martin's Press, 1999); Norman C. Thomas and Joseph A. Pika, *The Politics of the Presidency*, 4th ed. (Washington, D.C.: CQ Press, 1997); James P. Pfiffner, *The Modern Presidency*, 3rd ed. (Boston: Bedford/St. Martin's Press, 2000).

30. Robert E. DiClerico, *The American President*, 5th ed. (Upper Saddle River, N.J.: Prentice Hall, 2000), 349.

31. Michael Genovese, *The Presidential Dilemma: Leadership in the American System*, 2nd ed. (New York: Longman, 2003), 168.

32. Light, *The President's Agenda*, p.39.

33. Ibid., 66.

34. Ibid., 38–39.

35. Michael B. Grossman, Martha Joynt Kumar, and Frances E. Rourke, "Second-Term Presidencies: The Aging of Administrations," in *The Presidency and the Political System*, 6th ed., ed. Michael Nelson (Washington, D.C.: CQ Press, 2000), 223.

36. Ibid., 236.

37. Paul Brace and Barbara Hinckley, *Follow the Leader* (New York: Basic Books, 1992); Paul Brace and Barbara Hinckley, "Presidential Activities from Truman through Reagan: Timing and Impact," *Journal of Politics* 55 (May 1993): 382–98.

38. Brace and Hinckley, *Follow the Leader*, 61.

39. Ibid.

40. Brace and Hinckley, *Follow the Leader*. Also see John G. Geer, *From Tea Leaves to Opinion Polls* (New York: Columbia University Press, 1996). It should be noted that they are largely unsuccessful at maintaining these approval ratings, however (see Theodore J. Lowi, *The Personal President* [Ithaca, N.Y.: Cornell University Press, 1985]).

41. Lawrence R. Jacobs and Robert Y. Shapiro, "The Rise of Presidential Polling: The Nixon White House in Historical Perspective," *Public Opinion Quarterly* 59 (Summer 1995): 163–95; Diane Heith, "Staffing the White House Public Opinion Apparatus: 1969–1988," *Public Opinion Quarterly* 62 (Summer 1998): 165–89.

42. Jeffrey K. Tulis, *The Rhetorical Presidency* (Princeton: Princeton University Press, 1987), 4.

43. On the need to increase observations in order to identify patterns, see Gary King, "The Methodology of Presidential Research," in *Researching the Presidency*, ed. George C. Edwards III, John H. Kessel, and Bert A. Rockman (Pittsburgh: University of Pittsburgh Press, 1993), 406.

44. Communication researchers agree that two-sided refutational messages are the most persuasive. See, among others, James B. Stiff, *Persuasive Communication* (New York: Guilford Press, 1994); Steven E. Lucas, *The Art of Public Speaking*, 4th ed. (New York: McGraw-Hill, 1992); Richard M. Perloff, *The Dynamics of Persuasion* (Hillsdale, N.J.: L. Erlbaum, 1993). Petty and Wegener note that this rhetorical strategy is particularly effective with better-educated individuals who are more likely to be aware of counterarguments. See Richard E. Petty and Duane Wegener, "Attitude Change: Multiple Roles for Persuasion Variables," in *The Handbook of Social Psychology*, 4th ed., ed. Daniel T. Gilbert, Susan T. Fiske, and Gardner Lindzey (New York, McGraw-Hill, 1998), 355. I do not address this in the text because my argument has nothing to do with the *success* of the president's attempts to persuade. Nevertheless, since his speechwriters are undoubtedly aware of such research, it seems likely that they would employ such techniques in crafting the president's message.

45. All of these quotes are from *The Public Papers of the Presidents: William J. Clinton* (Washington, D.C.: U.S. Government Printing Office, 1993), 1918–20.

46. Heith, "Staffing the White House," 178.

47. Reported in Jennifer Barrett, "Iraq Attack Gains Momentum," *Newsweek Web Exclusive*, September 14, 2002, <http://www.msnbc.com/news/807985.asp> (accessed February 26, 2003). For a broad array of such polls, see *The Polling Report*, February 26, 2003, <http://www.pollingreport.com/iraq.htm> (accessed February 26, 2003).

48. All of these quotes are from the *Weekly Compilation of Presidential Documents* (Washington, D.C.: U.S. Government Printing Office, 2002), 1716–20.

49. See Lyn Ragsdale, *Vital Statistics on the Presidency*, rev. ed. (Washington, D.C.: CQ Press, 1998), 159–66.

50. Because Reagan did not give weekly radio addresses in 1981, I use the speeches from 1982.

51. Light, *The President's Agenda*.

52. *The Public Papers*, 61.

53. Ibid., 103.

54. *Weekly Compilation*, 196.

55. "Tone, Tenor of First Session Seemed Like Old Times," *CQ Almanac 1997* (Washington, D.C.: CQ Press, 1998), 1–6.

56. "Clinton Finds Support on Hill Despite GOP's Vocal Attacks," *CQ Almanac 1997* (Washington, D.C.: CQ Press, 1998), C-3.

57. Bert A. Rockman, "Cutting *With* the Grain: Is There a Clinton Leadership Legacy?" in *The Clinton Legacy*, ed. Colin Campbell and Bert A. Rockman (New York: Chatham House, 2000); see also Paul J. Quirk and William Cunion, "Clinton's Domestic Policy: The Lessons of a 'New Democrat,'" in *The Clinton Legacy*, ed. Colin Campbell and Bert A. Rockman (New York: Chatham House, 2000).

58. These quotes are from *The Public Papers of the President: Dwight D. Eisenhower* (Washington, D.C.: U.S. Government Printing Office 1953), 312–13.

59. Ibid., 313.

60. Ibid., 315.

61. These quotes are from *The Public Papers of the President: Dwight D. Eisenhower* (Washington, D.C.: U.S. Government Printing Office, 1957), 810–16.

62. Donald T. Regan, *For the Record* (San Diego: Harcourt Brace Jovanovich, 1988), 286.

63. Light, *The President's Agenda*, 66.

III

The Challenge of Presentation

Developing an effective communication strategy has become an institutionalized aspect of the day-to-day operation of the White House in recent decades. Important decisions must be made about the president's public activities and messages—where to go, what to say, and to whom to say it. Presidents must not only be able to gauge the public's mood on particular issues in crafting their public messages but must be attentive to the differences between addressing national audiences as opposed to specific groups of citizens. The four chapters in Part III consider the importance of the president's standing with the public, his use of public activities as part of the overall White House communication strategy, and his use of rhetorical strategies.

Although the public receives its information through the inevitable filter of the news media, citizens still retain their own attitudes and opinions. If the president wants to garner public support, more often than not he must deal with these ingrained policy preferences among citizens in order to demonstrate public leadership. Moving the public on some policy positions is often difficult and can require a significant expenditure of political capital. In "Presidential Ideology and the Public Mood: 1956–1994," Jeffrey E. Cohen and John A. Hamman argue that to meet this public challenge, presidents are best served by working with, and not against, the public agenda and mood. In effect, they argue that the public presents boundaries and end points, often warning the president to "go no further." When opinions already exist, presidents should remain responsive to the public mood, since staying more closely in step with the public can allow the president to retain more influence with other political actors.

In an attempt to gain favor among the American public, presidents in recent years have increasingly taken their policy message directly to citizens through a variety of public speaking venues. This campaign style of governing keeps presidents on center stage on a daily basis, from the start of the administration right on through reelection efforts. As Lori Cox Han shows in "The Rose Garden Strategy Revisited: How Presidents Use Public Activities," rarely do presidents have an opportunity to hide from the American public, which requires little adjustment when the president reemerges as a candidate for reelection during the fourth year in office. Presidents are extremely visible during an election and do not rely solely on Rose Garden or foreign appearances during the campaign in an attempt to appear more presidential than their opponent. However, presidents do appear to be speaking more often to fragmented populations through interest group appearances as opposed to national audiences, and more may not mean better in terms of the substance of messages to the American public.

In addition to selecting public venues, other rhetorical strategies come into play for presidents. Unlike members of the House of Representatives and the Senate, the president must be elected by a multitude of states and constituencies in order to win the White House. As such, the president faces a challenge directly born from the fact that he is the manager of the national identity. Therefore, while in office, the president must appeal to and deal with the nation as a whole and as a collection of subparts. This challenge of integration and diversity manifests itself in presidential rhetoric. How, then, do presidents speak to both the nation and to groups? In "Doing Diversity across the Partisan Divide: George H. W. Bush, Bill Clinton, and American National Identity," Mary E. Stuckey argues that neither Bush nor Clinton was able to use his unique position to build consensus. Instead, both denied the challenge to the status quo, albeit in distinct ways.

Crises and war are perhaps the most significant challenges to any president from a number of perspectives. Accordingly, the unprecedented terrorist attack on the United States in 2001 forced George W. Bush to place foreign policy at the forefront of his agenda, to become a frequent public speaker, and to lead a nation through the shock and mourning of the attack. Since Eisenhower, all modern presidents have faced the challenge of television, which requires presidents to be skilled public speakers. Prior to September 11, 2001, Bush's dearth of public skills led to a reduction in presidential appeals to the public. However, one of the unintended effects of this tragedy was to compel Bush to grow, respond, and lead within the public sphere. In "A President Transformed: Bush's Pre and Post-September 11 Rhetoric and Image," Jeremy D. Mayer and Mark J. Rozell give Bush a decidedly mixed midterm grade on growth, responsiveness, and public leadership. Bush's poor efforts to lead the public toward a war with Iraq in 2003 demonstrate that the public skills Bush developed in the aftermath of September 11 were not lasting or transferable.

8

Presidential Ideology and the Public Mood: 1956–1994

Jeffrey E. Cohen and John A. Hamman

Leadership of public opinion stands at the core of the modern presidency. Presidents believe that much of their political influence comes from their ability to lead public opinion. In particular, presidents believe that their influence with other political elites is enhanced when they are able to lead public opinion or are believed to be able to lead the public.[1] As a consequence, presidents invest considerable resources of both time and staff in activities intended to lead public opinion. By some accounts, more people in the White House are assigned to presidential public relations and image building than any other single activity.[2] Some scholars now contend that image building takes priority over policy making as a presidential goal.[3]

Despite its high priority, students of the presidency are somewhat skeptical about the president's ability to affect public thinking. Case studies of presidential leadership on specific issues present mixed findings. Some studies find presidential leadership effects, while others do not.[4] Studies that look across policies also fail to find consistent and strong presidential leadership effects over public opinion.[5] The most recent major examination contends that the president's bully pulpit is not all that it was once thought to be.[6]

Other research questions whether presidents can affect their own public approval, much less public thinking on policy issues. Evidence suggests that the president's public activities have only a modest and short-term impact on presidential approval. Ragsdale, for instance, reports that major, nationally televised addresses produce a mere three percentage point increase in approval.[7] This approval boost is short-lived, evaporating within several weeks. Brace and Hinckley also find that major speeches lift presidential approval by about three points, but only during a president's first term.[8] Ostrom and Simon find that another public activity, presidential trips abroad, does not improve the president's standing with the public.[9]

In contrast, the literature on agenda setting finds that presidents have a relatively strong impact on the public agenda. When presidents emphasize a policy area in their public rhetoric, the issue rises on the public's agenda as well.[10] Agenda setting often has been thought to be a key to presidential influence, and in this chapter we build a theory of presidential leadership of public opinion that is rooted in agenda setting. Going beyond the agenda-setting literature, which demonstrates that presidents can influence the public's agenda, we show that agenda-setting processes also can affect policy positions that the public holds. This effect is observable in global orientations to public affairs, such as the public mood,[11] and is contingent on public and presidential factors. By setting the public agenda, presidents can influence the public mood, steering it marginally but measurably in a liberal or conservative direction. In the next section we outline our theory of presidential leadership of public opinion, which we call "issue installation." Then we empirically demonstrate that presidential rhetoric affects the public mood. We conclude with some thoughts on presidential leadership of public opinion.

Building a Theory of Presidential Leadership of Public Opinion

Any theory of presidential leadership over public opinion must be rooted in an understanding of public opinion as well as presidential behavior. Much of the research on presidential leadership of public opinion has not given much attention to developing the public opinion side of the equation, focusing more on presidential variables. Here we begin with public opinion and build our theory on common understandings of the nature of public opinion and processes of opinion change. Presidential leadership of public opinion is observable when some aspect of public opinion changes due to the president's behavior, that is, the president's attempt to affect public thinking. Past research has detected presidential influence over the public's agenda. In this chapter, we build on agenda-setting research to investigate whether the president's influence over the public agenda may extend to the public's policy preferences.

We begin by focusing on opinion dynamics at the individual level and ask: What are the processes by which opinions change? Past public opinion research finds that many people do not hold well thought-out or considered opinions, nor are they highly attentive to political matters. Yet people still form opinions that are observable as answers to survey questions,[12] among other forms. Moreover, those opinions can change in systematic ways. As opposed to random change, we identify four ways in which a person's opinion may change systematically. These four processes are issue installation, priming, framing, and conversion. Conversion is the hardest type of change to accomplish. Presidential leadership research has mostly focused on conversion, and this has limited the possibility of locating strong presidential leadership effects. While it may be easier for the president to produce opinion change through either priming or framing, we argue that issue installation provides the president with his best opportunity to alter public opinion. Issue installation is a variant of agenda setting that creates a new opinion when one previously did not exist. It is the easiest type of change to effect, but possible only under certain conditions, which we specify later.

After addressing the ways in which opinions change, the analysis turns to an examination of how presidential leadership may produce change. We will show that global policy orientations, like the public mood, may be altered through issue installation processes. By altering the public mood, presidents may create an impression of public movement across a range of related policy issues. Such perceived movement may enable the president to convince other political leaders to follow this public movement and thus support his policy proposals. In this fashion, presidential leadership of public opinion may convert into other types of presidential influence. Next we define each of the four opinion change processes, discussing their implications for presidential leadership of public opinion.

1. Conversion: We define conversion as altering a person's opinion on an issue that exists in unidimensional space. Conversion shifts a person's opinion on that issue from some point to another location, for example, from a liberal leaning posture to a more conservative one. Under this definition of conversion, how an issue is defined does not change. Nor does it matter if the issue becomes more or less salient to an individual. Rather, conversion merely implies that on any existing and stable issue, a person changes his or her preference.

Conversion is difficult to achieve. If a person's opinion is well reasoned and deeply held, presidents will have a hard time changing it. When a person holds a strong preference or opinion, he or she often discounts, ignores, deflects, or misconstrues new information that counters the opinion. Opinions that are less strongly held are more subject to conversion effects, but the difficulty is gaining the person's attention in the first place. However, if presidents can convert these people, so can other elites. Presidents may have a hard time holding onto these new converts because they are so opinion malleable, and thus open to conversion by elites who compete with the president for public support. Given this, it is not surprising that studies that look at single issues have a hard time finding discernable and lasting presidential leadership effects.

2. Framing: Framing differs from conversion in that an issue is redefined. Instead of an issue being perceived as unidimensional, framing raises the possibility that an issue is multidimensional. Framing occurs when a person shifts the frame that is used to evaluate an issue and thus may alter his or her policy preference. Consider the health care debate of the period 1993–1994. Bill Clinton initially framed his proposal in terms of supplying equitable access to

health care at an affordable cost. Using that frame, he initially received majority support from the public. But his opponents offered a competing frame with which to judge his proposal—big government. The big government frame caught on in the public, and when people began to see the issue from that frame, Clinton lost public support for his proposal. Framing thus replaces one frame with another. When people shift the frame that they are using to structure their opinion, then their policy preferences also may shift.

Framing offers a president greater potential for leadership than conversion, but it still poses serious barriers for effective leadership. As the Clinton health care example illustrates, other frames may resonate more strongly with the public than the president's frame. Effective framing often requires that the president employ a frame already popular with the mass public. Sometimes such frames will not promote the policy options that he is offering; in fact, such popular frames may undercut his position. In other words, for framing to work, presidents cannot be too far out of step with the public. This also suggests limits to presidential leadership.

3. Priming: Priming entails bringing an opinion out of (deep) memory and making a person consciously aware of it. The theory of priming implies that people have opinions on issues, but not all are used all of the time. Some are recessed into memory but can be evoked when stimulated. A presidential speech or a news story may prime people to think about an issue that has been lying dormant in memory. Priming need not lead to opinion change. However, if the priming stimulant provides new information relevant to the opinion, then a person may reevaluate his or her opinion. Priming also may affect a person's public agenda, as the primed issue displaces previously activated issue(s). In this sense, priming may have an agenda-setting effect. Priming also may relate several issues to each other, unlike conversion or framing, which refers to single issues.

Priming affords presidents more potential for leadership than either conversion or framing, but it does not provide the president with unlimited leadership potential. Priming's main limitation is that presidents only can evoke issues stored in memory. Simple priming entails bringing an issue out of memory; it does not imply that issue position will be altered. Perhaps the new information that presidents present will be incorporated into the primed issue, and people will change their opinions, but that process looks a lot like conversion or framing, as discussed earlier, and the possibility exists that priming may occur simultaneously with either conversion or framing.

Presidents need to be careful what they prime. Surely presidents should not prime people to think much about issues for which they hold opinions opposed to the president. Priming's greatest impact may not be in leading to opinion change but in a newly primed issue displacing issues off of the public agenda. Through this process, presidents may help create a more congenial public opinion climate than previously existed. The diversionary hypothesis, in which leaders commit troops to divert public attention from domestic issues, is one variant of that theme.

4. Issue installation: Issue installation is the fourth process that may lead to opinion change. We argue that issue installation may, under certain circumstances, provide the president with perhaps his greatest potential for affecting public opinion. We define issue installation as the creation of an opinion that previously did not exist. Issue installation occurs when a person did not have an opinion on an issue and/or was unaware of an issue. Creating or activating a new issue opinion is akin to an agenda-setting process. Similarly, we can think of issue installation as a mobilization process. Studies find that it is easier to mobilize than to convert voters.[13] The comparative ease of issue installation (mobilization), in contrast to issue conversion, presents the president with a better opportunity to affect public thinking, although as we detail later, issue installation is not without its own barriers to opinion change.

Polls and surveys often find significant numbers of "Don't Know" or "No Opinion" responses on many issues. People may lack an opinion for many reasons. Classic ones include lack of information and inattention to politics, but new issues may arise, and existing issues may be redefined into entirely new, albeit related, issues. In the latter instance, consider how the issue of comprehensive health care in the early 1990s was transformed into many subissues, for instance, prescription drug benefits, regulation of HMOs, and patients' medical rights by the late 1990s. The point is that there are many reasons some people may not have an opinion on an issue. When people lack an issue opinion, then presidents and other leaders have the opportunity to instill a new opinion among people previously lacking one. Through issue installation, presidents not only affect the public agenda by putting a new issue on that agenda, but they also may alter the public's mood.

By illustration, assume that a person has opinions on seven issues but lacks opinion on three others. Of the seven issues on which he or she has an opinion, five are conservative and two are liberal. For illustration, score liberal positions equal to 1, conservative positions equal to negative 1, and no opinion equal to 0. Our individual will possess a net score of 3 (5 − 2 + 0). Summing issue positions in this manner is similar to the logic of Stimson's public mood indicator, which we will use to measure public opinion. Now assume that the president activates opinion on two issues for which the person previously held no opinion, and in both cases the activation leads the person to adopt the president's conservative stance. Our individual's net score, or mood, becomes 1 (5 − 4 + 0), a shift to the right more consistent with the conservative president's stand on these two issues.

Notice that in this example, we assume that presidents are unable to affect existing issue preferences. This is consistent with much of the literature that finds that presidents do not have an impact on public preferences for specific issues. Moreover, our example implies that presidents need not be able to activate opinions on all issues. Note that in the example our person retained his or her lack of opinion for one issue. The president could have been silent on the issue or could have spoken about it. The model allows both possibilities. As long as presidents can instill opinion in some people who lack opinions, and those people also adopt the president's preference in the process, then presidents can shift the public mood (and opinion on those select issues). Thus the combination of presidential rhetoric and lack of preexisting attitudes conditions whether presidents can move public opinion.

Priming alone cannot explain such a process. It suggests that presidents can alter the salience of an issue in the public, but not the position that a person holds. Thus priming may account for why the public's agenda is sensitive to emphasis in the president's major speeches, but it does not predict that public opinion on an issue will shift. Rather, priming brings to the fore attitudes that are deeper in memory, but for which a person may hold a preference. However, it does allow for the possibility that when an issue is primed, new information about that issue may be incorporated into the person's preferences. This new information may shift a person's preference for that issue. But as we discussed earlier, such processes are complex and create barriers to effective presidential leadership of public opinion.

Framing may account for opinion change on an issue, but it assumes a multidimensional issue space. Framing says that a person's preference on an issue changes if the frame of reference changes. The issue installation model suggested here does not assume a multidimensional issue space. Rather, it is compatible with a unidimensional space as conceptualized by Poole and Rosenthal[14] and Stimson's concept of the public mood,[15] who argue that a single dimension explains most of the structure among issues in American politics.

The issue installation model also accommodates literature that suggests that there are barriers to the extent to which presidents can influence public opinion.[16] One of the most difficult barriers for presidents to overcome is gaining public attention. The most attentive may be the hardest to influence because presidents tend to possess well-formed opinions on most issues. From framing and conversion perspectives, people with strong preexisting attitudes will be resistant to presidential rhetoric.[17] From an issue installation perspective, they also are unlikely candidates for opinion change, because their opinions were active prior to the president's attempt to create new issue preferences. Presidents can potentially affect only those lacking in opinion formation. Conversion cannot explain such change, since it begins with the assumption that one possesses a preference or an opinion to begin with.

Reaching the less attentive is an obstacle that potentially inhibits presidential-induced opinion change, regardless of which of the four change processes is considered. Presidents can gain the attention of the inattentive only under certain conditions. We focus on the presidential use of major speeches as one way that presidents may be able to overcome the inattentiveness of the public, giving speeches that signal to the public the importance of the issue(s) at hand. In a recent study, Andrade investigates the impact of Lyndon Johnson's public rhetoric on the public agenda.[18] Contrary to Cohen,[19] Hill,[20] and Lawrence,[21] she finds little impact. Two factors account for Andrade's inability to detect an agenda-setting effect. First, there is often little variance in presidential speech across an administration.[22] If a president's policy emphases and positions are relatively constant, then it will be hard, if not impossible, to find an effect. Variance in presidential rhetoric is necessary to determine whether the variance in rhetoric co-varies with the variance in public opinion. Second, and perhaps more important from the perspective offered here, is that few speeches command the kind of public attention that major speeches such as the State of the Union address can. It is not surprising that minor and less visible speeches have such little impact on public opinion.

The issue installation perspective, which is closely related to agenda setting, suggests that presidents can affect the public mood, but only incrementally. First, we are only likely to witness opinion impact from major presidential speeches that command considerable public attention. Second, the degree of presidential impact depends on the issues that the president speaks about and the number of people lacking opinions on those issues. So, from the issue installation perspective, we can witness several types of opinion change. First, on particular issues, the percentage of "Don't Know" responses will decline.

But on issues that were not already on the public agenda, that is, on new issues, we are likely to lack polling information, thus will be unable to assess the degree of impact that presidents had on preferences for those issues. To assess the degree of presidential influence on public thinking, we want to observe the distribution of opinion before and after the president speaks. If no polls on a topic exist prior to the presidential speech, then we cannot assess change in opinion. Thus we often are limited in assessing presidential influence on individual issues because we lack data.

However, we will be able to assess whether the public shifted to the right or left on the public mood, which incorporates information across all issues for which we possess polls. If a president successfully instills new opinions as a result of a major public address for those who do not have opinions on preferences made by that speech, then we should see the public mood moving in the direction of the president's rhetoric. Even if there is no poll on the issue prior to the president's speech, but there is one after the speech, the inclusion of this new poll data becomes useful information in assessing the degree of the aggregate shift in the public mood. Assume that at $t-1$, the period before the presidential speech, n issues were polled, producing a public mood of X/n. Now assume that because of the president's speech, $n + 1$ issues are polled, with the addition issue being the new one that the president spoke about in his speech. Further, assume that opinion stays the same on all of the original n issues. Now the calculation of the public mood becomes $(X + P)/ n + 1$, where P is public opinion on the new issue. If $X/n = (X + P)/n +1$, then the addition of the new issue has no impact on the public mood. While the president may have impacted the public by instilling opinion on the new issue, an alternative presents itself, that the previously held opinion directed opinion on the new issue. However, if they are not equal, then we can suggest that the difference is due to the president instilling opinion on the new opinion, and that those newly installed opinions differ from preexisting opinions.[23] Thus while we might not be able to observe the impact of the issue installation process on single issues because of the lack of polls, we should be able to observe its implications on aggregate opinion indicators such as the public mood.

Because of the highly aggregated nature of the data that we use next, we cannot truly distinguish which one of the four opinion change processes accounts for shifts in the public mood. Our argument is that conversion, framing, and priming are less likely to affect public opinion to the degree that issue installation can. Thus we assume that much of the change in public opinion that we detect, if we detect any, will most likely be a result of issue installation processes. Other kinds of data, however, are needed to test whether this assumption is true. But the issue installation process has the theoretical virtue of integrating the literature on presidential leadership of public opinion more coherently than conversion, framing, or priming theory seems able to accomplish.

Measuring Presidential Ideology

To test the notions developed earlier we need an indicator of presidential policy preferences as revealed in the president's rhetoric that parallels the public mood indicator, which will be our dependent variable. We introduce an indicator that we call "presidential ideology," which builds on the work reported in Cohen,[24] extending that data through 1994. We use the State of the Union address operationalized presidential ideology as the percentage of sentences in the State of the Union address (SUA),[25] in which the president indicates a liberal policy preference divided by the sum of the number of liberal- and conservative-directed sentences. To make the scale comparable with the public mood indicator, we shifted the midpoint from 50 to 0. The specific formula is:

Presidential Ideology = {(Number of liberal sentences in the SUA)/(Number of conservative sentences + number of liberal sentences)} − 50

Sentences in which no policy direction was ascertainable, or in which no policy preference was offered, are excluded from calculations. We use conventional definitions to determine the liberal and conservative position on issues, much as Stimson does in his construction of the public mood series.[26] Details of the operationalization and measurement are presented in Cohen.[27] The presidential ideology series appears quite valid, correlating at .85 (Pearson's r) with a measure of presidential position on Americans for Democratic Action (ADA) roll calls and .80 with the Stimson, MacKuen, and Erikson measure of presidential policy positions.[28] Table 8.1 presents comparative data for each president.

ANALYSIS

To test the ideas put forth earlier we adopt a conservative research strategy and ask whether presidential rhetoric adds anything to our understanding of the public mood in addition to factors already known to influence it. Prior research suggests that the public seems to counterreact to governmental policies: as policies veer too far to the right or left, the public moves in the opposite direction.[29] We operationalize this by replicating and extending Durr's policy index back to 1956 and up through 1994. We also expect that the economy will affect the public mood. In particular, we expect the public to move left as unemployment rises.[30]

Research shows that the public mood is slow to change and does so only incrementally, rarely abruptly. In assessing the impact of presidential ideology, there is a possibility that there might be a "simultaneous" adjustment between

TABLE 8.1
Presidential Ideology, 1956–1994

President	Mean	Minimum	Maximum	Standard Deviation
All	44	0	92	27
Democrats	66	47	92	17
Republicans	32	0	80	23
Eisenhower	66	53	80	12
Kennedy	83	69	91	13
Johnson	70	48	92	18
Nixon	35	6	50	18
Ford	26	20	31	8
Carter	57	49	69	8
Reagan	10	0	20	7
Bush	30	17	43	11
Clinton	51	50	52	1

Note: See Cohen, "Presidential Rhetoric and the Public Agenda," and text for details.

Source: Collected by the authors from the State of the Union address.

the president and the public reflected in this incremental movement of the public mood over time. Fortunately, our design allows us to locate the presidential ideology and public mood variables in temporal sequence.[31] Presidential ideology, being recorded through the SUA, comes early in each calendar year. Public mood is an aggregate indicator built from surveys taken throughout the year. Most of the surveys occur after the SUA is delivered. We enter into the equation a lagged public mood variable both to control for inertia in the public mood and for possible presidential responsiveness to changes in the public mood.[32] Hence, the presidential ideology variable that we employ is net of the impact of the public mood on it; because of this control variable, public mood lagged one year.

BASELINE EFFECTS

Table 8.2 presents the results of the baseline model. The OLS estimation is used because we did not detect any serial or correlated error problems.[33] The baseline model accounts for 82 percent of the variance. All three of the base-

TABLE 8.2
Regression Results of Presidential Ideology on Public Mood, 1956–1994

Variable	Model 1		Model 2		Model 3	
	b (se)	t	b (se)	t	b (se)	t
Constant	10.57 (3.54)	2.98	10.95 (3.89)	2.81	10.86 (3.33)	3.27
Public Mood $_{(t-1)}$	.73 (.09)	8.09	.73 (.09)	7.95	.73 (.09)	8.59
Policy Index	−.29 (.07)	−3.94	−.30 (.08)	−3.69	−.29 (.07)	−4.11
Unemployment	.70 (.28)	2.52	.69 (.28)	2.43	.62 (.26)	2.37
Presidential Ideology—Levels	xxxx		−.004 (.015)	−.26	xxxx	
Presidential Ideology—Changes	xxxx		xxxx		.03 (.01)	2.38
R^2/Adjusted R^2	.83/.82		.83/.81		.86/.84	
n	38		38		38	

Note: See Cohen, "Presidential Rhetoric and the Public Agenda," and text for details.
Source: Collected by the authors from the State of the Union address.

line variables are statistically significant, and their signs point in the correct direction. As predicted, past public mood strongly affects the current public mood (b = .73), displaying the inertia quality of this public opinion indicator. Also as expected, unemployment moves the public to the left. Lastly, the public reacts negatively to government policy, confirming Durr's finding on quarterly data. So we arrive at a three variable baseline equation that includes government policy index, average annual unemployment, and public mood that lagged one year.[34] The baseline model's large adjusted R^2 shows that the equation is well specified. Finding presidential effects given controls for this baseline would thus be a significant result.

PRESIDENTIAL EFFECTS ON THE PUBLIC MOOD

The presidential ideology series contains both a long-term and a short-term component; either or both may affect the public mood. The long-term component can be thought of in administration or presidential epochs.[35] At times such epochs are distinctive and identifiable, denoted by such labels as Johnson's Great Society and Reaganomics. The short-term component refers to the particulars of the speech, the policies and issues that are emphasized, and the liberal or conservative tendencies of those emphases. Using first differences to represent short-term shifts and levels to represent long-term trends,[36] we model these two alternatives by estimating each in separate equations.[37] The results, reported in Table 8.2, show that the level of presidential ideology does not affect the public mood, but that change does. Inclusion of the change in presidential ideology boosts the equation adjusted R^2 about 2 percent over the baseline model. An F test shows that the improvement in the adjusted R^2 is statistically significant.[38] Addition of the change variable does not affect any of the baseline variables. When both variables for levels and changes are entered in the same equation (not shown), change is a positive and statistically significant influence on the public mood, while level is not. Thus the remainder of the analysis focuses upon short-term effects and uses changes rather than levels.

Although the impact of ideology change appears substantively small, the restricted range of the public mood variable and the greater potential range in presidential ideology need to be taken into account to accurately gauge the impact. The public mood generally ranges from −10 to +10 (with 0 as the neutral midpoint). A shift from the most liberal to the most conservative president (or vice versa) translates into a three-point swing of the public mood. While small, this represents about 15 percent of the total range (3/20) that the public mood has historically taken. Although potentially great, presidential ideology, on average, shifted only 20 percent of its historical range (18/92), but with a maximum change of 63 points.

The impact of presidential ideology on the public mood is felt swiftly and soon exhausts itself. About two-thirds of the impact of change in presidential ideology occurs in a little over a year (1.03 years). Fully 99 percent of the impact of presidential rhetoric is felt in a little over three years' time (3.09). Presidential effects do not build across time, but the impact begins to fade not long after the speech has been delivered.[39] This makes substantive sense too. Many other factors, including public opinion campaigns by presidential antagonists, new events, changing world conditions, and the like, may come into play and affect public opinion. With the appearance of these other change agents, we should expect the impact of presidential rhetoric to fade over time. So, in the short term, change in presidential ideology and public mood generally tends to be quite small and may not be noticeable to the political world, as these presidential impacts may not be substantively important.

We also considered whether the effect of the SUA speech in public mood we are detecting might be due to changes in presidents or presidential party instead of the SUA speech itself. There is general stability in presidential ideology within administrations, but often there are strong shifts between administrations. To test for this likelihood, we added into the equation dummy variables for president and/or party change. Neither shows an effect, while the effects of presidential ideology do not diminish. Moreover, regressing president and party change on change in presidential ideology unearths no statistical relationship. Thus the effects of presidential ideology are not merely the result of a new president or a different party coming into office. Presidential ideology affects the public mood within and across administrations. Still, we must contend with the issue of the modesty of those presidential effects. In the next section we argue that the potency of presidential impacts is conditional upon the credibility of the president.

SOURCE CREDIBILITY EFFECTS AND THE PUBLIC MOOD

The analysis thus far finds a small but statistically significant effect of presidential ideology on the public mood. That analysis, however, assumes that this effect is constant across presidents and within administrations. This is much like saying that Jimmy Carter and Ronald Reagan could equally influence public opinion. Such a simple comparison highlights the absurdity of such an assumption. Different presidents and different contexts may affect the persuasiveness of presidential communications. We focus on two source credibility effects that a substantial literature has shown modulate the persuasiveness of political communications.[40] Furthermore, the source credibility approach allows us to identify within and between administration effects.

The source credibility literature emphasizes that people do not necessarily learn from credible sources; rather, they accept the opinion leadership of credible sources and adopt the positions of those they view as credible. This issue installation framework is entirely consistent with this. We focus on two factors that might affect the source credibility of presidents and, hence, the persuasiveness of their communications: (1) the policy distance between president and public, and (2) the popularity of the president.[41]

First, presidents who generally are felt to be in touch with the public may have more impact on the public mood than those who are viewed as being out of touch. For example, Bill Clinton offered a massive health care reform package that was based on governmental regulation and management, while the public was in more of an anti-government mood. Clinton had a hard time sustaining public support for that program. In effect, he was out of step with the public, or was viewed as being out of step with the public, and thus limited in his ability to mold public opinion on health care. This leads to our hypothesis that the greater the policy distance between the president and the public, the less impact the president will have on the public mood.[42]

Popular approval is another plausible indication of presidential credibility. In fact, it may be hard conceptually to separate approval from credibility. A key hypothesis in the literature on presidential leadership of the public's policy preferences looks at the effects of popularity. At the very least, popular presidents are thought to be doing a good job in office.[43] Thus our second source credibility hypothesis is that more popular presidents will have greater impact on the public mood than less popular presidents.

The "source credibility" effects are used as a weight on change in presidential ideology. For policy distance, we compute the policy distance between the president and the public by subtracting standardized public mood from standardized presidential ideology, and then by computing the absolute value of the difference. The standardized variables are used because of the different metrics of the two indicators. Then we multiply this distance variable against the change in presidential ideology. For popularity, we multiply change in presidential ideology by popularity at the time of the delivery of the SUA.[44] Since these weighted terms are essentially interaction ones, the unweighted terms (i.e., policy distance, presidential popularity, and change in presidential ideology) tend to be statistically insignificant in fully specified equations. This is expected when noninteraction and interaction forms of variables are included in the same equation, and if interaction is truly present.[45] For ease of interpretation and presentation, we only report the results of the equation with the interaction terms in Table 8.3.

The results confirm our hypotheses. As the president gets farther away from the public, his ability to lead diminishes; as his popularity improves, his leadership of public opinion rises. Source credibility clearly helps explain more variation in public mood. The adjusted R^2 increases to .88, fully 6 percent more than the baseline model and 4 percent higher than the model that

TABLE 8.3
Regression Results of Presidential Ideology Public Mood,
Controlling for Source and Congress, 1956–1994

Variable	Model 4		Model 5		Model 6	
	b (se)	t	b (se)	t	b (se)	t
Constant	12.58 (2.96)	4.25	10.92 (2.67)	4.09	13.64 (3.10)	4.39
Public Mood $_{(t-1)}$	.65 (.08)	8.34	.64 (.07)	9.21	.58 (.08)	7.26
Policy Index	−.29 (.06)	−4.71	−.29 (.05)	−5.43	−.32 (.06)	−5.21
Unemployment	.48 (.23)	2.05	.30 (.21)	1.40	.25 (.24)	1.05
Presidential Ideology—Changes						
*Policy Distance	−.065 (.02)	−3.21	−.06 (.02)	−3.61	−.06 (.02)	−2.97
*Presidential Popularity	.001 (.0003)	4.31	.001 (.0003)	5.02	.001 (.0003)	4.23
Conservative Coalition Wins—Senate	xxxx		.04 (.01)	3.16	xxxx	
Conservative Coalition Wins—Senate $_{(t-1)}$	xxxx		xxxx		.04 (.02)	2.23
R^2/Adjusted R^2	.90/.88		.92/.90		.91/.89	
n	38		38		38	

Note: See Cohen, "Presidential Rhetoric and the Public Agenda," and text for details.

Source: Collected by the authors from the State of the Union address.

includes (unweighted) changes in presidential ideology. F tests show that both increments are statistically significant.

COMPETITIVE ELITES, PRESIDENTIAL IDEOLOGY, AND THE PUBLIC MOOD

Relatively, presidents may possess the loudest single voice in American politics, but many other actors also speak, often in opposition to the president. Can this chorus of voices drown out or weaken the presidential leadership effects unearthed earlier? In this section we make an initial attempt to answer this question.

We were not able to measure the tone of these competing voices as easily and cleanly as we were the president's because of the tremendous diversity and decentralization of the nonpresidential elite. No single forum for opposition (or support) of the president exists, nor is it even easy to identify the membership of this alternative "elite." Also, the network of political communications, while elite based, is characterized by many elites, located in many institutional settings, with a multitude of channels of communication to the mass public. Even mass media reporting of these other voices is decentralized. Many media venues exist, from national and local print media to the specialized press and the electronic media. Further, within those reporting media, there is no one place to go to find the voice of these other elites—their voices may be reported throughout the many news stories that appear, as well as on the opinion and editorial pages of the press.

Given all of this, we argue that Congress is the most suitable, and practical, place for identifying the tenor of discourse among nonpresidential elites. First, Congress's position in the governmental structure makes it perhaps the most important competing elite to the president. Second, Congress may be fairly representative of the mainstream elite in the nation due to its recruitment structure, which emphasizes, at least for the House, frequent elections. Moreover, members of Congress are opinion leaders in their own right. Their trips home to meet with constituents and explain their decisions and votes provide one important opportunity and avenue to influence local public opinion.[46] Aggregated across all districts, such behavior may affect national opinion. And lastly, while not as heavily covered by the press as the presidency, Congress, as an institution and as individuals, is well covered. Thus Congress provides us with a location where competitor elites express their views publicly and have an opportunity to affect public opinion.

Congress also provides a practical setting for measuring the tenor or tone of discourse among the nonpresidential elite. Members express their public opinions in floor debates. Once publicly expressed, they are then generally bound to vote on roll calls in ways consistent with their rhetoric. Too much deviation between rhetoric and roll calls may be politically untenable and leave members more vulnerable to challengers in subsequent election contests. In this way, public rhetoric and roll call behavior are linked. If one accepts such a connection, then we can use roll calls as a summary indicator of the tenor of policy debates and rhetoric in Congress. The particular measures that we use are the percentage of conservative coalition victories for the House and Senate. Table 8.3 presents the results of the equation, including the percentage of conservative coalition wins in the Senate (House victories had no impact and thus are not shown).[47]

The fit of Model 5 in Table 8.3 improves over Model 4, explaining 2 percent more of the variance in public mood. Each 1 percent change in the Senate conservative coalition victory rate leads to a shift of about .04 percent in the public mood, which is comparable to some of the presidential effects. Although shifts in the conservative tone of Congress tend to be much smaller, a change from the most conservative Congress (100 percent) to the least conservative (39 percent) results in a shift of about 2.4 percent in the public mood, a small, though statistically significant increment.

Since the conservative coalition and public mood variables are both aggregated by year, it is possible that Congress might be responding to the public mood rather than influencing it. Sorting out causality requires a more intricate specification of the relationship between Congress and the public, something beyond the scope of this chapter. Still, we initially explore the relationship by lagging the congressional variable by one year as a way to test for the temporal ordering of the two variables (Model 6, Table 8.3). The congressional results essentially remain unaltered, though they are slightly weakened. More work, however, needs to be done on this side of the congressional-public mood linkage.

More importantly for our purposes, the impact of the presidential variables is not affected when the congressional variables are entered into the equation. Inclusion of the congressional variables does not diminish the impact of the presidency on the public mood, and the significance level of the presidential variables improves as the size of their standard errors decreases. So, adding the congressional variable improves the fit of the model and does not alter the presidential effects. The only variable in our original model that is affected by the congressional variable is unemployment. The value of the coefficient for unemployment decreases, and it becomes statistically insignificant.

CONCLUSIONS

The major tasks in this chapter were (1) to develop a theory that specifies the conditions under which presidents can influence public opinion on policies and issues, and (2) to empirically determine whether presidential leadership effects exist. Our theoretical perspective distinguishes among four processes of opinion change—conversion, framing, priming, and issue installation—and argues that issue installation offers the president perhaps the best opportunity to influence public thinking about issues of the day. We empirically demonstrate that presidents can move the public mood, and we offer a rationale that suggests that much of that movement may be due to issue installation processes.

The theoretical model presented here and the empirical results echo findings in much of the literature that argues that it is hard for presidents to lead public opinion. Thus we emphasize that certain conditions must hold in the mass public. In particular, there must be issues for which the president can gain the attention of a sufficiently large number of people who lack preexisting preferences on them. Furthermore, not all presidents are equally able to influence the public. We focus in particular on two aspects of presidents, presidential popularity and the distance between the president's policy preferences and the public mood. More popular presidents and those closer to the public mood are more influential with the public than less popular and policy distant presidents.

This latter point is ironic and deserves greater attention. Presidents cannot be too far from the public if they intend on leading it. Previously, we identified Clinton and health care reform as an example of how presidents lose influence with the mass public when their policies are out of step with the public. FDR seems to have understood this predicament—to lead public opinion, the president cannot be too far ahead of it. One of the most important challenges for FDR was preparing the public for eventual war with Germany. However, during the late 1930s, the public remained in an isolationist mood that dated from the end of the First World War. Rather than embark on a radical move toward war preparation, FDR took a series of small measured steps from 1938 to 1941. He sought lend-lease support for Great Britain, followed later by a modest draft and increases in the military budget. With each move he modestly "pushed" public opinion in the direction of war, but not going so far as to suggest war. By the time of the Japanese attack on Pearl Harbor, antiwar voices were essentially silenced, and the public shifted gears from peace to war practically overnight.[48]

Our results fit nicely with the comparison of these two stories of attempted presidential leadership and provide us with a nuanced understanding of the context of presidential leadership. Opportunities for presidential leadership exist, but presidents cannot be too bold in what they attempt. Leadership is most effective when presidents do not stray too far from what is acceptable to the public, from what it is ready to do. Thus the public, while being willing to be led, constrains presidential leadership. Give and take, mutual accommodation, thus best describes the potential for presidential leadership.

Given that straying too far from public sentiment undermines presidential leadership over public opinion, why would presidents even take positions that the public opposes? First, presidential policy preferences are not a function of public opinion alone. Presidents come into office with their own agendas, and some have their own vision or ideology to guide their behavior and policy choices. In pursuing the office, presidential contenders make promises to party and interest groups to garner their electoral support. Once elected, presidents may have to deliver on these campaign promises, which may be at variance with public preferences. As these personal attitudes and commitments to party and interest groups become stronger, the tug of public opinion on the president weakens. Furthermore, presidents may overestimate their ability to lead public opinion, leading them to miscalculate their ability to move the public. All of this suggests that there are important limitations to presidential leadership of public opinion, that there is potential for presidential leadership, but that such leadership should not be taken as a given or be assumed always to be effective.

NOTES

1. George C. Edwards III, "Aligning Tests with Theory: Presidential Approval as a Source of Influence with Congress," *Congress and the Presidency* 24 (Autumn 1997): 113–30.

2. See Michael B. Grossman and Martha Joynt Kumar, *Portraying the President: The White House and the News Media* (Baltimore, Md.: Johns Hopkins University Press, 1981); John Anthony Maltese, *Spin Control: The White House Office of Communications and the Management of Presidential News*, 2nd ed. rev. (Chapel Hill: University of North Carolina Press, 1994).

3. Richard W. Waterman, Robert Wright, and Gilbert St. Clair, *The Image-Is-Everything Presidency: Dilemmas in American Leadership* (Boulder, Colo.: Westview Press, 1999).

4. See George C. Edwards III, *The Public Presidency: The Pursuit of Popular Support* (New York: St. Martin's Press, 1983); Samuel Kernell, *Going Public: New Strategies of Presidential Leadership*, 2nd ed. (Washington, D.C.: CQ Press, 1993), 168–82; Jeffrey J. Mondak, "Source Cues and Policy Approval: The Cognitive Dynamics of Public Support for the Reagan Agenda," *American Journal of Political Science* 37 (February 1993): 186–212; Corey M. Rosen, "A Test of Presidential Leadership of Public Opinion: The Split-Ballot Technique," *Polity* 6 (Winter 1973): 282–90; Lee Sigelman, "Gauging the Public Response to Presidential Leadership," *Presidential Studies Quarterly*, 10 (Summer 1980): 427–33; Lee Sigelman and Carol K. Sigelman, "Presidential Leadership of Public Opinion: From Benevolent Leader to Kiss of Death?" *Experimental Study of Politics* 7:3 (1981): 1–22; Dan Thomas and Lee Sigelman, "Presidential Identification and Policy Leadership: Experimental Evidence on the Reagan Case," in *The Presidency and Public Policy Making*, ed. George C. Edwards III, Steven A. Shull, Norman C. Thomas (Pittsburgh: University of Pittsburgh Press, 1985), 37–49; Richard A. Brody and Catherine R. Shapiro, "Policy Failure and Public Support: The Iran Contra Affair and Public Assessments of President Reagan," *Political Behavior* 11:4 (1989): 353–69. Sigelman and Sigelman, "Presidential Leadership," even contend that unpopular presidents may repel public opinion.

5. Benjamin I. Page, Robert Y. Shapiro, and Glenn R. Dempsey, "What Moves Public Opinion?" *American Political Science Review* 81 (March 1987): 23–43.

6. George C. Edwards III, *On Deaf Ears: The Limits of the Bully Pulpit* (New Haven, Conn.: Yale University Press, 2003).

7. Lyn Ragsdale, "Presidential Speechmaking and the Public Audience: Individual Presidents and Group Attitudes," *Journal of Politics* 49 (August 1987): 704–36.

8. Paul Brace and Barbara Hinckley, *Follow the Leader: Opinion Polls and the Modern Presidency* (New York: Basic Books, 1992).

9. See Charles W. Ostrom Jr. and Dennis M. Simon, "Promise and Performance: A Dynamic Model of Presidential Popularity," *American Political Science Review* 79 (June 1985): 334–58; see also Paul Brace and Barbara Hinckley, "Presidential Activities from Truman through Reagan: Timing and Impact," *Journal of Politics* 55 (May 1993): 382–93; Richard J. Powell, "'Going Public' Revisited: Presidential Speechmaking and the Bargaining Setting in Congress," *Congress and the Presidency* 26 (Fall 1999): 153–70.

10. Jeffrey E. Cohen, "Presidential Rhetoric and the Public Agenda," *American Journal of Political Science* 39 (February 1995): 87–107; Kim Quaile Hill, "The Policy Agendas of the President and the Mass Public: A Research Validation and Extension," *American Journal of Political Science* 42 (October 1998): 1328–34; Adam B. Lawrence, "Does It Really Matter What Presidents Say? The Influence of Presidential Rhetoric on the Public Agenda, 1946–2002," paper presented at the 2002 Annual Meeting of the American Political Science Association, Boston, August 29–September 1, 2002; but also see Lydia M. Andrade, "When to Lead and When to Follow: Presidential Speeches and Public Opinion," paper presented at the Annual Meeting of the American Political Science Association, Boston, August 29–September 1, 2002.

11. James A. Stimson, *Public Opinion in America: Moods, Cycles, and Swings* (Boulder, Colo.: Westview Press, 1991).

12. John R. Zaller, *The Nature and Origins of Mass Opinion* (New York: Cambridge University Press, 1992); John R. Zaller and Stanley Feldman, "A Simple Theory of the Survey Response: Answering Questions versus Revealing Preferences," *American Journal of Political Science* 36 (August 1992): 579–96.

13. Jeffrey E. Cohen, Michael A. Krassa, and John A. Hamman, "The Impact of Presidential Campaigning on Midterm U.S. Senate Elections," *American Political Science Review* 51 (March 1991): 165–78.

14. Keith T. Poole and Howard Rosenthal, *Congress: A Political-Economic History of Roll Call Voting* (New York: Oxford University Press, 1997).

15. Stimson, *Public Opinion in America*.

16. George C. Edwards III, "Can the President Focus the Public's Attention?," paper presented at the Midwest Political Science Association, Chicago, April 18–20, 2001; George C. Edwards III and Matthew Eshbaugh-Soha, "Presidential Persuasion: Does the Public Respond?," paper presented at the 2000 Annual Meeting of the Southern Political Science Association, Atlanta, November 8–11, 2000.

17. Zaller, *The Nature and Origins of Mass Opinion*.

18. Andrade, "When to Lead."

19. See Cohen, "Presidential Rhetoric and the Public Agenda"; Jeffrey E. Cohen, *Presidential Responsiveness and Public Policy Making* (Ann Arbor: University of Michigan Press, 1997).

20. Hill, "The Policy Agendas."

21. Lawrence, "Does It Really Matter . . . ?"

22. See Cohen, *Presidential Responsiveness and Public Policy Making*.

23. It also may be the case that the president is able to shift the public mood by affecting opinion on issues for which previous polls existed. When the public mood shifts, then, we cannot truly distinguish between issue installation and other types of opinion change. But for reasons presented earlier, we suggest that presidents might have an easier time affecting opinion through issue installation than through other opinion change processes.

24. Cohen, *Presidential Responsiveness and Public Policy Making*.

25. In several instances, presidents did not issue State of the Union addresses. In those cases, we substituted a major national address presented close to the time that the State of the Union address would normally be given. There are four such cases across this series: April 14, 1969 (Plan for Domestic Legislation), February 27, 1977 (Report to the American People), February 21, 1981 (Economic Proposal Text), and February 9, 1989 (Address to Congress and the Nation).

26. Stimson, *Public Opinion in America*, 35.

27. See Cohen, *Presidential Responsiveness and Public Policy Making*.

28. James A. Stimson, Michael B. MacKuen, and Robert S. Erikson, "Dynamic Representation," *American Political Science Review* 89 (September 1995): 543–65.

29. Robert H. Durr, "What Moves Policy Sentiment?" *American Political Science Review* 87 (March 1993): 158–70; Christopher Wlezien, "The Public as Thermostat: Dynamics of Preferences for Spending," *American Journal of Political Science* 39 (November 1995): 981–1000; Robert S. Erikson, Michael B. MacKuen, and James A. Stimson, *The Macropolity* (New York: Cambridge University Press, 2002).

30. We experimented with a host of economic variables, including average annual inflation and public confidence and expectations about the economy, the latter being measures of the "perceptual" economy. Only the unemployment variable was found to affect the public mood.

31. By doing this, we are able to avoid the problems associated with true simultaneous processes.

32. See Stimson, MacKuen, and Erikson, "Dynamic Representation"; Erikson, MacKuen, and Stimson, *The Macropolity*.

33. In all estimations, we checked for time-dependent problems by using both Durbin h statistics and Lagrange multiplier procedures, as well as the Dickey-Fuller test. No equation was found to be so disturbed, thus we were able to proceed with OLS estimation throughout.

34. We experimented with several other variables derived from existing research, including the inflation rate, indicators of the perceptual economy (consumer confidence and expectations), the occurrence of war, and several scandal dummy variables (Watergate and the Iranian hostage crisis). None of these other factors showed impact on the public mood, thus to preserve degrees of freedom in a time series analysis with a limited n (1956 to 1994, n = 39), they were excluded form further analysis. However,

after building our model with the presidential variables included, we experimented with each of these excluded variables, singularly and in various combinations, to determine whether the presidential results would hold up under further control. In no case were any of these other factors found to be statistically significant, nor did any affect the presidential effects detailed later. Our results differ slightly from Durr's, because our time series is longer than the one he used, and because our time units are measured in years, while Durr's are measured in quarters. Still, two of our three baseline variables are included in Durr's model (government policy, past public mood); only the specification of the economic variable differs.

35. Other possible epochs might relate to party control of the presidency or party system eras.

36. See Stimson, MacKuen, and Erikson, "Dynamic Representation," 558.

37. An analysis of the relationship between presidential ideology and the public mood in levels from our long-term component could yield spurious results if both series are nonstationary. Dickey-Fuller unit root tests indicate that we should reject the null hypothesis that the series has a unit root (i.e., that the series was nonstationary) for the presidential ideology variable, as well as the variables and interaction terms we enter into the subsequent equation, which we report in Tables 8.3, 8.4, and 8.5. See Robert S. Pindyck and Daniel L. Rubinfeld, *Econometric Models and Economic Forecasts*, 2nd ed. (New York: McGraw-Hill, 1981), 459–62; D. A. Dickey and W. A. Fuller, "Distribution of the Estimates for Autoregressive Time Series with a Unit Root," *Journal of the American Statistical Association* 74 (June 1979): 427–31.

38. The F test is described in Pindyck and Rubinfeld, *Economic Models and Economic Forecasts*, 116–26.

39. We calculate the speed of impact of presidential ideology by using the following formula: $1/(1-B)$, where B is the regression coefficient for changes in presidential ideology. The resulting quantity, in this case, 1.03 $\{1/1-.03)\}$, represents the time it takes for about two-thirds of the effect of presidential ideology to be felt. Multiplying that quantity by three gives the time it takes for almost all (99 percent) of the impact of presidential ideology to be felt ($3 * 1.03 = 3.09$). See Stimson, MacKuen, and Erikson, "Dynamic Representation," 558, for more on this technique.

40. Zaller, *The Nature and Origins of Mass Opinion*, 45–46.

41. We also examined several other source credibility effects: first year in office, whether elected, and extremism, with the idea that presidents may have greater source credibility in their first year in office, if they were elected (as opposed to succeeding from the vice presidency), and if they were moderate politically as opposed to being liberal or conservative. None of these showed any impact on the public mood.

42. One could argue that policy extremism on the part of the president, not distance from the public, is the better specification. John Zaller, "Monica Lewinsky's Contribution to Political Science," *Political Science and Politics* (June 1998): 182–88, argues and demonstrates that policy moderation affects presidential election results. We tried this alternative and found that policy distance, but not moderation, affects the public mood.

43. However, Cohen, "Presidential Rhetoric and the Public Agenda," shows that popularity does not seem to affect the president's ability to influence the public's agenda, and presidents seem only marginally able to boost their popularity.

44. Using average annual popularity produces essentially the same results.

45. Robert J. Friedrich, "In Defense of Multiplicative Terms in Multiple Regression Equations," *American Journal of Political Science* 26 (November 1982): 797–833.

46. Richard F. Fenno Jr., *Home Style: House Members in Their Districts* (Boston: Little Brown, 1978).

47. This equation fits best. Equations that used either percentage of coalition victories in the House and/or averaged for both Houses attributed much less effect to the congressional variables.

48. Doris Kearns Goodwin, *No Ordinary Time: Franklin and Eleanor Roosevelt: The Home Front in World War II* (New York: Simon & Schuster, 1994).

9

The Rose Garden Strategy Revisited

How Presidents Use Public Activities

Lori Cox Han

Many scholars have documented the shift during recent decades to a style of presidential leadership that is increasingly based on rhetorical skills and the effective use of public activities. Those public efforts have become increasingly important for presidents who have occupied the White House during the last fifty years, as the expansion of media technology has contributed to the expansion of the rhetorical presidency and the need to develop successful communication strategies. As it has evolved with recent administrations, a communication strategy consists of various components, including the presidential and press relationship, presidential public activities, the presidential policy agenda, and the leadership style of the president. "To understand how a president communicates is to understand an important base of power for the modern presidency."[1] A successful communication strategy can determine the relationship that the president has with both the press and the public. As the essential link between the president and the public, the news media have contributed to the expansion of the executive branch as an institution; the extent to which the White House handles both press and public relations is evident by the number of people now employed in both the press and communication offices.[2] Presidents of the modern era also have utilized public support by increasingly "going public," a style of presidential leadership where the president sells his programs directly to the American people.[3]

Given all that is now known about how presidents utilize public activities and the strategy that is developed within the White House in an attempt to capitalize on the president's effective use of the bully pulpit, an important question still remains as to how presidents rely on public aspects of the office during their reelection efforts. As Lammers wrote in 1982, presidents now rely so much on attention-focusing activities that they do not necessarily need to change their public strategies during the reelection campaign at the end of the first term. In general, presidents now partake in extensive public exposure efforts such as public addresses and other appearances throughout their first term in office, not just during the reelection campaign, due in part to the increased media attention of the presidency over the past forty years. Presidents are now "motivated by a realization that public exposure can be more helpful to them for reelection when it is undertaken in their role as president rather than in the role of a candidate for reelection."[4] The overall goal here is to determine how often, and in which formats, presidents choose to go public, and if differences exist in that pattern during their reelection efforts. This chapter also considers the major developments within the public presidency during the twentieth century, and how those developments contributed to the patterns in public activities that have emerged for Presidents Hoover through Clinton.

PRESIDENTIAL PUBLIC ACTIVITIES THROUGHOUT THE TWENTIETH CENTURY

The start of the rhetorical presidency and the president's use of the bully pulpit are credited to Theodore Roosevelt. He advanced the president's role as the national leader of public opinion and used his rhetorical skills to increase the power of the presidency through popular support. Roosevelt believed that the president was the steward of the people, and that weak presidential leadership during the nineteenth century had left the American system of government open to the harmful influence of special interests. Roosevelt's use of the presidency as a bully pulpit changed American's view of the office and helped shift power from the legislative to executive branch during the twentieth century. Later presidents, though not all, would follow Roosevelt's strategy of relying on the bully pulpit to elevate the power of the office as an attempt to lead democratically as the spokesperson for the American public. Use of the bully pulpit has become especially important since the start of the television age, where a president's overall success or failure as a leader can be determined by his rhetorical skills and public influence. Since the 1950s, three presidents stand out as successful in their use of the bully pulpit—John F. Kennedy, Ronald Reagan, and Bill Clinton. Other presidents during the twentieth century either abdicated the bully pulpit or used it ineffectively, which diminished presidential power during their terms and curtailed their leadership potential by allowing other political actors to shape the public debate.[5]

In Neustadt's classic study of the presidency, presidential power is defined as the power to persuade, with successful presidents relying on a leadership style based on bargaining.[6] Many scholars have since further examined and some have redefined how presidential communication and public activities can impact a president's success with policy making, relations with Congress and other political actors, attempts to control the political agenda, and overall public relations with American citizens. Presidents now enjoy more power over shaping the national agenda by rapidly reaching the American audience through the mass media.[7] Presidential rhetoric is a means for mobilizing the masses and is a primary tool used by presidents in their attempts to implement policy objectives. The current political culture now demands presidents to be popular leaders, with "a duty constantly to defend themselves publicly, to promote policy initiatives nationwide, and to inspirit the population."[8] The rhetorical presidency is viewed by some scholars as a constitutional aberration, a "tool of barter rather than a means of informing or challenging a citizenry,"[9] while others see the trend as a positive institutional and constitutional feature that allows presidents to speak directly to the public.[10] Regardless of one's view of the constitutional ramifications of the rhetorical presidency, the modern rhetorical president functions as an "interpreter in chief" and the "nation's chief storyteller," and the emphasis on communication strategies and public activities has led to an emphasis on ceremonial, rather than deliberative, speech.[11]

Several recent studies have documented how, when, and why presidents participate in public activities. Going public is defined as "a class of activities that presidents engage in as they promote themselves and their policies before the American public."[12] Addresses to the nation, press conferences, and other public appearances are examples of how a president attempts to sell his agenda or other presidential actions to not only the public but other political actors as well. Certainly the technological developments of the mass media in recent years have allowed presidents to go public more often, and with much greater ease. However, more recent presidents have gone public with much more frequency.[13] Other recent presidents, most notably Clinton, also have relied on the "perpetual campaign" approach to governing, which results from, among other things, the decline of party influence during elections that "personalize[s] the presidency and make[s] imagery one of its cornerstones."[14] Key predictors also exist to determine when a president is likely to deliver a national address, as well as when he is not. Changes in public attitudes toward the president, as well as a change in national conditions, increase the likelihood of a presidential address, whereas a worsening economic condition or announcing an increase in military activities decreases the chance of a president addressing the nation.[15]

Other studies on presidential public activities have focused on distinct time periods of a president's tenure in office. Presidential transitions prior to first taking office, a time traditionally spent staffing administrations, developing congressional relationships, and building coalitions to gain support of a new policy agenda, often find presidents relying heavily on public rhetoric to develop support for their policy agendas and to shape the political context of their administration, especially if the incoming president is a member of the opposite party of the incumbent he is replacing.[16] Presidential inaugurals also provide the president with a critical rhetorical moment at the start of his administration,[17] and since the first inaugural address by George Washington in 1789, most presidents still follow the original script set forth by the first president to outline goals and discuss the constitutional duties of the office.[18] Presidents also have used press conferences as a tool to promote their agendas, although some more frequently than others. However, since these are not controlled events and include other participants, the ability to control the agenda is not always predictable. The president's opening statement may include several minor policy announcements, or it may be a reaction to a single event, such as an international crisis.[19] Since the days of Franklin Roosevelt and Harry Truman, presidents overall have relied less on frequent and regular press conferences due to such factors as an increase in international involvement, presidential personalities, and the advent of televised news conferences during the 1960s.

Presidents also are likely to avoid the press during times of national uncertainty, when major policy options are being considered within the White House, or when a situation arises that could embarrass the administration.[20] A president also can affect the public's policy agenda through public speeches, with a specific policy often rising on the public's agenda if a president gives a high-profile speech on that issue. The public responds to the emphasis a president gives to a particular policy during multi-policy speeches, especially the State of the Union address, and the president's popularity in public opinion polls seems to not affect his ability to place an issue on the public's agenda.[21]

RESEARCH QUESTIONS AND STRATEGIES

In revisiting the questions that emerged in Lammers's initial study of presidential attention-focusing activities and the impact on campaign strategies, all remain relevant, particularly during the past two decades, when two incumbents who were perceived as successful communicators won reelection (Reagan and Clinton), and one incumbent not known for his communication skills lost his bid for reelection (Bush). The questions include:

- Have recent presidents tended to hide in Washington refusing to campaign during the reelection year?
- Are they likely to engage more extensively in White House-based activities in the reelection year?
- Are presidents more apt to use the device of major national addresses and to focus on foreign policy matters in the context of their reelection year?
- In the years prior to their reelection campaign, are presidents actually traveling more extensively, and are they engaging in more extensive White House exposure and routine appearances throughout the nation?

- Has there been a continuing shift in the attention-focusing activity of all presidents, thus suggesting a systemic explanation, or are there marked deviations which would indicate the importance of individual presidential personalities and perhaps historic events?
- Insofar as the forces producing change are systemic, are there indications of the relative impact of such factors as increases in American international involvement, the growing importance of television, improved transportation opportunities, and the increasing range of particularistic interest groups in a less party-oriented political system?[22]

For presidential scholars, the office of the presidency, as well as the men who have held it, seems to provide a never-ending set of research questions regarding the role of executive leadership within the American political system. Specifically, providing a better understanding of the nature of the public presidency has been a goal of many scholars during recent years, as the mass media have played an increasingly influential role in presidential politics. Also in recent years, a robust discussion has emerged among presidency scholars on how to develop a more rigorous and systematic approach more befitting the traditions of political science to study both the president and the presidency. Many scholars have maintained an emphasis on presidential leadership and its importance in understanding the role of the president in both policy making and governing, yet at the same time began to change the direction of research by relying on a broader theoretical perspective and including extensive data for comparative analysis.[23]

When considering the use of public activities by recent presidents, Ragsdale's methodological approach to studying the presidency is particularly influential in the development and design of this study. Ragsdale relies on three dimensions to describe the parameters of the presidency as an institution: organization, behavior, and structure. She recognizes that presidents can make marginal changes to the organization of the presidency, but that the office is not reinvented with each new occupant in the White House. Also, presidents tend to behave in similar ways, since they are faced with a similar political and institutional environment. It is through rigorous data analysis across several presidencies that explanations can be found to define the president's role within the institution of the presidency; ultimately, "the institution of the presidency shapes presidents as much as presidents, during their short tenures, shape the institution."[24]

In adding to Lammers's initial data set, the eight most recent presidents to run for reelection and the three accidental presidents who sought office in their own right emerge as appropriate candidates for analysis. The eleven presidents included are Herbert Hoover, Franklin D. Roosevelt, Harry S. Truman, Dwight Eisenhower, Lyndon Johnson, Richard Nixon, Gerald Ford, Jimmy Carter, Ronald Reagan, George H. W. Bush, and Bill Clinton.

The principal data for this analysis have been drawn from the official presidential records. Started in 1957, the *Public Papers of the Presidents of the United States* series is the official annual compilation of presidential papers. The *Public Papers* series is considered a comprehensive public source of data on the American presidency and has aided those presidency scholars interested in a more institutional approach to studying the office, since current data span numerous administrations. This allows researchers to employ a comparative methodological approach to understanding the institution of the American presidency. Administrations included in the series of *Public Papers* are Hoover, Truman, Eisenhower, Kennedy, Johnson, Nixon, Ford, Carter, Reagan, Bush, and Clinton. The papers of President Franklin Roosevelt were published privately prior to the creation of the official *Public Papers* series. The papers and speeches of the president of the United States that were issued by the Office of the Press Secretary during the specified time period are included in each volume of the *Public Papers*. These include press releases, presidential proclamations, executive orders, addresses, remarks, letters, messages, telegrams, memorandums to federal agencies, communications to Congress, bill-signing statements, transcripts from presidential press conferences, and communiqués to foreign heads of state. While some changes have occurred in the compilation of presidential documents in these volumes, particularly with information about audiences for particular presidential addresses, the level of comparability for the more public aspects of presidential appearances through the past seventy years is nevertheless quite high. However, a number of coding steps were undertaken to minimize problems of differing thoroughness in the official records due to the lack of complete comparability.

To determine the total number of public activities of each president, as well as the different forums used, each public event chronicled in the *Public Papers of the President* was grouped into the following categories: major addresses or routine addresses and location of address (White House appearance, Washington area appearance, U.S. appearance, and foreign appearance). Major addresses include State of the Union and other addresses to a joint session of Congress, addresses to the nation that are broadcast live on television, and other major addresses that presidents use to outline policy goals, including addresses to business, labor, or other major interest groups. Each inaugural address and the nomination speech at a national convention also were included. Routine appearances include press conferences, radio addresses, addresses that did not include major policy statements (for example, many graduation speeches and some appearances at colleges or universities), signing ceremonies, teleconference and roundtable remarks, town meetings, remarks to or exchanges with reporters, partisan appearances, and other brief statements. (Since all presidential interviews are not included in the various sets of the *Public Papers*, these public activities were not included in the data for this study.)[25]

The advantage of the methodological approach used in this study is that it allows for a comparison across a nearly seventy-year time span and involves the public activities of eleven different presidents. The data give initial answers to basic questions about institutional change, and along with more recent studies on presidential communication strategies, this data can provide a contextual basis for more detailed case studies of presidential approaches to public activities.

PUBLIC-EXPOSURE PATTERNS

The public-exposure patterns of presidents since the Hoover administration show a substantial change in recent decades, but much continuity exists in the patterns as well. The data, as presented in Tables 9.1 and 9.2, allow comparisons of yearly totals, first-term totals, and the relative distribution of activity within each four-year period.

As the data suggest, presidential use of major addresses has been remarkably consistent throughout the entire time period, and as Lammers pointed out in his original study, the preemption of national television for major presidential addresses has been an infrequent phenomenon. When that does occur, foreign policy news has consistently dominated the message for all presidents. The four pre-television-age presidents[26] reflect consistent use of major addresses, and major policy statements and messages to the American public were used sparingly. Even Roosevelt did not go to the well too often with his fireside chats. Starting with Johnson, a trend emerges for presidents to increasingly rely on major addresses as a means of communicating their policy goals as television increased its dominance in the political arena. By the 1980s, the number of yearly major addresses shows another consistent increase for Reagan, Bush, and Clinton, suggesting that the era of mediated politics had changed presidential communication strategies to require each president to go public even more frequently. It is striking, however, that presidents do not rely more heavily on major addresses during their reelection efforts, with several giving fewer major addresses during their fourth year in office than in their first three.

The number of routine presidential addresses also has steadily increased throughout the time period, which can be attributed to the influence of television, changes in the political environment that have encouraged presidents to go public more often, and each president's public leadership style. Presidents also make more routine public appearances during an election year while campaigning for themselves or for other members of their party. As for public appearance venues, a steady increase is noticeable for presidents throughout the time period studied in all four categories (see Table 9.2). White House appearances increase throughout the television age as presidents hold more "photo op" events for news coverage in an attempt to govern from center stage. Washington appearances increase during the Eisenhower years, and continue

TABLE 9.1
Public Addresses

	Major Addresses	Routine Addresses	Total Public Activities
Hoover			
1929	3	93	96
1930	6	114	120
1931	5	104	109
1932	17	152	169
Total	31	463	494
Roosevelt			
1933	10	103	113
1934	5	116	121
1935	2	130	132
1936	3	201	204
Total	20	550	570
Truman			
1945	8	51	59
1946	6	76	82
1947	8	63	71
1948	7	383	390
Total	29	573	602
Eisenhower			
1953	10	85	95
1954	10	127	137
1955	6	83	89
1956	14	81	95
Total	40	376	416
Johnson			
1964	17	461	478
Nixon			
1969	14	250	264
1970	11	219	230
1971	9	160	169
1972	10	146	156
Total	44	775	819
Ford			
1975	23	380	403
1976	2	691	693
Total	25	1071	1096

(continued on next page)

TABLE 9.1 *(continued)*

	Major Addresses	Routine Addresses	Total Public Activities
Carter			
1977	12	312	324
1978	7	350	357
1979	7	279	286
1980	9	448	457
Total	35	1389	1424
Reagan			
1981	13	239	252
1982	11	369	380
1983	9	400	409
1984	8	447	455
Total	41	1455	1496
Bush			
1989	16	413	429
1990	7	473	480
1991	11	482	493
1992	8	562	570
Total	42	1930	1972
Clinton			
1993	16	625	641
1994	9	634	643
1995	8	532	540
1996	8	628	636
Total	41	2419	2460

Source: Collected by the author from the Private Papers of F. D. Roosevelt and the Presidential Papers of Truman, Eisenhower, Johnson, Ford, Carter, Reagan, Bush, and Clinton.

to increase steadily thereafter as presidents make more major policy addresses, often to major interest groups holding their annual conventions in the nation's capitol, as part of their overall communication strategy. Appearances throughout the U.S. also steadily increase, and most presidents show a dramatic increase in this category as they campaign around the country during their fourth year in office. Foreign policy appearances have also increased as transportation became more reliable and efficient throughout the twentieth century.

IMPLICATIONS

When assessing how often, and in which forums, each president engaged in public activities, several patterns emerge. The increase in presidential activities

TABLE 9.2
Presidential Venues

	White House Appearances	Washington Appearances	U. S. Appearances	Foreign Appearances
Hoover				
1929	83	8	5	0
1930	72	43	5	0
1931	77	13	17	2
1932	47	16	106	0
Total	279	80	133	2
Roosevelt				
1933	91	13	8	1
1934	81	12	21	7
1935	110	7	15	0
1936	83	9	106	6
Total	365	41	150	14
Truman				
1945	44	5	9	1
1946	72	3	7	0
1947	54	5	7	5
1948	34	11	342	3
Total	204	24	365	9
Eisenhower				
1953	42	24	28	1
1954	67	32	38	0
1955	41	17	25	6
1956	40	20	33	2
Total	190	93	124	9
Johnson				
1964	272	27	177	2
Nixon				
1969	126	40	42	56
1970	95	13	94	28
1971	67	28	71	5
1972	56	23	55	22
Total	344	109	262	107
Ford				
1975	164	60	133	46
1976	206	49	436	2
Total	370	109	569	48

(continued on next page)

TABLE 9.2 *(continued)*

	White House Appearances	Washington Appearances	U. S. Appearances	Foreign Appearances
Carter				
1977	212	38	55	19
1978	171	31	104	51
1979	149	29	76	32
1980	195	47	198	17
Total	727	145	433	119
Reagan				
1981	163	40	41	8
1982	206	42	95	37
1983	234	72	88	15
1984	205	65	156	29
Total	808	219	380	89
Bush				
1989	201	59	112	57
1990	226	43	162	49
1991	266	55	127	45
1992	171	48	320	31
Total	864	205	721	182
Clinton				
1993	402	72	141	26
1994	299	68	183	93
1995	258	79	152	51
1996	226	58	298	54
Total	1185	277	774	224

Source: Collected by the author from the Private Papers of F. D. Roosevelt and the Presidential Papers of Truman, Eisenhower, Johnson, Ford, Carter, Reagan, Bush, and Clinton.

over the years can be attributed to not only the historical context of the role and capability of the news media during each administration but the president's public style as well. Since many presidential activities are now planned for optimum coverage on television, the White House relies more heavily, as especially witnessed during the Reagan and Clinton administrations, on using photo opportunities to achieve its few seconds of airtime on network newscasts. The increase in short presidential events and appearances, rather than a greater emphasis on major addresses, clearly reflects presidential concern with maximum footage on the evening news. Receptions for foreign guests, clips of foreign travel, and visits to disaster areas, for example, are likely targets for television coverage.

The institutional nature of the presidency, and the role that the press plays within it, can limit a president's options in the development and implementation of strategies, but attempts to influence the public's perception of the president are not always futile. Most presidents in recent years have attempted to improve upon their early mistakes while in office, especially when dealing with the press and other public activities, and most also experience somewhat of a learning curve as they become accustomed to the responsibilities of the office. But the uniqueness of each president's leadership style cannot be completely ignored, since each leaves his mark, in one way or another, on the Oval Office, especially where communication strategies are concerned. As a result, each administration, at least in recent years, has served in developing an institutional learning curve on press and public relations for future presidents to follow. Presidents also learn important lessons from their successors in office about the use of public activities, and as this study shows, a general increase in public activities exists for presidents during the television age.

Television coverage during a presidential campaign is crucial for candidates to reach millions of viewers, so it is not surprising to see presidential public exposure activities increase during presidents' reelection efforts. How each president relies on public activities as part of his reelection campaign differs based on public leadership style as well as how intensely he may have feared defeat. However, one important trend has emerged that not only dictates presidential reelection behavior but governing as well—the perpetual campaign. No longer do presidents shift their public strategies during their fourth year in office to match that of their opponent, as presidents since the Ford and Carter years have increased their public efforts throughout their first terms, with an even greater increase in public activities as traditional campaign activities begin. Presidents have become so dependent on public activities as a day-to-day strategy in communicating with the American public through the news media that, as witnessed during the Clinton years, it is often difficult to tell when they are governing or campaigning.

As Lammers concluded in 1982, three important factors have contributed to the influence of presidential exposure patterns. The most important of the three is obviously television, followed by air travel, and the rise of particularistic interest groups. Foreign policy matters have only minimally altered public exposure activities, and presidents simply alter their existing public strategies to include campaign events during their reelection efforts. Presidents now go public more than ever before, in part because there are more outlets for presidential communication than ever before. The definition of what constitutes a major presidential address also has changed throughout the twentieth century. All presidents continue to address a joint session of Congress for annual State of the Union messages or when other events necessitate such an address. Presidents also continue to address the nation from the Oval Office or perhaps other settings within the White House for issues of national importance. But other public venues, such as national conventions for interest groups or other organizations, have become increasingly popular for presidents to deliver major addresses. Over the years, presidents have attended even more national conventions, both in and out of Washington, and they participate in more speaking engagements for the purpose of delivering a major address or even for just brief remarks. This allows them to stay on center stage and maintain a dominant presence on television news broadcasts and on the front page of the nation's leading newspapers.

To restate Lammers's conclusions, "Presidential linkages with the electorate have undergone a basic transformation." Presidents do not hide from the public during their first years in the White House, waiting to reemerge as candidates for reelection. The good news for voters is that presidents are extremely visible during an election, and since most do not rely extensively on foreign appearances, one is to assume that a discussion of a broad range of issues is being presented to the American public. The bad news, however, is that presidents may be speaking more often to fragmented populations through interest group appearances and not national audiences. Also, more may not necessarily mean better in terms of the substance of messages from the president, and certainly how those messages are portrayed to the American public through the news media.

NOTES

Author's note: The late Bill Lammers, professor of political science at the University of Southern California, wrote one of the chapters that appeared in *The President and the Public*, titled "Presidential Attention-Focusing Activities." The chapter examines how presidents use public activities during their first three years in office compared to the fourth year—their reelection effort. I was fortunate to study with Bill during my time in graduate school at USC, and my dissertation was the last that he chaired prior to his death in 1997. With the blessing of his wife, Mary Lammers, I have updated his research in this chapter and reconsider the "Rose Garden strategy," upon which incumbent presidents rely during their reelection efforts.

1. Lori Cox Han, *Governing From Center Stage: White House Communication Strategies during the Television Age of Politics* (Cresskill, N.J.: Hampton Press, 2001), 2.

2. For example, see John Anthony Maltese, *Spin Control: The White House Office of Communications and the Management of Presidential News* (Chapel Hill: University of North Carolina Press, 1994).

3. See Samuel Kernell, *Going Public: New Strategies of Presidential Leadership*, 3rd ed. (Washington, D.C.: Congressional Quarterly, 1997); Richard Rose, *The Postmodern President* (Chatham, N.J.: Chatham House, 1991).

4. William W. Lammers, "Presidential Attention-Focusing Activities," in *The President and the Public*, ed. Doris Graber (Philadelphia: Institute for the Study of Human Issues, 1982), 145–71.

5. For a further discussion of the rhetorical presidency, see Jeffrey K. Tulis, *The Rhetorical Presidency* (Princeton: Princeton University Press, 1987), and Carol Gelderman, *All the Presidents' Words: The Bully Pulpit and the Creation of the Virtual Presidency* (New York: Walker & Co., 1997).

6. Richard Neustadt, *Presidential Power and the Modern Presidents: The Politics of Leadership From Roosevelt to Reagan* (New York: Macmillan, 1990).

7. See Elmer E. Cornwell Jr., *Presidential Leadership of Public Opinion* (Westport, Conn.: Greenwood Press, 1965); Theodore J. Lowi, *The Personal President: Power Invested, Promise Unfulfilled* (Ithaca, N.Y.: Cornell University Press, 1985).

8. Tulis, *The Rhetorical Presidency*, 4–23.

9. Roderick P. Hart, *The Sound of Leadership: Presidential Communication in the Modern Age* (Chicago: University of Chicago Press, 1987), 110, 212.

10. Karlyn Kohrs Campbell and Kathleen Hall Jamieson, *Deeds Done in Words: Presidential Rhetoric and the Genres of Governance* (Chicago: University of Chicago Press, 1990), 1, 213–19.

11. Mary E. Stuckey, *The President as Interpreter-in-Chief* (Chatham, N.J.: Chatham House, 1991), 1–3.

12. Kernell, *Going Public*, ix.

13. Ibid., 104–107.

14. Lyn Ragsdale, *Vital Statistics on the Presidency: Washington to Clinton* (Washington, D.C.: Congressional Quarterly, 1996), 145–54.

15. Lyn Ragsdale, "The Politics of Presidential Speechmaking, 1949–1980," *American Political Science Review* 78 (December 1984): 971–84.

16. A. L. Crothers, "Asserting Dominance: Presidential Transitions From Out-Party to In-Party," *Polity* 26 (Summer 1994): 793–814.

17. Campbell and Jamieson, *Deeds Done in Words*, 15.

18. Lee Sigelman, "Presidential Inaugurals: The Modernization of a Genre," *Political Communication* 13 (January–March 1996): 81–92.

19. Carolyn Smith, *Presidential Press Conferences: A Critical Approach* (New York: Praeger, 1990), 79–85.

20. William W. Lammers, "Presidential Press-Conference Schedules: Who Hides, and When?" *Political Science Quarterly* 96 (Summer 1981): 261–78.

21. See Roy L. Behr and Shanto Iyengar, "Television News, Real-World Cues, and Changes in the Public Agenda," *Public Opinion Quarterly* 49 (1985): 38–57; Jeffrey E. Cohen, "Presidential Rhetoric and the Public Agenda," *American Journal of Political Science* 39 (February 1995): 87–107.

22. Lammers, "Presidential Attention-Focusing Activities," 147.

23. Many scholars still rely on Richard Neustadt's classic work *Presidential Power*, first published in 1960, for at least a starting point in their research, while also recognizing the limitations that an individual president can face in effecting political

change. Examples include works such as George C. Edwards III, *At the Margins: Presidential Leadership of Congress* (New Haven, Conn.: Yale University Press, 1989), and Mark A. Peterson, *Legislating Together: The White House and Capital Hill from Eisenhower to Reagan* (Cambridge, Mass.: Harvard University Press, 1990), and Kernell, *Going Public*, just to name a few.

24. Ragsdale, *Vital Statistics on the Presidency*, 7–13.

25. The methodology used for categorizing speeches was modified somewhat from Lammers's initial study due to the increased use of public activities and the variety of venues for Reagan, Bush, and Clinton. Therefore, additional public appearances were included in the data set for earlier presidents to maintain more consistency with later presidents, which explains the higher totals for Presidents Hoover through Carter when compared to Lammers's original data. Also, the total number of major addresses and routine appearances are slightly different than Ragsdale's totals in *Vital Statistics on the Presidency* due to a slightly different coding technique. I also have fine-tuned my own methodology for coding presidential public activities since the publication of *Governing From Center Stage*, which explains any slight differences in totals for these two categories when comparing the two data sets.

26. Eisenhower is included in this category, along with Hoover, Roosevelt, and Truman. While television was gaining prominence throughout the 1950s, it was Kennedy, not Eisenhower, who first used the medium extensively to communicate with the American public.

10

Doing Diversity across the Partisan Divide

George H. W. Bush, Bill Clinton, and American National Identity

Mary E. Stuckey

Each generation of Americans must define what it means to be American.[1]

Issues of national identity—how the *"unum"* is to be constituted out of the *"pluribus"*—have always troubled our nation. Consequently, all presidents have had to contend with these issues, and they have done so in a variety of ways.[2] Short of war, they have rarely been so fraught or so central to the national agenda as in the last days of the twentieth and the early days of the twenty-first centuries. This chapter presents an analysis of presidential rhetorical constructions of national identity, using the public speeches of George H. W. Bush and the first term of Bill Clinton as exemplars of rhetoric from each side of the partisan aisle.[3] Every public utterance of the presidents was included, the policy driven and the ceremonial—the kind of speech that is often considered trivial or "mere pandering"—without intent or substance. Because my concern is with epideictic rhetoric—that which is based on the character of a speaker and serves to create a political community through language—all presidential rhetoric is given equal weight.

Bush and Clinton represent mirror images of each other, images that derive both from the personal predilections of the presidents and from their institutional locus as representatives of particular parties. In outlining these images, my argument proceeds in three parts: I first provide some historical context, which is followed by a comparison of the two presidents along four dimensions: approaches to policy making, orientations toward the political process, their understandings of the roles government can usefully play in that process, and finally their speech toward minority communities. I conclude with some discussion about what this case study tells us about presidents as managers of national diversity and articulators of national identity.

DOING DIVERSITY IN THE CONTEMPORARY UNITED STATES

One of the few things that seemed generally accepted by the late 1980s was the fragmentation of American life. With the end of the cold war, the United States lost its unifying enemy and was cast adrift as the sole remaining "superpower." At home, the tumultuousness of the late 1960s and 1970s had given rise to a number of vociferous social movements, many of which had calcified (along with the organized and powerful interests of the mighty) into "special interests" whose power in Congress and the bureaucracy was making them an ever-more popular target of politicians and diagnosticians of the nature of the problem of American life.[4] As both the interests of those who sought to maintain the national hierarchies and those who sought to join it (or overthrow it) became increasingly organized and vocal, they also became increasingly engaged in public duels with one another, most often in the halls of Congress, but for a time also on the streets, then in the courts,[5] and finally throughout the polity, a phenomenon most often referred to as the "culture wars."[6]

John F. Kennedy was briefly present at the contemporary creation of tensions between these groups, but the focus during his abbreviated term in office was more international than national; Lyndon Johnson attempted to govern as these forces gathered enough momentum to affect national politics; Richard Nixon alternately tried to harness their power and diffuse their impact; and Jimmy Carter made a feckless attempt to discuss the consequences of their influence, and consequently he was accused of blaming the American people for the disunity he deplored. That speech, in which he never used the word, has become infamous as the "malaise speech," and it is often blamed for Carter's loss of the presidency to the sunnily optimistic Ronald Reagan.[7]

The national disunity was not purely domestic however. "Vietnam" joined "malaise" as a convenient shorthand for national fragmentation; it was blamed for everything from loss of faith in American national government to the problems attendant on certain military strategies, and it was a powerful example to some of the corrosive power that the mass media had assumed since the 1960s.[8] Vietnam was to international affairs what "malaise" was to domestic concerns: a way to discuss the fear that the nation had become too complex, too fragmented, and too oppositional to be governed.

"Malaise" became the label for the problems at home as Vietnam served for the problems abroad, and Reagan offered a solution to both: optimism regarding "America" at home and the use of military power overseas.[9] In pursuing these policies, Reagan "brought America back," only to plunge it into the deepest budget deficits in the nation's history.[10] Even putting the deficit aside, Reagan's policies have been described as "crass," involving as they did "cutting benefits to poor people, lowering taxes for the wealthy, increasing the military budget, filling the federal court system with conservative judges, actively working to destroy revolutionary movements in the Caribbean."[11] In short, he was heavily criticized for fulfilling all or part of the contemporaneous conservative agenda.

Bush, by contrast, although "a stepchild in the Reagan White House,"[12] was nonetheless elected as Reagan's heir,[13] but he had a much lower ideological profile:[14] "In nearly thirty years of public life—as a member of Congress from Texas, as ambassador to the United Nations and minister to China, as director of the CIA, head of the Republican National Committee, and finally, vice president—Bush had identified himself clearly with no major issue and could take credit for no major accomplishment."[15] Bush had no real public identity except that of Reagan's successor,[16] and he was widely considered, in Richard Rose's terms, to be more a guardian than a leader.[17] "Politically, Reagan bequeathed Bush an ideological commitment to a reduced federal role in the affairs of the nation. Financially, Reagan left a deficit that limits government spending. Popularly, Reagan's style of rhetoric and communication . . . would challenge any successor."[18] Reagan was, in nearly all respects, a hard act to follow.

In the wake of Reagan's presidency, and crippled by Reagan's budget deficits,[19] Bush came to offer a more pallid version of Reaganism. Among the issues left for Bush by Reagan, and shared by all contemporary Republicans, was a certain suspect attitude on issues of national diversity. Four elements of Bush's rhetoric were relevant to these issues: an emphasis on cautious policy making, a focus on the importance of process, an explicit preference for the private over the public sphere, and the inclusion of various groups based on their ability to exemplify certain specific values. These four elements combined to apparently include all groups even as they excluded them, for as these groups represented "us," they were prevented from becoming "us," and their experiences and histories were erased even as they ostensibly were brought into the national polity.

Clinton, whose campaign against Bush often seemed to be based on being that which Bush was not,[20] presented a mirror image of his predecessor on matters of diversity.[21] Where Bush was cautious, Clinton promised to be bold; where Bush relied on established processes, Clinton identified those processes as part of the problems he had been elected to solve; where Bush depended upon distinguishing between the public and private spheres, Clinton proposed a partnership between those spheres; and where Bush used the language of "celebratory othering," or symbolic inclusion, Clinton tended more toward using language that reflected inclusion of a less distant kind.

Neither model has proved a satisfactory basis for a national consensus on issues of national diversity, but each reflects idiosyncratic tendencies peculiar to these two chief executives and also the partisan predilections that remain an important part of the differences that we continue to see reflected in the national conversations on national identity and race.

The Mirror Images of Diversity

Bush had the unenviable task of following Reagan into the Oval Office, but despite his harsh anti-Reagan rhetoric during the 1980 campaign[22] and his generally more moderate politics, by 1988 he seemed to have little quarrel with the general tone and content of Reaganism.[23] Stylistically, of course, Bush could not hope to compare with Reagan,[24] and "more importantly, he lacked Reagan's simple clarity and will."[25] He also attained office after a bitter, and according to some, a racially charged but otherwise an empty campaign.[26] Bush entered office with a political legacy of conservatism and a specific rhetorical strategy on issues of race. There are four elements of Bush's approach to diversity: cautious policy making, a commitment to rules and process, a preference for the private sphere, and a use of minority communities as exemplars of shared values. All of these combine to produce a single effect of maintaining the status quo while diffusing opposition to it. It is a powerfully legitimating rhetorical strategy, relied upon in an age when political legitimacy is hard to acquire and maintain.

Clinton, on the other hand, a pragmatist, or "New Democrat," followed a discredited Bush into the White House, in part based on his promises to approach policy making in a different, less ideologically driven, and more conciliatory way—he would end gridlock and govern from the center, changes that would require a bold approach to policy, changes in process, the use of government as a partner with the private sphere, and an attempt to focus on minorities as an important part of the American identity. This approach to diversity raised expectations in minority communities and created a certain discomfort among those in many white communities; he thus seemed to function as a catalyst for polarization rather than as a manager of diversity.[27] Thus neither president was able to forge a national consensus on issues of national diversity and national identity. The fissures that both presidents sought to direct will therefore help define American politics for some time to come.

Policy Making: Caution versus Change

Caution is both a rhetorical strategy and a preferred approach to life for Bush, who "was primarily interested in defending the status quo," which he understood as "the established social and economic order at home and American leadership abroad."[28] In both arenas, he sought to maintain and protect the existing structures of power and the social hierarchies that accompanied those structures. A believer in the old ways of doing things, Bush often talked about change and its proper management. Probably the most frequently cited instance in his inaugural, where he referred to change through such gentle metaphors as a page turning and a breeze blowing and softened its potentially threatening nature by saying "on days like this we remember that we are all part of a continuum, inescapably connected by the ties that bind."[29] Change for Bush was natural, inevitable, and progressive, not radical nor disruptive.

Bush's presidency, in short, was not one that offered dramatic change in any policy realm. In fact, "George Bush provided no leadership in regard to highly salient issues like health care, and his uncertainty bred uncertainty. He chose not to lead when he might have done so. To lead would have required presenting plausible proposals that could win enough political support among enough people to shift the median opinion in the president's direction."[30] Bush had neither the political interest nor the personal will to engage in that brand of leadership. He did declare that, "the Presidency does provide an incomparable opportunity to set a tone, to lead a movement,"[31] and on at least one occasion he told blue-collar workers, "And I just wanted you to know: One, I know you're hurting; two, I care about it; three, I've been wrong about how long this recovery would take; but, four, I am determined to use the role as leader of the free world, leader of the United States, to make things better."[32] These occasions were rare. His understanding of the office was procedural. As a result, his presidency is widely considered to be characterized by "a series of dramatic developments in international affairs and an almost complete absence of initiatives or ideas on domestic issues."[33] His policies were incremental and often uninspired. His policy rhetoric was equally uninspiring, for caution does not make for inspirational rhetoric.

This cautious approach in addition to his limited domestic agenda[34] may well have suited Bush both personally and politically, but it had powerful downsides as well: "Only seven weeks into his term, Bush felt obliged to call a press conference to deny that his administration suffered from 'drift' or 'malaise.'"[35] This issue never abated; in time it became known, in Bush's own contemptuous phrase, as "the vision thing."[36] Bush's inability to forge a public argument defending his lack of action sat uneasily with the American public, as accustomed as it was to cold war presidents, for whom forcefulness and activity were indications of strength vis-à-vis the Soviet Union.

Clinton took advantage of that unease in running for the presidency, and, in keeping with the imperatives that drive a president of one party replacing a chief executive of the other, he stressed the need for change more or less continually during the first term. In a typical example, he told a gathering of Democratic governors, "As you and I learned from the elections last year, the

American people want their political system and their Government to end gridlock, to face problems, and to make progress.... They sent us to the statehouse and to the White House to change America. And they want action now. That is our mandate and we must never forget it."[37] Change needed to be deep, dramatic, and immediate. Rather than envisioning change as something that would proceed naturally, as in Bush's rhetoric, for Clinton, change would be "forced,"[38] the product of active and intentional human agency.

He also articulated his policy accomplishments in terms of change—both in substance and in process. Clinton cited FDR often, especially with reference to his preference for "bold, persistent experimentation,"[39] and he talked about the need for change in explicit terms: "Change is never easy. It requires us to forsake the old order and to embrace a new one. Change means asking everyone to pull his or her own weight for the common good. But change is our only choice."[40] This was the locution that got Clinton elected as a "New Democrat," who would strive to see that all those "who worked hard and played by the rules" would be rewarded. The locution was vague enough that members of minority groups could hear it as promising a version of social justice that resonated in their communities. Members of the socially conservative white middle class also could hear a call for their version of social justice—an end to "government handouts" and "free rides" for "welfare cheats."

Clinton promised "change," but he left the specifics of a policy that would emanate from that change open to interpretation. Given that this president had difficulty prioritizing, he rapidly lost control of the public agenda. His chaotic leadership style and lack of discipline encouraged him to advocate action on multiple fronts, often without fully grasping the complexity of the issues before him.[41] The result was heightened expectations, increased pressures on the White House to act on even more issues, and ideologically visceral reactions to nearly every action he did take. Increasingly unable to contend with the existing structures, Clinton looked ever more to reinventing and recreating those structures.

Rules and Process: The Status Quo versus Reinventing Government

In keeping with his cautious approach to policy making, Bush's administration was characterized by a dedication to rules and process, which also meant a reliance on fairness and decency. In emphasizing the fairness of the process, Bush maintained the status quo. In advocating change, Clinton directly challenged that status quo. Both presidents were damaged by their approaches, a fact that underlines the difficulties presidents face on these issues.

Bush, by most accounts, was a sincerely decent man.[42] For him, the rules of decency, honor, and fair play were important and deeply embedded in the

American character. In a typical statement, he said: "More than anything else, democracy depends on the decency of its people. And I am convinced that there is in this country a deep reservoir of democratic decency—a respect for others, a sense of responsibility, a solid recognition that values matter. This reservoir of decency is there for us to draw on to renew our dedication to the fundamental ideals of a free government."[43] Bush's approach to issues of diversity was grounded in such decency, in the argument that courtesy was more important than policy, in the belief that good people could not knowingly damage others; that while governments, democratic or not, could forget this principle, the American people, *en masse*, could not. Thus for Bush, civility was not just a personal value, it was a national goal, the very bedrock of democracy. In his inaugural, he said, "America today is a proud, free nation, decent and civil, a place we cannot help but love."[44] That character was worth defending: "We didn't stand together to see moral values rise in Russia only to be ignored here at home. We did not sacrifice so that personal responsibility could triumph in totalitarian regimes only to become passé here in this great Nation. It's time to get back to some basic American values. So I am going to defend the principles for which you stand so firm."[45] One pillar of these principles was playing by the rules.

Bush's commitment to "playing fair" did not involve an equal commitment to the protection of civil rights.[46] While Bush has always claimed to be a supporter of civil rights in general, there is little evidence for any specific support.[47] Indeed, his veto of the 1990–1991 Civil Rights Act signaled the weakness of any such support within the administration.[48] Defending his veto via his history on civil rights, he said, "I have long stood for civil rights. I think anybody in public life knows that I have long stood for civil rights. But I just don't think it's fair to sign a bill that will result in quotas. The day I vetoed that bill I attached to it a civil rights bill challenging all these proponents of civil rights. Pass a real civil rights bill. And they didn't even permit the House and Senate to vote on it because they wanted to try and embarrass the President. I am for civil rights and I am against quotas."[49] The defensiveness of his tone here was remarkable; it is reflective of the informal occasion (an exchange with reporters rather than a formal press conference) and the degree to which he understood the significance of the veto in terms of his public image vis-à-vis civil rights.

That veto touched off something of a national debate on the issue and created some furor over his handling of the matter. As a result, Bush's approval among American blacks, which had been higher than that of any other modern Republican president, dropped to more predictable levels of support.[50] In response, Bush first sought to minimize the debate by arguing that "we" were all in substantial agreement about the principle upon which his veto was based: "And we all know quotas aren't right. They are not fair. They divide society instead of bringing people together."[51] According to this argument,

Bush was simply doing his duty as the national protector of fair play and decency by vetoing the bill.

Bush next tried to straddle the issue by claiming support for "civil rights" but an opposition to "quotas,"[52] but this is unconvincing at best, and duplicitous at worst.[53] In an address at West Point, Bush said, "Black and white, the great civil rights leaders of the fifties and sixties deplored intolerance, demanded equality of opportunity, and equality under the law.... And today, some talk not of opportunity but of redistributing rights. They'd pit one group against another, encourage people to think of others as competitors not colleagues. That's not the way to achieve justice and equality here in America. We need to adopt a more unifying, moral, and noble approach."[54] This attempt to demonize his opponents and justify his veto as moral in the tradition of the "great civil rights leaders of the past" was, to say the least, implausible.

The nadir of his argumentation on this issue was undoubtedly his claim that congressional Democrats were trying to turn the civil rights bill into a "women's issue" because of the Equal Rights Amendment.[55] Not only did this fail to address the actual issues relevant to the bill in question, but it also was "the only separate reference to gender during his first three years,"[56] indicating that women were well below the presidential radar. Bush did appoint more women (and fewer non-whites) as district court judges than had any previous contemporary president except Jimmy Carter,[57] suggesting that perhaps there were a given number of "minority appointments" available and that members of those groups could squabble amongst themselves for access to those appointments.

Bush attempted to deflect some attention away from the civil rights bill and toward other policy areas, especially to the economic realm, where he was surer of his ground: "Civil rights," he said, "are also crucial to protecting economic opportunity. Every one of us has a responsibility to speak out against racism, bigotry, and hate. We will continue our vigorous enforcement of existing statutes, and I will again press the Congress to strengthen the laws against employment discrimination without resorting to the use of unfair practices."[58] Bush tried to argue that the civil rights bill meant quotas, and quotas, not the absence of real, enforceable civil rights, were what constituted "unfairness," not the discrimination the civil rights bill purported to address.

Despite the weakness of his record on African American civil rights, Bush never faltered in support for one group: America's disabled. The Americans with Disabilities Act (ADA) was "an unprecedented piece of legislation,"[59] for which Bush perhaps received more credit than he was due,[60] but it is legislation he vaunted as one of the administration's main accomplishments. The ADA was the subject of Bush's most impassioned defense of civil rights: "The quest for civil rights is not a zero-sum game. It shouldn't mean advancing some at the expense of others. The quest for civil rights is a quest for individual rights and equal opportunity. And it's a crusade to throw open the doors of opportunity and tear down the walls of bigotry. The ADA works because it calls upon the best in the American people, and then Americans respond."[61] The ADA exemplified Bush's belief in the essential decency of Americans, in the importance of freedom and opportunity, and in the understanding that if the government makes it possible for people to enter America's mainstream, that is exactly where they will go. Because of our commitment to this shared history of freedom, opportunity, and independence, it is possible to welcome members of all groups into the American mainstream, as long as they can be used to exemplify those values. Civil rights for Bush meant inclusion and assimilation into the mainstream—and on the terms set by the mainstream.

Clinton, on the other hand, seemed more than willing to challenge the values of the mainstream. The issue of gays in the military in particular created for Clinton problems similar to the ones caused for Bush by the civil rights bill, indicating the peculiar weaknesses each president had on issues of national diversity. Just as for Bush, the civil rights bill fed into suspicions that Republicans wished to roll back advances on civil rights for blacks, the issue of gays in the military fed concerns that Clinton was more of an "old liberal" than a "New Democrat."[62] Many feared that he was more concerned with advancing the narrow agenda of a "special interest group" than with protecting the economic rights of the mainstream American middle class.

The evidence is that Clinton was taken by surprise by the reaction to the issue. He had campaigned on the rights of gay personnel to serve in the armed forces and in his initial action was simply acting on that promise. He failed to realize, however, that while he could change some aspect of the treatment of gays by executive order, congressional action would be required to change the Military Code of Conduct. He quickly realized that there was not sufficient support for any such action. Clinton thus faced a bind: he could not fulfill the letter of his campaign promise, and any action designed to accomplish part of that promise would alienate both gays and their supporters and opponents of his policy.

In facing this difficult situation, Clinton first tried to frame the issue in his preferred terms, arguing that it was not "identity" but "behavior" that was the appropriate focus. In an exchange with reporters during his first week as president, he said, "The principle behind this for me is that Americans who are willing to conform to the requirements of conduct within the military services, in my judgment, should be able to serve in the military and that people should be disqualified from serving in the military based on something they do, not based on who they are."[63] Note that the president claimed to be operating on the basis of principle, not out of expediency. He made this argument consistently. The problem was that the principle seemed to change from one demanding inclusion to one advocating compromise.

Note also that this position directly contradicts the conception of homosexuality as a fundamental part of an individual's identity. This understanding was clear among members of the Christian communities opposed to removing the ban; it also was clear among gay rights groups as well, who argued that homosexuality was inherent not in what one does, but in who one is. Clinton thus offered a compromise that was no real compromise, and that contravened the commonly held understanding of homosexuality.[64] His frame was untenable from the start.

When it became obvious that this issue would continue to dominate news, Clinton then tried to duck the issue. He referred the issue to a committee for study, refused to answer questions,[65] and became increasingly short-tempered as the issue seemed to control more and more of the attention the media paid to his presidency. Still, he tried to have it both ways, and he portrayed himself both as the protector of gays and their rights and as a moderate member of the mainstream. When challenged by gay advocacy groups for his unwillingness to participate in a march for gay rights, he replied to a question on whether he was "snubbing" gays, by saying, "I don't see how any serious person could claim that I have snubbed the gay community in this country, having taken the position I have not only on the issue of the military but of participation in Government. I have, I believe it is clear, taken a stronger position against discrimination than any of my predecessors. . . . It had nothing to do with politics and everything to do with the fact that I grew up in a segregated society and have very strong feelings about the right of everybody who is willing to work hard and play by the rules to participate in American life."[66] Note the qualification of his critics. No "serious person" would question him on this; no one should question that he acted on principle alone. Finally, note his attempt to imbue the fight over gays in the military with the legitimacy of the fight to end segregation, casting opponents of removing the ban as equals to those attempting to fend over removal of the ban to allow gays to serve in the military.

He continued to temporize on the issue, arguing even in the same speech both that "This is not about embracing any lifestyle," and "I think the only way our country can make it is if we can find somehow strength in our own diversity, even with people with whom we profoundly disagree, as long as we can agree on how we're going to treat each other and how we're going to conduct ourselves in public forums [sic]. That is the real issue."[67] Ignoring the fact that the debate was over exactly the question of "How we're going to conduct ourselves in public forums," these positions are not inconsistent, nor were they that hard to reconcile. But there is enough of an attempt to placate both sides of this complicated issue that when combined with Clinton's increasing reputation for "waffling"[68] made his position unclear enough to support challenges from both sides. Vagueness both worked for Clinton—audiences could read their preferred meanings into his words—and against him—they were liable to the rage of betrayal when they considered his actions less than fully accommodating of their preferred policies.

Clinton continued to insist that he did not propose any changes in the Code of Military Conduct[69] as a way of deflecting criticism that he was "too liberal." In contrast to his earlier equation of the fight to include gays in the military with desegregation, he argued that the situation of gays was not analogous to that of blacks, and that the situation was vastly more complicated than most realized. He tried to portray the "compromise" as reasonable, fair, and equitable.

> The real thing you ought to ask is how long did it take before African Americans, in this case, were treated fully equally in the service? It didn't just happen snap with Truman's order. It didn't happen after Truman's order and it developed a long time after Truman's order. There was an explicit open involvement of the military culture with blacks in a segregated way for a very long time before this order was issued. The same thing happened with women. . . . It happened over a period of years as the military culture adapted to it. Now if I had done what you suggest, if I had just said that gays could serve and whatever they do in private is their own business—which I never committed to do in the campaign—I'll tell you exactly what would have happened. Congress would have overturned it immediately and done it on the defense bill and in ways that would have been difficult, if not impossible, for me to veto. So the situations simply aren't analogous. Congress had no intention of overturning President Truman's position, and it's something that built up over a long period of time, not something that just entered the public debate, in effect, about a year ago.[70]

So for Clinton it was not really a matter of principle but of what he could get through Congress; not a matter comparable to the civil rights movement or to segregation in the military, despite his earlier imputation that the situations were analogous. In effect, he was replying to gays in the military as whites long did to blacks in the segregated South—telling them that they needed to be patient, and when they had earned admission into the mainstream, they would be admitted therein.

Clinton's actions—and his rhetorical justifications of those actions—satisfied no one. He alienated devout Christians, threatened any conservative to middling supporters, and disappointed liberals.[71] He also raised doubts as to his leadership style, which many saw as neatly—and disastrously—encapsulated in his bumbling management of this issue.[72]

Bush sought to deal with minorities by incorporating them into the mainstream. Initially, Clinton attempted the less often tried route of bringing the mainstream around to one minority's way of thinking, and he found that change was considerably "easier to promise than to deliver."[73] Both presidents sought to render the process "fair"—given their differing opinions on what constituted "fairness." Neither answer worked for either president; neither proved a viable way of creating a national consensus.

The Role of Government: The Private Sphere Versus Government as Partner

In every issue area that did not explicitly involve foreign policy, George Bush preferred private to public action. Bush was a firm supporter of federalism, and like Reagan he sought to lessen Washington's influence over policy in a wide variety of domestic matters.[74] He supported returning programs to the states[75] and removing Washington from policy altogether in favor of the private sphere. For Bush, "The simple truth is this: Democracy and the freedoms it enshrines can never be the gift of government."[76] They were instead most properly understood as the province of the private sector, an understanding Bush traced back to the earliest days of the republic:

> Nineteen eighty-nine was an important year for another reason: because it reminded us of the role that government should and shouldn't play in enterprise. It set off a collective movement toward democracy worldwide that has all of us looking up from our work for a moment in wonder, bearing witness as the world confirmed the wisdom of our forefathers. They understood the importance of a limited government—those forefathers—so they fought for a social order that gave free reign [sic] to ambition and unleashed the power of individual aspiration. We rose, in fact, as a nation of upstarts who didn't know their place. This was a new idea: that government, far from fearing private initiative, should be all for it. It still seems like a new idea.[77]

What was true for the economy also was true for other areas of governmental policy. On education, for instance, he said, "You want to ensure that parents, not bureaucrats, decide how to care for America's children. And Wyomingites don't want to expand the budget of the bureaucracy, you want to expand the horizons of your kids."[78] By positing a world in which the horizons of children exist in diametric opposition to governmental bureaucracies and their budgets, Bush also constructed a world in which government was unlikely to be the appropriate response to a national domestic problem.

In relying upon the private sphere, Bush individuated both virtue and exclusion, used voluntarism to make the government less responsible for continued inequality, reconciled individualism with community, and set the frame for minorities as representatives but not members of the nation. Voluntarism came naturally to Bush, about whom it was said that "he was a deeply reactive man who has always been less interested in doing anything specific as president than in just *being* president. He had entered politics without a desire to accomplish anything, but rather just to *serve*."[79] Voluntarism gave Bush a way to extend his personal preferences into policy.

Voluntarism served other purposes as well: it individuated virtue, and it maintained existing hierarchies while reconciling the tensions between the individual and the community. Bush said: "We all have something to give. So, if you know how to read, find someone who can't. If you've got a hammer, find a nail. If you're not hungry, not lonely, not in trouble, seek out someone who is. Join the community of conscience. Do the hard work of freedom. And that will define the state of our Union. Since the birth of our nation, 'We the People' has been the source of our strength. What government can do alone is limited, but the potential of the American people knows no limits."[80] Private, not public, action is the answer to whatever problems America may face. This tactic blurred disparate and unequal things into a single mass; it also blurred the potential solutions to those things. Loneliness is not necessarily the province of governmental action; hunger, at least potentially, is. Bush made them equal, and equally amenable to private, not public, solutions.

For Clinton, the private sphere was not the locus of solutions to public problems. Instead, government needed to work with the private sphere as a partner. He argued this both in general and in the specifics of policy making. In terms of the general argument, Clinton said, "What I believe is that our problems are both personal and cultural and political and economic. And I don't intend to use the personal and cultural nature of our problems as an excuse to walk away from our common responsibility to do better."[81] In this 1995 quotation, he was arguing specifically against the Republican advocacy of privatizing many of government's functions, and for his own relevance as president,[82] but his commitment to making government a positive force rather than the demonized actor of the Republican rhetoric was real and ran throughout his administration.[83]

In terms of specifics, he advocated a National Service program, a sort of Clintonian version of Bush's "Points of Light" program, that would provide governmental incentives such as scholarships for national service: "National service is a challenge for Americans from every background and walk of life, and it values something far more than money. National service is nothing less than the American way to change America. It is rooted in the concept of community: the simple idea that none of us on our own will ever have as much to cherish about our own lives if we are out here all alone as we will if we work together . . . each of us has an obligation to serve."[84] Unlike Bush's program, Clinton's did not depend purely upon voluntarism, and thus provides a good example of the sort of partnership he advocated. Yet the National Service program garnered little public attention, and there were few other examples of such programs.[85] Clinton was happy, as in the case of welfare reform, to talk about the need to provide opportunity while demanding responsibility,[86] but the cases when he could actually point to specific legislation that did this were few and far between. If government was a partner to the private sector, then by the end of Clinton's first term it seemed to be something of a silent one.

The Language of Governing: "Celebratory Othering" versus Local Vernaculars

Those who were previously defined as being "outside" the mainstream were welcomed into that mainstream with rhetoric that I call "celebratory othering." This rhetoric has been increasingly practiced by presidents and has by now become something of an art form. Bush relied heavily on "American values" in his public speech, which he used as a way of including those who were otherwise somehow foreign or alien to him—and therefore to America.[87] As with other presidents who have based inclusion on shared values, it is important to note that the dominant culture controls which values are central, which groups are allowed to represent them, and on what occasions. These occasions are generally ethnic holidays, which function to both include certain groups as "their" holidays become "our" holidays and to underline the contingent nature of their inclusion—what is ceremonially given can be taken away without remark.

As a conservative and a member of the "greatest generation," it is no surprise that his most important value is freedom. In Bush's understanding, we are free, in part, because the Christian God blessed us. Bush often expressed his own faith and encouraged others to practice theirs. "Prayer," he said, "has a place not only in the life of every American but also in the life of our Nation, for we are truly one Nation under God."[88] Christianity formed an important part of his rhetoric on values, and he celebrated groups for their devotion to a Christian God: "Your good works and your faith and your beliefs are an inspiration to this country." He told the National Baptist Convention, "And it was the first American Baptists in Rhode Island who led the campaign for religious tolerance. And it was the Baptists who played an important role in securing our freedom of religion in the American Constitution. And it was the Baptists who, as pioneers, built sturdy new churches on the empty prairies and the plains of the West."[89] Without the Christian God, there could be no freedom. Even ignoring the exclusionary effects of this prose on American Indians and non-Christians, the president was essentially stating that those who failed to worship the Christian God also failed in their support for American freedom.[90] Freedom, Bush's most central value, depended upon the Christian God.

Bush, possibly because of his problems on racial questions, spoke relatively often to African American audiences, although almost always in celebration of "black" events. In all of these occasions, he worked to show that

"Black history is, in fact, America's history."[91] His narrative of "the black experience" was a fairly traditional one: "Despite first slavery and then segregation, African Americans have overcome seemingly insurmountable odds to be at the cutting edge of change in American society. From the winning of independence—when Crispus Attucks gave his life in the Boston Massacre and Benjamin Banneker helped draw the plans for our nation's capital—to the present day, black Americans have played a vital role in the development of the United States."[92] This narrative glossed over much of the pain and sorrow of the early history and nearly all of the struggle since; it selected certain African Americans who contributed to mainstream historical events and celebrated them as if they also celebrated mainstream black experiences. Crispus Attucks and Benjamin Banneker were important because they were present at events that are important to mainstream history. Few of us can name the white people who were killed in Boston or the white man who designed the Capitol, because for them, it is the event, not the individuals present at it, that matters. If, however, we argue that African Americans were present at these events, then we include them as equal actors in historical events at times when their exclusion was specific and largely uncontested. This is not an argument intended to demean African American contributions to mainstream America; it is simply to point out that to discuss "their" contributions to "our" history is to both include and to underline their continued exclusion. This is the heart of celebratory othering.

African Americans are not the only groups to be treated this way. American Jews, for example, remind us "that the enduring spirit of liberty can never be crushed by the cruel hand of tyranny and enslavement,"[93] the Irish "have long demonstrated a capacity for hard work, as well as a strong penchant for full, spirited, and upright living,"[94] and Hispanics and Latinos and Latinas are given credit for a history that "arose out of risk and romance,"[95] cherishing the values of "discipline, caring, patriotism, love of God."[96] All of these groups were celebrated in ways that were functionally interchangeable; ethnic pride was emphasized, and ethnicity was trivialized. Bush went so far as to call Columbus, a Genoan who sailed in the service of Spain, an "American." He said, "The American adventure has always had the capacity to inspire others and to astonish the world: the voyages of Columbus, the taming of a continent, the invention of flight. America's democracy is the world's greatest experiment that continues to unleash the creative energy of the world's most diverse population. It's what took American pioneers to the Moon and back. It's what will take you as far as your dreams can soar."[97] In this narrative, so satisfyingly a part of the dominant ideology, all immigrants were the same immigrants, with the same experiences, and they all revealed the same laudable things about America.

In the absence of knowledge of specific groups, Bush tended to include by listing: "Men, women, immigrants, Americans of every kind"[98] was a typical locution. Absent the sort of insensitivity made famous by Reagan's Interior Secretary James Watt, this sort of listing offends no one, ostensibly includes everyone, and costs nothing. But note that its use conflated different experiences of different groups and put all experiences of all groups into the terms and experiences of the dominant culture: "The story of America has been the story of opportunity. Throughout our history, we've pioneered the frontiers of liberty for all humanity.... The story of opportunity in America is the story of Thomas Paine and Frederick Douglass, Clara Barton, the Wright Brothers, Rosa Parks."[99] As should be obvious, the experiences of the people in this group are simply not condensable to one story without rendering those experiences meaningless. They are not one story but many stories, and each of them highlights something different about the nation and its history. This does not mean that common ground is not possible, but that truly common ground may not be the ground determined by the dominant culture and its attendant hierarchies, a possibility ignored and rendered inconceivable in Bush's rhetoric.

To his credit, Bush also spoke out against racism and in favor of diversity. During the Iraqi war, for instance, he said, "But I want to take this opportunity to tell you something that bothers me because I've heard from some and then I've read accounts that suggest Arab Americans in this country, because of the conflict abroad, are being discriminated against, and it's causing pain in families in this country. And there is no room for discrimination against anybody in the United States."[100] His statements against racism, prejudice, and bigotry were not confined to situations resulting from military conflict but formed a consistent pattern in his discussions to and about minority groups. In a typical example, he said, "Discrimination, whether on the basis of race, national origin, sex, religion, or disability, is worse than wrong. It's an evil that strikes at the very heart of the American ideal."[101] Bush backed up these words with some action: he put minorities in his cabinet, including two Hispanics (Lauro Cavanos and Manuel Lujan) and the controversial African American, Louis Sullivan. Arguably, this reflects more the representative nature of the cabinet than the politics of the Bush administration,[102] but in Bush's defense, he also appointed Colin Powell as chair of the joint chiefs of staff.

But such actions aside, celebratory othering is a distortion—of American history, and of the American present. This is true even when Bush was ostensibly correcting the historical record. In the middle of the Iraqi war, for instance, he took the occasion of Black History Month to celebrate the Tuskegee Airmen: "And they never received the credit, they never received the credit they deserve for their devoted patriotism, for their vision, and their sacrifices ... for two centuries, black soldiers have established a record of pride in the face of incredible obstacles."[103] This made it appear that now that credit was being given, there were no longer any race-related problems in the American military, no discrimination, because all of that was safely in the past. Bush could talk about past discrimination; current discriminatory practices were erased.

Clinton had no interest in erasing past discrimination, and he evinced no reluctance to discuss discrimination in the present. He was proud of assembling the most diverse cabinet in history, and issues of formal representation were crucial, if not fully determinative, of his cabinet appointees.[104] Indeed, his emphasis on diversity led to more than a few problems, as the bungled nominations of Zoe Baird and Lani Gunier attest.[105] In addition to these well-publicized problems, the emphasis on diversity brought others as well, including a delayed appointments process. There also is some evidence that the diversity went only so deep, and that most of the important decisions were made by a small group of white men.[106]

Despite his emphasis on diversity, Bill Clinton did his fair share of celebratory othering,[107] and he also danced a fine line between the inclusion of immigrants as "real" Americans and promising to defend our borders against illegal immigrants, whom he tended to associate with terrorists and other threats to the national well-being.[108] Interestingly, and in an impressionistic comparison with other recent presidents, it seems that Clinton was actually less inclined than others to speak to minority groups constituted as minority groups. By this I mean that while he did address Islamic, Jewish, and other groups—and tended to do so on holidays or other occasions special to those groups—he was more likely to speak to communities constituted by geography (the citizens of Milwaukee) than by ethnicity or religious affiliation (the Knights of Columbus). Thus while he showed no reluctance to engage in this rhetoric, his opportunities for celebratory othering were rather more limited than those of other presidents. Thus, and especially when talking with, to, or about African Americans, Clinton validated both past and continuing discrimination, and he tended to talk to minority groups in their local vernaculars.

Even in his first term, and before his Initiative on Race, Clinton was willing to talk about diversity and how troubling it was to the nation. He talked about the problems of being a diverse nation, and he talked about opening up conversations on these problems. In remarks at American University, given in his first months as president, Clinton said:

> Look now at our new immigrant Nation and think of the world which we are tending. Look at how diverse and multiethnic and multilingual we are, in a world in which the ability to communicate with all kinds of people from all over the world and to understand them will be critical. Look at our civic habits of tolerance and respect. They are not perfect in our own eyes. It grieved us all when there was so much trouble a year ago in Los Angeles. But Los Angeles is a country with 150 different ethnic groups of widely differing levels of education and access to capital and income. It is a miracle that we get along as well as we do. And all you have to do is look at Bosnia, where the differences were not so great, to see how well we have done in spite of our difficulties.[109]

As this quotation makes clear, Clinton was aware of the problems; he also saw in them a cause for celebration, because they were so much more often manageable than not; Los Angeles, for all its troubles, was not Bosnia. He sounded this theme again and again.[110]

While Clinton tended to locate the problems of diversity in the structures of governance and the private sphere—that is, like most liberals, he considered them systemic rather than individual—he was not averse to calling upon members of minority communities to improve their individual conduct. His rhetoric, especially on matters of race and equality, was charged with both compassion and exhortations for individual responsibility. In Memphis, for instance, in one of the best speeches of his speech-laden presidency,[111] Clinton imagined a conversation with Martin Luther King Jr., who would "give us a report card on the last 25 years."[112] King, according to Clinton, would have praise for the considerable progress we have made as a nation since 1968. But he would also express sorrow:

> "But," he would say, "I did not live and die to see the American family destroyed. I did not live and die to see 13-year-old boys get automatic weapons and gun down 9-year-olds just for the kick of it. I did not live and die to see people destroy their own lives with drugs and build drug fortunes destroying the lives of others. That is not what I came here to do." "I fought for freedom," he would say, "but not for the freedom of people to kill each other with reckless abandon, not for the freedom of children to impregnate each other with babies and then abandon them, nor for the freedom of adult fathers of children to walk away from the children they created and abandon them, as if they didn't amount to anything." He would say, "This is not what I lived and died for. I fought to stop white people from being so filled with hate that they would wreak violence on black people. I did not fight for the right of black people to murder other black people on a daily basis."[113]

For a white president to go to the city where Dr. King was assassinated, and from there to put words into Dr. King's mouth, was an act breathtaking in its audacity. Yet it worked, and it worked at least in part because Clinton was adept in his use of the local vernacular—he could speak to blacks in the tones and cadences of their traditions; and in Memphis he spoke of "us" in a way that usefully constituted a white president as part of the "us" of the struggle for civil rights. He made the problems many whites relegate exclusively to "the black community" the problems of "America."

Memphis was not the only, nor even the most eloquent, example of this. Near the end of his first term, Clinton spoke at the University of Texas: "When a child is gunned down on a street in the Bronx, no matter what our race, he is an American child. When a woman dies from a beating, no matter what our race or hers, she is our American sister. And every time drugs course through the veins of another child, it clouds the future of all our American children. Whether we like it or not, we are one nation, one family, indivisible. And for us, divorce or separation are not options."[114] Through this language, Clinton did seem to be, in Toni Morrison's famous phrase, "America's first black president," and there did seem to be a promise of the capacity for national consensus. Yet he was not as faithful to the promise that this identity seemed to hold when it came to the details of policy, as his stance on affirmative action and welfare reform indicated.[115] He left the white middle class confused, ambivalent, and resentful[116] without cementing any real gains for minority constituencies. The gains African Americans may have made under his administration were largely symbolic, and all too easily eroded.

CONCLUSION: DIVERSITY ACROSS THE PARTISAN DIVIDE

As this is being written, Senate Majority Leader Trent Lott (R-MS) has just resigned his position as majority leader of the United States Senate because of remarks he made ostensibly in honor of Strom Thurmond—remarks that had definite racial overtones. And the chairman of the Augusta, Georgia, golf course where the master's tournament is played is continuing his defiant refusal to allow women members into the club. Such events remind us all too painfully that matters of national identity and the place of minorities in that identity remain contested. The difficulties of addressing these matters directly also remain considerable.[117]

Yet they also remain the province of the president, the only nationally elected leader, the only one who represents all of "the people." No president, of course, has ever represented all of us; presidents respond to their coalitions, both electoral and governing, and with very few exceptions, most of them in wartime, the degree of national unity has been far short of overwhelming. As Clinton pointed out, however, the degree of national disunity also is far less than one might suppose from watching the headlines.

Presidents are institutional actors. They protect national institutions even while seeking to bend those institutions to their individual will. Presidents are thus also conservative political actors. And importantly, institutions tend to be significantly stronger than the individuals who temporarily inhabit them, thus forcing presidents and other elected officials into even more conservative positions. Institutions, by definition, resist change.

Presidents thus face a daunting task when it comes to articulating issues of diversity, inclusion, and national identity. It is significantly easier to criticize presidential policy and rhetoric than it is to derive positive alternatives to those actions. These are difficult problems, and sorting through them will likely continue to absorb significant presidential attention well into the twenty-first century.

NOTES

1. William J. Clinton, "Inaugural Address," January 20, 1993, *Public Papers of the President, William J. Clinton* (Washington, D.C.: U.S. Government Printing Office, 1994), 1.

2. This chapter is based in part on material included in *Americans in Light and Shadow: Presidential Articulations of National Identity*, a book manuscript in progress. The arguments here are abbreviated versions of the longer discussions available in that manuscript.

3. In order to keep the amount of data both equitable and reasonable, I used Clinton's first term; this allowed me to do a cleaner comparison between Bush and Clinton but also kept the furor of Monica Lewinsky and the President's Initiative on Race from skewing the data.

4. Alan Brinkley, *The Unfinished Nation: A Concise History of the American People* (New York: McGraw-Hill, 1993), 897–98. See also Robert M. Stein and Kenneth N. Bickers, *Perpetuating the Pork Barrel: Policy Subsystems and American Democracy* (New York: Cambridge University Press, 1995).

5. See Jo Freeman and Victoria Johnson, eds., *Waves of Protest* (New York: Rowman and Littlefield, 1999); David S. Meyer and Sidney Tarrow, eds., *The Social Movement Society* (New York: Rowman and Littlefield, 1997); Herbert Simons, "Requirements, Problems, Strategies: A Theory of Persuasion for Social Movements," *Quarterly Journal of Speech* 56 (1970): 1–11.

6. Brinkley, *The Unfinished Nation*, 911–12.

7. Carol Gelderman, *All the Presidents' Words: The Bully Pulpit and the Creation of the Virtual Presidency* (New York: Walker and Co., 1997), 139–43; Mary E. Stuckey, *Strategic Failures in the Modern Presidency* (Cresskill, N.J.: Hampton Press, 1997), 116–26.

8. Richard Morris and Peter Ehrenhaus, eds., *Cultural Legacies of Vietnam: Uses of the Past in the Present* (Norwood, N.J.: Ablex, 1990); George N. Dionisopoulos and Steven Goldzwig, "The Meaning of Vietnam: Political Rhetoric as Revisionist Cultural History," *Quarterly Journal of Speech* 78 (1992): 61–78.

9. See, among many others, Robert Dallek, *Ronald Reagan: The Politics of Symbolism* (Cambridge, Mass.: Harvard University Press, 1984); Robert E. Denton Jr., *The Primetime Presidency of Ronald Reagan: The Era of the Television Presidency* (New York: Praeger, 1994); Paul D. Erickson, *Reagan Speaks: The Making of an American Myth* (New York: New York University Press, 1985).

10. David A. Stockman, *The Triumph of Politics: Why the Reagan Revolution Failed* (New York: Harper and Row, 1986).

11. Jerry Hagstrom, *Beyond Reagan: The New Landscape in American Politics* (New York: Penguin, 1988), 19; Howard Zinn, *A People's History of the United States 1492–Present*, revised and updated ed. (New York: Harper Perennial, 1995), 561.

12. Bob Woodward, *The Commanders* (New York: Simon and Schuster, 1991), 47.

13. Erwin C. Hargrove, *The President as Leader: Appealing to the Better Angels of Our Nature* (Lawrence: University Press of Kansas, 1998), 62; Paul Johnson, *A History of the American People* (New York: Harper Collins, 1997), 931.

14. Bush did try to appease conservatives, who remained suspicious of him. See, for example, Matthew C. Moen and Kenneth T. Palmer, "Poppy and His Conservative Passengers," in *Leadership and the Bush Presidency: Prudence or Drift in an Era of Change?*, Ryan J. Barilleaux and Mary E. Stuckey (New York: Praeger, 1992), 133–46.

15. Brinkley, *The Unfinished Nation*, 889.

16. Sidney Blumenthal, *Pledging Allegiance: The Last Campaign of the Cold War* (New York: HarperCollins, 1990), 51.

17. Richard Rose, *The Post-Modern Presidency: George Bush Meets the World* (Chatham, N.J.: Chatham House, 1991). See also David Mervin, *George Bush and the Guardianship Presidency* (New York: St. Martin's Press, 1996).

18. Mary E. Stuckey, *The President as Interpreter-in-Chief* (Chatham, N.J.: Chatham House, 1991), 124.

19. John Robert Greene, *The Presidency of George Bush* (Lawrence: University Press of Kansas, 2000), 5, 79.

20. Stanley Greenberg, *Middle Class Dreams: The Politics and Power of the New American Majority*, revised and updated ed. (New Haven, Conn.: Yale University Press, 1995), 13; Koichi Suzuki, L. Alexander Norsworthy, and Helen C. Gleason, *The Clinton Revolution: An Inside Look at the New Administration* (Lanham, Mass.: University Press of America, 1993), xi, 1; John Kenneth White, *Still Seeing Red: How the Cold War Shapes the New American Politics* (New York: Westview Press, 1997), 219.

21. On the importance of these matters to understanding at least the Clinton administration, see Virginia Sapiro and David T. Canon, "Race, Gender, and the Clinton Presidency," in *The Clinton Presidency*, ed. Colin Campbell and Bert A. Rockman (New York: Chatham House, Seven Bridges Press, 2000), 207–41.

22. See, for example, William W. Lammers and Michael A. Genovese, *The Presidency and Domestic Policy: Comparing Leadership Styles, FDR to Clinton* (Washington, D.C.: CQ Press, 2000), 279.

23. Stephen Skowronek, in fact, refers to Bush as Reagan's "faithful son." See Skowronek, *The Politics Presidents Make: Leadership From John Adams to George Bush* (Cambridge, Mass.: Belknap Press of Harvard University Press, 1993), 429. See also Michael Duffy and Dan Goodgame, *Marching in Place: The Status Quo Presidency of George Bush* (New York: Simon and Schuster, 1992), 70.

24. On the contrast between the Reagan and Bush styles, see, among many others, Lance Blakesley, *Presidential Leadership From Eisenhower to Clinton* (Chicago: Nelson-Hall, 1995); George C. Edwards III, "George Bush and the Public Presidency: The Politics of Inclusion," in *The Bush Presidency: First Appraisals*, ed. Colin Campbell and Bert Rockman (Chatham, N.J.: Chatham House, 1991), 129–54; Kerry Mullins and Aaron Wildavsky, "The Procedural Presidency of George Bush," *Political Science Quarterly* 107 (1992): 39–40; Rockman, "The Leadership Style of George Bush," in

The Bush Presidency; Mary E. Stuckey and Frederick J. Antczak, "Governance as Political Theater: George Bush and the MTV Presidency," in *Leadership and the Bush Presidency*, 24–34.

25. Johnson, *A History of the American People*, 931. See also Gelderman, *All the Presidents' Words*, 143.

26. Blumenthal, *Pledging Allegiance*; Hargrove, *The President as Leader*, 171; Woodward, *The Commanders*, 47.

27. Charles O. Jones, *Clinton and Congress, 1993–1996: Risk, Restoration, and Reelection* (Norman: University of Oklahoma Press, 1999), 45, 75.

28. Duffy and Goodgame, *Marching in Place*, 65–66.

29. Bush, Inaugural Address, January 20, 1989, *The Public Papers of the Presidents of the United States: George H. W. Bush* (Washington, D.C.: Government Printing Office, 1989–92), 3.

30. Hargrove, *The President as Leader*, 70.

31. Bush, Remarks at a White House Luncheon for Business Leaders, February 2, 1989, *Public Papers*, 50.

32. Bush, Remarks to Davidson Interior Trim Employees in Dover, New Hampshire, January 15, 1992, *Public Papers*, 100.

33. Brinkley, *The Unfinished Nation*, 890. See also Duffy and Goodgame, *Marching in Place*, 63; Greene, *The Presidency of George Bush*, 61; Robert J. Thompson and Carmine Scavo, "The Home Front: Domestic Policy in the Bush Years," in *Leadership and the Bush Presidency*, 150–64; John W. Winkle III, "George Bush and Inertial Federalism," in *Leadership and the Bush Presidency*, 81–88.

34. Greene, *The Presidency of George Bush*, 61. See also Byron W. Daynes and Glen Sussman, "The Presidency and Social Policy," in *Presidential Frontiers: Underexplored Issues in White House Politics*, ed. Ryan J. Barilleaux (Westport, Conn.: Praeger, 1998), 99–118; Lammers and Genovese, *The Presidency and Domestic Policy*, 281–82.

35. Duffy and Goodgame, *Marching in Place*, 56–57.

36. Greene, *The Presidency of George Bush*, 184. See also Gelderman, *All the President's Words*, 143–54.

37. Clinton, Remarks at the Democratic Governor's Association Dinner, February 1, 1993, *Public Papers*, 30.

38. Clinton, Inaugural Address.

39. Clinton, Remarks at the Democratic Governor's Association Dinner, February 1, 1993, *Public Papers*, 31.

40. Clinton, The President's Radio Address, February 13, 1993, *Public Papers*, 102.

41. Jeffrey H. Birnbaum, *Madhouse: The Private Turmoil of Working for the President* (New York: Random House, 1996), 7; Elizabeth Drew, *Showdown: The Struggle between the Gingrich Congress and the Clinton White House* (New York: Simon and Schuster, 1996), 190; Charles O. Jones, "Campaigning to Govern: The Clinton Style," in *The Clinton Presidency: First Appraisals*, ed. Colin Campbell and Bert A. Rockman

(Chatham, N.J.: Chatham House, 1996), 26; Stanley Renshon, *High Hopes: The Clinton Presidency and the Politics of Ambition* (New York: New York University Press, 1996), 56–65.

42. Greene, *The Presidency of George Bush*, 144.

43. Bush, Remarks at the American Spectator Annual Dinner, January 22, 1990, *Public Papers*, 72.

44. Bush, Inaugural Address, January 20, 1989, *Public Papers*, 1.

45. Bush, Remarks to the Knights of Columbus Supreme Council Convention in New York City, August 5, 1992, *Public Papers*, 1307.

46. Steven A. Shull, *American Civil Rights Policy From Truman to Clinton: The Role of Presidential Leadership* (Armonk, N.Y.: ME Sharpe, 1999), xiii.

47. For example, as a member of Congress, Bush denounced the Civil Rights Act of 1964 but did create something of a stir in conservative circles with his support for the Fair Housing Act of 1968. See Phillip A. Klinkner, with Roger A. Smith, *The Unsteady March: The Rise and Decline of Racial Inequality in America* (Chicago: University of Chicago Press, 1999), 284–85.

48. Shull, *American Civil Rights Policy*, 96–100.

49. Bush, Exchange with Reporters in San Francisco, California, *Public Papers*, 1487.

50. Shull, *American Civil Rights Policy*, 4.

51. Bush, Remarks to the National Council of La Raza, July 18, 1990, *Public Papers*, 1023.

52. Duffy and Goodgame, *Marching in Place*, 100. See also Klinkner, with Smith, *The Unsteady March*, 305.

53. David Zarefsky, "George Bush and the Metamorphosis of Civil Rights Discourse, 1965–1990," paper presented at the Annual Conference on Presidential Rhetoric, College Station, Texas, March 1999.

54. Bush, Remarks at the United States Military Academy Commencement Ceremony in West Point, N.Y., June 1, 1991, *Public Papers*, 591.

55. Shull, *American Civil Rights Policy*, 63.

56. Ibid.

57. Ibid., 141.

58. Bush, Address before a Joint Session of Congress on the State of the Union, January 29, 1991, *Public Papers*, 77.

59. Shull, *American Civil Rights Policy*, 42; Zinn, *A People's History*, 617.

60. Greene, *The Presidency of George Bush*, 71.

61. Bush, Remarks Commemorating the First Anniversary of the Signing of the Americans with Disabilities Act of 1990, July 26, 1991, *Public Papers*, 963–64.

62. James MacGregor Burns and Georgia J. Sorenson, with Robin Gerber and Scott W. Webster, *Dead Center: Clinton-Gore Leadership and the Perils of Moderation* (New York: Scribner, 1999), 99; Jones, *Clinton and Congress*, 76; White, *Still Seeing Red*, 221.

63. Clinton, Remarks Honoring the School Principal of the Year and an Exchange with Reporters, January 28, 1993, *Public Papers*, 18.

64. Denise M. Bostdorff, "Clinton's Characteristic Issue Management Style: Caution, Conciliation, and Conflict Avoidance in the Case of Gays in the Military," in *The Clinton Presidency: Images, Issues, and Communication Strategies*, ed. Robert E. Denton, Jr., and Rachel L. Holloway (New York: Praeger, 1996),199.

65. Clinton, The President's News Conference, March 23, 1993, *Public Papers*, 337–38; Clinton, Interview with Dan Rather of CBS News, March 24, 1993, *Public Papers*, 352–53; Clinton, Remarks on the Appointment of Kristine M. Gebbie as AIDS Policy Coordinator and Exchange with Reporters, June 25, 1993, *Public Papers*, 933.

66. Clinton, Remarks to Law Enforcement Organizations and an Exchange with Reporters, April 15, 1993, *Public Papers*, 443–44.

67. Clinton, Remarks to the Newspaper Association of America in Boston, Massachusetts, April 25, 1993, *Public Papers*, 504.

68. Colin Campbell, "Management in a Sandbox: Why the Clinton White House Failed to Cope with Gridlock," in *The Clinton Presidency: First Appraisals*, 64; George C. Edwards III, "Frustration and Folly: Bill Clinton and the Public Presidency," in *The Clinton Presidency: First Appraisals*, 241; Renshon, *High Hopes*, 75.

69. Clinton, Question and Answer Session with the Cleveland City Club, May 10, 1993, *Public Papers*, 610.

70. Clinton, Interview with Larry King, July 20, 1993, *Public Papers*, 1146.

71. Rita K. Whillock, "The Compromising Clinton: Images of Failure, a Record of Success," in *The Clinton Presidency*, 134; Graham K. Wilson, "The Clinton Administration and Interest Groups, in *The Clinton Presidency: First Appraisals*, 223.

72. Bostdorff, "Clinton's Characteristic Issue Management Style," 203; Jones, *Clinton and Congress*, 76; Whillock, "The Compromising Clinton," 131.

73. Burns and Sorenson, *Dead Center*, 121; Jones, *Clinton and Congress*, 39; Michael Waldman, *POTUS Speaks: Finding the Words That Defined the Clinton Presidency* (New York: Simon and Schuster, 2000), 69.

74. Duffy and Goodgame, *Marching in Place*, 97.

75. Bush, Remarks to Members of the National Conference of State Legislators, March 6, 1998, *Public Papers*, 199. For a discussion of Bush on federalism, see John Winkle, "George Bush and Inertial Federalism," in *Leadership and the Bush Presidency*, ed. Ryan J. Barilleaux and Mary E. Stuckey (Westport, Conn.: Greenwood, 1992), 81–88.

76. Bush, Remarks at the Annual Meeting of the United States Chamber of Commerce, April 30, 1991, *Public Papers*, 585.

77. Bush, Remarks at a White House Briefing for the Leadership of National Small Business United and the National Association of Women Business Owners, May 1, 1990, *Public Papers*, 597.

78. Bush, Remarks at the Frontier Days and State Centennial Parade in Cheyenne, Wyoming, July 20, 1990, *Public Papers*, 1039.

79. Duffy and Goodgame, *Marching in Place*, 21, emphases in original. See also Lammers and Genovese, *The Presidency and Domestic Policy*, 282.

80. Bush, Address before Congress on the State of the Union, January 29, 1991, *Public Papers*, 75.

81. Clinton, Remarks at a Fund-raiser in Chicago, Illinois, June 29, 1995, *Public Papers*, 983.

82. Drew, *Showdown*, 181.

83. See, for example, Clinton, Remarks on National Service at Rutgers University in New Brunswick, March 1, 1993, *Public Papers*, 225; Clinton, Remarks at Cal State University Northridge, January 17, 1995, *Public Papers*, 56.

84. Clinton, Remarks on National Service at Rutgers University in New Brunswick, March 1, 1993, *Public Papers*, 225.

85. There are some important exceptions to this general rule, as in the establishment of the Holocaust Museum in Washington, D.C. At its opening reception, Clinton argued eloquently for the public sphere as a place where values such as tolerance are fostered. See Clinton, Remarks at a Reception for the Opening of the United States Holocaust Memorial Museum, April 21, 1993, *Public Papers*, 473–74.

86. See, for example, Clinton, Remarks at a Town Hall Meeting in Detroit, February 10, 1993, *Public Papers*, 81; Clinton, Address before a Joint Session of Congress on Administration Goals, February 17, 1993, *Public Papers*, 114; Clinton, Remarks on the Withdrawal of Lani Gunier To Be Assistant Attorney General and an Exchange with Reporters, June 3, 1993, *Public Papers*, 808.

87. Stuckey, *The President as Interpreter-in-Chief*, 125.

88. Bush, Remarks at the National Prayer Breakfast, January 30, 1992, *Public Papers*, 169.

89. Bush, Remarks to the National Baptist Convention in New Orleans, Louisiana, September 8, 1989, *Public Papers*, 1169. See also, Bush, Remarks at Mount Zion Missionary Baptist Church in Los Angeles, California, May 7, 1992, *Public Papers*, 715.

90. Bush, Remarks at the Frontier Days and State Centennial Parade in Cheyenne, Wyoming, July 20, 1990, *Public Papers*, 1023.

91. Bush, Message on the Observance of National Afro-American (Black) History Month, February 25, 1991, *Public Papers*, 129.

92. Bush, Message on the Observance of National Afro-American (Black) History Month, February 1, 1989, *Public Papers*, 39.

93. Bush, Message on the Observance of Passover, March 29, 1991, *Public Papers*, 319.

94. Bush, Message on the Observance of St. Patrick's Day, March 7, 1991, *Public Papers*, 224; see also Bush, Message on the Observance of St. Patrick's Day, March 6, 1989, *Public Papers*, 176; Bush, Message on the Observance of St. Patrick's Day, March 13, 1990, *Public Papers*, 364.

95. Bush, Remarks at the Annual Convention of the United States Hispanic Chamber of Commerce in Chicago, Illinois, September 20, 1991, *Public Papers*, 1195–96; see also Bush, Remarks at a Cinco De Mayo Celebration, May 5, 1989, *Public Papers*, 520; Bush, Remarks to the United States Hispanic Chamber of Commerce, September 8, 1989, *Public Papers*, 1165.

96. Bush, Remarks to the Hispanic-American Community in Los Angeles, California, April 25, 1989, *Public Papers*, 477.

97. Bush, Remarks at the Texas A&I Commencement Ceremony in Kingsville, Texas, May 11, 1990, *Public Papers*, 643.

98. Bush, Remarks at a White House Briefing for the Leadership of Small Business United at the National Association of Women Business Owners, May 1, 1990, *Public Papers*, 597.

99. Bush, Remarks at a Meeting of the American Society of Association Executives, February 27, 1991, *Public Papers*, 184.

100. Bush, Remarks to Arab-American Leaders, January 25, 1991, *Public Papers*, 62.

101. Bush, Remarks on Signing the Civil Rights Act of 1991, November 21, 1991, *Public Papers*, 1502; see also, Bush, Statement on the Meeting with Benjamin Hooks, Executive Director of the NAACP, January 9, 1990, *Public Papers*, 28; Bush, Remarks at the Minority Business Development Week Awards Ceremony, September 25, 1991, *Public Papers*, 1211.

102. Greene, *The Presidency of George Bush*, 48.

103. Bush, Remarks on the Observance of Afro-American (Black) History Month, February 25, 1991, *Public Papers*, 172.

104. Joel D. Aberbach, "The Federal Executive under Clinton," in *The Clinton Presidency: First Appraisals*, 168; Burns and Sorenson, *Dead Center*, 80; Campbell, "Management in a Sandbox," 68; Jones, "Campaigning to Govern," 25.

105. Aberbach, "The Federal Executive," 172–74; Birnbaum, *Madhouse*, 39; Burns and Sorenson, *Dead Center*, 80, 95; David M. O'Brien, "Clinton's Legal Policy and the Courts: Rising from Disarray or Turning Around and Around?" in *The Clinton Presidency: First Appraisals*, 130–31; Waldman, *POTUS Speaks*, 25; Wilson, "The Clinton Administration," 224.

106. Birnbaum, *Madhouse*, 154.

107. See, for example, Clinton, Remarks at the Ireland Fund Dinner, March 16, 1993, *Public Papers*, 312; Clinton, Remarks on Signing the Greek Independence Day Proclamation, March, 25, 1993, *Public Papers*, 357–58; Clinton, Remarks on Signing the Asian/Pacific American Heritage Month Proclamation, May 3, 1993, *Public Papers*, 554.

108. See, for example, Clinton, Remarks and an Exchange with Reporters on Immigration Policy, July 27, 1993, *Public Papers*, 1194; Clinton, Interview with the California Media, July 30, 1993, *Public Papers*, 1245; Clinton, Interview with the Nevada Media, August 3, 1993, *Public Papers*, 1319.

109. Clinton, Remarks at the American University Centennial Celebration, February 26, 1993, *Public Papers*, 214.

110. Clinton, Remarks and a Question and Answer Session at the Adult Learning Center in New Brunswick, N.J., March 1, 1993, *Public Papers*, 220; Clinton, Remarks to the Community in Milwaukee, Wisc., June 1, 1993, *Public Papers*, 788; Clinton, Remarks at a Children's Town Meeting, March 19, 1994, *Public Papers*, 490.

111. Renshon, *High Hopes*, 2.

112. Clinton, Remarks and a Question and Answer Session at the Adult Learning Center in New Brunswick, N.J., March 1, 1993, *Public Papers*, 220.

113. Clinton, Remarks to the Convocation of the Church of God in Memphis, November 13, 1993, *Public Papers*, 1983.

114. Ibid., 1983–84.

115. Burns and Sorenson, *Dead Center*, 228–29; Peter Edelman, *Searching for America's Heart: RFK and the Renewal of Hope* (New York: Houghton Mifflin, 2001), 142; Sapiro and Canon, "Race, Gender, and the Clinton Presidency," in *The Clinton Presidency*, 192–93; Waldman, *POTUS Speaks*, 128.

116. Greenberg, *Middle Class Dreams*, 21; Harold W. Stanley, "The Parties, the President, and the 1994 Midterm Elections," in *The Clinton Presidency: First Appraisals*, 194.

117. White, *Still Seeing Red*, 267.

11

A President Transformed

Bush's Pre- and Post-September 11 Rhetoric and Image

Jeremy D. Mayer and Mark J. Rozell

> The real measure of a person is how he responds to bad news.
> —George W. Bush's 2000 campaign memoir[1]

An examination of the rhetoric and the public image of President George W. Bush reveals a number of paradoxes. First, during an era in which the public aspects of the job had become by many accounts omnipresent, the public elected a president who was notably unskilled at public speaking. Second, Bush won an electoral contest that revolved around a medium, television, with which he is particularly uncomfortable. Third, Bush has sought to reduce the public role the presidency plays, while at the same time seeking to expand presidential power and restore executive prerogatives in other areas. This development is all the more surprising given that many political scientists now believe that the public role of the president is an increasingly vital source of executive power. Fourth, stylistically, this scion of wealth and privilege presents Bush as an anti-elitist and anti-intellectual.

One predictable aspect of Bush's rhetorical presidency is the role of religion in his speeches. The first born-again president since Jimmy Carter, Bush rode to the Republican nomination and onto victory in large part because of the fervor of his Christian Right base, and this is evident in the rhetoric of his most important speeches. However, there remains a final paradox: the man who had little more than average skill in rhetoric and who had sought to reduce the public role of the presidency was soon faced with the monumental task of speaking almost daily to a distraught and an anxious nation in the midst of one of our greatest crises. Should the presidency of George W. Bush ultimately be judged a successful one, it will be in no small part because of his growth as a rhetorician.

In this chapter, then, we will discuss Bush's general rhetorical skills, his initial attempt to reduce the public role of the president, his presentation of self as a commoner and an anti-intellectual, the role of religion in his speeches, and the successful changes in his rhetoric in the aftermath of September 11, 2001.

BUSH AS ORATOR: AN IMPERFECT SPEECHIFIER

The rhetoric and oratory of a president has typically been one of the measures of presidential excellence. Great presidents are almost always those who have rallied the nation with their speeches and oratory. The words of Franklin Delano Roosevelt in the midst of the Great Depression and on the eve of World War II set a modern standard perhaps matched only by Kennedy's inaugural speech or Reagan's D-Day anniversary rhetoric. It was once possible for the occupant of the White House to pursue a successful "textual presidency," the term historian Joseph Ellis applied to the notoriously shy Thomas Jefferson, who may have given only two speeches during his eight years in office. However, since the dawn of television, presidents have been increasingly judged by their ability to speak in public. Indeed, political scientists have given increasingly greater attention to the public aspects of the presidency since the Reagan era. Earlier studies of the presidency had focused some attention on the importance of a president maintaining his standing in public opinion.[2] Today, many scholars see the modern president as, by necessity, using the mass media to speak over the heads of the Washington establishment to rally public support to bring about his agenda.[3]

George W. Bush entered the Oval Office in 2001 with perhaps more disadvantages than any modern elected president. Having lost the popular vote to Al Gore, Bush could not claim a mandate. Although his party initially held razor-thin majorities in both Houses of Congress, Bush lacked electoral coattails. The bizarre events surrounding the more than month-long contested presidential election outcome gave Bush the briefest transition period in the modern presidency. Bush also had the unenviable task of following a very popular president who had dominated the political landscape for eight years. Leading political observers tended to be dismissive of Bush's abilities, with many writing him off as an intellectual lightweight without serious leadership experience at the national level. To say that Bush entered office amidst low expectations may be something of an understatement. To top it all off, early in Bush's term when a GOP senator abandoned the part to become an Independent, the president's party lost control of the chamber to the Democrats.

Perhaps nowhere were the expectations so low as for Bush's potential for public leadership. Even his staunchest defenders have never made the case that he is a Reagan-like "great communicator" or a gifted speaker like Bill

Clinton. Indeed, Bush's public speaking has been a staple of political comedy ever since he hit the national scene. Frequent misstatements, malapropisms, and mangled sentences by candidate Bush in 2000 opened him up to ridicule by both political opponents and comedians. Hilarious skits on "Saturday Night Live" and the nightly mocking of Bush by late-night comedians contributed to his overall reputation for having serious troubles with the English language. Jay Leno likes to quip that when Bush meets with a foreign leader, there are two persons in the room whose second language is English. This line never fails to elicit a hearty laugh from the audience.

To the extent that Bush's supporters defended him against charges of poor communications, they often said that his verbal slipups were part of his "charm"—that he seemed more real than other politicians who tended to appear just a little too coached in their use of language. Furthermore, polls in 2000 revealed that whatever shortcomings people saw in Bush as a potential leader, he had the reputation for being an honorable person. Bush never hesitated subtly and sometimes not too subtly to draw out a contrast between his reputation and that of his predecessor Bill Clinton, who was widely perceived as a moral failure and a liar.

Bush's lack of oratorical skills did not prevent him from the effective use of short, evocative phrases that conveyed important messages to voters. During the campaign Bush made a point of emphasizing that he was "a uniter, not a divider" and a "compassionate conservative." Again, much of this rhetoric was intended to draw a contrast with the politics of the Clinton years and to appeal to Americans who yearned for a less contentious environment in Washington.

George W. Bush actually has sought to learn from the political weaknesses and rhetorical mistakes of the two previous administrations—those of his father and those of Bill Clinton. By the end of Clinton's presidency, there was a credibility gap in his rhetoric; according to many polls, he had sacrificed the dignity of the office to his personal appetites. In the case of Bush's father, he had been attacked for a rhetorical style that was too distant from the concerns of average Americans. The challenge for Bush would be to harness his minimal oratorical skills to craft a rhetoric that was at once connected but dignified.

REDUCING THE PUBLIC FACE OF THE PRESIDENCY

In his first months in office, George W. Bush sought to be a very different type of national leader than his predecessor. Clinton had dominated the news media, in times of triumph and scandal. His aides worried that he was overexposed, but the constant presence of Clinton on television seemed to be part of his success. Political scientist Samuel Kernell had argued that increasingly modern presidents would "go public" in pursuit of power of the nation's agenda, and Clinton seemed to be the apotheosis of this tactic. In contrast, Bush set a far less frenetic media pace. He reduced the presence of the president in the nation's media life and seemed to suffer no public relations penalty for that. Although it is highly unlikely that President Bush stays current on trends in political science, his actions meshed well with the insights of leading presidential scholar George C. Edwards III, who has recently argued that national speeches and "going public" generally are far less effective than many observers believe.[4] Bush's inaugural address, at a mere twelve minutes, was a stunning contrast to the attention-grabbing actions of his predecessor, who seemed to relish every last minute in the spotlight and commanded much of it even on Bush's first day in office.

Perhaps because of his poor oratorical skills and his lack of fluency with complex policy questions, Bush has held fewer press conferences than almost any modern president in a comparable period of his presidency. By one count, Bush, in his first six months, held fewer press conferences than any president since William Howard Taft.[5] At midterm, Bush had held only seven solo press conferences, a pace that set the path for Bush to possibly establish a record for presidential inaccessibility.[6] Bush has frequently gone months without holding a formal meeting with the press. While Presidents Clinton and Reagan also did this, their longest periods without press conferences occurred in the midst of scandals. The few times Bush has formally met with the press, he has performed reasonably well, and he has certainly avoided major gaffes. But in his impromptu interactions with reporters during photo opportunities, he has occasionally made headlines for poor word choices, such as "crusade" in reference to the war on terror, which attracted a great deal of attention in the Muslim world for its painful historical meaning. Also, Bush's off-the-cuff remarks to reporters have continued to feature the malapropisms and poor grammar that were typical of his campaign rhetoric. Media scholar Richard Davis observed that Kennedy, the modern master of the televised press conference, "enjoyed press conferences because of his skill in bantering with reporters; his press conferences reinforced the image of a president in command of the issues."[7] It seems that the Bush White House has made a strategic decision that Bush would be unlikely to convey the image of a president in command of the issues if he held regular press conferences. It also is unlikely that Bush enjoys press conferences; even during the campaign, he tended to avoid situations that might feature hostile or detailed questions. Moreover, Bush is said to "despise the preening by correspondents that he believes is an inescapable part of televised question sessions."[8] Bush much prefers staged interactions, such as his economic conference in Waco, Texas, in which his discussions with business and finance leaders were scripted in advance.[9]

Bush's rhetoric also has downplayed the personal aspects of the presidency. In many ways, John F. Kennedy politicized the First Family by inviting the media to broadcast images of his youthful, large, and attractive family, with the certain knowledge that it would reap a political benefit. Later presidents were forced to become more personal in their rhetoric. For example, George H. W. Bush was coaxed by aides into finally talking about the death of his toddler daughter decades before. Although it went against his upbringing to include such a personal matter in a public speech, the elder Bush did so. Compared to previous presidents, the current president tends to downplay his family and himself in speeches.

Some observers criticized Bush for perhaps turning away from the spotlight during periods when presidents are supposed to be highly visible. He did not visit the site of a school shooting near San Diego, nor did he attend the April 14, 2001, ceremony welcoming home the twenty-four military personnel who had been detained by China after their plane made an emergency landing in that country. Even a race riot in Cincinnati failed to attract either a visit by the president or a speech.[10] It was almost unthinkable that Clinton would have passed up such opportunities for symbolic leadership. According to presidential scholar Fred I. Greenstein, Bush behaved "almost as if he doesn't realize that the president is the symbolic leader of the nation, the head of state," as well as the head of government.[11]

PRESENTATION OF SELF: THE UNCOMMON COMMONER

Part of the job of presidential rhetoric is to shape the public impression of the man in the White House. American presidents have often struggled to remain perceived as being part of the common people. This phenomenon in American politics goes back to some of our earliest campaigns, in which candidates competed to have a more humble "log-cabin" childhood. The majority of our presidents have come from wealthy backgrounds, including some from the wealthiest families in the country (Washington, Roosevelt, and Kennedy, to name just a few). In this century, only two presidents were raised in deep poverty, Nixon and Reagan. Yet Kennedy, the richest of Bush's immediate predecessors, most frequently used humor to acknowledge his privileged past, and far from portraying himself as anti-intellectual, he purposefully brought the academic elite and the highest culture to the White House. Of course, the rules of the game may be different for wealthy Democratic presidents than for rich Republican ones. A Democrat from an elite background plays against type, at least on economic politics, while a Republican all too easily fits the stereotype of a fat cat captured by corporate and moneyed interests.

Bush's rhetoric, perhaps unwittingly, has worked well to insulate him from being perceived as elitist and privileged. The second son of a president to rise to the White House, Bush was raised amid extraordinary wealth and political access. He attended two Ivy League institutions, Harvard and Yale, and graduated from perhaps the most rarefied prep school in the country. In his 1978 campaign for Congress, Bush's election hopes were gravely damaged by the perception that he was the product of elite Northeastern schools, and thus out of touch with the concerns of real Americans.[12] Bush has successfully avoided that image in all subsequent elections, in part through his speeches and phrases. Like many recent presidents, Bush frequently criticizes Washington and emphasizes in his speeches on the road how happy he is to be outside the capital. The major domestic policy speech of his presidency was delivered from his Crawford, Texas, ranch, and Bush peppers his speeches with references to the heartland, as well as the values of Midland, Texas, or Crawford, Texas.

Bush also watched his own father wrestle with handling a privileged background at a time of economic crisis. The elder Bush went to great lengths to publicize his love of country music and pork rinds, and he attacked his opponent for his "boutique Harvard liberalism." These tiny adjustments to his image and his speeches did not prevent the public perception of the elder Bush as being an out-of-touch elitist. Democrats also tried to accuse him of not being a real Texan, since he owned homes in several other states. George H. W. Bush also concealed from reporters that he spoke fluent French, which only came out during his presidency. The contrast with his son is instructive. The younger Bush's light Texas drawl is not feigned; he really is a product of Midland, Texas. And he does not have to pretend that he does not speak French, to say the least. When he mispronounces and mangles words of medium complexity, such as "subliminal," it may actually send a subliminal message to voters; despite his name and his background, he is one of us, not one of the elite. The anti-intellectualism in Bush's rhetoric works against the facts of his upbringing in a way that pays political dividends. If Bush sounded like a better-educated man, he possibly would be a less effective president.

GOD ON HIS SIDE: THE RELIGIOUS RHETORIC OF BUSH

Another aspect of Bush's rhetoric separates him from many other presidents: the vibrant role that religious phrases play in his speeches. Bush has never hidden his deep religious faith from the public. Again, in contrast with his father, an adherent of the famously stiff and cold Episcopalian faith, George W. Bush is an evangelical Methodist who speaks easily about his religious faith and experience. During the campaign, Bush identified Jesus Christ as his most influential political philosopher, a choice that few other presidents, save perhaps Carter, would have made. While all modern presidents have ended major addresses by calling on the deity to bless the country, and many, including Clinton, would refer to biblical passages, Bush's speeches are quite distinctive in their use of born-again rhetoric. In addition to direct quotes from the Bible, Bush often uses phrases that contain deep meaning for his co-religionists but fly beneath the radar of nonevangelical Americans. For example, he referred to "wonder-working power" in his second State of the Union address, a phrase laden with meaning for born-again Christians. Another example of biblical phrases encoded into a speech without attribution was contained in Bush's speech on the anniversary of September 11. "Our prayer tonight is that God will see us through and keep us worthy. . . . Hope still lights our way, and the light shines in the darkness, and the darkness will not overcome it." Many Christians would immediately recognize the language as a paraphrase of the Gospel of John's famous metaphor of Christ as the light of the world.[13]

In Bush's major domestic policy speech in 2001 on stem cell research, the religious emphasis was obvious. It was to be expected that a speech by a deeply Christian man on a topic of bioethics would contain religious references, and Bush did not disappoint. In addition to saying that "I . . . believe that human life is a sacred gift from our creator," Bush referred to prayer twice. Significantly, at least one phrase of Bush's speech was subtly exclusionary. "The issue is debated within the church, with people of different faiths, even many of the same faith, coming to different conclusions." The "church" is mentioned, as if it were singular, and no mention is made of synagogues, mosques, or temples.

The role of religion in Bush's speeches is even greater than that played by church and God in the speeches of Ronald Reagan. Reagan was the only president whose popularity with the Religious Right rivals that of Bush, and like Bush he spoke of God with ease and frequency. However, when faced with a similar situation, the loss of a space shuttle, the speeches given by the two men differ in the prominence given to religion. In Reagan's moving address, God was only present at the very end, in a quote from a poem. In contrast, the last quarter of Bush's speech was consumed with religion:

> Yet farther than we can see there is comfort and hope. In the words of the prophet Isaiah, "Lift your eyes and look to the heavens. Who created all these? He who brings out the starry hosts one by one and calls them each by name. Because of His great power and mighty strength, not one of them is missing." The same Creator who names the stars also knows the names of the seven souls we mourn today. The crew of the shuttle Columbia did not return safely to Earth; yet we can pray that all are safely home.[14]

Not only did Bush, unlike Reagan, quote from the Bible, he also made it clear that a singular creator had welcomed all seven astronauts safely home, including one who was a polytheistic believer in reincarnation.

The enhanced place that religion has in Bush's speeches may be an outgrowth of his speechwriting team. Bush's main speechwriter, Michael Gerson, is, like his employer, a born-again Christian. Knowing of Bush's deep faith, poor speaking abilities, and dislike of intellectual language, Gerson has crafted a simple but effective style of writing that conveys moral absolutes with clarity. Bush's frequent references to "evil" and "evil doers" are yet another sign of his religiously influenced rhetoric. Indeed, the first Bush insider to write an account of life in the administration, speechwriter David Frum, found out very early how religion suffused the place when he overhead a colleague questioned about missing a Bible study: "The news that this was a White House where attendance at Bible study was, if not compulsory, not quite uncompulsory, either, was disconcerting to a non-Christian like me."[15]

Bush's religious rhetoric plays well with his attempt to be nonelitist in his presentation of self. Religious faith, particularly of the born-again variety, is far less common among the highly educated than among the hoi polloi. Many of the intellectuals whom Bush disdains probably have less than positive views toward his faith and his blunt references about it. Yet in sprinkling the words of faith throughout many of his presidential speeches, Bush succeeds in signaling not only his faith but also his distance from the intellectual elite. Those who would be alienated by Bush's "God talk" were probably already opposed to much of his agenda, while those who are enthusiastic about it will forge a deeper bond with their leader. In 1992, Clinton used the language of the Southern Baptist church to win back an important faction of the evangelical vote for his party. In part, he was able to do this because he was running against Bush's father, who had little ability to speak with sincerity about religion. Had the Democrats nominated yet another Southern Baptist (only Southern Baptists have won the presidency for the Democrats since 1968) instead of John Kerry, a Catholic, Bush would have been much better positioned rhetorically than his father had been to struggle to maintain a solid Republican majority among born-again Christians and Evangelicals.

MEETING HIS MOMENT AND FINDING HIS MESSAGE: BUSH AS WAR ORATOR

The attacks of September 11, 2001, forced Bush to change gears and to speak to the nation on an almost daily basis. His early efforts at leading the nation in crisis were not successful. In his first comments from Florida that morning, Bush appeared shaky and unable to reassure the nation. He referred to the perpetrators as the "folks who committed this act" and promised that after his remarks, he would return to Washington. But he did not return directly to Washington. On advice from the Secret Service and from Vice President Cheney, the president traveled first to a secure bunker in Nebraska before finally arriving in Washington late at night. When the president finally arrived at the White House that night, muted criticism of him was already emerging. Many wondered if the president who had avoided military service in Vietnam lacked the courage to be commander in chief of a nation under attack.

Bush did little to reassure the doubters with his first evening address to the nation. Similarly, when he arranged for news cameras to witness a phone call with Mayor Rudy Giuliani and Governor George Pataki of New York State, his attempts to convey his sympathy and resolve did not seem at all presidential. For *Time* correspondent Margaret Carlson, Bush "looked like a teenager making weekend plans," hardly an uplifting description.[16] Yet during his visit to Ground Zero, the smoking wreckage that had once been the World Trade Center (WTC), Bush seemed to find his voice in talking to the rescue workers. As the president stood among the rubble of the collapsed World Trade Center, his arm draped around a firefighter, he declared through a bullhorn, "I can hear you. The rest of the world hears you. And the people who knocked down these buildings will hear all of us soon." In this impromptu speech and in his address at a national prayer service at the National Cathedral in Washington, he began to rise to the moment, to comfort a nation reeling from a sudden and an unprecedented attack.

Some observers cautiously criticized some of Bush's rhetoric in the early days after the attacks as bellicose. Indeed, he made comments about wanting to hunt down the terrorists and catch them "dead or alive," or to "smoke" the terrorists "out of their holes." Some news reports suggested that First Lady Laura Bush was privately asking her husband to tone down some of his rhetoric. On September 19, the *New York Times* criticized Bush's rhetoric as overheated: "The hotter the rhetoric is now, the harder President Bush will find it later if his better judgment winds up telling him to delay action, or to concentrate for a while on diplomatic and economic sanctions rather than military force."[17] Nonetheless, Bush was reflecting the intense public anger at the terrorist attacks, and he balanced his heated rhetoric with appeals to the public to be patient and to not expect some precipitous action by the government.

By the time Bush spoke to Congress on September 20, the stakes were as high as they had been for any presidential address since 1941. Not only had the initial assaults undermined Americans' sense of security, but also the economy seemed to be in free fall. The New York Stock Exchange, located not far from the WTC, reopened days after the attack but immediately lost $1.4 trillion in share values, and consumer confidence dropped. Bush also would have to address the question of domestic security; many Americans feared further terrorist attacks and wanted their government to take radical new steps to prevent them.

Bush's September 20 nationally televised speech before a special joint session of Congress was masterful, and his subsequent statements, including a powerful speech at the United Nations, were measured and reassuring to the public. In one telling moment after the end of his speech to Congress, the president walked over to his chief congressional rival, Democratic Senator Tom Daschle, and embraced him. The rhetoric and the bipartisan symbolism fit the occasion perfectly. Americans felt that their president was in control of the situation, and that the country would not only survive the crisis but even strengthen its common bonds of nationalism, civic duty, and charity.

Bush rightfully received high marks for his carefully measured rhetoric in these speeches. One of his goals was to ensure that Arab and Muslim Americans would not be singled out in the United States for discriminatory treatment, and he went to great lengths to distinguish for the American public the evil of terrorism and the true teachings of Islam. In his speech to Congress the president addressed the Muslim world as well as the American people:

> We respect your faith. It's practiced freely by many millions of Americans, and by millions more in countries that America counts as friends. Its teachings are good and peaceful, and those who commit evil in the name of Allah blaspheme the name of Allah. The terrorists are traitors to their own faith, trying, in effect, to hijack Islam itself. The enemy of America is not our many Muslim friends; it is not our many Arab friends. Our enemy is a radical network of terrorists, and every government that supports them.[18]

The only other time an American president spoke to a joint session and the nation following a sudden attack on the nation was when FDR had failed to distinguish between the empire of Japan and Japanese Americans. Shortly afterward, many acts of mob violence, vandalism, and discrimination occurred against Japanese Americans. Eventually, tens of thousands of Asian citizens were rounded up and put into concentration camps for much of the war. Bush's rhetoric on religion and ethnicity attempted to prevent Americans in their anger over September 11 from taking action against innocent fellow citizens. In this, he was largely successful. Few acts of hatred were committed against Muslims or Arabs, and Bush deserves a great deal of the credit. Had his rhetoric not praised Islam and Arab Americans, it is likely that more violence against innocent scapegoats would have occurred.

The surge in public support for Bush after the terrorist attacks was dramatic. The last Gallup Poll prior to the terrorist attacks showed Bush with a presidential approval of only 51 percent, but in the weeks following the tragedy, his support soared to almost 90 percent, with a scant 6 percent disapproving of his handling of the presidency. Although it is not unusual for presidents to win widespread support during wartime—Bush's father had reached nearly 90 percent job approval at the end of the Gulf War—this surge was more than a public rally. Many of Bush's staunchest critics praised his performance, with some Democratic leaders even privately telling media sources that they were glad that Bush was president during the crisis. Unlike past public opinion rallies, this one effected a lasting change in approval for the president. The president instructed the American people that the struggle against terrorism was long term, and the public responded with sustained support for Bush, even as the economy sank into recession.

PRESIDENTIAL RHETORIC DURING CRISES: A COMPARISON OF FDR AND BUSH

One of the most famous speeches ever given by an American president was Franklin Delano Roosevelt's December 8, 1941, address to Congress. Among the many burdens placed on George W. Bush in the aftermath of September 11 was to measure up to the standard set by FDR's war oration. Michael Gerson wrote Bush's September 20 speech to Congress with the help of Karen Hughes and input from many other staffers. The president was involved during each step of the process, rejecting drafts and making suggestions. The two speeches are quite different. First, Bush's speech was nearly six times the length of Roosevelt's (3,023 words to 515). The length and complexity of Bush's speech may reflect that he had nine days in which to prepare, whereas FDR spoke to Congress as soon as it could be gathered.

These two historic speeches provide interesting contrasts. FDR chose to open with blunt simplicity:

> Yesterday, December 7, 1941—a date which will live in infamy—the United States of America was suddenly and deliberately attacked by naval and air forces of the Empire of Japan.

Bush, however, opened with a more indirect approach. Only in his tenth sentence did he begin to express the nation's anger:

> Tonight we are a country awakened to danger and called to defend freedom. Our grief has turned to anger, and our anger to resolution. Whether we bring our enemies to justice, or bring justice to our enemies, justice will be done.

In his brief remarks, FDR several times mentioned the nature of the Japanese sneak attack, reminding Americans that up until the very minute of the attack, Japanese diplomats were engaged in negotiations with U.S. authorities. In so doing, he rallied the country's anger.

> Always will we remember the character of the onslaught against us. No matter how long it may take us to overcome this premeditated invasion, the American people in their righteous might will win through to absolute victory.

Bush also emphasized the malicious character of the assault upon the country, but he spent at least as much time on the beliefs of America's new opponents, which FDR largely ignored:

> Al Qaeda is to terror what the Mafia is to crime. But its goal is not making money; its goal is remaking the world—and imposing its radical beliefs on people everywhere. The terrorists practice a fringe form of Islamic extremism . . . a fringe movement that perverts the peaceful teachings of Islam. The terrorists' directive commands them to kill Christians and Jews, to kill all Americans, and make no distinction among military and civilians, including women and children.

FDR's speech was impersonal compared to Bush's. He did not, for example, mention Emperor Hirohito or any Japanese politicians or military leaders. In contrast, Bush mentioned Osama bin Laden by name, personalizing the enemy in America's new war. He also introduced to the nation and to Congress the widow of a murdered passenger, and he ended his speech by holding up the badge of a police officer lost in the rubble of the World Trade Center. Presidential speeches since Reagan have often included "real Americans" to illustrate the president's points and to tug at the heartstrings of the public. This approach would have struck many Americans as maudlin in 1941, but today it is expected and praised.

Bush included many other nations in his address, using his speech to continue the work of building an international coalition against terror. He had even invited the prime minister of America's most faithful ally, Great Britain, to attend the speech so he could thank the British personally for their support. FDR, in contrast, did not mention that Japan also had attacked the forces of Great Britain, perhaps because the attack on Pearl Harbor had already made a coalition against fascism inevitable.

Bush used his speech to announce a new American policy, now known as the Bush Doctrine:

> Every nation, in ever region, now has a decision to make. Either you are with us, or you are with the terrorists. From this day forward, any nation that continues to harbor or support terrorism will be regarded by the United States as a hostile regime.

One of the most important differences was that Bush included in his speech a call on Americans not to take out their anger on Muslim or Arab citizens:

> We are in a fight for our principles and our first responsibility is to live by them. No one should be singled out for unfair treatment or unkind words because of their ethnic background or religious faith.

Roosevelt, however, did not warn Americans against mistreating citizens of Japanese descent. Quickly, many Japanese Americans suffered from acts of violent revenge. Japanese businesses were attacked, and many Japanese either lost all of their possessions or were forced to sell their belongings at fire-sale prices.

Both presidents ended their addresses to Congress by predicting victory and calling on God for assistance:

> FDR: There is no blinking at the fact that our people, our territory, and our interests are in grave danger. With confidence in our armed forces, with the unbounding determination of our people, we will gain the inevitable triumph. So help us God.

> Bush: The course of this conflict is not known, yet its outcome is certain. Freedom and fear, justice and cruelty, have always been at war, and we know that God is not neutral between them. Fellow citizens, we'll meet violence with patient justice—assured of the rightness of our cause, and confident in the victories to come. In all that lies before us, may God grant us wisdom, and may He watch over the United States of America.

It is too early to tell if Bush's speech to the nation on September 20 will achieve the legendary status of FDR's December 8 address. The key may well be whether journalists and the public identify a single phrase or sentence from Bush's speech as capturing the mood of the nation. FDR's "a day that will live in infamy" has become one of the most famous phrases in presidential rhetoric, while much of the rest of his speech is forgotten. (FDR inserted the word "infamy" at the last minute, in place of the far blander "live in world history.") The phrase captured the sense of outrage that Americans felt at the sneaky nature of the Japanese attack. Perhaps the most likely phrases to endure from Bush's speech are the ones about bringing al Qaeda to justice or bringing justice to them, or the outline of the Bush Doctrine, quoted earlier.

Bush as War Leader, Part II: The War on Iraq

While Bush's rhetoric in the aftermath of September 11 and during the Afghanistan war won plaudits from Democrats and pundits, similar praise was not received for his speeches leading into the war on Iraq. It may be simply that the task facing Bush was much greater; after the devastation of September 11, it required little persuasive skill to convince Americans to attack the Taliban that was sheltering Osama bin Laden. In contrast, it required a great deal of salesmanship to get America behind a large war against a country that had never attacked the United States. Many of the claims made in speeches by Bush and his administration have since been revealed as erroneous or at least questionable. One speech by Bush on the eve of the use of force vote by Congress in the fall of 2002 illustrates how his rhetoric aided his political aim of a war on Iraq. Bush made several assertions about Iraq that have turned out to be false: that Iraq possessed large quantities of chemical and biological weapons, that it had unmanned delivery vehicles capable of launching these weapons hundreds of miles (and were exploring using them against the United States), that it had sought to purchase specific materials for an active nuclear weapons development program, and that it had strong links to al-Qaeda. In addition, the president raised the specter of a mushroom cloud rising over an American city if swift action against Saddam were not taken soon. In a relatively short speech of just over 3,000 words, Bush used some form of the word "terror" thirty-five times, and he used "weapons" in reference to weapons of mass destruction another thirty-two times.[19] Bush's simple rhetorical style had been turned into a bludgeon, beating misinformation into the heads of the American public.[20] The speech "worked"; polls showed that Americans believed that Iraq was connected to al-Qaeda, and that Saddam was involved in the September 11 attacks. Congress, buoyed by rising fear in the public, voted for war against Iraq.

Similarly, Bush's rhetoric of victory in the aftermath of the swift defeat of Iraq was momentarily quite effective at rallying support for him. Speaking to the nation and to the armed forces in a speech following an unprecedented jet landing on a carrier, Bush called the defeated Baathist regime an "ally of al-Qaeda," contradicting his own CIA and the best information produced by the intelligence community. Under a banner reading "Mission Accomplished," Bush's rhetoric clearly suggested that the most difficult aspects of the conflict with Iraq were over. His simple and clear style was evident throughout the speech: "Major combat operations in Iraq have ended. In the battle of Iraq, the United States and our allies have prevailed. . . . The battle of Iraq is one victory in a war on terror that began on September the 11, 2001." While Bush did say that "difficult work" of reconstruction and finding weapons of mass destruction lay ahead, it was not a speech that prepared the nation for losing many more soldiers in the occupation of Iraq than in the "victory" that Bush celebrated. The subtle linking of Saddam to al-Qaeda and September 11 continued.

Yet the speech on the carrier represented something of a shift in tone for President Bush. As a candidate, Bush had rejected "nation building" and called for a more humble America, but since the end of the war in Iraq, Bush has increasingly touched on Wilsonian themes of universal democracy and America's role in bringing about positive change in the world, by force if necessary. Particularly since the failure to find any evidence to support his allegations about weapons of mass destruction, Bush has increasingly grounded his defense of the occupation of Iraq in the necessity of creating a democratic and free Iraq. This represents a rare thematic shift for Bush, who has typically stayed with the same messages as president.

Conclusion: Grade, Incomplete

The great difficulty of evaluating the effectiveness of presidential rhetoric is of course separating substance from skillful presentation. Now that Bush's approval ratings (as of May 2004) are the lowest in his presidency, it would be far too facile to conclude that his rhetorical shortcomings are to blame. The questions that Bush has been forced to address in his infrequent press conferences have simply become far more pointed and difficult. The pictures on the news that precede and follow his presidential addresses have become much less consonant with his rhetoric. It is entirely possible that Bush's sober, dogged, and inelegant expressions of confidence in the rightness of his foreign and domestic policies have helped maintain his solid base of support.

But the success of a president as communicator must take into account his ability to persuade audiences far beyond his domestic partisan base. In March 2003, the president persuaded a majority of Americans to support an invasion of Iraq. But recent polls show that a majority of Americans now believe the invasion to have been a mistake, despite Bush's continued advocacy of it. He has strong GOP support, but Democratic leaders are becoming increasingly bold in criticizing the president's foreign policies. Most discouraging of all, the president's rhetoric has failed to stop the free fall in respect for the United States. Public opinion polling in every region of the world shows that America has never been more unpopular. The foreign image of President Bush is also not, to say the least, positive. Even in Great Britain, Germany, France, and Canada, opinion polls suggest that significant percentages of citizens see Bush as a threat to world peace.

Thus we are left with a mixed picture. A president never credited as a good speaker, a man constantly lampooned in the entertainment media for making pratfalls all over the English language, ultimately rose to the occasion and communicated remarkably well during a national crisis. If the measure of a president's success is his performance during extraordinary times, then Bush not only exceeded all expectations in the post-September 11 months, he clearly earned high grades. Bush's ability to crystallize complex situations down to their existential core suited well the battle against Osama bin Laden and the Taliban. Using similar rhetorical techniques, Bush masterfully convinced the nation to support his war against Iraq. In the immediate afterglow of swift victory, Bush's style seemed again to fit the moment. In confronting the far more complicated and nuanced problem of Iraqi occupation, Bush's Manichean rhetoric style of evil versus good has not served him as well. In 2004 Bush was not forced to adopt a new, more sophisticated style in order to convince his fellow citizens to give him another four years as the dominant voice in American politics. Clearly, Bush will continue to speak to the nation in the same raw, unvarnished rhetoric that has characterized his speeches since his first run for Congress in 1978.

NOTES

1. George W. Bush, *A Charge to Keep* (New York: William Morrow, 2001).

2. Richard Neustadt, *Presidential Power* (New York: Wiley, 1960), 99–100.

3. Samuell Kernell, *Going Public: New Strategies of Presidential Leadership*, 3rd ed. (Washington, D.C.: CQ Press, 1997).

4. See George C. Edwards III, *On Deaf Ears: The Limits of the Bully Pulpit* (New Haven, Conn.: Yale University Press, 2003).

5. Rick Shenkman, "What George W. Bush and William Howard Taft Have in Common," *History News Network* (August 2001): 1.

6. Martha Joynt Kumar, "'Does This Constitute a Press Conference?' Defining and Tabulating Modern Presidential Press Conferences," *Presidential Studies Quarterly* 33 (March 1, 2003): 221–38.

7. Richard Davis, *The Press and American Politics*, 3rd ed. (New York: Prentice Hall, 2000).

8. Mike Allen, "President Bush to Hold News Conference Tonight," *Washington Post*, March 6, 2003, p. A20.

9. Ron Suskind, *The Price of Loyalty* (New York: Simon and Schuster, 2004), 269–73.

10. Quoted in John F. Harris, "On the World Stage, Bush Shuns the Spotlight," *The Washington Post National Weekly Edition*, April 23–29, 2001, p. 11.

11. Fred I. Greenstein, "The Changing Leadership of George W. Bush: A Pre and Post 9-11 Comparison," *Forum* 1 (2002): 8.

12. Lois Romano and George Lardner Jr., "Young Bush, a Political Natural, Revs Up," *Washington Post*, July 29, 1999, p. A1.

13. David L. Greene, "Bush Turns Increasingly to Language of Religion," *Baltimore Sun*, February 10, 2003, p. 11A.

14. President addresses nation on space shuttle Columbia tragedy, February 1, 2003, Public Papers of the Presidents, George W. Bush 2001–2004, Washington D.C., Government Printing Office.

15. David L. Greene, "Bush Turns Increasingly to Language of Religion," *Baltimore Sun*, February 10, 2003, p. 11A.

16. Jeremy D. Mayer, *9–11: The Giant Awakens* (New York: Wadsworth, 2002).

17. "Wartime Rhetoric," *New York Times*, September 19, 2001, p. A26.

18. http://www.whitehouse.gov/news/releases/2001/09/20010920-8.html (accessed March 1, 2003).

19. "Bush: Don't Wait for Mushroom Cloud," Transcript, October 8, 2002. http://www.edition.cnn.com/2002/ALLPOLITICS/10/07/bush.transcript/ (accessed March 1, 2003).

20. Bush repeated "terror" and "weapons" to sell the nation on a war against a country that had not directly engaged in terrorism since 1993, and had, apparently, no large stockpiles of any weapon of mass destruction.

IV

The Challenge after the White House

During a president's tenure in office, managing, relating to, and using the public remain a priority. Once the president leaves office, there should be a natural transition—the president leaves behind the often challenging, sometime combative relationship with the news media and the public to start a new era in his public life in the benign elder statesman role that most former presidents serve. However, Bill Clinton's actions upon leaving office, and George W. Bush's actions upon entering office, suggest that post-presidency public management resembles in-office behavior more closely than previously suspected.

The smooth transition of power from one elected official to another is a hallmark of the United States' constitutional system of government. As a president leaves office, whether he has served one or two terms, he presumably leaves behind the day-to-day wrangling with the news media and concerns over the latest approval ratings. In the public realm, the biggest challenge for a new former president is how to gracefully leave center stage as the news media and public begin to focus on the new president. In most cases, the presidential inauguration marks the time in which the former president courteously disappears into retirement, allowing the new president, regardless of his party affiliation, to step into the presidential spotlight. What if that does not occur? Persistent media coverage of the departing president can potentially impact on the presidential legacy, but more significantly, it can hinder the transfer of power and the development of a new relationship between the new president and the public. In "Life after the White House: The Public Post-Presidency and the Development of Presidential Legacies," Lori Cox Han and Matthew J. Krov discover that Clinton's persistence in the spotlight upon leaving office might not permanently harm his legacy, but it did have a comparative influence on Bush's public introduction as president.

Clinton's work on his post-presidency legacy began while in office, as he devoted considerable time and attention to the building of his presidential museum and library. The presidential library houses all of the personal papers and materials from his administration, supposedly in the spirit of openness and government transparency. Access to important documents within each library also provides an important link between presidents and the scholars and journalists who will help shape the president's public legacy. However, the existence of the libraries (and the exuberant investigation into White House behavior during the 1980s and 1990s) created fears of subpoenas and tarnished legacies. The White House loses control of the material once it falls under the auspices of the National Archives. The current Bush White House has challenged the lack of post-presidential management while in office by attacking the law that governs the archives (the Presidential Records Act). In "Not Going Public: George W. Bush and the Presidential Records Act," Nancy Kassop argues that the Bush administration has undertaken an unprecedented effort to replace openness with secrecy and control. Thus if the Bush administration continues along this path, the post-presidency relationship with the public will not abandon any of the challenges of management, perception, and presentation cited in previous chapters.

12

Life after the White House

The Public Post-Presidency and the Development of Presidential Legacies

Lori Cox Han and Matthew J. Krov

> An ex-President of the United States occupies a unique position in our national life.... His countrymen cannot forget that he was once their chosen chief of state. Interested in him for this special reason, as in no other person, they are naturally curious to know what course he will mark out for himself, now that he has become an ex-President. Will he retire into quiet seclusion, to occupy himself with his favorite pursuits, or, perchance, to write memoirs of his times and of his part in them? Or, if a lawyer, will he once more hang out his shingle and resume the practice of his profession? Will he continue to be a national figure, gracing many a public occasion with high thinking and eloquent speech, or will he pass into the twilight zone of the "Has-beens," who have had their day and no longer attract followers?[1]
> —Winthrop Dudley Sheldon, *The Ex-Presidents of the United States*

Presidential inaugurations represent a unique feature of the American constitutional system of government—a peaceful transition of power from one administration to the next. The incoming president faces many daunting tasks in his early days in office—creating a legislative agenda, building working relationships with his newly appointed cabinet members and staff as well as key congressional leaders, and developing an effective means of communicating his goals and vision to the American public. The tasks that the outgoing president faces are much different as he looks to the development of his legacy, a legacy that usually includes building a presidential library, writing memoirs, speaking engagements, and worrying about how presidential scholars will view his years in office. And while there are no guidelines, constitutional or otherwise, for how former presidents should spend their time, most gracefully step back from the national spotlight of the presidency while Americans, and especially the news media, focus on the new occupant of the White House.

The inauguration of George W. Bush on January 20, 2001, was just as newsworthy as any previous inaugural, with perhaps a slightly heightened public interest following the November 2000 election controversy. The day would mark not only the start of the Bush administration but also the end of the Clinton era in Washington. From the time he announced his candidacy for the presidency in 1991 until his last moments in office, Bill Clinton had dominated the political center stage. His eight years in office included some big political wins and losses and plenty of scandal; his relationship with both the American press and public was nothing if not complex. Clinton has been described by friends as "a tornado that roars through people's lives,"[2] and his presidency tells a similar tale, "full of ironic twists and turns, of a president whose mixed record of accomplishment and failure illuminates the point that the historical process is never static and that it unfolds in ways that are often unanticipated."[3] His last day in office was no different. Having promised to "work until the last hour of the last day,"[4] Clinton managed to deliver the last of his 416 weekly radio addresses and granted 140 presidential pardons (including the controversial pardon to fugitive financier Marc Rich) during his last hours in the Oval Office. Shortly after witnessing Bush take the oath of office, Clinton promised a crowd of supporters gathered at the airport for his departure from Washington that "I'm not going anywhere." And during the first weeks of the new Bush administration, Clinton's promise turned out to be an accurate prediction. The "comeback kid" kept coming back in the news media, time after time, to rival the new president as the nation's top political news maker.

This chapter considers two distinct yet related issues: first we examine the role that continuing press coverage of a former president plays in the development of a presidential legacy, and second, we consider the impact of Clinton's lingering presence in the news media in the first year after he left office and how that has shaped the early phase of his legacy. While the historical rankings and public approval ratings of former presidents can and do shift—sometimes dramatically—in the years after leaving office, news coverage during the first year can be important in setting a tone as to how the president will be viewed and the public role that he will assume, as well as what news organizations view as significant from his time in office. A recent study on press coverage of former presidents Gerald Ford, Jimmy Carter, Ronald Reagan, and George H. W. Bush suggests that the amount of post–White House coverage decreases after the first year out of office; once both the press and the public are satisfied in knowing how the former president is adjusting to his new responsibilities, then he is no longer viewed as being tremendously newsworthy. Therefore, the first year of coverage is important if the former president hopes to create positive coverage through his public activities by working "toward the goals in which he believes in the hopes of drawing both media and public attention . . . [since] an ex-president with a rigorous agenda is bound to capture more media attention than one with a less rigorous postpresidential schedule."[5]

The activities of former presidents in the modern era (beginning with Harry S. Truman) also are considered here in order to assess the process of building a presidential legacy through its various participants, in particular, the news media, which provide an ongoing link between the former president and the public even after he has left office. We also provide a comparative analysis of Clinton's first year out of office with that of former presidents Reagan and Bush through the watchful, and sometimes critical, lens of the news media. Finally, we consider whether or not Clinton upstaged George W. Bush's honeymoon with the American press and public during the early days of the new administration in 2001.

Specifically, this research focuses on the following questions: First, what comprises a presidential legacy, and how does it take shape during a president's years out of office? Second, how have modern presidents spent their time after leaving office, and how has this contributed to public expectations for former presidents? Third, what type of news coverage did former President Clinton receive during his first year out of office compared to former presidents Reagan and Bush? And, finally, did Clinton's coverage preempt national news coverage of President George W. Bush's first 100 days in office?

To answer the last two questions, news stories on Clinton in the *New York Times* and on the nightly newscasts on ABC, CBS, and NBC were content analyzed for story topic from January 21, 2001, through December 31, 2001. For comparison, the same news media sources were content analyzed for Reagan from January 21, 1989, through December 31, 1989, and for Bush from January 21, 1993, through December 31, 1993. Widely recognized as the nation's "newspaper of record" and a trendsetter in coverage for which other news outlets often follow, the *New York Times* was selected as an appropriate representation of print coverage due to the influence that the paper wields as an important political player within Washington.[6] Television coverage also was included for comparative analysis due to the expanding influence that television news has enjoyed on presidential politics for the past several decades, which became particularly evident in the 1980s as the Reagan administration made imagery and symbolism through television coverage a vital part of its communication strategy. A separate comparison also will be made of front-page coverage in the *New York Times* of Clinton and George W. Bush between January 21, 2001, and February 28, 2001.

Ex-Presidents: Of Legacies and Greatness

To determine a president's true legacy—that is, understanding the political, institutional, and policy implications of an administration on the American system of government—can take years, even decades, to sort out. Numerous participants can play a role, including presidential scholars, the news media (which capture the day-to-day events during the administration, as well as initial assessments as the president is leaving office and ongoing coverage over the years), pollsters (who determine one measure of presidential "greatness" both during the administration and after), the American public (both as participants in public opinion polls and voters during subsequent elections), and the president himself (assuming that he has not died in office). However, a magic formula for determining presidential greatness, or lack thereof, does not exist, but news coverage during a president's first year out of office can indicate the early mood of the news media as to their view of the president and how that may impact subsequent public opinion.

Several political scientists have attempted in recent years to more clearly define presidential legacies and to clarify which factors contribute to their development. According to Cronin and Genovese, many presidential "experts," including the news media, rely on the following factors in determining a legacy: the scope of problems faced while in office, the actions to deal with those problems and their long-term effects, overall accomplishments, and a judgment of the president's character.[7] Similarly, Neustadt states that a legacy can be understood in three ways: the conventional wisdom that defines presidential successes and failures, the opportunities and constraints facing the president's immediate successor, and a "retrospective view in the sense of place in history."[8] Skowronek offers a different approach to understanding the presidency and the legacies of particular presidents by shifting from an "individual-centered perspective on leadership" to looking at presidential leadership in political time: "To catch the patterns and sequences in the politics of leadership, we need to adopt a much broader view of the relevant historical experience than is customary."[9] In all three scholarly discussions, the news media play a significant role in communicating relevant information about a president's tenure to not only the public at large but also to those participants directly involved in the creation of a president's legacy.

The news media also have long been fascinated by scholarly discussions of presidential rankings, always eager to promote the latest findings by scholars as to how past presidents have fared in the latest polls. Since the time of historian Arthur Schlesinger's initial survey published in *Life* in 1948[10] and his subsequent book *Paths to the Present*,[11] both historians and political scientists have debated the methodological approach of determining so-called "presidential greatness." Through a poll of fifty-five "students of American history and government," Schlesinger sought the opinions of his fellow scholars in determining the assessment of former presidents and their places in American history. With no specific criteria, the respondents selected six "great" presidents—Abraham Lincoln, George Washington, Franklin D. Roosevelt, Woodrow Wilson, Thomas Jefferson, and Andrew Jackson. Arthur

Schlesinger Jr. conducted a second poll among seventy-five scholars in 1962 published in the *New York Times Magazine* with similar rankings.[12] According to James MacGregor Burns, a participant in the second poll, "historians are a profoundly important constituency indeed" in determining how the accomplishments of a president will be viewed and that agreement existed over the criteria for Schlesinger's polls—"strength in the White House."[13]

Since then, other surveys have been conducted in an attempt to rank former presidents,[14] and several articles and books have debated both the methodologies and usefulness of such scholarly endeavors,[15] including Dean Keith Simonton's *Why Presidents Succeed*,[16] a quantitative analysis that offers a means for predicting presidential greatness before (who will win the general election?), during (approval ratings and legislative performance), and after ("the president's ultimate standing with posterity") an administration. Two new polls emerged during the end of Clinton's time in office in 2000—one conducted by the Federalist Society and the *Wall Street Journal* and the other conducted by C-SPAN—which both ranked Clinton as an average president.[17] A study of the C-SPAN survey, which also included the opinions of informed citizens as well as presidential experts, showed great stability in how each group rated presidents. Interestingly, in the wake of the Clinton scandals during his administration, character traits have not become more important in rating presidents, showing "great temporal stability in how presidents are rated."[18]

When Bill Clinton became president on January 20, 1993, until Richard Nixon's death on April 22, 1994, Americans enjoyed the presence of five former presidents (Nixon, Ford, Carter, Reagan, and Bush). Such an event had only occurred once before in American history in 1861 following Lincoln's inauguration (with former presidents Martin Van Buren, John Tyler, Millard Fillmore, Franklin Pierce, and James Buchanan). While the activities of a former president are usually considered newsworthy, a public gathering of several former presidents can make for a great news media photo opportunity. This has occurred several times in recent years, usually at presidential library openings and dedications, or at more solemn occasions such as Nixon's funeral or the national day of prayer in Washington following the September 11, 2001, terrorist attacks.

By the 1980s, with three former presidents in the public eye and many presidential observers looking ahead to the formation of "the Reagan legacy," public discussions began about the role, if any, that former presidents should play in the operation of the federal government, since "the men who have served as our presidents are significant enough political figures for us to be concerned with them after they have left office."[19] Unlike some of their earlier counterparts, this new breed of former presidents in the latter half of the twentieth century did not show interest in seeking other elected or appointed positions, yet still remained newsworthy. (Upon leaving the White House, William Howard Taft became chief justice of the U.S. Supreme Court, John

Quincy Adams served in the House of Representatives, Andrew Johnson served briefly in the Senate, and three former presidents—Martin Van Buren, Millard Fillmore, and Theodore Roosevelt—ran for their former office representing third parties.) By the early 1990s, some members of Congress had begun to criticize the federal funds appropriated to former presidents as an "extravagant retirement, complete with Secret Service protection for widows and children, 'fat' book deals, handsome offices, and bloated staffs as well as presidential libraries that more nearly resemble monuments than research institutions."[20]

At a conference debating the question of "What to do with ex-presidents?" historian Daniel J. Boorstin urged Americans to embrace former presidents for the knowledgeable public servants that they had both been and could continue to be through the creation of an official council of former presidents: "Who is better qualified to help us focus on enduring national issues than our former presidents with their experience and their feeling for the nation's unfinished business?"[21] However, not many have subscribed to this official role for former presidents. Several journalists, as participants at this conference, also weighed in with their opinions on the issue of former presidents. According to broadcast journalist Roger Mudd, with no constitutional or legal mandate, a former president's role in public life has remained unofficial based on his "reputations, accomplishments, wisdom, believability and political credibility."[22] Perhaps ironically, Mudd pointed out that all new presidents also wish to be free of their predecessors, stating "The new headmaster does not want Mr. Chips living on campus," yet it is his colleagues in the news media that can create this problem as they continue to find these men to hold tremendous news value.

Many political observers—scholars and journalists alike—have nearly institutionalized the "legacy watch," with a president's legacy "debated, constructed, and reconstructed long before he leaves office"[23] through scholarly articles, books, conference panels, newspaper editorials, and other news media coverage about the impending finale of a president's time in office. Perhaps no president, especially during the modern presidential era, has left a greater legacy, with the help of scholars and journalists, than Franklin D. Roosevelt, whose "legacy for his successors would be the shadow he cast on them. . . . He personally dominated the political landscape, and his polices changed American society permanently."[24] Still, scholars and other interested presidency observers also have pointed to other contemporary presidents who have left an indelible mark on the presidency as an institution. Two noteworthy examples include Nixon, whose resignation following Watergate left the modern presidency "limited and diminished,"[25] and Reagan, whose legacy has received much attention since as early as his last year in office, as he was credited with closing "the gap between the public and its leader"[26] and putting "a stamp upon his party and upon the nation's political culture that shapes it still."[27]

According to presidential communications advisor David Gergen, who worked in the Nixon, Ford, Reagan, and Clinton administrations, the ability to create a legacy is a lesson in presidential leadership for future presidents to ponder, since "the most effective presidents create a living legacy, inspiring legions of followers to carry on their mission long after they are gone."[28]

LIFE AFTER THE WHITE HOUSE IN THE MODERN ERA: DOES TIME HEAL ALL WOUNDS?

Since FDR's death in 1945, only one other president, John F. Kennedy, died while in office. The remaining nine presidents (some longer than others) enjoyed their time in the exclusive club of ex-presidents, fondly called "my exclusive trade union" by former president Herbert Hoover. (Hoover was the only former president when he left office in March 1933, and he enjoyed the longest tenure as an ex-president, thirty-one years until his death in 1964.) Various factors can impact the activities of and public expectations for a former president, including his age when leaving office (leaving the presidency as a relatively young man can create much higher expectations about contributions to public life), his length of tenure in office (a two-term president presumably contributed more to policy changes during his time in office and can receive more attention as a policy "expert"), and whether or not he leaves office in good standing with the public (some presidents have left office with low approval ratings and/or under the cloud of a scandal, leaving even more legacy-related questions to debate than usual). The activities in which former presidents have engaged during the past half century have varied tremendously due not only to the circumstances already stated, but also due to the individual's desire to be publicly active and viewed as making a useful contribution to society and, therefore, also viewed as a successful former president.

Harry Truman, while not a young man when he left office in 1953, would spend twenty years as a former president until his death in 1973. Truman relished his return to life as a private citizen in Independence, Missouri, and it was this simple life as a former president that allowed his low public approval ratings upon leaving office to slowly begin to rise during his post-White House years through the public's glimpses, via news coverage, of his daily activities. He spent a good deal of his time going for walks, playing the piano, driving, writing his memoirs, and working at his library—for many years, the "most memorable exhibit on display was Truman himself." Truman left the White House with no Secret Service protection, and no expense accounts or staff funded through the federal treasury; he also did not work as a lobbyist or consultant and never attempted to cash in on his fame as a former president. His return to life as a citizen was considered one of the happiest periods of his life,[29] and his public approval resurgence by the late 1970s led to many politicians and citizens alike longing for the simplicity and directness of Truman's political style.

Upon leaving the White House in 1961, Dwight Eisenhower also enjoyed his chance to return to life as a private citizen, and at age seventy he did not have a high public expectation for continued service. Instead of remaining active on the political scene, Eisenhower played golf, visited with friends, and wrote both formal and informal memoirs of his life and presidency. His political visibility remained low key; he gave advice on foreign and military affairs when asked by Presidents Kennedy and Johnson, and months before his death in 1969, Eisenhower had endorsed Nixon in his 1968 bid for the presidency. Eisenhower's ranking as a great president has steadily risen among historians since first being rated "average" in Schlesinger's 1962 survey, with more recent surveys placing him in the top ten and labeling him "near great."[30] According to biographer Stephen Ambrose, the eight years of peace and prosperity during the Eisenhower years will continue to improve his public standings as a great president: "No other President in the twentieth century could make that claim. No wonder that millions of Americans felt the country was damned lucky to have him."[31]

The next two former presidents—Johnson and Nixon—would leave office under much different circumstances. Johnson, whose initial legacy could be summed up by one word—Vietnam—spent his four years out of office, prior to his death in 1973, building his library, writing his memoirs, and working on his ranch. His public appearances were limited but did include some speaking engagements (most notably at the LBJ Library) and interviews with Walter Cronkite. The press, however, portrayed him as "a sullen, bitter, brooding, unhappy man, retreating to the isolation of his ranch to lick his wounds."[32] By the 1990s, Johnson was enjoying a resurgence in public standing in spite of Vietnam, in part through efforts of the Johnson Library, family members, former colleagues, and even scholars who began to pay more attention to his achievements in the domestic policy arena.[33] According to Richard Goodwin, former speechwriter during the early years of the Johnson administration, scholars and commentators were finally reassessing Johnson's domestic agenda, which had long been obscured because of Vietnam: "[F]or years afterward, the moans of the battlefield have obscured the narrative of achievement and spacious vision that may ultimately rank Lyndon Johnson among our very great leaders."[34]

After his resignation from office in August 1974, Nixon began a twenty-year effort of rehabilitating his public image and shaping his legacy while "running for ex-president." He traveled around the world, wrote several books (mostly on foreign policy), gave lectures, wrote newspaper editorials, and counseled presidents on the state of foreign affairs. Public passions about Nixon, both good and bad, continued throughout his twenty-year tenure as a former president; however, slight improvements in his rankings by historians have been slow in coming, as he is still rated "below average" and at the bottom third in recent surveys.³⁵ According to biographer Melvin Small, Nixon did restore some of his image as a knowledgeable resource for national and international concerns: "Whatever people may have thought of Watergate and Nixon personally, by the time [his] library opened [in July 1990], many considered him a wise elder statesman whose ideas about foreign policy, particularly relating to the communist bloc, were worth listening to."³⁶ Upon his death in 1994, many political observers discussed the Nixon legacy, which was muddled at best even two decades after Watergate: "At Nixon's death, nothing about him was perfectly clear anymore. Like children standing at the grave of a deeply flawed father, Americans began to construct a more complex picture of his strengths and weaknesses."³⁷

According to Gerald Ford, who once described his post-presidential years as being "without prescribed activities and [enjoying] a marvelous array of choices," five themes have characterized his return to public life, including education, advocacy, partisanship, the celebrity status accorded a former president, and former presidents as symbols.³⁸ In addition to writing his memoirs and remaining somewhat active in Republican politics (including Ronald Reagan's 1980 presidential campaign), Ford was criticized during the early 1980s for his ability to make large sums of money from business consulting and his service on a variety of corporate boards.³⁹ However, Ford's legacy, like that of many of his predecessors, has improved with time. After his appearance, at age eighty-seven, at the 2000 Republican National Convention, where his political colleagues paid him tribute, political observers in the press also began to cast a different light on his political legacy as "underrated" for his role in helping the nation recover from Watergate, which has been considered "one of America's darkest periods."⁴⁰

Jimmy Carter's role as a former president represents a unique schism in the pattern of his contemporary colleagues—his accomplishments as an ex-president in many ways rival those of his presidency. Carter also was relatively young when he left office in January 1981; at age fifty-six, he had many viable years in which to remain publicly active. Through his work with Habitat for Humanity, international human rights, overseeing elections, and other diplomatic foreign missions, there has been continuity in the issues that Carter pursued both during and after his years in the White House. Carter has "redefined the ex-presidency" by adding a new dimension "to the traditional roles of ex-presidents—the retired statesman who simply returned to his home, from which he offered sage advice, or, more rarely, the occasional public servant who ran for office again or accepted a presidential appointment." In just over a decade after his presidency, Carter's record, particularly in foreign policy, had begun to look better in retrospect as he solidified "the political resurrection that had turned 1980's malaise-ridden loser into 1994's distinguished global peacemaker."⁴¹ According to historian Douglas Brinkley, Carter used his time in the White House "as a stepping-stone to greater *global* achievement. . . . What Carter really wanted was to find some way to continue the unfinished business of his presidency. . . . Nothing about the White House so became Carter as having left it."[42]

Ronald Reagan, as the longest living ex-president (he was ninety-three when he died in 2004) and first two-term president to leave office since Eisenhower, remained newsworthy throughout his tenure as a former president. Each year his birthday in February was a ready-made news story recollecting the achievements of the Reagan administration, and much press attention was paid to the announcement in 1994 that Reagan was battling Alzheimer's. By the end of the decade the press was following closely the efforts to name a variety of federal venues after Reagan, including National Airport in Washington and the Reagan Federal Building. Initially, his legacy was discussed in terms of his skills as a communicator and the changes that he brought to presidential leadership during the 1980s, that in addition to policy changes "his more important legacy is in how much he changed our minds."[43] The successful public image of strong leadership cultivated by the Reagan administration, in spite of the perceived manipulation of the news media, continues to mold Reagan's legacy, exemplifying the fact that "Americans felt good about Reagan generally, if not about the presidency itself. If Reagan had alienated reporters, it had not affected his bond with the public."[44]

In contrast to his immediate predecessor and former boss, the initial assessment of George H. W. Bush's legacy was formed, without the lead time in the press of a second term, following his reelection loss in 1992. And while his pardons of Casper Weinberger and others involved in the Iran-Contra scandal during the last weeks of his administration threatened to tarnish his legacy, Bush has maintained a somewhat low profile as a former president and has been "deeply ambivalent about trying to shape his own legacy."[45] Bush has participated in the usual activities of former presidents, including speeches and publishing books. At the dedication of his library in 1997, however, he made it clear that it was the job of historians, not his or the library's, to assess his legacy. Bush has remained off the national stage, having stated "we only have one president at a time," particularly since the election of his son as president in 2000. He has been reluctant to use his library "to erect a monument to himself," sees much of his legacy in the political careers of his sons, George W. and Jeb, and sets himself apart as a former president in his "calm indifference to his place in history."[46]

CLINTON'S LEGACY: THE PERPETUAL PARADOX

Even before Clinton officially left office, presidential scholars and the news media began considering the question of the Clinton legacy. As the youngest man to leave the White House since Teddy Roosevelt in 1909, and as a two-term president, Clinton faced different and perhaps greater public expectations as a former president than some of his predecessors. By most accounts, Clinton was a complex president during a "turbulent" political era in American history; during the 1990s, Americans witnessed both tremendous economic growth and partisan polarization in Washington while trying to sort out the complexities of where America fit into the post-cold war "New World Order."[47] The Clinton years also have been described as a paradox and a time of missed opportunities—a skilled politician governing at a time of economic prosperity, yet one whose personal scandals diminished his ability to command leadership over the national agenda. Clinton is viewed as "a politician of extraordinary talent [who] missed the opportunity to be an extraordinary president."[48]

In spite of the economic growth during the 1990s, the achievement of producing a balanced budget, and policy victories such as welfare reform, the impeachment in 1998 will forever cast a dark cloud over the Clinton presidency, as it "continued the long-term loss of presidential prestige" that began during the imperial presidencies of Johnson and Nixon.[49] The economic boom of the 1990s also may work against the ultimate legacy of the Clinton years, since facing a crisis provides a better opportunity for strong leadership: "Except for the scarlet letter of impeachment, Clinton's presidency is not particularly likely to stand out because the times in which he governed denied much opportunity to make a bold mark."[50] But some remain optimistic for a positive legacy based on Clinton's policy accomplishments, once the memory of the impeachment has begun to fade, which "might eventually outweigh his lack of personal judgment. Historians tend to be more concerned generations later with the impact a president has on a country from the long view."[51]

In the waning days of the Clinton presidency, the national news media also began to weigh in with their early assessment of the Clinton legacy, particularly how to view the personal failings of such a skilled politician. But in one of his last acts as president, Clinton extended the national discussion about his lack of moral judgment by granting a presidential pardon to Marc Rich, a wealthy financier-turned-fugitive, whose ex-wife had donated millions of dollars to Democratic Party coffers and whose attorney was once employed by the Clinton administration. Others who received a pardon included Susan McDougal (who served eighteen months in jail for refusing to testify against the Clintons in the Whitewater scandal), Patricia Hearst (the publishing heiress kidnapped in the 1970s), and Roger Clinton (the president's half-brother, who once received a conviction on drug charges). The Rich pardon remained the most controversial; Rich had been living in Switzerland since 1983, having fled the country when he was indicted on federal charges of evading more than $48 million in income taxes and illegally buying oil from Iran during the 1979 hostage crisis.[52] Other negative stories also followed

Clinton out of office, including those about gifts that the former president and First Lady had not properly reported, rumored misdeeds and pranks by Clinton staffers in their last hours in the White House, the cost and location of Clinton's post-presidential offices, and Clinton's negotiation of a deal with the special prosecutor to end legal problems stemming from the Monica Lewinsky scandal. But it was the flap over the Marc Rich pardon, as well as other questionable pardons that had been solicited by Clinton's brother-in-law, Hugh Rodham, that led the *New York Times* in an editorial to declare Clinton's last presidential acts a "redoubled effort . . . to plunge further and further beneath the already low expectation of his most cynical critics and most world-weary friends."[53]

FORMER PRESIDENT CLINTON AS NEWS: THE GIFT THAT KEEPS ON GIVING

Stories in the national news media about Clinton's ongoing problems kept the former president in full public view for months after he left the White House with much coverage that presented a critical and negative tone[54] about the end-of-administration scandals and how his legacy would be adversely affected. Other studies have documented the finding of the prevalent coverage of Clinton once he left office. According to a study by the Center for Media and Public Affairs (CMPA),[55] published in March 2001, during the period January 21, 2001–February 28, 2001, 101 stories about Clinton were broadcast on the nightly network news shows, compared to only fourteen stories that had been aired about former president George H. W. Bush during the same time span in 1993.[56] A second study by the CMPA, published in May 2001, found that during the first 100 days of the new Bush administration in 2001, stories related to the Rich pardon ranked sixth in a study of top-ten news stories on the nightly network news shows (in number of minutes). And if late-night television is any indication of news prominence on the national level, Clinton also beat out Bush during the first 100 days in the number of jokes; Jay Leno, David Letterman, Conan O'Brien, and Bill Maher "barely seemed to notice the presidential transition" as Clinton garnered 293 jokes compared to Bush's 200, according to the same study.[57] The potential damage to Clinton's legacy resulting from the pardons also remained a topic of discussion on the op-ed pages of America during Bush's honeymoon. For example, a column in the *Christian Science Monitor* stated: "Permanent damage to Clinton's legacy and future is possible, but unlikely, say some analysts. Virtually every previous president who left office under some sort of cloud eventually recovered standing with the American people. But for now the ex-president's travails have damaged his ability to provide a countering view to President Bush's initial policy proposals."[58]

Coverage in the *New York Times*

An analysis of Clinton stories in the *New York Times* from January 21, 2001, through December 31, 2001, shows several negative stories about Clinton in early 2001, but as the frequency of the stories decreased throughout the year, the tone of the coverage began to turn more positive. The shift toward more neutral or positive coverage is consistent with the coverage, considered "largely favorable in tone," that each of his four predecessors received after leaving office.[59] During the time period studied here, a total of 174 news stories (excluding editorials and columns) appeared in which Clinton or one of his actions was the subject. (A breakdown of topics covered in these stories is provided in Table 12.1).

A more focused look at the tone of coverage shows that in his first weeks out of office, stories on Clinton were mostly negative in tone, which is not surprising when considering the conditions in which Clinton left office. The focus of early Clinton coverage is centered on basically two issues: last-minute pardons and the taking and returning of White House gifts and other property. During Clinton's first month out of office, eighty-four news stories appeared in the *Times* (from January 21 to February 21) focusing on the former president; of those, forty stories were related to the pardons, and seven

TABLE 12.1
New York Times Coverage By Topic
(Former Presidents Reagan, Bush, and Clinton—
Total Stories First Year Out of Office)*

Topic	Reagan	Bush	Clinton
Legacy	10	5	7
Pardons	0	0	85
Travel/Speeches	9	2	4
Memoirs	0	0	1
Presidential Library	0	0	5
Office	0	0	20
Life After White House	4	1	10
Policies	16	18	15
Honors	0	0	0
Health	8	0	0
Ongoing Scandals	29	5	16
Miscellaneous	9	18	11
TOTAL	85	49	174

*These data also appear in Lori Cox Han and Matthew J. Krov, "Out of Office and in the News: Early Projections of the Clinton Legacy," *Presidential Studies Quarterly* 33:4 (December 2003): 925–933.

focused on White House gifts. Negative coverage of Clinton in the *Times* peaked in mid-February, with ten front-page stories in a sixteen-day span, from February 9 to February 25 (including four stories on the Rich pardon and subsequent investigation, two stories on Roger Clinton's role in the pardons, one story about Hugh Rodham's role in the pardons, one story about the pardons in general, and two stories about Clinton's initial choice of office space in Manhattan). Negative news coverage of Clinton during his first six weeks out of office prompted *New York Times* columnist Adam Nagourney to document the irony of Clinton's political isolation while perhaps enjoying the notoriety as the world's most famous man. Nagourney described Clinton on March 1 as "a man who so craves attention and company and is [now] described by friends as adrift and often isolated," concluding that "the incessant controversy over a series of last-minute pardons has exacerbated his forced isolation."[60]

By May, stories appearing in the *Times* about Clinton were mostly neutral in tone for several weeks, turning to mostly positive stories by late July, taking a more human-interest perspective on the former president that described more typical activities that Americans had come to expect (for example, a story appearing on May 16 discussed Clinton's attendance at a New York high school graduation). Previously critical story lines about the end-of-administration scandals also began to neutralize somewhat in May; for example, staff writer Christi Marquis wrote on May 19 that the vandalism reported in the White House by Clinton staffers was overblown. A front-page story on Clinton's Harlem office appears on July 31, followed by another front-page story about his book deal on August 7. In a twelve-day period, from July 31 through August 11, Clinton received a total of thirteen news stories in the *Times*, as well as a column by Maureen Dowd on August 1 about his public relations strategy as a former president: "Trying to move past the fiasco about the Marc Rich pardon and the china and silver heist, Mr. Clinton emerged from a funk and reintroduced himself this week. He has reintroduced himself so many times after overstepping and screwing up . . . [that] his old White House aides laugh at the fact that the Protean Pol is still doing it after his presidency is over."[61]

Coverage of Clinton decreases after the spring and early summer months, with only thirteen stories from August 11 through December 31. Coverage of Clinton during 2001, however, ends with a familiar theme from earlier in the year—a December 21 front-page story on Clinton's attempt to repair his public image and the strategy for building his legacy. In describing the aggressive public relations campaign to strengthen Clinton's image during his first year out of office, staff writer Richard Berke wrote, "No modern president has ever mounted such an aggressive and organized drive to affect the agenda after leaving the White House." The strategy consisted of "efforts to deploy surrogates to speak out for him [which were] reminiscent of his vaunted war rooms in the White House, which were established for him to seize the political offensive on matters that included Whitewater and health care." Berke also noted that Clinton was careful not to attempt to upstage Bush, but that Clinton still faced an uphill battle to repair his public image.[62]

In contrast, both Reagan and Bush received much less coverage in the *Times* during their first years out of office. Between January 21, 1989, and December 31, 1989, a total of eighty-five stories appeared in the *Times* about Reagan, nearly one-half the number of stories for Clinton during the same time period. Approximately one-third of those stories dealt with the ongoing legal actions stemming from the Iran-Contra scandal, including speculations as to whether Reagan would testify in court during the trials of those indicted (Oliver North, John Poindexter, etc.). Other stories focused on typical post-White House topics, such as travel and speeches (in particular, Reagan's visit to and speeches in Japan, for which he received $2 million); Reagan's health also was covered (a fall from his horse and subsequent medical procedures). With the exception of Iran-Contra scandal coverage and two critical stories of the Reagan legacy on domestic policies such as Medicare and welfare, the remaining news coverage of Reagan in the *Times* presented a mostly positive view of the former president and his legacy.

Bush, a one-term president, received just over half the coverage in the *Times* as Reagan, with a total of forty-nine stories from January 21, 1993, through December 31, 1993. Of those, a total of eleven stories focused on the Iraqi assassination plot against Bush in early 1993. Bush also faced lingering coverage from the Iran-Contra scandal, which received a total of five stories, mostly critical of Bush's connection to the scandal while vice president. Most of Bush's remaining coverage was positive, and like Reagan's, focused on his post-presidential activities.

Coverage on Network News

A similar analysis of Clinton stories on the nightly network newscasts from January 21, 2001, through December 31, 2001, shows that while the *New York Times* had begun to soften its critical stance toward Clinton by the end of the year, the television coverage from the three major networks (ABC, CBS, and NBC) had remained harshly critical. (These data were accessed from the Vanderbilt University Television News Archive.)[63] Each of the three networks began its coverage of the former president with critical stories during Clinton's first months out of office but rarely acknowledged his existence during the latter half of 2001. *ABC World News Tonight* dedicated just over seventy-nine minutes of its national nightly newscast to Clinton, with approximately fifty-five minutes focusing on the pardon controversies, approximately eight minutes on the Harlem office, and the remaining sixteen minutes focusing on various topics such as his book deal, his trip to India, and the controversy over taking gifts from the White House. A story on Clinton led the ABC newscast nine times after he left office in 2001. The *CBS Evening News* dedicated nearly seventy-five minutes of airtime to Clinton (the lowest total of all three networks). Approximately forty-seven minutes focused on the pardon controversies, while approximately ten minutes went to the Harlem office and the remaining eighteen minutes to other topics, including the Clinton administration's policy on terrorism and Osama bin Laden. Like ABC, CBS led its newscast nine times with stories on Clinton.

The *NBC Nightly News* dedicated a network-high 102 minutes to Clinton coverage during this time period—approximately seventy-one minutes to the pardon scandals, eight minutes to the Harlem Office, eight minutes to the taking and returning of White House gifts, and the remaining fifteen minutes to various other topics, such as the India trip and Chelsea Clinton's college graduation. NBC also had a regular segment in its program from February 1 to March 2 dubbed the "Clinton Watch," in which various aspects of Clinton's post-presidency were discussed. NBC also led its broadcast nine times with stories on Clinton. In general, most network coverage of Clinton during 2001 came within his first six weeks after leaving office. From January 21 through March 7, Clinton received eighty-three total stories on the three networks, including twenty-five of his twenty-seven lead stories. During this time, topics relating to Clinton received 215 minutes of coverage for all three networks out of 255:50 minutes of total airtime on Clinton through the end of 2001. After March 7, Clinton received only thirty-nine stories, two of which were lead stories.

Compared to Reagan and Bush, Clinton again eclipsed his two predecessors in amount of coverage on network news shows during the first year out of office (see Table 12.2). During the period January 21, 1989–December 31, 1989, Reagan received a total of 141:40 minutes of coverage on all three net-

TABLE 12.2
Total Airtime on Nightly Network News Shows
(Former Presidents Reagan, Bush, and Clinton—
First Year Out of Office)*

Total Airtime Minutes	Reagan	Bush	Clinton
ABC World News Tonight	51:20	5:00	79:10
NBC Nightly News	40:20	6:50	102:00
CBS Evening News	50:00	4:10	74:40
TOTAL	141:40	16:00	255:50

*These data also appear in Lori Cox Han and Matthew J. Krov, "Out of Office and in the News: Early Projections of the Clinton Legacy," *Presidential Studies Quarterly* 33:4 (December 2003): 925–33.

works—ABC had the most, with 51:20 minutes, followed by CBS, with 50:00 minutes, and NBC, with 40:20 minutes. Each network had brief stories on Reagan's travel to and speeches in Japan, as well as other typical post-presidency stories on topics such as his memoirs, other travels, and his daily routine after the White House. Reagan's health (the fall off the horse) also made news, including three lead stories on NBC and one each on ABC and CBS. Most of Reagan's network coverage, however, focused on the ongoing Iran-Contra scandal court cases. On ABC, fifteen stories totaling 21:50 minutes focused on the Iran-Contra scandal; similarly, NBC devoted thirteen stores totaling 22:10 minutes, and CBS devoted eighteen stories totaling 42:40 minutes to the ongoing story. Bush enjoyed much less coverage on the network news during the period January 21, 1993–December 31, 1993. A total of only sixteen minutes is devoted to Bush on all three networks—NBC had the most coverage, with 6:50 minutes, followed by ABC, with five minutes, and CBS, with 4:10 minutes. Speeches and travels by Bush received occasional coverage, but most of the network airtime was devoted to updates on the Iran-Contra scandal and the uncovering of the Iraqi assassination plot against the former president. A total of 8:10 minutes was devoted to the assassination plot on all three networks, with 4:40 minutes devoted to the Iran-Contra scandal on all three networks.

Analysis

When assessing the comparisons of coverage for each of the three former presidents considered here, it is interesting to note the approval ratings of each just prior to leaving office. Clinton enjoyed a 65 percent approval rating, according to a Gallup Poll, just days before leaving office in January 2001, while Reagan had a 63 percent approval rating in late December 1988, and Bush's approval rating in January 1993 was 56 percent.[64] While both Reagan and Clinton left office with high approval ratings, each received different news coverage during his first year out of office. Also important to consider is the fact that as a one-term president, Bush had just lost a presidential election, and the news media had not been preparing for his exit from center stage for four years throughout a second term. As a result, much of the coverage in the last weeks of the Bush administration served as a summation of his four years in office. However, without the coverage of the Iran-Contra scandal during 1989, Reagan's coverage in both the *Times* and on the networks does not differ that much from Bush's, at least by topic. Former presidents remain important public figures, and their activities—speeches, honors, travels, and health—rightly remain newsworthy.

Reagan did have the ongoing story of the Iran-Contra scandal shaping the first phase of his legacy in the news media during his first year out of office, but the significance of this "scandal" coverage differs greatly in its focus than ongoing scandals for Clinton throughout 2001. Critical news coverage of the Reagan administration dealt with just that—the administration and the various political actors within it—and not necessarily with Reagan the man. Clinton's troubles with the news media, and throughout his administration, were most often focused on him personally, not his administration as a whole. This continued during his first year out of office, with most of the coverage focusing on pardons and concluding activities surrounding the Whitewater and Lewinsky investigations. The personal angle of Clinton's troubles highlighted his ongoing press coverage, while Reagan's coverage while out of office suggests the validity of the oft-quoted nickname "The Teflon President."

Given the national furor among the press and the American public over Clinton's last-minute pardons, particularly the Rich pardon, it is interesting to note that Bush received no news coverage in the sources considered here once he left office on his controversial pardons of Casper Weinberger and five other Iran-Contra scandal participants on Christmas Eve, 1992. While many in the press suggested that the pardons would tarnish his legacy, Bush was not hounded by ongoing questions in the press about his actions. (He also did not wait until his last hours in office to grant the pardons, which gave the news media time to move on to other stories by January 1993.)

The amount of coverage received by Clinton during his first year out of office, unlike Reagan and Bush, suggests two explanations. First, Clinton, at age fifty-four, was the youngest president to leave office since 1909 (Reagan was seventy-seven, and Bush was sixty-eight) and was not at the typical retirement age, which left much speculation as to how he would spend his time. Also, his connection to Washington politics remained stronger than most other former presidents with his wife's election to the U.S. Senate in 2000. Second, and perhaps most importantly, much of the coverage of the post-Clinton presidency maintained a critical, somewhat sensational tone about ongoing scandals and controversies, which certainly proves the adage that "old habits die hard." From the early days of the presidential campaign in 1992, the news media had been in perpetual scandal mode while covering Clinton throughout his entire eight years in office, making the possibility of the news media suddenly seeing former President Clinton in a new light unlikely. The nation may have been suffering from "Clinton fatigue" by the time he left office, but the nation's news media were still going strong in their coverage of ethical questions, legal problems, and allegations surrounding Clinton.[65] The American press has always enjoyed a good story; as such, Clinton is perhaps the most newsworthy ex-president in American history.

Crashing Bush's Honeymoon: The Tale of the Uninvited Guest?

One final question must be considered when looking at the first phase of Clinton's legacy—what is a new president to do with a former president who is still dominating center stage? Presidents during the modern era usually have experienced a "honeymoon" period when first taking office—a brief time when both the news media and political adversaries allow the new administration to settle into its new surroundings.[66] The honeymoon also has been defined as the "courteous manners and procedural accommodations" that most incoming presidents receive from Congress during their first weeks in office, which can be affected by outside sources as well: "The answer seems to lie in public opinion, or more accurately in public sentiment as gauged by Members of Congress themselves and by their party leaders, drawing upon polls and on press treatment of the new regime downtown."[67] This follows the eleven-week transition period between the election in November and the inauguration in January, which the president-elect spends making top-level appointments to his cabinet and staff and laying the groundwork for his legislative agenda. (In 2000, however, Bush experienced a shortened transition period due to the contested presidential election. Vice President Al Gore officially conceded the election on December 13, one day after the Supreme Court's historic ruling in *Bush v. Gore*.) Timing is especially crucial for newly elected presidents who must have an effective strategy to "hit the ground running" to achieve policy agenda success. The power to control the political agenda must be seized early in an administration; only constitutional authority is automatic, since the "power of the presidency—in terms of effective control of the policy agenda—must be consciously developed."[68]

What a presidential candidate talks about during the general election campaign, especially if he discusses specific domestic policy proposals, is a good indication of what his agenda will look like once in office. However, presidents alone do not control their destinies, since outside political actors such as Congress or interest groups, among others, are important players in the agenda-building process. Presidents only have control over the policies they choose to initiate and the strategy behind that initiation.[69] An important tool for that strategy is the use of public activities, since a president can affect to some degree the public's policy agenda through public speeches. Developing an effective strategy for press relations also must be a top priority for new administrations, since the news media are the primary link between the president and the public, especially in terms of setting the national political agenda. Communication strategies have become an important and a permanent part of the everyday operation of the White House. As such, the expanding role of the rhetorical presidency in American politics and the growing technology and influence of the mass media have forever changed the definition of presidential leadership. Most often, the mass media provide the primary means of presidential communication.[70]

The traditional honeymoon period for new presidents, however, is no longer a guarantee. Both Clinton in 1993 and Bush in 2001 experienced predominantly negative news coverage during their first weeks in office, and Bush received less media attention overall than did Clinton or his father,

George H. W. Bush, did in 1989, which "illustrates the shriveling of the honeymoon period."[71] Research on the Clinton and Bush honeymoons, or lack thereof, substantiates the claim. According to a study by the Project for Excellence in Journalism, published in April 2001, Bush received less positive coverage overall in his first 100 days in office during 2001 than did Clinton in 1993; Bush also was "dramatically less visible" than Clinton, with 41 percent fewer stories appearing in major newspapers, on network television, and in a major newsweekly magazine. A trend also has emerged in how the press follows the first 100 days: initial coverage looks at whether the president is up to the job, then moves to the policy agenda, particularly budget issues; presidents also appear to receive less coverage overall on the front pages of newspapers as the press continues a trend of "lighter," meaning less political, news.[72] A similar study by the CMPA, published in May 2001, found that television news coverage of Bush during the first 100 days was substantially less than the amount of airtime given to Clinton during his first 100 days in office.[73]

The lingering media presence of Clinton during the Bush honeymoon period raises the question of whether the former president edged out the new president in terms of press coverage. According to the CMPA in March 2001, Clinton garnered 101 stories on the nightly network news shows compared to 201 stories for Bush through the end of February 2001, suggesting that in spite of the unprecedented coverage for a former president, Clinton had not completely "elbowed [Bush] off the stage." Nonetheless, Bush staffers seemed "annoyed that Clinton [was] hogging the limelight," but they hoped that their administration's "orderly launch" presented a positive public image in "contrast with the final, frenetic days of the Clinton presidency."[74] Clinton, however, seemed to have lost the opportunity to present the Democratic voice as a former two-term president who could still speak as a leader of his party in the early dialogue on Bush's legislative agenda. The news media were more interested in the scandal-plagued last days of the Clinton administration, which allowed the Bush administration to focus more intently on its early policy messages.

An analysis of front-page stories in the *New York Times* for both Bush and Clinton from January 21, 2001, through March 1, 2001 (the first forty days of the Bush administration), suggests that the former president did, at times, rival his successor in the White House for the national news media's attention. During this time period, sixteen front-page stories focused on Clinton, while fifty-one front-page stories focused on Bush. The former and current presidents shared front-page headlines fourteen times during the forty-day period. During the week of February 13, both Clinton and Bush earned five front-page stories apiece. During this week, Bush was attempting to push his defense policies to center stage, but stories of Clinton's plans to move his office from Manhattan to Harlem and the Rich pardon scandal countered the new administration's attempts to dominate the national news agenda. Clinton

TABLE 12.3
New York Times Coverage of Clinton and Bush
(Comparison of Front-Page Stories)

Date	Topic: Clinton	Topic: Bush
1/23/2001	Foreign Policy	Abortion Policy
1/29/2001	Pardons	Church Groups
2/3/2001	White House Gifts	
2/6/2001	Pardon Inquiry	Tax Cut
2/9/2001	Rich Pardon	Tax Cut
		Defense Policy: Iraq
2/13/2001	NY Office	Energy Policy
2/14/2001	NY Office	Defense Policy
2/15/2001	Rich Pardon	
2/17/2001	Rich Pardon	Drug Policy
		Missile Defense
		Defense Policy: Iraq
2/19/2001	Rich Pardon	
2/22/2001	Pardons	Missile Defense
2/23/2001	Pardons	Foreign Policy: China
	Rodham Pardons	
2/25/2001	Pardons	Missile Defense
3/1/2001	Pardons	Budget
	Rodham Pardons	

Source: Collected by the authors from the *New York Times,* January 21, 2001–March 1, 2001.

earned front-page headlines in the *Times* on February 16 and 19 while Bush received no front-page billing. (On Sunday, February 18, Clinton also made national news with an op-ed column in the *Times* defending his last-minute pardons.) Finally, on March 1, Clinton received two front-page headlines to Bush's one, at a time when Bush was attempting to promote plans for his first budget proposal to Congress. However, it should be noted that the Bush administration employed a targeted news coverage strategy in its early months on specific policy topics, therefore the quantity of coverage was not necessarily the overall goal. Also, the continuing coverage of Clinton's problems provided a positive contrast for Bush in highlighting the differences in leadership styles and personalities.

CONCLUSION

In 1989, George H. W. Bush was quoted in the *New York Times* as saying, "History is basically kind to American Presidents. Everybody looks better over time. Herbert Hoover looks better today than he did 40 years ago, doesn't he?

Time is generous to people."[75] Most scholars considering presidential legacies have come to similar conclusions. Historian Marie B. Hecht wrote in 1976 that former presidents should be allowed to choose how to spend their retirement years without the designation of a formal role in government. However,

> [N]o ex-president can hope for obscurity. A sense of history drives them to protect and defend their administrations in statements and writings. This influences their actions and their behavior in retirement. . . . For the people, an ex-president is a link with the past, a symbol of continuity, and an exercise in nostalgia. If he lives long enough, no matter how unpopular on leaving office, he acquires respect. The public is fickle in its bestowal of favors but also has a short memory for those it disliked. Retired chief executives become sages, nestors, beloved elder statesmen, or even folk heroes.[76]

The question of defining Bill Clinton's legacy, and his continued role in American public life, remains unanswered. Well into his third year out of office, Clinton continued to make headlines, as the newsworthiness of the former president did not wane. In March 2002, upon the release of independent counsel Robert Ray's final report about the Whitewater and Lewinsky investigations, a March 10, 2002, editorial in the *Washington Post* declared that while "the official era of Clinton scandals is finally over," it appears unlikely for a "meeting of the minds about the Clinton presidency" to appear any time soon.[77] In May 2002, the topic of Clinton again dominated political talk shows and op-ed pages with the news that he was considering a network television deal to host his own talk show on NBC or CBS, reportedly worth $50 million.[78] This news prompted much criticism in the press that Clinton was once again tarnishing the integrity of the presidency; however, Richard Cohen of the *Washington Post* defended Clinton in his comparison to money-making efforts by other former presidents, most notably Ford's $1 million deal with NBC in 1977 to offer his commentary on current events, suggesting that unless Clinton decided on a "Montel Williams-style show" that he could be a "great teacher" on important domestic and foreign policy matters.[79]

There is little doubt that both the press and public remain fascinated with Bill Clinton. In its April 8, 2002, edition, *Newsweek* ran a cover story by Jonathan Alter on the former president and his life since leaving the White House—his numerous speeches around the world, his work on his memoirs, and his life as husband to a U.S. senator. The conclusion, at least in terms of the unfolding legacy, was that Clinton still has "star power," and while talk of the initial overshadowing of George W. Bush has faded, "the incumbent can't possibly match his predecessor as a figure of fascination."[80] In making a first assessment of Ronald Reagan's legacy in 1988, Charles O. Jones wrote that it was not too early to analyze the "extraordinary" political events of the Reagan administration, since a more in-depth analysis would emerge as time went by: "All Presidents leave something of themselves behind, to be sure, but whatever that legacy may be, it is fitted into larger, ongoing political developments. No President is forgotten. But all leave town when it is over."[81] Clinton may have left Washington, but he left center stage later than most former presidents. The impact that the continuing coverage will have on Clinton's longer-term legacy is yet to be determined. However, the image left in the minds of Americans during his initial days out of the White House was not an overly positive one.

Newsweek columnist Jonathan Alter provided an accurate summation of the news media's ongoing obsession with the Clinton story on February 26, 2001, during the early days of the Bush administration:

> At first I was puzzled by why the latest installment of the Bill Clinton Story has been so big. Yes, the Marc Rich pardon was inexcusable by any standard, and the Bush honeymoon a tepid media affair by comparison. But week after week of it? The man's a former president, after all; even Richard Nixon didn't dominate the news this way from his Elba in San Clemente. . . . It's clear that Clinton is more than just another addiction in a nation of substance abusers. He's the gift that keeps on giving—to the media, the lip-smacking Republicans, and anyone with any appreciation of the subtleties of character and motivation.[82]

Even out of office, Clinton is still a good story, and this will undoubtedly impact future assessments of his legacy as it has the early projections of his years in the White House. And in the final analysis, at least one aspect of Clinton's legacy has probably already been determined. As the nation's first baby boomer president born during the television age, Clinton set a new standard for turning "the personal" into "the political" in news coverage of the White House, which is likely a difficult path that future presidents must navigate as well.

NOTES

1. Winthrop Dudley Sheldon, *The Ex-Presidents of the United States: How Each Played the Role* (Philadelphia: 1925), 3.

2. Peter Grier, "Clinton's Suspect Pardons," *Christian Science Monitor*, February 23, 2001, p. 2.

3. William Berman, *From the Center to the Edge: The Politics and Policies of the Clinton Presidency* (Lanham, Md.: Rowman & Littlefield, 2001), 2.

4. William J. Clinton, "The President's Radio Address," *Weekly Compilation of Presidential Documents*, January 20, 2001.

5. Clement E. Asante, *Life after the White House: Press Coverage of Four Ex-Presidents* (Westport, Conn.: Praeger, 2002), 75.

6. The influence of the *New York Times*, both politically and within the journalism industry, has been well documented. For example, see Michael Emery and Edwin Emery, *The Press and America: An Interpretive History of the Mass Media*, 8th ed. (Needham Heights, Mass.: Simon & Schuster, 1996), and Dean E. Alger, *The Media and Politics*, 2nd ed. (Belmont, Calif.: Wadsworth, 1996).

7. Thomas E. Cronin and Michael A. Genovese, *The Paradoxes of the American Presidency* (New York: Oxford University Press, 1998), 88–96.

8. Richard E. Neustadt, "Looking Back: Meanings and Puzzles," in *Looking Back on the Reagan Presidency*, ed. Larry Berman (Baltimore: Johns Hopkins University Press, 1990), 319.

9. Stephen Skowronek, "Presidential Leadership in Political Time," in *The Presidency and the Political System*, 6th ed., ed. Michael Nelson (Washington, D.C.: CQ Press, 2000), 164.

10. Arthur M. Schlesinger Sr., "Historians Rate U.S. Presidents," *Life* (November 1, 1948): 65–74.

11. Arthur M. Schlesinger Sr., *Paths to the Present* (New York: Macmillan, 1949), 94–96.

12. Arthur M. Schlesinger Jr., "Our Presidents: A Rating by 75 Historians," *New York Times Magazine*, July 29, 1962, pp. 40–43.

13. James MacGregor Burns, *Presidential Government: The Crucible of Leadership* (Boston: Houghton Mifflin, 1966), 80–81.

14. For example, see Thomas A. Bailey, *Presidential Greatness* (New York: Appleton-Century, 1966); Robert K. Murray and Tim H. Blessing, *Greatness in the White House: Rating the Presidents from George Washington through Ronald Reagan*, 2nd ed. (University Park: Pennsylvania State University Press, 1994); Gary M. Maranell, "The Evaluation of Presidents: An Extension of the Schlesinger Polls," *Journal of American History* 57 (1970): 104–13; Steven Neal, *Chicago Tribune Magazine*, January 10, 1982, pp. 9–13, 15, 18; Arthur M. Schlesinger Jr., "The Ultimate Approval Rating," *New York Times Magazine*, December 15, 1996, pp. 46–51.

15. For example, see Arthur B. Murphy, "Evaluating the Presidents of the United States," *Presidential Studies Quarterly* (Winter 1984): 117–26; Jack E. Holmes and Robert E. Elder Jr., "Our Best and Worst Presidents: Some Possible Reasons for Perceived Performance," *Presidential Studies Quarterly* (Summer 1989): 529–57; Patrick J. Kenney and Tom W. Rice, "The Contextual Determinants of Presidential Greatness," *Presidential Studies Quarterly* (Winter 1988): 161–69; Dean Keith Simonton, "Predicting Presidential Greatness: An Alternative to the Kenney and Rice Contextual Index," *Presidential Studies Quarterly* (Spring 1991): 301–305.

16. Dean Keith Simonton, *Why Presidents Succeed: A Political Psychology of Leadership* (New Haven, Conn.: Yale University Press, 1987), 5–6.

17. The Federalist Society/*Wall Street Journal* Survey on Presidents, May 5, 2003, which ranked Clinton number 24 out of 39 presidents in the "average" category, can be accessed at http://www.opinionjournal.com/hail/rankings/html. The C-SPAN Survey of Presidential Leadership, which ranked Clinton number 21 out of 41 presidents, can be accessed at http://www.americanpresidents.org/survey/historians/overall.asp.

18. Jeffrey E. Cohen, "Presidential Greatness as Seen in the Mass Public: An Extension and Application of the Simonton Model," paper presented at the 2002 American Political Science Association meeting, Boston, Mass.

19. Alan Evan Schenker, "Former Presidents: Suggestions for the Study of an Often Neglected Resource," *Presidential Studies Quarterly* 12 (1982): 545–51.

20. Richard Norton Smith and Timothy Walch, "Introduction," in *Farewell to the Chief: Former Presidents in American Public Life* (Worland, Wyo.: High Plains Publishing, 1990), xi–xii.

21. Daniel J. Boorstin, "Saving a National Resource: An Address on the Role of Former Presidents in American Public Life," in *Farewell to the Chief: Former Presidents in American Public Life*, ed. Richard Norton Smith and Timothy Walch (Worland, Wyo.: High Plains Publishing, 1990), 21–33.

22. Roger Mudd, Comments in "Former Presidents in American Public Life: A Symposium," in *Farewell to the Chief: Former Presidents in American Public Life*, ed. Richard Norton Smith and Timothy Walch (Worland, Wyo.: High Plains Publishing, 1990), 5–8.

23. John M. Murphy and Mary E. Stuckey, "Never Cared to Say Goodbye: Presidential Legacies and Vice Presidential Campaigns, *Presidential Studies Quarterly* 32 (2002): 46–66.

24. See Larry Berman, *The New American Presidency* (Boston: Little, Brown and Company, 1987), 209; William E. Leuchtenburg, *In the Shadow of FDR: From Harry Truman to Ronald Reagan* (Ithaca, N.Y.: Cornell University Press, 1983).

25. Bob Woodward, *Shadow: Five Presidents and the Legacy of Watergate* (New York: Simon & Schuster, 1999), 514.

26. Charles O. Jones, *The Reagan Legacy: Promise and Performance* (Chatham, N.J.: Chatham House, 1988), vii.

27. David Gergen, *Eyewitness to Power: The Essence of Leadership from Nixon to Clinton* (New York: Simon & Schuster, 2000), 351.

28. Ibid.

29. David McCullough, "The Man of Independence: Harry S. Truman in Retirement," in *Farewell to the Chief: Former Presidents in American Public Life*, ed. Richard Norton Smith and Timothy Walch (Worland, Wyo.: High Plains Publishing, 1990), 47–54.

30. See both the Federalist Society/*Wall Street Journal* and C-SPAN surveys from 2000.

31. Stephen E. Ambrose, *Eisenhower: Soldier and President* (New York: Simon & Schuster, 1990), 573.

32. Robert L. Hardesty, "With Lyndon Johnson in Texas: A Memoir of the Post-Presidential Years," in *Farewell to the Chief: Former Presidents in American Public Life*, ed. Richard Norton Smith and Timothy Walch (Worland, Wyo.: High Plains Publishing, 1990), 97.

33. Brian D. Sweany, "LBJ's Living Legacy," *Texas Monthly* (August 2000): 108.

34. Richard N. Goodwin, "LBJ's Forgotten Legacy," *Boston Globe*, February 22, 1999, p. A15.

35. See both the Federalist Society/*Wall Street Journal* and C-SPAN surveys from 2000.

36. Melvin Small, *The Presidency of Richard Nixon* (Lawrence: Kansas University Press, 1999), 307–308.

37. Jonathan Alter, "Growing Up with Nixon," *Newsweek* (May 2, 1994): 31.

38. Gerald R. Ford, "Personal Reflections on My Experiences as a Former President," in *Farewell to the Chief: Former Presidents in American Public Life*," ed. Richard Norton Smith and Timothy Walch (Worland, Wyo.: High Plains Publishing, 1990), 173.

39. Tom Morganthau and Thomas M. DeFrank, "Jerry Ford, Incorporated," *Newsweek* (May 11, 1981): 28.

40. *Newsweek*, "Gerald Ford's Underrated Legacy" (August 14, 2000): 5.

41. Douglas Brinkley, *The Unfinished Presidency: Jimmy Carter's Journey beyond the White House* (New York: Penguin Books, 1998), xi–xii.

42. Ibid., xvi.

43. David Gergen, "Ronald Reagan's Most Important Legacy," *U.S. News and World Report* (January 9, 1989): 28.

44. Louis Liebovich, *The Press and the Modern Presidency: Myths and Mindsets from Kennedy to Election 2000*, rev. 2d ed. (Westport, Conn.: Praeger, 2001), 148.

45. Ann McDaniel, "Bush's Legacy Thing," *Newsweek* (November 10, 1997): 50.

46. Kenneth T. Walsh, "The Mount Rushmore Complex," *U.S. News and World Report* (November 17, 1997): 7.

47. Steven E. Schier, "A Unique Presidency," in *The Postmodern Presidency: Bill Clinton's Legacy in U.S. Politics*, ed. Steven E. Schier (Pittsburgh: University of Pittsburgh Press, 2000), 1–16.

48. E. J. Dionne, "The Clinton Enigma: Seeking Consensus, Breeding Discord," in *The Election of 2000*, ed. Gerald Pomper (New York: Chatham House, 2001), 1–11.

49. Berman, *From the Center to the Edge*, 123.

50. Colin Campbell and Bert A. Rockman, "Introduction," in *The Clinton Legacy*, ed. Colin Campbell and Bert A. Rockman (New York: Chatham House Publishers, 2001), ix–xviii.

51. Liebovich, *The Press and the Modern Presidency*, 229.

52. Robert A. Rosenblatt and Debora Vrana, "Clinton Pardons: McDougal and Hearst but Not Milken," *Los Angeles Times*, January 21, 2001, p. A1.

53. *New York Times*, "Between Two Eras," February 11, 2001, sec. 4, p. 6.

54. For this study, critical and negative news coverage consists of scandal-related coverage or other issues that reporters suggest may harm the development of a positive presidential legacy. Neutral and/or positive coverage consists of stories about a president's post-White House activities that keep him in the public eye without harming his potential legacy.

55. The Center for Media and Public Affairs is a nonpartisan research and educational organization that conducts scientific studies of the news. Its goal is to provide an empirical basis for ongoing debates over media fairness and impact through studies of media content.

56. The Center for Media and Public Affairs, "Clinton Coverage Doesn't Eclipse Dubya," March 2001, available from http://www.cmpa.com (accessed March 21, 2001).

57. The Center for Media and Public Affairs, "The Disappearing Honeymoon: TV News Coverage of President George Bush's First 100 Days," *Media Monitor* (May–June 2001), available from http://www.cmpa/com (accessed March 30, 2003).

58. Grier, "Clinton's Suspect Pardons," 2.

59. Asante, *Life after the White House*, 74.

60. Adam Nagourney, "His Perks and Power Gone, Clinton Faces Storm Alone," *New York Times*, March 1, 2001, p. A1.

61. Maureen Dowd, "Liberties; One More for the Road," *New York Times*, August 1, 2001, p. A17.

62. Richard L. Berke, "Clinton and Aides Lay Plans to Repair a Battered Image," *New York Times*, December 21, 2001, p. A1.

63. The Television News Archive collection at Vanderbilt University holds more than 30,000 individual network evening news broadcasts from the major U.S. national broadcast networks—ABC, CBS, NBC, and CNN—and more than 9,000 hours of special news-related programming, including ABC's *Nightline*, since 1989.

64. Data from *The Gallup Poll, Public Opinion 1989* (Wilmington, Del.: Scholarly Resources, 1990); *The Gallup Poll, Public Opinion 1993* (Wilmington, Del.: Scholarly Resources, 1994); *The Gallup Poll, Public Opinion 2001* (Wilmington, Del.: Scholarly Resources, 2002). An analysis for soon-to-be former presidents also states, "Historically, incumbent presidents tend to receive a boost in their job approval ratings in the month following an election," *The Gallup Poll, Public Opinion 2000* (Wilmington, Del.: Scholarly Resources, 2001), 422.

65. For a discussion of the legacy of scandals during the Clinton administration, see Stanley A. Renshon, "The Polls: The Public's Response to the Clinton Scandals, Part 2: Diverse Explanations, Clearer Consequences," *Presidential Studies Quarterly* (June 2002): 412–27.

66. Michael Baruch Grossman and Martha Joynt Kumar, *Portraying the President* (Baltimore: Johns Hopkins University Press, 1981).

67. Richard Neustadt, "The Presidential 'One Hundred Days:' An Overview," in *Triumphs and Tragedies of the Modern Presidency: Seventy-Six Case Studies in Presidential Leadership*, ed. David Abshire (Westport, Conn.: Praeger, 2001), 47–52.

68. James P. Pfiffner, *The Strategic Presidency: Hitting the Ground Running*, 2d ed. (Lawrence: University Press of Kansas, 1996), 3.

69. Jeff Fishel, *Presidents & Promises: From Campaign Pledge to Presidential Performance* (Washington, D.C.: CQ Press, 1985), 187–88.

70. Lori Cox Han, *Governing From Center Stage: White House Communication Strategies during the Television Age of Politics* (Cresskill, N.J.: Hampton Press, 2001).

71. Doris A. Graber, *Mass Media & American Politics*, 6th ed. (Washington, D.C.: CQ Press, 2002), 282–83; The Center for Media and Public Affairs, "No News Is Good News for Dubya," April 2001, available from http://www.cmpa.com (accessed February 24, 2003).

72. The Project for Excellence in Journalism, "The First 100 Days: How Bush versus Clinton Fared in the Press," April 2001.

73. The Center for Media and Public Affairs, "The Disappearing Honeymoon: TV News Coverage of President George Bush's First 100 Days," *Media Monitor* (May–June, 2001), available from http://www.cmpa/com (accessed March 30, 2003).

74. Howard Fineman, "The Longest Goodbye," *Newsweek* (February 26, 2001): 26.

75. Bernard Weinraub, "Bush Sees History as 'Basically Kind' to Presidents," *New York Times*, April 1, 1989, p. A8.

76. Marie B. Hecht, *Beyond the Presidency: The Residues of Power* (New York: Macmillan, 1976), 313.

77. *Washington Post*, "An Ending," March 10, 2002, p. B8.

78. Sallie Hofmeister, "Clinton Said to Want TV Talk Show," *Los Angeles Times*, May 2, 2002, p. A1.

79. Richard Cohen, "Clinton on TV? Why Not?" *Washington Post Weekly Edition*, May 13–19, 2002, p. 27.

80. Jonathan Alter, "Citizen Clinton Up Close," *Newsweek* (April 8, 2002): 34.

81. Jones, vii–x.

82. Jonathan Alter, "Why We Can't Let Elvis Go," *Newsweek* (February 26, 2001): 36.

13

Not Going Public

George W. Bush and the Presidential Records Act

Nancy Kassop

What seems to be coming out of the administration is the idea that public information is a dangerous thing.
—Tom Connors, Society of American Archivists[1]

George W. Bush has a fetish for secrecy. And unless this executive order . . . is overturned, it will be a victory for secrecy in government—a victory so total that it would make Nixon jealous in his grave.
—Hugh Graham, historian[2]

There are some things that, when I discuss in the privacy of the Oval Office . . . , that just should not be in the national arena.
—President George W. Bush, in a speech to the
American Society of Newspaper Editors, April 5, 2001[3]

Never? That could be a possible effect of Executive Order (EO) 13233 issued by President George W. Bush on November 1, 2001, entitled "Further Implementation of the Presidential Records Act."[4] That order, which made considerably more restrictive the already existing procedures for releasing official records of prior presidential administrations, elicited a swift, critical, and overwhelmingly negative response. It enraged scholars, archivists, journalists, editors, and public interest organizations dedicated to open government, spawned three sets of congressional hearings and a bill that would strip it of force and effect, and provoked a lawsuit by scholars who feared that its consequences would impose costly litigation on researchers and lengthy delays or even close completely public access to some records of a president's administration after he has left office.[5] To those who depend upon open access to government documents in order to analyze and interpret history, and to anyone with an interest in reading primary source materials from the Oval Office as a way to understand how government operates, this executive order represented an enormous (and unexpected) setback from what had been a twenty-five-year trend of far greater openness in government.[6] Why would President Bush do this? How much of a change to existing law did the order actually make? Was there a need for this order, or did the administration create a solution for a nonexistent problem? If it had done so, what motivated it to do this, and had it calculated the depth of the uniformly hostile response this order would generate—and did it even care? And, finally, are there lessons from this episode that illuminate President Bush's views about the relationship that the *office* of the presidency should maintain with the public?

This is not an inquiry into how a president manages his day-to-day standing with the public. Nor is it a look into short-term approval ratings that provide evidence of public opinion about a chief executive's contemporary actions, statements, and policies. It is, instead, an examination of one official action taken by a president that suggests a striking set of attitudes held by the nation's chief executive about the contours of his own public leadership: attitudes toward the public, toward the amount of information he believes that democracy requires for an informed citizenry and for governmental accountability, and, ultimately, toward whether he cares about openness and accuracy in the writing of history. The consequences of this action are deep and long lasting, and they affect not only a sitting president's efforts to control his own legacy but also that of his predecessors.

These are solemn and weighty matters. They strike at the heart of what it means to be an open society that holds its leaders responsible for its policy choices and that wants to understand why these officials choose some policies over others. Presidential legacies are at issue here—but so is national heritage, as seen through the lens of public history. If people are shielded from knowledge of the elements that created that history, then they will be unable to learn from its successes and its failures.

Most of the controversy sparked by EO 13233 has occurred beneath the national radar screen, with adverse reactions from scholars, authors, journalists, and open government organizations (as well as from members of Congress)—those people who are either most directly impacted by or suspicious of the new procedures. Although opinion editorials have appeared in major newspapers, the general public has not directed much attention to this issue.[7] However, the warnings from historians as to the potentially restrictive effect the EO will have on their accessibility to official presidential records and thus on their ability to produce accurate historical analysis suggest that the public also will ultimately feel the impact, once it realizes the consequences of lost access.

Presidents and their subordinates may harbor an understandable reluctance to lay bare the inner workings of their administrations. But once Congress made clear in the Presidential Records Act (PRA) of 1978 that the official papers of former presidents are public property and not the private possession of the person who once occupied the office, that reticence was required to give way to this federal law mandating public access, with only limited exceptions. It is this law with which the Bush order conflicted and those exceptions that it broadened, despite the order's stated purpose in its title "Further Implementation of the Presidential Records Act."

SECRECY IN THE BUSH ADMINISTRATION

As this chapter will discuss, the provisions of EO 13233 operated in such a way as to raise suspicions among its critics that it would further secrecy rather than openness.[8] As a working presumption, that was not unreasonable, given that the Bush administration had already been embroiled in a number of controversies over confidentiality and secrecy by late fall 2001 (e.g., the Justice Department's refusal to give documents to a congressional committee regarding prosecutorial decisions in a Boston organized crime case from the 1960s and in the 1996 inquiry of possible campaign finance violations by the Democratic Party; Vice President Dick Cheney's refusal to comply with a request from the Government Accounting Office (GAO) for records of his energy task force meetings; Attorney General Ashcroft's reversal of the burden of proof for Freedom of Information Act (FOIA) requests from one that withheld information only when there was foreseeable harm that would result from disclosure to one where he assured federal officials of Justice Department support if they resisted FOIA requests, essentially going from a policy of "withhold rarely" to one of "withhold whenever possible"; and Bush's decision not to house his gubernatorial papers in a Texas state repository but rather in his father's presidential library where they would not be subject to the Texas Public Information Act). The executive order on access to presidential records was yet another example in a growing number of Bush administration actions criticized for their propensity to wall off the public or Congress from executive branch information. It might well serve as a metaphor for the administration's approach generally to protecting the prerogatives of the presidency, and, more specifically, when those relate to information management.

Both President Bush and Vice President Cheney have expressed their belief that some prior administrations, particularly that of Bill Clinton, had allowed, regrettably, for the weakening of executive privilege, the limited constitutional principle that, under certain conditions, insulates a president from having to comply with demands from the other two branches for records of internal White House communications. Bush and Cheney have reiterated that an important mission of their administration is to restore confidentiality to the presidency and protect it against encroachments from Congress or the courts.[9] The administration has pursued this objective with single-minded fervor, and the breadth of its efforts and thrust of its arguments have been stunning, prompting more than one commentator on this matter to suggest that "Nixon's ghost" is lurking somewhere within the mind-set of the present administration.[10] In fact, four federal court cases from the Nixon era on either executive privilege or the interpretation of presidential records legislation form the backdrop against which the present issue emerged.[11] Nixon lost all four cases, and yet the Bush administration has surprisingly resurrected and relied upon many of the same legal arguments and implementation procedures that had been urged, unsuccessfully, by Nixon decades ago.

The question that looms over Bush's executive order is that of motivation, or, more precisely, political objective. For what purposes did he impose additional restrictions on public access, and what does such a willingness to restrict the public from reading its historical record suggest about how Bush would wish his own legacy in the future to be viewed? Some have suggested that an evident purpose of the order might be to protect (1) Bush's father when the latter was Reagan's vice president and was a key player in the Iran-Contra scandal, (2) current administration officials who had served under Reagan, for example, Secretary of State Colin Powell, and (3) those such as Vice President Dick Cheney and Secretary of State Colin Powell, who had served in the George H. W. Bush administration, whose presidential records would be due for release in January 2005.[12] Prospectively, Bush may be preparing for the day when his own presidential records will, under the 1978 law, become ready for release to the public, and he may want a vigorous mechanism in place to ensure his firm control over such a release. Even if these speculations are correct, they are misguided and misplaced, according to historians who testified before congressional committees, because it is rare that the opening of presidential records damages a former president's reputation.[13]

Scholars caution that the threat of diminished access to presidential records under the present order is occurring at a time when there are other reasons for concern among those who "write" presidential history. Michael Beschloss notes that the experiences of recent presidents who were confronted with subpoenas under the now-lapsed independent counsel statute, newspaper leaks, and memoirs of White House aides published while an administration was still in office increase the likelihood that presidents will be quite circumspect about creating any paper trail in the first place.[14] Thus the sources that scholars have used traditionally to explore presidential motivations, such as memos, letters, records, and diaries, are already drying up and will make the job much harder for scholars of the Clinton and George W. Bush presidencies. It is conventional wisdom in Washington that no one in the White

House takes notes anymore. Beschloss calls this the "Page One of the *Washington Post*" atmosphere, that is, anyone working in the White House is instructed not to put anything down on paper that they "would not wish to read on Page One of the *Washington Post*."

One unfortunate irony noted by Beschloss is that with expanded public rights to governmental information under the FOIA and the PRA, the opposite effect has occurred. As presidents began to realize that they would be forced to surrender their documents under these laws, they fought back by putting less on paper. Thus the laws that guaranteed *more* government openness have, in fact, resulted in *less* transparency, as presidents have found ways to frustrate them.[15] Robert Dallek notes that presidents, to make wise decisions, must be able to learn from their predecessors, but that will be less likely if fewer records are created or made available.[16] Historians will find it harder to research and write, and history will be impoverished.

At the same time, there have been recent efforts, with some rich payoffs, to counteract this ominous trend and to find additional avenues to document history. The Miller Center of the University of Virginia has done extensive work in its Presidential Oral History Project and in its transcribing of presidential audiotapes and recorded phone conversations.[17] Similarly, the White House 2001 Project has compiled seventy-eight interviews with former White House staff members from six administrations, and it too has created an invaluable source of information that will eventually be deposited in the National Archives and made available to the public.[18] If the Bush executive order survives in its present form, and if it, as feared, hampers public access to presidential documents, then these alternative sources of presidential history will become even more critical and precious. But the real loss here would be the sense that the president does not acknowledge the public's *right* to the work of his office, which was, after all, the whole premise for the PRA and its predecessor legislation, the Presidential Recordings and Materials Preservation Act (PRMPA)—that these materials *belonged* to the American people. This circumstance surely represents one of the greater "challenges" of the public presidency—that the president must perform the functions of his office, knowing all the time that under the law he will be obligated to reveal the chain of events and advice that led to his administration's policy choices. Beyond obligation, however, one would hope that a president would recognize the inherent, central significance in a democracy of public ownership of and access to governmental records as the ultimate symbol of accountable leadership.

Who Controls Presidential Records?

Upon leaving office, presidents prior to Ronald Reagan considered their official White House papers their own private property, and, with the exception of Richard Nixon, either they or their heirs maintained personal control over them. Traditionally, some materials were donated to historical societies, libraries, or private collections, and some went to the Library of Congress, while in 1939, President Franklin Roosevelt was the first to donate his records to the federal government and to ask the National Archives to administer his library at his Hyde Park, New York, estate. By 1955, Congress enacted the Presidential Libraries Act, which encouraged presidents to donate their papers to the government and provided for the creation of presidential libraries that would be funded privately but maintained by the federal government. Today, presidents from Hoover through Clinton have established their own presidential libraries under this act, administered by the National Archives and Records Administration (NARA).[19]

The resignation of Richard Nixon in August 1974 presented a unique and an extraordinary circumstance that provoked close scrutiny over the key issues surrounding the disposition of a president's White House records. It set in motion a series of executive actions, congressional enactments, and judicial decisions over the next fifteen years that eventually resulted in the development of a legal framework governing the handling of presidential records. This succession of governmental actions consisted of the following:

- The 1974 Supreme Court decision of *U.S. v. Nixon* that ruled that executive privilege is constitutionally based, deriving from "the supremacy of each branch within its own assigned area of constitutional duties."[20] The Court rejected Nixon's claim of an absolute, unqualified privilege of confidentiality between a president and his advisors, while acknowledging instead a qualified privilege that was constitutionally based when it related to "the effective discharge of a President's powers." The Court also held that the president's claim of a generalized assertion of privilege in this case must be balanced against the need for evidence in a criminal trial, and that when those two interests are pitted against each other, "the generalized assertion of privilege must yield to the demonstrated, specific need for evidence in a pending criminal trial." This standard applied to claims of executive privilege against requests for information from the president by the courts or Congress. The Court did *not* address whether this standard applied to requests from private citizens (but the Bush EO 13233 contained, for the first time under law, that exact standard).
- The 1974 agreement concluded between Nixon and Arthur F. Sampson, administrator of general services, known as the Nixon-Sampson agreement, that granted the former president legal ownership of his official papers with conditions on future access and ultimately permitted the eventual destruction of the audiotapes at Nixon's request or upon his death.[21]
- An opinion in September 1974 by Attorney General William Saxbe on the question of ownership of Nixon's White House records, at the request of

President Ford, who had been informed by the Watergate special prosecutor that the government had a continuing need for these materials.[22] The attorney general's opinion concluded that ownership rested, with a limited exception, with the former president, based on historical practice and the lack of any contrary statute. That exception stemmed from recognition throughout history that "Presidential materials are peculiarly affected by a public interest," and that limitations on a former president's absolute rights of ownership may be justified when they are "directly related to the character of the documents as records of government activity."[23]

- Passage by Congress in December 1974 of the PRMPA, for the purpose of abrogating the Nixon-Sampson agreement and in its place authorizing the administrator of general services to take custody of Nixon's presidential materials, thus guaranteeing their availability for future judicial proceedings and eventually for public access. In conjunction with the National Archives and Records Administration Act of 1984, the responsibility for issuing regulations governing the preparation of materials for public access fell to the NARA. The PRMPA was the first law to make clear that presidential materials (at least those of Nixon) were the property of the U.S. government, and that the public was entitled to have access to them, pursuant to regulations drawn up by, at first, the administrator of general services and later by the NARA.

- The Supreme Court decision (7–2) in *Nixon v. Administrator of General Services* (1977), found Nixon's constitutional challenge to the PRMPA on five separate grounds without merit, and that upheld the law but injected some ambiguity into two key issues: Who owns a former president's official records?[24] What is the proper scope of a former president's assertion of executive privilege with regard to these records? Two footnotes in the Court's opinion were mysteriously ambivalent about the ownership issue and appeared to "invite" a congressional response for clarification.[25] The Court's majority opinion also was noteworthy for reaffirming from *U.S. v. Nixon* a president's right to claim a qualified executive privilege and for furthering that right by acknowledging that it "survives the individual President's tenure." However, a former president's right to assert privilege was limited by two further qualifications: (1) it lessens over time; in the Court's words, "The expectation of the confidentiality of executive communications thus has always been limited and subject to erosion over time after an administration leaves office"; and (2) "a former President is in less need of it than an incumbent. In addition, there are obvious political checks against an incumbent's abuse of the privilege." The Court added for emphasis that "the incumbent President is . . . in the best position to assess the present and future needs of the Executive Branch, and to support the invocation of the privilege accordingly." Thus this ruling established two important precedents: (1) that former presidents possess the constitutional right, though qualified, to claim privilege; and (2) the strength of that claim diminishes with time. The first element is the crucial reference for *all* former presidents in any future actions regarding presidential records. The second element works against former presidents and therefore is one that they prefer to ignore.

• Congressional enactment of the PRA in 1978, which established definitively that with the departure from office of a president and vice president, ownership and control of their official records reside exclusively in the federal government. The PRA contained detailed provisions outlining the administration of these records and authorized the NARA to promulgate implementing regulations, subject to congressional oversight. The first president to whom these provisions would apply fully would be the person who would assume office on January 20, 1981. That distinction would fall to Ronald Reagan, who was elected in 1980 and left office on January 20, 1989. Under the terms of the PRA, those categories of Reagan's presidential records that would be closed for the subsequent twelve years would become publicly available on January 20, 2001.

• A 1982 D.C. Circuit Court of Appeals decision, *Nixon v. Freeman*, which rejected the position urged by Nixon, that under the PRMPA a requester provide proof of a specific need for presidential materials from a former president's records.[26] Precisely *because* the privilege erodes over time, the court deemed it appropriate for material from the archives to be available to all requesters, without a showing of need. The court agreed that the regulation permitting a former president to challenge in court an archivist's adverse decision denying his privilege claim and to establish that disclosure would violate the privilege provided to him with "a meaningful opportunity to contest disclosure" (*Nixon v. Freeman* began where *Nixon v. Administrator of General Services* ended: former President Nixon challenged only the government custody arrangement of the PRMPA in the earlier case in 1977, while he charged in the later case in 1982 that the archivist screening and public access provisions of the 1974 law violated his constitutional rights of privacy and associational privacy under the First Amendment. All of his claims in both cases were rejected by the courts). The court emphasized the importance to the act of furthering "the congressional goal of providing the public with full information about the Nixon Presidency."

• A 1986 memorandum opinion by Charles Cooper, assistant attorney general, Office of Legal Counsel (OLC) in the Department of Justice, which (1) reviewed the NARA's proposed regulations under the PRMPA for use in further processing of the Nixon materials, (2) interpreted the PRMPA in ways that undermined the objectives of the law, and (3) in retrospect, provided the model and the doctrinal foundation for the most significant features of the Bush executive order that would be issued fifteen years later in November 2001.[27] For Cooper, the key provision in the PRMPA was Section 104 (a)(5), which recognized the need "to protect any party's opportunity to assert any legally or constitutionally based right or privilege which would prevent or otherwise limit access to such recordings and materials." From this recognition that Cooper viewed as a "statutory mandate" flowed interpretations about the role of the archivist and about procedures for public access that were contrary to the terms of the PRMPA. Most pointed was Cooper's interpretation that although the archivist may make "the final administrative determinations on questions of executive privilege, those determinations must be made under the supervision and control of the incumbent president. Thus, while the Archivist is certainly free to offer advice as to whether particular documents, in his judgment, are or should be protected by executive privilege, the Archivist has no legal authority to make a determination inconsistent with the President's assertion of executive privilege." A review of the classic cases addressing a president's power to control his subordinates *(Myers v. US.; Humphrey's Executor v. U.S.; Wiener v. U.S.)* led Cooper to this conclusion, based on his interpretation of a president's Article II, Section 3, duty "to take care that the laws be faithfully executed." This conclusion was extended to also include within the *incumbent* president's protection any assertion of executive privilege by a *former* president.

• A 1988 D.C. Circuit Court of Appeals decision, *Public Citizen v. Burke*, which soundly rejected as "erroneous" Cooper's constitutional interpretation of the requirements of Article II, Section 3, and his statutory construction of the PRMPA regulations that he interpreted as requiring the archivist to acquiesce in any claim of executive privilege by a former president.[28] The court held that such an interpretation was "contrary to PRMPA and, therefore, could not be sustained." Cooper's position, had it been upheld, maintained that both the incumbent president and the archivist must honor and accept a former president's claims without judging them on the merits. Thus any challenge to the decision to withhold documents would come from a requester, who would then take the former president to court to contest the claim. This process would have reversed the burden of proof, as established in the PRMPA, which provides for a former president to contest an adverse ruling by the archivist and *not* for a requester to challenge a favorable ruling to a former president. The court noted, "We read the statute . . . as imposing on the Archivist the responsibility to arrange for disclosure of a category of the Nixon papers. The burden to seek disclosure is not . . . placed upon the public." The court further stated that the statute provided that "the Archivist must afford an 'opportunity' for Mr. Nixon to *assert* his privileges, but the implication of the statute is that Mr. Nixon's assertion must be directed to that individual whom Congress has entrusted with the affirmative duty to disclose" (emphasis in original). The significance of this ruling is that the positions that Cooper advocated in his interpretation, discredited by the court, of the PRMPA, (1) that the archivist and incumbent president must accept, unquestioningly, the claims of a former president, and (2) that the requester, not the former president, must go to court to get a favorable decision on contested documents, are the exact ones that appear in the Bush executive order in November 2001.

- Promulgation of Executive Order 12667 by President Reagan in January 1989, as he was preparing to leave office, detailing criteria and procedures for former and incumbent presidents to use to determine executive privilege claims in their review of confidential advice records (P-5) before they were released to the public.[29]
- Three requests by Bush White House Counsel Alberto Gonzales for extensions of the January 20, 2001, release date of the Reagan presidential materials. These requests were granted in February, May, and August 2001.
- Issuance of Executive Order 13233 by President Bush on November 1, 2001, which rescinded Reagan's 1989 executive order and replaced it with new procedures that enhanced considerably the roles of the former and incumbent presidents and the representatives of a former president after his death, broadened the definition of executive privilege, diminished the role of the archivist, reversed the burden of proof onto researchers for determining executive privilege claims, and extended to former vice presidents an independent (and unprecedented) right to claim executive privilege. Not only were these revised procedures notable for the increased control of White House records by the two presidents at the expense of the archivist, but critics charged that the order violated the very Presidential Records Act that it declared it was, in fact, "implementing."
- Critical reaction by the scholarly community and members of Congress to Bush's executive order, resulting in legislative efforts to overturn it and a lawsuit to declare it in violation of the PRA. Both of these challenges are still ongoing, and neither has reached a conclusive outcome as of this writing.

Key Developments in the Handling of Presidential Records

The central issues in the matter of presidential records are those of (1) legal ownership, and (2) control over public access and the related claims of executive privilege that would restrict such access. The Supreme Court decision in *Nixon v. Administrator of General Services* upheld the provisions of the PRMPA, which directed the administrator of general services to take custody of Nixon's White House papers and recordings. Government archivists would screen and return any personal or private materials to Nixon before processing the rest of the records. Nixon challenged the statute as an unconstitutional infringement of his rights, but the Court ruled against him on all of the five separate grounds urged by him. It left dangling in two tantalizing footnotes, however, the ultimate question of whether the government or the former president had legal title to the records. In footnote 8, the Court said, "We see no reason to engage in the debate whether appellant has legal title to the materials." It reiterated the lack of resolution of this matter in footnote 39, noting "In fact, it remains unsettled whether the materials in question are the property of appellant or of the Government. See n. 8, supra."

That uncertainty, as it would relate to future presidents, was finally resolved by the passage of the Presidential Records Act in 1978, which states that "the United States shall reserve and retain complete ownership, possession, and control of Presidential records."[30] Section 2203 directs the archivist of the United States to "assume responsibility for the custody, control, and preservation of, and access to, the Presidential records of that President," and also imposes upon the archivist "an affirmative duty to make such records available to the public as rapidly and completely as possible." Section 2204 constitutes the heart of the statute, permitting a former president to restrict public access for up to twelve years for records in six categories: those "properly classified" as national security information, relating to federal appointments, trade secrets, records specifically exempt from disclosure by law, confidential communications between a president and his advisors (known as P-5 records), and personal information where disclosure would constitute an invasion of privacy. After twelve years, formerly restricted records may be released, subject to FOIA exemptions, except that the deliberative process exemption for confidential advice between a president and his advisors (P-5 category) does *not* apply, rendering those materials publicly accessible at that point. Records that fall outside of the six categories shall be made public five years from the end of an administration, subject to FOIA exemptions. However, during the five-year restriction on access, records subpoenaed by the courts or requested by Congress or the incumbent or former president *will* be available in those circumstances. Denial of access may be appealed to the archivist, who is required to respond within thirty days with a written determination that specifies the reasons for denial. Finally, the PRA did not specify any definition of executive privilege but provided for the archivist to notify the former president "when the disclosure of particular documents may adversely affect any rights and privileges which the former President may have."[31]

The 1989 executive order issued by President Reagan filled in the gaps in the PRA by defining executive privilege and providing new procedures for asserting such claims. "Executive privilege" was defined the following way:

> A "substantial question of Executive privilege" exists if NARA's disclosure of Presidential records might impair the national security (including the conduct of foreign relations), law enforcement, or the deliberative processes of the Executive branch.[32]

The procedures for determining if a claim of executive privilege is warranted are different for incumbent and former presidents under the order. The most notable and consequential difference is that an incumbent president's assertion of executive privilege over a former president's records can be absolute, whereas a former president's claim of privilege over his *own* records can be overridden by the archivist. It is this distinction that the Bush executive order in 2001 changes so as to make a former president's claims *greater* than they were under the Reagan order—and essentially equal to the incumbent president's. The reason for an incumbent president's veto power over a former president's claims is that, as the Court noted in *Nixon v. Administrator of General Services*, a former president's power to claim executive privilege "is subject to erosion over time." Additionally, an incumbent president is in a better position, in practical terms, to judge whether there is a contemporary need for restricting access and is a government official, operating under the Constitution and the laws; the former president is a private citizen and no longer in any official capacity.

Under the Reagan EO, the archivist notifies both the former and incumbent presidents when he believes that disclosure of material "may raise a substantial question of executive privilege." The former and incumbent presidents have thirty days in which to inform the archivist if either wishes to claim executive privilege. Additionally, the incumbent president may request an extension of time.

The major difference in how the EO treats executive privilege claims of a former president versus those of an incumbent president occurs when an actual claim of privilege is made. When an incumbent president invokes executive privilege and through his White House Counsel notifies the former president, the archivist, and the attorney general, "the Archivist shall not disclose the privileged records unless directed to do so by an incumbent president or by a final court order." In contrast, when a former president asserts executive privilege, the archivist shall determine "whether to honor the former President's claim of privilege or instead to disclose the Presidential records notwithstanding the claim of privilege." Furthermore, the archivist is bound to follow "any instructions given him by the incumbent president or his designee unless otherwise directed by a final court order. Thus the Reagan EO extends greater discretion and coverage to an *incumbent* president's claim of privilege over a former president's records than a *former* president has over his *own* records, for the reasons noted earlier.

President Reagan was the first president whose White House records would be released to the public under the terms of the PRA, the archivist's regulations pursuant to it, and Reagan's EO 12667. With his departure from office in January 1989, his confidential advice files (P–5) would become eligible for release in January 2001, twelve years after the end of his administration.

Both President George W. Bush, as incumbent president, and former President Reagan were notified by the archivist that 68,000 pages of documents in the P–5 category of the Reagan records were scheduled for release at this time, pending review by both the former and incumbent presidents. It was at this point, through a series of three requests for time extensions and, ultimately, issuance of an entirely new EO (13233), that President Bush signaled his will to change substantially the process for release of a former president's records.

The effect of these changes was to extend significantly more discretion and control over executive privilege claims to the former president than he had under the Reagan EO and the PRA, in effect equalizing control of both the former and incumbent presidents. That change, as well as others in the Bush order, raised the issue of whether the order violates the 1978 law. Affected by these changes were the following:

- the roles of the incumbent and former presidents, and the time frame for their review of records
- the role of the archivist
- the definition of executive privilege
- the addition of the former president's representatives to act on his behalf after his death
- the burden of proof for researchers wishing access to records where executive privilege has been claimed—researchers would now be required to go to court to claim access rather than leaving it to former presidents to ask for a judicial review of an archivist's decision unfavorable to that former president
- a new and an unprecedented extension of the right to claim executive privilege to former vice presidents

The salient features of the Bush order include the following:

- A reassertion that "constitutionally based privileges survive the individual President's tenure" *(Nixon v. Administrator of General Services)*. The order then builds upon this declaration by expanding the rights of former presidents farther than *Nixon v. Administrator* provides and beyond the statutory limits in the PRA.
- Expansion of the categories for which executive privilege can be claimed from the PRA's "confidential communications . . . between the president and his advisers" to "legal advice, legal work, presidential communications, or the deliberative processes of the President and the President's advisers" by providing in the opening clause of the Bush EO that "constitutionally based privileges . . . apply to . . ." these new categories (EO 13233). This extension of the application of executive privilege contradicts the PRA and was not contemplated by the Supreme Court in *U.S. v. Nixon*, where the Court first articulated the constitutional grounding for a president's invocation of privilege.

- Imposition of the requirement, never mandated previously for *private* requesters, that the party seeking to overcome a constitutionally based privilege must establish a "demonstrated, specific need for the records," the standard imposed in *U.S. v. Nixon* for requests of presidential information from Congress or the courts.
- Providing the former president with ninety days to review and indicate withholding of records for those requests that are not "unduly burdensome," as contrasted with thirty days for all records under the Reagan EO, and then providing the incumbent president, either concurrently with or after the former president, with an unspecified amount of time to review. No provision exists for a time frame for "burdensome" records, leaving open the possibility that such records could be withheld forever.
- Permitting the incumbent president to review or "utilize whatever other procedures the incumbent deems appropriate to decide whether to concur" in a former president's decision (either way). In effect, a sitting president could delay indefinitely (and permanently) the release of a former president's records.
- When a former president wants to withhold records, the incumbent may concur, and then the agreement of *both* is required to release records; not concur, but the former president "independently retains the right to assert constitutionally based privileges," and then the agreement of *both* is needed to release records.
- When a former president agrees to release records, the incumbent may concur; and the archivist then permits access; not concur, but the incumbent "may independently order the Archivist to withhold privileged records." In order for release of the records to occur, agreement of *both* is needed.
- But Section 4 of the EO provides that "Absent compelling circumstances, the incumbent President will concur in the privilege decision of the former President in response to a request for access." Thus the likely effect of Sections 3 and 4 is that, except for those rare circumstances, the incumbent president will permit the former president's decision to release records or withhold records to govern. Even if an incumbent president finds "compelling circumstances" to disagree with a former president's decision to withhold records, the archivist is bound to honor the former president's decision and may not release the records until both the incumbent and former presidents agree, "because the former President independently retains the right to assert constitutionally based privileges." Furthermore, Section 4 mandates that when the incumbent president concurs in the former president's decision to withhold records, "the incumbent President will support that privilege claim in any forum in which the privilege claim

is challenged." This provision requires an incumbent president to automatically uphold the claims of the former president without first determining the validity of those claims. Such a mandate is contradictory to a sitting president's Article II, Section 3, constitutional duty to "take care that the laws be faithfully executed" and was specifically rejected by the court of appeals in its 1988 ruling in *Public Citizen v. Burke*.

- "The former President may designate a representative . . . to act on his behalf for purposes of the Presidential Records Act and this order" upon his death or disability (Section 10). Critics claim that this provision further eviscerates the archivist's role, contrary to the requirements of the PRA, but even more importantly, it leaves the decision regarding the release of public records in the hands of private citizens who never held office and who have no official status (nor ever did) to determine the disposition of government property.[33]
- Extension to former vice presidents of the same right as former and incumbent presidents to claim privilege. Section 11 of the EO states "this order shall also apply with respect to any such records that are subject to any constitutionally based privilege that the former Vice President may be entitled to invoke, . . . references in this order to a former President shall be deemed also to be references to the relevant former Vice President."[34]

REACTION TO THE BUSH ORDER

The response to the Bush order was an immediate and openly suspicious one. Journalists, researchers, and open governmental organizations recognized the obstacles to public access that it would create. Members of Congress, on a bipartisan basis, criticized it. The House Committee on Government Reform held hearings to review the order and propose legislation to overturn it and reinstate the Reagan EO. Scholars, journalists, and public interest organizations filed a lawsuit asking the court to declare the Bush EO in violation of the PRA and to order the archivist to administer the PRA without regard to the order.

The Bush administration responded to this barrage of criticism and efforts to undo the order by explaining its reasons for the EO through statements by the press secretary at daily briefings and by an opinion article by White House Counsel Alberto Gonzales in the *Washington Post*.[35] The administration's explanation was that the EO would "provide for an orderly process, so that information can be shared, releasing the records of former presidents to historians, to the public, and to the press."[36] Gonzales, in his opinion piece for the *Washington Post*, defended the order as ensuring "expeditious disclosure of documents to provide historians, scholars, and the public valuable insights into the way our government works."[37] The language and justifications offered by administration officials are striking for their effort to minimize and to dismiss any substantial—and substantive—importance of the new EO. All explanations of its purpose speak only of changes of "process" and suggest, rhetorically, that these changes are of insignificant proportions. When M. Edward Whelan III, acting assistant attorney general, Office of Legal Counsel in the Department of Justice, testified before the House subcommittee, he stated, "Let me emphasize, moreover, that the executive order is wholly procedural in nature."[38] Even the title of the order, "Further Implementation of the Presidential Records Act," presumes that it *is* enforcing or carrying out the act rather than changing and countermanding it, which is precisely what its critics claim it does.

The administration also claimed that the order was needed to protect national security,[39] but this explanation was soundly rejected by opponents, who asserted that the national security interests of presidential records were already fully protected by the applicable FOIA exemptions and thus there could be no further national security purpose served by the order.[40]

Finally, the administration responded in a very tangible way by eventually, and gradually, releasing most of the Reagan records throughout 2002, perhaps hoping to defuse and moot the issue entirely. On January 3, 2002, 8,000 pages were released to the public, without any claims of executive privilege. In March 2002, the White House agreed to release most of the remaining 60,000 pages of the Reagan presidential and Bush vice presidential records, minus about 150 pages that were believed to include memoranda concerning Supreme Court and other presidential appointments. These 150 pages were finally authorized for release in July 2002, along with forty pages of outstanding Bush vice presidential documents, also relating to presidential appointments that had been withheld from about 800 pages of Bush records released in June. At that time, plaintiffs in the lawsuit were informed that there were an additional 1,654 pages of Reagan documents whose existence had not been previously disclosed by the National Archives and which had been scheduled for release in January 2001. Scott Nelson, attorney for Public Citizen, claimed that the release of most, but not all, of the Reagan records did not, in fact, close the controversy, since the order was still the operative law, and it was still in violation of the PRA. Nelson stated, "The White House desperately wants to avoid having a court decide whether its executive order is lawful, so it has made every effort to dodge the issue. But the government is continuing to implement the executive order and is using it to hold up release of other documents, so the legal challenge to the order remains a live issue."[41] On April 29, 2003, Nelson filed notice in U.S. District Court that representatives of President Reagan had, for the first time, claimed executive privilege for seventy-four pages of the 1,654 pages and fifteen minutes of video, thus negating the defendant's prior position that the absence of any assertion of privilege by a former president deprived the issue of justiciability. With this privilege claim, as well as with the continuing operation of the EO, Nelson urged the court that the issue was, indeed, a live one, ripe for the court to resolve on the merits.[42]

The Nixon Connection

The most curious and revealing aspect of all is the connection between the Bush EO and the legal arguments offered by former President Nixon in his many efforts, all unsuccessful, to litigate the presidential records issue in the courts. Of the four federal court cases brought by Nixon concerning this issue, the Bush administration relied on selective parts or statements in two of these cases (*U.S. v. Nixon* and *Nixon v. Administrator of General Services*) that gave *some* qualified support to Nixon's claims in the abstract, though not to him personally, but it completely ignored the other two cases (*Public Citizen v. Burke* and *Nixon v. Freeman*) and the rulings or statements in them that pointedly rejected interpretations of provisions that were either (1) in the PRMPA and were similar to those in the PRA, or (2) that had been struck down in those two cases and that suddenly reappeared in the Bush EO, as if they had never been litigated previously. That is why the 1986 OLC memo by Assistant Attorney General Charles Cooper is so intriguing, since it could have easily been written by his counterpart in the Bush Justice Department, as it justifies the same provisions that show up anew in the Bush EO fifteen years later.

What could be the reason for the reemergence of provisions that had been rejected in the Nixon litigation decades ago? Critics have suggested that the effect of the Bush EO would be to return to the pre-PRA (and the pre-PRMPA) days and to reverse these laws by executive order. For all practical purposes, that would mean that presidents would now, once again, retain personal control of their records and could, if they chose, deny public access permanently. Thus EO 13233, borrowing liberally from the positions articulated in the 1986 Cooper OLC memo, would overturn the PRA. Kutler notes that "the executive order constitutes nothing less than a wholesale emasculation of the Presidential Records Act of 1978."[43]

CONGRESSIONAL AND JUDICIAL RESPONSES

Within days of the issuance of the order, the Subcommittee on Government Efficiency, Financial Management, and Intergovernmental Relations of the House Committee on Government Reform held hearings, chaired by Rep. Steve Horn (R-CA). In all, hearings were held on November 6, 2001, and two more rounds on April 11 and 24, 2002. Testimony was provided by a wealth of scholars, legal experts, and government officials, including historians Stanley Kutler, Robert Dallek, Richard Reeves, Anna Nelson, and Joan Hoff: political scientist and executive privilege specialist Mark Rozell; law professors Peter Shane and Jonathan Turley; attorneys Scott Nelson (Public Citizen), Edward Whelan (Department of Justice), and Todd Gaziano (Heritage Foundation); and John Carlin, archivist of the United States. The outgrowth of that testimony was the introduction of HR 4187 on April 11, 2002, the "Presidential Records Act Amendments of 2002," sponsored by Rep. Horn, with forty-four co-sponsors, which repealed the Bush EO and replaced it with streamlined provisions of Section 2208 of the PRA that addressed executive privilege claims. Thus all of the other new provisions in the Bush EO would be canceled out by this act. The bill was reported out of the Committee on Government Reform on November 22, 2002, but it was never considered by the full House and died at the end of the session.

On March 27, 2003, Rep. Doug Ose (R-CA) introduced HR 1493, a scaled-down version of the previous effort that would simply repeal the Bush EO and restore the Reagan EO as the operative implementing provisions. The bill was referred to the House Committee on Government Reform and then to the Subcommittee on Technology, Information Policy, Intergovernmental Relations, and the Census on April 2, 2003. No further action has been taken on that bill in the House. On the Senate side, Senators Jeff Bingaman (D-NM) and Bob Graham (D-FL) introduced S1517 on July 31, 2003, which was referred to the Committee on Governmental Affairs. This bill was a companion to HR 1493, with identical wording, revoking EO 13233 and replacing it with the Reagan EO 12667. No further action has been taken on this bill.

Most of the people directly involved with efforts to overturn the Bush EO expect that the courts will be the place where the issue will ultimately be determined. Plaintiff organizations, including the American Historical Association and Public Citizen, filed a complaint in federal district court against the NARA on November 28, 2001, asking for injunctive relief and a declaratory judgment that the EO is contrary to law. The case of *AHA et al. v. NARA et al.* was assigned to Judge Colleen Kollar-Kotelly of the U.S. District Court in Washington, D.C., but the judge delayed her consideration of it while she was preoccupied with two other cases of huge proportions on her docket at the same time (the Microsoft and campaign finance reform cases).

On March 29, 2004, Judge Kollar-Kotelly dismissed the case as nonjusticiable on the grounds that the plaintiff organizations did not have standing to sue, and that the issue was not ripe. Soon thereafter, on April 12, 2004, Scott Nelson, attorney for Public Citizen, filed a motion with the court to "alter or amend" the judgment because (1) the court failed to understand that the EO "is *currently* being applied on an ongoing basis to all requests for releases of Reagan presidential and Bush vice presidential documents," and therefore the plaintiffs' injuries are not at all speculative or hypothetical, as the court ruled (emphasis in original), and (2) the court also was incorrect to assume that plaintiffs were *not* challenging the assertion of privilege as to the remaining seventy-four pages of Reagan materials, when in fact they were but were caught in a time lag while waiting to first exhaust their administrative remedies under the FOIA against the NARA before proceeding to file an action on the privilege claim.[44]

Thus the issue is still very much a live one in the courts, and it is likely to reappear more publicly as of January 20, 2005, when the records of the George H.W. Bush administration are released. President Bush will need to decide whether to implement EO 13233 in processing the Bush administration materials or supercede it with a new executive order with different provisions.

In addition, the Bush administration took another action related to presidential records recently, though not directly connected to EO 13233, that has generated still more controversy. On April 8, 2004, President Bush nominated historian Allen Weinstein the archivist of the United States, succeeding John Carlin in that position.[45] Historians, researchers, and archivists were critical of the selection of Weinstein and questioned his scholarship, credentials, and research practices. They also complained about the selection process. Scholars raised questions about whether the administration was forcing Carlin out before his publicly stated intention to leave, and they also pointed to language in a House report that accompanied passage of the NARA Act of 1984 (P.L. 98–497), which stated that "the committee expects that (determining professional qualifications) will be achieved through consultation with recognized organizations of archivists and historians."[46] In addition, the NARA Act provides that when there is a change of archivist, the president "shall communicate the reasons for such removal to each House of Congress." There was no consultation with professional groups, and the president has given no reason for the change in the position that will occur earlier than Carlin's previously announced date of departure. There is no readily apparent connection to President Bush's 2001 executive order on the handling of presidential records, but cynics could suggest that the two actions are indeed related, since the archivist Weinstein will be the one to administer the release of the George H.W. Bush papers.

Presidential Records as Presidential Legacy— From the Bush Administration's Perspective

This examination began with speculation about the motives of the Bush administration in its promulgation of the executive order pertaining to the disposition of presidential records. Critics of it have not been timid to suggest that the true purpose of the order might be to protect (1) the vice presidential records of George H.W. Bush during the Reagan years, (2) the presidential records of George H.W. Bush, released in January 2005, (3) Reagan records that may include material on current Bush administration officials, such as Colin Powell, or (4) the process that would be in place when President George W. Bush leaves office, to which his own presidential records would be subjected. Since the administration has not admitted and will not admit to any of these possible purposes, then there is no way to know, with any accuracy, its motivation. If, in fact, the underlying and unstated concern is that a twelve-year period of nondisclosure is too short of a time frame, as some archivists have noted, then it might be preferable to address that issue directly and seek to revise the PRA through the normal legislative process. Instead, the Bush administration is using a strategy of undermining the current law by imposing, by executive fiat, controversial and unjustifiable obstacles to public access to reach the same goal of lengthening or delaying the release of records that a longer restrictive period, by law, could accomplish. The only purpose served by the Bush strategy is to antagonize those very people who will one day write the history of this administration.

Without a doubt, the recognition by a sitting president that the official records generated by his administration will be bared to the public at some future date is a daunting burden with which to live, but not if the validity of the underlying principle of public ownership is accepted. Presidents who understand that they are only temporary guardians of the Oval Office until it gets passed on to the next occupant and, furthermore, who recognize that the people are the ultimate sovereigns in a democracy should have no difficulty acknowledging the passage of their records from their White House office into governmental ownership. The true challenge of the public presidency is for a president to live with the inevitability that what is said in private for four to eight years will be exposed in public at some later time. But in this era of rapid production of memoirs by presidents and the officials (some sympathetic, some not) who served with them, there are plenty of opportunities to explain the context in which those words were expressed. As a public officer who can expect his actions to come under intense scrutiny, a president bears a heavy responsibility for what is said and decided behind closed doors; but when those doors are flung open and the sunshine flows in, there is no better illustration of a system that prides itself on open government and official accountability than easy access to the public records belonging to all of us. That is why the Bush administration's effort to restrict access and impose greater obstacles on researchers raises so many questions, as it turns toward the exact opposite direction—because its effect will be to retard rather than to promote openness, and because the philosophy supporting it returns us to the days when presidents, not the public, controlled official records.

NOTES

1. Alison Leigh Cowan, "Battling over Records of Bush's Governorship," *New York Times*, February 11, 2002, p. A14.

2. Carl M. Cannon, "For the Record," *National Journal* (January 12, 2002): 90.

3. Ibid.

4. Executive Order 13233, "Further Implementation of the Presidential Records Act," *Public Papers of the President: George W. Bush*, November 1, 2001, 1581–84, Washington, D.C. Government Printing Office.

5. The Subcommittee on Government Efficiency, Financial Management and Intergovernmental Relations and the Committee on Government Reform held hearings on November 6, 2001, and on April 11 and April 24, 2002. The House Committee on Government Reform reported H.R. 4187, the "Presidential Records Act Amendments of 2002," to the full House on November 22, 2002 (H. Rept. 107-790). The House never acted on it. A revised and streamlined version of the bill, H.R. 1493, was introduced in the House by Rep. Doug Ose (R-CA) on March 27, 2003, and referred on April 2 to the Subcommittee on Technology, Information Policy, Intergovernmental Relations, and the Census. No further action has been recorded on this bill. Senators Bingaman (D-NM) and Graham (D-FL) introduced S1517 in the Senate on July 31, 2003: the bill was referred to the Committee on Governmental Affairs at that time, and no further action has been recorded on this bill. Public Citizen filed a lawsuit in federal district court on February 8, 2001, on behalf of itself and the American Historical Association, historians Hugh Davis Graham and Stanley Kutler, the National Security Archive, the Organization of American Historians, and the Reporters Committee for Freedom of the Press, as plaintiffs, against the National Archives and Records Administration and John Carlin, Archivist of the United States, as defendants, in *AHA et al. v. NARA et al.* (01-CV02447). The case was assigned to Judge Colleen Kollar-Kotelly in the U.S. District Court for the District of Columbia; the court issued a ruling on March 29, 2004, dismissing the case as nonjusticiable, on the basis that the plaintiffs lacked standing, and the issue was not ripe. Plaintiffs filed a motion on April 12, 2004, to request that the court "alter or amend" its judgment because they claimed that the court had acted on mistaken assumptions and an incorrect interpretation of the facts.

6. Cannon, "For the Record," 90.

7. Emily Eakin, "Presidential Papers as Smoking Guns," *New York Times*, April 12, 2002, p. 7; Steven Hensen, "The President's Papers Are the People's Business," *Washington Post*, December 16, 2001, p. B1; Stanley I. Kutler, "Classified! George W. Uses 9/11 as a Pretext to Reverse the Will of Congress and Wall Off Presidential Records," *Chicago Tribune*, January 2, 2002, p. 1.

8. See Cannon, "For the Record," p. 90; David G. Savage, "Group Fights Shield on Executive Records," *Los Angeles Times*, November 29, 2001, p. A31; Kutler, "Classified!," p. 1; Charles N. Davis, "George II Protects the Court of George I," *St. Louis Post-Dispatch*, November 19, 2001, p. C7; Don Wycliff, "Top Secret: Just Whose Government Is It, Anyway?," *Chicago Tribune*, January 17, 2002, p. 23; Hensen, "The Pres-

ident's Papers Are the People's Business," p. B1; Russ Baker, "What Are They Hiding?" *The Nation*, February 25, 2002, p. 14; Mike Allen and George Lardner Jr., "A Veto over Presidential Papers: Order Lets Sitting or Former President Block Release," *Washington Post*, November 2, 2001, p. A1; Francine Kiefer, "Backlash Grows against White House Secrecy: In Congress and the Courts, Challenges to Bush's Tight Control of Information Rise," *Christian Science Monitor*, March 25, 2002, p. 3.

9. See Ari Fleischer, White House Press Briefing, November 1, 2001, www.whitehouse.gov/news/releases (accessed June 4, 2003); Ari Fleischer, White House Press Briefing, January 28, 2002, www.whitehouse.gov/news/releases (accessed June 4, 2003); Ari Fleischer, White House Press Briefing, January 30, 2002, www.whitehouse.gov/news/releases (accessed June 4, 2003); Vanessa Blum, "Why Bush Won't Let Go," *Legal Times*, February 6, 2002, p. 18; Elisabeth Bumiller, "Cheney Is Set to Battle Congress to Keep His Enron Talks Secret," *New York Times*, January 28, 2002, pp. A1, 11; Adam Clymer, "Judge Says Cheney Needn't Give Energy Policy Records to Agency," *New York Times*, December 19, 2002, pp. 1, 33. Vice President Cheney was outspoken on this issue in a series of comments in a January 27, 2002, interview on Fox News Sunday: "What I object to, and what the president objected to . . . is (to) make it impossible for me or future vice presidents to ever have a conversation in confidence with anybody without having, ultimately, to tell a member of Congress what we talked about" (quoted in Bumiller, "Cheney Is Set to Battle," pp. A1, 11). "We've seen it in cases like this before, where it's demanded that presidents cough up and compromise on important principles . . . we are weaker today as an institution because of the unwise compromises that have been made over the last 30 to 35 years" (quoted in ibid.). "There has been a constant, steady erosion of the prerogatives and the power of the Oval Office and a continual encroachment by Congress . . . where presidents have given up, if you will, important principles. So, the office is weaker than it was 30, 35 years ago. What we're committed to is to make sure we preserve the office, at least as strong as we found it, for our successors" (quoted in Clymer, "Judge Says," p. 33). "Time after time administrations have traded away the authority of the president to do his job. We're not going to do that in this administration" (quoted in Blum, "Why Bush Won't Let Go," p. 18). Similarly, Ari Fleischer, White House press secretary, parroted similar comments in his responses to reporters in his daily news briefings, such as, "And it's time for somebody in the administration, somebody in the executive branch, to stop the slide, where Presidential authority, constitutionally vested, has been yielded to the Congress, since Watergate, since Vietnam. That's been a steady erosion of constitutional authority, granted to the President" (January 28, 2002).

10. See Bruce P. Montgomery, "Nixon's Ghost Haunts the Presidential Records Act: The Reagan and George W. Bush Administrations," *Presidential Studies Quarterly* 32:4 (2002): 789–809; Baker, "What Are They Hiding?," p. 14; Cannon, "For the Record," p. 31.

11. See *U.S. v. Nixon*, 418 U.S. 683 (1974); *Nixon v. Administrator of General Services*, 433 U.S. 425 (1977); *Public Citizen v. Burke*, 843 F.2d 1473 (1988); *Nixon v. Freeman* 670 F.2d346 (1982). The Bush administration relied selectively on the favorable parts of *U.S. v. Nixon* and *Nixon v. Administrator of General Services* and ignored the unfavorable rulings in *Nixon v. Freeman* and *Public Citizen v. Burke*. See also Montgomery, "Nixon's Ghost," 789–809; Scott Nelson, "Memorandum of Points and

Authorities in Support of Plaintiff's Motion for Summary Judgment in *AHA v. NARA*," 01–CV02447, filed February 8, 2002 (on file with author).

12. See Cannon, "For the Record," p. 31; Kutler, "Classified," p. 1; Baker, "What Are They Hiding?," p. 14; Wycliff, "Top Secret," p. 23.

13. Joan Hoff, Testimony at Hearings Regarding Executive Order 13233 and the Presidential Records Act, Subcommittee on Government Efficiency, Financial Management, and Intergovernmental Relations and the Committee on Government Reform, House of Representatives, 107th Congress, Second Session, April 11, 2002.

14. Michael Beschloss, "Knowing What Really Happened," *Presidential Studies Quarterly* 32:4 (2002): 642–46.

15. Ibid.

16. Robert Dallek, Testimony at Hearings Regarding Executive Order 13233 and the Presidential Records Act, Subcommittee on Government Efficiency, Financial Management, and Intergovernmental Relations and the Committee on Government Reform, House of Representatives, 107th Congress, Second Session, April 11, 2002.

17. See http://www.millercenter.virginia.edu/recordings.html (accessed June 10, 2003).

18. See http://www.whitehouse2001.org (accessed June 10, 2003).

19. See the NARA presidential library Web page at http://www.archives.gov/presidential_libraries/about/history.html.

20. *U.S. v. Nixon*, 418 U.S. 683 (1974).

21. See *Nixon v. Administrator of General Services*, 433 U.S. 425, 431–33 (1977).

22. 43 *Op. Atty. Gen.* No. 1 (1974), App. 220–230.

23. As quoted in *Nixon v. Administrator of General Services*, 433 U.S. 425, 431 (1977).

24. *Nixon v. Administrator of General Services*, 433 U.S. 425 (1977).

25. See 433 U.S. 425, Brennan, majority, notes 8 and 39.

26. *Nixon v. Freeman*, 670 F.2d 346 (1982).

27. Charles J. Cooper, Memorandum for Robert P. Bedell re: Nixon Papers and Regulations, Office of Legal Counsel, Department of Justice, February 18, 1986.

28. *Public Citizen v. Burke*, 843 F.2d 1473 (1988).

29. Executive Order 12667, *Public Papers of the President: Ronald Reagan*, January 16, 1989.

30. Presidential Records Act (P.L. 95–591) 44 U.S.C. 2201–2208, et seq. (1978).

31. See also Martha Joynt Kumar, "Executive Order 13233 Further Implementation of the Presidential Records Act," *Presidential Studies Quarterly* 32:1 (2002): 194–209.

32. EO 12667, 54 F.R. 3403, Section 1[g].

33. See Robert D. Putnam and Robert J. Spitzer, "American Political Science Association Response to Executive Order 13233," *Presidential Studies Quarterly* 32:1 (2002): 190–92.

34. See Nelson, "Memorandum," Montgomery, "Nixon's Ghost," pp. 789–809; Kumar, "Executive Order," pp. 194–209.

35. See Fleischer, White House Press Briefing, November 1, 2001; Alberto R. Gonzales, "Freedom, Openness, and Presidential Papers," *Washington Post*, December 20, 2001, p. A43.

36. Fleischer, White House Press Briefing, November 1, 2001.

37. Gonzales, "Freedom," p. 43.

38. Edward Whelan, Testimony at Hearings Regarding Executive Order 13233 and the Presidential Records Act, Subcommittee on Government Efficiency, Financial Management, and Intergovernmental Relations and the Committee on Government Reform, House of Representatives, 107th Congress, First Session, November 6, 2001.

39. See Fleischer, White House Press Briefing, November 1, 2001; Gonzales, "Freedom," p. 43.

40. See Scott Nelson, Testimony at Hearings Regarding Executive Order 13233 and the Presidential Records Act, Subcommittee on Government Efficiency, Financial Management, and Intergovernmental Relations and the Committee on Government Reform, House of Representatives, 107th Congress, First Session, November 6, 2001; Putnam and Spitzer, American Political Science, pp. 190–92; Kumar, "Executive Order," pp. 194–209; Stanley I. Kutler, Testimony at Hearings Regarding Executive Order 13233 and the Presidential Records Act, Subcommittee on Government Efficiency, Financial Management, and Intergovernmental Relations and the Committee on Government Reform, House of Representatives, 107th Congress, Second Session, April 11, 2002; Mark Rozell, Testimony at Hearings Regarding Executive Order 13233 and the Presidential Records Act, Subcommittee on Government Efficiency, Financial Management, and Intergovernmental Relations and the Committee on Government Reform, House of Representatives, 107th Congress, Second Session, April 24, 2002.

41. Quote accessed at www.citizen.org (accessed June 10, 2003).

42. Scott Nelson, Plaintiffs' Response to Defendants' "Notice with Respect to Processing of Records," *AHA et al. v. NARA et al.* (01CV02447[CKK]), April 29, 2003.

43. Kutler, "Classified," 1.

44. Scott Nelson, Plaintiffs' Motion to Alter or Amend the Judgment, *AHA et al. v. NARA et al.* (01–CV02447 [CKK]), March 29, 2004.

45. Sheryl Gay Stolberg and Felicia R. Lee, "Bush Nominee for Archivist Is Criticized for His Secrecy," *New York Times*, April 20, 2004, p. A14.

46. Society of American Archivists, "Statement on the Nomination of Allen Weinstein to Become Archivist of the United States," April 14, 2004, available at www.archivists.org/statements/weinstein.asp (accessed June 1, 2004).

Contributors

MATTHEW A. BAUM is Assistant Professor of Political Science and Communication Studies at the University of California, Los Angeles. His current research focuses on the domestic sources of foreign policy, including the influence of the mass media and public opinion on U.S. presidential decision making. He is the author of *Soft News Goes to War: Public Opinion and American Foreign Policy in the New Media Age*. His work has appeared in the *American Political Science Review*, the *American Journal of Political Science, International Studies Quarterly, Public Opinion Quarterly*, and *Comparative Political Studies*.

JEFFREY E. COHEN is Professor of Political Science at Fordham University. His book *Presidential Responsiveness and Public Policy Making: The Public and the Policies That Presidents Make* won the 1998 Richard E. Neustadt Award from the Presidency Research Group of the American Political Science Association. He has been published in numerous journals, including the *American Political Science Review*, the *American Journal of Political Science*, and the *Journal of Politics*.

WILLIAM CUNION is Assistant Professor of Political Science at Mount Union College in Alliance, Ohio. His teaching and research interests include the American presidency, voting behavior, and political psychology. His work has appeared in *White House Studies* and in several edited volumes on the presidency.

MICHAEL A. GENOVESE is Professor of Political Science and Loyola Chair of Leadership Studies and Director of the Institute for Leadership Studies at Loyola Marymount University. He has written fourteen books, including *The Paradoxes of the American Presidency* (with Thomas E. Cronin), *The Presidency and Domestic Policy* (with William W. Lammers), and *The Power of the American Presidency 1789–2000*, and he is the editor of *The Encyclopedia of the American Presidency*. He has won more than a dozen university and national teaching awards.

DORIS A. GRABER is Professor of Political Science at the University of Illinois, Chicago. She has written and edited numerous books and articles on the mass media and public opinion, including *Mass Media and American Politics*, *Media Power in Politics*, *Processing Politics: Learning from Television in the Internet Age*, and *The Power of Communication: Managing Information in Public Organizations*.

TIM GROELING is Assistant Professor of Communication Studies at the University of California, Los Angeles. His research interests include the presidency, Congress, political communication, parties, computer-mediated communication, new media, and collective action. His forthcoming book is *Breaking the Eleventh Commandment: Divided Partisan Communication and Unified Government*.

JOHN A. HAMMAN is Associate Professor of Political Science at Southern Illinois University, Carbondale. His research interests focus on the American presidency, elections, and public opinion. His work has appeared in such journals as *Presidential Studies Quarterly*, *American Politics Quarterly*, *Legislative Studies Quarterly*, and *Political Research Quarterly*.

LORI COX HAN is Professor of Political Science at Chapman University. She is the author of *Governing From Center Stage: White House Communication Strategies during the Television Age of Politics*. Her research interests include the American presidency, media and politics, and women and politics. Her work has appeared in *Presidential Studies Quarterly* and *White House Studies*.

DIANE J. HEITH is Associate Professor of Government and Politics at St. John's University. She is the author of several works on polling and the presidency, including *Polling to Govern: Public Opinion and Presidential Leadership*. Her work has appeared in *Public Opinion Quarterly*, *Presidential Studies Quarterly*, *Political Science Quarterly*, and *White House Studies*. Recent research includes an examination of gender, ethnicity, and media coverage. She also has coauthored an article on the health care debate and political advertising for *The Journal of Health Politics, Policy, and Law*.

SHARON E. JARVIS is Assistant Professor in the Department of Communication Studies and Associate Director of the Annette Strauss Institute for Civic

Participation at the University of Texas, Austin. She has published articles and chapters on partisan rhetoric, presidential discourse, and media and politics.

EMILY BALANOFF JONES is a doctoral student in the Department of Communication Studies at the University of Texas, Austin.

NANCY KASSOP is Professor of Political Science and International Relations at the State University of New York, New Paltz. Her research addresses issues of the presidency and law. Recent articles include "The War Power and Its Limits," in *Presidential Studies Quarterly*; "The Power to Make War," in Katy Harriger, ed., *Separation of Powers: Documents and Commentary*; "The White House Counsel's Office," coauthored with Karen Hult and MaryAnne Borrelli, in Martha J. Kumar and Terry Sullivan, eds., *The White House World: Transitions, Organization and Office Operations*; and the forthcoming "The View from the President," in Mark C. Miller and Jeb Barnes, eds., *Putting the Pieces Together: American Lawmaking from an Inter-Branch Perspective*.

MATTHEW J. KROV is a 2002 graduate of Austin College and plans to major in political science in graduate school.

JEREMY D. MAYER is Assistant Professor in the School of Public Policy at George Mason University. He is the author of *Running on Race: Racial Politics in Presidential Campaigns 1960–2000*, as well as the brief textbook *9–11: The Giant Awakens*. Mayer recently received the Rowman & Littlefield Award in Innovative Teaching for the American Political Science Association, the only national teaching award in political science. He is currently working on a textbook on media politics.

DANIEL E. PONDER is Associate Professor of Political Science at the University of Colorado, Colorado Springs. He is the author of *Good Advice: Information and Policy Making in the White House*. His work also has appeared in *Congress and the Presidency* and *PS: Political Science and Politics*.

MARK J. ROZELL is Professor in the School of Public Policy at George Mason University. He is the author of four books on media and American politics and is the editor of the text *Media Power, Media Politics*.

MARY E. STUCKEY holds a joint appointment as Professor of Communication and Political Science at Georgia State University. She works in the area of political communication, with a special emphasis on presidential rhetoric, the media, and how American Indians are treated in both. She is the author, editor, or coeditor of six books and over thirty articles and book chapters.

Index

ABC World News Tonight, 57, 58, 60, 61, 65, 229, 241–243
Abe Lincoln in Illinois, 15
Aberbach, Joel D., 204n
Abraham Lincoln, 15
Abraham Lincoln's Clemency, 15
Abshire, David, 254n
Advice and Consent, 16
Abrahams, Darcy, 70n
Adams, John Quincy, 232
Agenda setting, 141–142, 147
Air Force One, 13, 18, 20
Albert, Stuart, 47n
Aldrich, John, 32, 45n, 48n
Alger, Dean E., 250n
Allen, Mike, 222n, 276n
All the President's Men, 16
Alter, Jonathan, 249, 252n, 254n
Ambrose, Stephen, 234, 251n
American Historical Association, 272
The American President, 17
Americans with Disabilities Act (ADA), 186–187
Andrade, Lydia, 147, 159n
Antczak, Frederick J., 200n
Aronson, Elliot, 70n
Articles of Confederation, 116
Asante, Clement E., 250n, 253n
Asch, Soloman, 69n

Ashcroft, John, 257
Ashforth, Blake E., 46n, 47n
Attucks, Crispus, 193
Atwater, Lee, 79

Bai, Matt, 86n
Bailey, Thomas A., 250n
Baird, Zoe, 195
Baker, Russ, 276n, 277n
Balz, Dan, 86n
Banneker, Benjamin, 193
Barger, Harold, 26n
Barilleaux, Ryan J., 199n, 200n, 202n
Barrett, Jennifer, 137n
Barton, Clara, 194
Baum, Matthew, 6, 12, 50, 51, 56, 57, 64, 68n, 69n, 70n, 71n
Beavis and Butthead Do America, 18
Bedtime for Bonzo, 17
Behr, Roy L., 176n
Being There, 17
Benoit, William L., 46n, 47n
Bergen, Polly, 19
Berger, Peter L., 45n
Berke, Richard L., 240–241, 253n
Berman, Larry, 250n, 251n
Berman, William, 249n, 252n
Bernstein, Carl, 16
Beschloss, Michael, 258, 277n

The Best Man, 16
Bicaud, Ann-Marie, 26n
Bice, Amy A., 45n
Bickers, Kenneth N., 68n, 198n
Bingaman, Jeff, 272
bin Laden, Osama, 218, 220, 222, 242
Birk, Thomas S., 47n
Birnbaum, Jeffrey H., 200n, 204n
Black History Month, 194
Blakesley, Lance, 199n
Blaney, Joseph R., 47n
Blechman, Barry M., 56, 70n
Blessing, Tim H., 250n
Blum, Vanessa, 276n
Blumenthal, Sidney, 199n, 200n
Bond, Jon R., 110n
Boorstin, Daniel J., 232, 251n
Bostdorff, Denise M., 202n
Brace, Paul, 111n, 121, 136n, 141, 159n
Brinkley, Alan, 198n, 199n, 200n
Brinkley, Douglas, 235, 252n
Brock, Timothy C., 68n
Brody, Richard A., 49, 50, 51, 65, 68n, 69n, 70n, 71n, 72n, 158n
Brownlow, Louis, 119, 135n
Buchanan, James, 231
Bullock, Bob, 29
Bully pulpit, 2, 164
Bumiller, Elisabeth, 86n, 276n
Burgoon, Michael, 47n
Burke, Kenneth, 34, 46n
Burns, James MacGregor, 202n, 204n, 205n, 231, 250n
Bush, Barbara, 16
Bush Doctrine, 218
Bush, George H. W., 16, 21, 23, 31, 49, 50, 64, 84, 90, 94, 140, 166, 167, 169, 171, 173, 179, 181–187, 189, 190–191, 192–194, 200n, 201n, 202n, 203n, 204n, 211, 212, 214, 216–217, 228, 229, 231, 236, 238, 241, 242–244, 246, 247, 258, 270, 273, 274
Bush, George W., 3, 18, 29, 39, 40, 42, 49, 50, 64, 73, 44n, 76, 77–84, 125–126, 140, 207–222, 222n, 223n, 225, 226, 228–229, 238, 245, 248, 255–259, 266–267, 269–270, 273–274
Bush, Laura, 215

Caddell, Patrick, 79, 82
Cain, Becky, 135n
Campbell, Angus, 33, 46n
Campbell, Colin, 137n, 199n, 200n, 202n, 204n, 252n
Campbell, Karlyn Kohrs, 176n
Candidate-centered campaign, 30, 31–33, 43–44
Cannon, Carl M., 275n, 277n
Canon, David T., 199n, 205n
Cappella, Joseph N., 69n
Capra, Frank, 15, 16
Card, Andrew, 78, 79, 80
Carey, John M., 134n
Carlin, John, 272, 273
Carlson, Margaret, 215
Carmines, Edward G., 47n
Carter, Jimmy, ix, 20, 23, 82, 94, 99, 152, 167, 171, 173, 174, 180, 186, 207, 212, 228, 231, 235–236
Cavanos, Lauro, 194
CBS Evening News, 229, 242–243
Celler, Emanuel, 119
Chaiken, Shelly, 68n, 70n
Cheney, Dick, 214, 257, 258
Cheney, George, 46n
Christian Science Monitor, 238
Chubb, John E., 109n
Civil Rights Act (1990–1991), 185
Clines, Francis, 86n
Clinton, Bill, 5, 13, 16, 18, 23, 76, 79, 80, 81, 82, 84, 94, 95, 113–115, 121, 124, 127, 128–131, 133, 137n, 140, 143–144, 153, 157, 164, 165, 166, 167, 169, 171, 173, 174, 179, 181, 182, 183–184, 187–190, 191–192, 195–197, 198n, 200n, 202n, 203n, 204n, 205n, 209, 212, 214, 225, 226, 228–229, 231, 236–249, 250n, 257, 260
Clinton, Chelsea, 242
Clinton, Hillary, 23
Clinton, Roger, 237, 240

Clymer, Adam, 276n
CNN, 8, 24
Cohan, George M., 15
Cohen, Jeffrey E., 90, 107n, 109n, 110n, 112n, 139, 147, 148, 149, 159n, 160n, 162n, 176n, 251n
Cohen, Richard, 254n
Collier, Kenneth, 108n, 109n, 110n, 112n
Columbus, Christopher, 193
Communication strategy, 75, 139, 163, 245
Connaughton, Stacey, 33, 46n
Connors, Tom, 255
Constitutional Convention, 116
Converse, Philip E., 46n
Conversion (of public opinion), 142–143, 146, 156
Cooper, Charles J., 262–263, 271, 277n
Cornwell, Elmer E., Jr., ix, 75, 85n, 176n
Corwin, Edward S., 119, 135n
Covington, Cary R., 110n
Cowan, Alison Leigh, 275n
Coyne, James K., 135n
Crane, Edward H., 135n
Crano, William D., 68n, 70n
Crawford, Vincent P., 70n
Cronin, Thomas E., x, xii*n*, 21, 26n, 230, 250n
Cronkite, Walter, 234
Crothers, A. L., 176n
Crowdus, Gary, 26n
C-SPAN, 231
Cuban Missile Crisis, 24
Cunion, William, 74, 137n

Dallek, Robert, 198n, 259, 272, 277n
Daschle, Tom, 216
Dave, 17
Davis, Charles N., 275n
Davis, Richard, 210, 222n
Daynes, Byron W., 200n
Deaver, Michael, 21, 26n
DeFrank, Thomas M., 252n
Dempsey, Glenn R., 158n
Denton, Robert E., Jr., 198n, 202n

Dewey, Thomas, 39, 47n
Dick, 16
Dickey, D. A., 161n
DiClerico, Robert, 120, 136n
DiIulio, John Jr., 79
Dionisopoulos, George N., 198n
Dionne, E. J., 252n
Dole, Bob, 39
Douglas, Frederick, 194
Dowd, Matthew, 79
Dowd, Maureen, 87n, 240, 253
The Dramatic Life of Abraham Lincoln, 15
Drew, Elizabeth, 200n, 203n
Druckman, James N., 70n
Duffy, Michael, 199n, 200n, 201n, 202n, 203n
Dupuex, Georges, 46n
Durr, Robert H., 149, 160n, 161n
Dutton, Donald, 68n
Dutton, Jane E., 47n

Eagly, Alice H., 68n, 70n
Eakin, Emily, 275n
Edelman, Murray, 7, 10n, 27n, 30, 31, 44n, 45n
Edelman, Peter, 205n
Edwards, George E. III, x, 109n, 110n, 136n, 158n, 159n, 177n, 199n, 202n, 210, 222n
Ehrenhaus, Peter, 198n
Eisenhower, Dwight D., 29–30, 39, 44n, 47n, 113, 127, 128, 131–132, 133, 137n, 138n, 140, 167, 169, 170, 172, 234, 236
Eisinger, Robert M., 85n
Elder, Janet, 86n, 87n
Elder, Robert E., Jr., 250n
Electoral College, 8–9, 74, 77, 81, 82, 116–117
Ellis, Joseph, 208
Ellis, Richard J., 135n
Elsbach, Kimberly D., 46n
Emery, Edwin, 250n
Emery, Michael, 250n
Entman, Robert, x
Equal Rights Amendment, 186

Erickson, Paul D., 198n
Erikson, Robert S., 111n, 149, 160n, 161n
Eshbaugh-Soha, Matthew, 159n
Executive Order 12667, 264, 266, 268, 269
Executive Order 13233, 255–259, 260, 264, 266–274
Executive privilege, 265–266

Fail-Safe, 16
Family and Medical Leave Act, 130
Federal Farmer, 117
Federalist 71, 117
Feeding frenzy, 23
Feldman, Stanley, 159nFett, Patrick J., 110n
Fenno, Richard F. Jr., 162n
Fillmore, Millard, 231, 232
Fineman, Howard, 254n
Finer, Herman, 119, 135n
Fiorina, Morris P., 46n
First Daughter, 19
First Family, 19
First Kid, 19
First Lady, 18
Fishel, Jeff, 254n
Fishkin, James, 134n
Fiske, Susan T., 137n
Fleischer, Ari, 276n, 278n
Fleisher, Richard, 110n
Ford, Gerald, 3, 23, 39, 47n, 77, 167, 170, 172, 174, 228, 231, 235, 248, 252n, 261
Ford, Harrison, 13
Foster, Preston, 18
Framing, 6, 142, 143–144, 146, 156
Francis, Kay, 18
Freedom of Information Act (FOIA), 257, 259, 265, 270, 273
Freeman, Jo, 48n, 198n
Friedenberg, Robert, 44n, 47n
Friedrich, Robert J., 162n
Fromkin, Victoria, 45n
Frum, David, 214
Fuller, W. A., 161n
Fund, John H., 135n

Gabriel Over the White House, 15
Gays in the military, 187–189
Gaziano, Todd, 272
Gelderman, Carol, 176n, 198n, 200n
Geer, John G., 136n
Genovese, Michael A., 4, 10, 25n, 26n, 112n, 120, 136n, 199n, 200n, 230, 250n
Gerber, Robin, 202n
Gergen, David, 233, 251n, 252n
Gerson, Michael, 214, 217
Gilbert, Daniel T., 137n
Gingrich, Newt, 76
Gipp, George, 17
Giuliani, Rudy, 215
Gleason, Helen C., 199n
Godfrey, Paul C., 46n
Going public, 2, 22, 98, 163, 165, 210
Goldwater, Barry, 40, 47n
Goldzwig, Steven, 198n
Gonzales, Alberto, 264, 269, 278n
Goodgame, Dan, 199n, 200n, 201n, 202n, 203n
Goodwin, Doris Kearns, 162n
Goodwin, Richard N., 234, 252n
Gore, Al, 77, 124, 208, 245
Graber, Doris, ix, x, xii*n*, 10n, 175n, 254n
Graham, Bob, 272
Graham, Hugh, 255
Green, Joshua, 80, 86n
Greenberg, Stanley, 199n, 205n
Greene, David L., 223n
Greene, John Robert, 199n, 200n, 201n, 204n
Greenstein, Fred I., 211, 222n
Grier, Peter, 249n, 253n
Groeling, Tim, 6, 12, 50, 51, 52, 68n, 69n, 70n
Groseclose, Tim, 110n
Grossman, Michael B., x, 27n, 120, 136n, 158n, 253n
Guarding Tess, 19
Gunier, Lani, 195

Habitat for Humanity, 235
Hager, Gregory L., 109n

Hagstrom, Jerry, 198n
Hail to the Chief, 17, 25
Haldeman, H.R., 22
Hall, Mimi, 86n
Hall of Presidents, Disneyworld, 14
Hallin, Daniel, 27n
Hamilton, Alexander, 117, 135n
Hamman, John A., 139, 159n
Han, Lori Cox, 3, 75, 85n, 140, 175n, 226, 254n
Hannum, Kristen, 48n
Hansen, John Mark, 134n
Hard Copy, 20, 23
Hardesty, Robert L., 252n
Hargrove, Erwin C., 107n, 108n, 111n, 199n, 200n
Harris, John F., 82, 86n, 87n, 222n
Hart, Roderick P., 47n, 176n
Hearst, Patricia, 237
The Heart of Lincoln, 15
Heith, Diane J., 3, 73, 85n, 125, 136n, 137n
Hensen, Steven, 275n
Hepburn, Katherine, 15
Hess, Stephen, 86
Hecht, Marie B., 248, 254n
Hibbing, John R., 108n
The Highest Law, 15
Hill, Kim Quaile, 107n, 147, 159n
Hinckley, Barbara, 111n, 121, 136n, 141, 159n
Hirohito, Emperor, 218
Hobbs, Sam, 119
Hodge, Robert H., 45n
Hoff, Joan, 272, 277n
Hoffman, Dustin, 16
Hofmeister, Sallie, 254n
Holloway, Rachel L., 202n
Hollywood blacklist, 16
Holmes, Jack E., 250n
Holsti, Oli, 71n
Hoover, Herbert, 5, 164, 167, 169, 170, 172, 233, 260
Hopkins, Anthony, 13
Horn, Steve, 271, 272
Horton, Willie, ads, 31
Hughes, Karen, 78, 79, 217

Hurley, Norman L., 69n
Hussein, Saddam, 220

Independence Day, 13, 17–18, 20, 25
Initiative on Race, 195
Internet, 7, 8
Iran-Contra scandal, 13, 16, 94, 236, 241, 243, 244, 258
Iraq War, 6, 64, 65, 77, 80, 81, 82–83, 125–126, 140, 220–222
Issue installation, 143, 145, 156
Iyengar, Shanto, 176n

Jackson, Andrew, 19, 230
Jackson, Rachel, 19
Jacobs, Lawrence R., 76, 80, 85n, 136n
Jacobson, Gary C., 134n
Jamieson, Kathleen Hall, 31, 42, 45, 69n, 176n
Jarvis, Sharon, 7, 12, 45n, 47n
Jay, John, 135n
Jefferson, Thomas, 208, 230
Jennings, M. Kent, 46n
JFK, 17
Johnson, Andrew, 232
Johnson, Lyndon B., 16, 94, 100, 146, 151, 167, 169, 170, 172, 180, 234, 237
Johnson, Paul, 199n, 200n
Johnson, Victoria, 198n
Jones, Charles O., 107n, 108n, 110n, 200n, 202n, 204n, 248, 251n, 254n
Jones, Emily Balanoff, 7, 12
Jordan, Donald L., 68n
Joyner, James H., 68n

Kalb, Bernard, 69n
Kamber, Victor, 135n
Kaplan, Robin, 32, 41
Kaplan, Stephen S., 70n
Kassop, Nancy, 226
Keating, Kenneth, 119
Kenney, Patrick J., 250n
Kernell, Samuel, x, 10n, 22, 27n, 68n, 69n, 108n, 110n, 111n, 158n, 175n, 176n, 177n, 209, 222n

Kennedy, John F., 3, 4, 16, 20, 23, 24, 75, 122, 164, 180, 208, 210, 211, 233, 234
Kerry, John, 214
Kessel, John H., 109n, 110n, 136n
Kiefer, Francine, 276n
Kilgore, Harley, 118
King, Gary, 111n, 136n
King, Martin Luther, Jr., 196
Kinney, Rhonda, 110n
Kisses For My President, 19
Klinkner, Phillip A., 201n
The Knute Rockne Story, 17
Koenig, Louis W., 119, 135n
Koeske, Gary F., 68n, 70n
Kollar-Kotelly, Colleen, 272
Kolodony, Robin, 45n, 46n, 48n, 56
Korean War, 121
Kornblut, Anne, 86n
Krassa, Michael, 159n
Krehbiel, Keith, 101, 110n, 111n
Kress, Gunther K., 45n
Krov, Matthew J., 226
Krutz, Glen S., 110n
Kuklinski, James H., 69n
Kumar, Martha Joynt, x, 27n, 120, 136n, 158n, 222n, 253, 277n, 278n
Kurtz, Howard, 27n, 69n
Kutler, Stanley I, 272, 275n, 278n

Lame duck president, 74, 114–115, 120
Lammers, William W., 163, 166, 169, 174, 175, 175n, 176n, 177n, 199n, 200n
LaMontagne, Margaret, 79
Lardner, George, Jr., 222n, 276n
Larry King Live, 20
Lawrence, Adam B., 147, 159n, 160n
Lee, Felicia R., 278n
Leham, Chris, 26n
Leno, Jay, 209, 238
Letterman, David, 238
Leuchtenburg, William E., 251n
Levine, Lawrence, 26n
Levitt, Steven D., 110n
Levy, Jack S., 72n
Lewinsky, Monica, 238, 244, 248

Lian, Bradley, 68n, 69n
Library of Congress, 260
Liebovich, Louis, 252n
The Life of Abraham Lincoln, 15
Life Magazine, 230
Light, Paul C., 107n, 110n, 111n, 120, 127, 133, 134n, 136n, 137n, 138n
Lincoln, Abraham, 4, 25, 230, 231
The Lincoln Cycle, 15
Lincoln in the White House, 15
Lincoln the Lover, 15
Lincoln's Gettysburg Address, 15
Lincoln's Thanksgiving Story, 15
Lindsey, Lawrence B., 79
Lindzey, Gardner, 137n
Logan, Angela, 45n
Long, Samuel, 68n
Lott, Trent, 197
Lowi, Theodore, x, 106, 112n, 136n, 176n
Lucas, Scott, 118
Lucas, Steven E., 137n
Luckman, Thomas, 45n
Luhan, Manuel, 194
Lupia, Arthur, 68n

MacKuen, Michael B., 110n, 111n, 149, 160n, 161n
MacLaine, Shirley, 19
Madison, Dolly, 19
Madison, James, 135n
Mael, Fred, 46n
Magnificent Doll, 19
Maher, Bill, 238
Maisel, L. Sandy, 32, 45n
Maltese, John Anthony, 26n, 158n, 175n
The Man, 26
The Manchurian Candidate, 16
Manoff, Robert Karl, 69n
Maranell, Gary M., 250n
Marquis, Christi, 240
Mars Attack, 18
Mason, George, 117
Matalin, Mary, 79
Mayer, Jeremy D., 140, 223n
Mayhew, David, 101, 110n, 111n

Index 289

McAllister, Bill, 86n
McCarthyism, 16
McCombs, Maxwell, 47n
McCubbins, Mathew D., 32, 45n, 68n
McCullough, David, 251n
McDaniel, Ann, 252n
McDougal, Susan, 237
McIver, John P., 47n
McMurray, Fred, 19
McPhee, Robert D., 46n
McWilliams, Wilson Carey, 85n
Media, 2, 20–21, 23–24, 51–53, 139, 155, 163, 165, 167, 210, 225, 228–229, 230, 238–243
Medicare, 114, 115, 133, 241
Mervin, David, 199n
Meyer, Davis S., 198n
Micheletti, Patrick, 48n
Milbank, Dana, 85n, 86n
Milkis, Sidney, M., 119, 135n
Miller, Arthur, 27n
Miller, Warren E., 46n
Miroff, Bruce, 26n
Moe, Terry M., 109n
Moen, Matthew C., 199n
Mondak, Jeffrey J, 158n
Mondale, Walter, 115
Montgomery, Bruce P., 276n, 278n
Moore, Mark P., 47n
Morgan, Clifton T., 68n
Morganthau, Tom, 252n
Morris, Richard, 79, 82, 198n
Morrison, Toni, 197
Mount Rushmore, 14
Mouw, Calvin, 110n
MTV, 24
Mudd, Roger, 232, 251n
Mueller, John E., 56, 68n, 70n, 96, 109n, 111n
Mullins, Kerry, 199n
Murphy, Arthur B., 250n
Murphy, John M., 251n
Murray, Robert K., 250n

Nagourney, Adam, 86n, 240, 253n
Naked Gun 2 1/2: The Smell of Fear, 16
Nathan, Richard, 109n

National Archives and Records Administration (NARA), 260, 261–262, 273
National identity, 179
National Service Program, 191
NBC Nightly News, 229, 242–243
Neal, Steven, 250n
Nelson, Anna, 272
Nelson, Candice J., 45n
Nelson, Michael, 26n, 107n, 108n, 111n, 119, 135n, 136n, 250n
Nelson, Scott, 270, 272, 276n, 278n
Neustadt, Richard, x, 2, 10n, 107n, 134n, 135n, 164, 176, 222n, 230, 250n, 254n
Newhart, Bob, 19
News media. *See* media
Newsweek, 125, 248
New York Stock Exchange, 215
New York Times, 215, 229, 238, 239–241, 246–247
New York Times Magazine, 231
Nie, Norman H., 46n
Niemi, Richard G., 46n, 134n
Nixon, Richard M., 14, 16, 23, 39, 47n, 73, 75, 76, 79, 93, 94, 120, 122, 127, 167, 170, 172, 180, 211, 231, 232, 234–235, 237, 249, 258, 260–261, 263, 264, 271
Nixon, 13, 16, 17
Nixon v. Administrator of General Services (1977), 261, 262, 264, 265, 267, 271
Nixon v. Freeman (1982), 262, 271
Norsworthy, L. Alexander, 199n
North American Free Trade Agreement (NAFTA), 124–125
North, Oliver, 241
Northrup, Alana, x, xii*n*

O'Brien, Conan, 238
O'Brien, David M., 204n
Office of Legal Counsel, 262, 270
Office of Political Affairs, 78–79
Office of Public Liaison, 79
Office of Strategic Initiatives, 79, 82
Of Human Hearts, 15
Oneal, John R., 56, 68n, 69n, 70n

Operation Desert Storm (Persian Gulf War), 49, 64, 65, 94, 194
Orman, John, 26n
Ornstein, Norman, 26n, 82
Ose, Doug, 272
Ostrom, Charles W., 108n, 109n, 111n, 141, 159n
Ostrom, Thomas M., 68n

Page, Benjamin I., 68n, 158n
Paine, Thomas, 194
Paletz, David L., x
Palmer, Kenneth T., 199n
Parker, Suzanne L., 68n
Parks, Rosa, 194
Party identification, 33–34, 43
Party labels, 36–38
Pastor, Gregory S., 45n
Pataki, George, 215
Patterson, Kelly D., 45n
Patterson, Thomas E., 32, 45n, 69n
Peake, Jeffrey S., 107n
Pearl Harbor (Japanese attack on, 1941), 217–219
Perloff, Richard M., 137n
Permanent (or perpetual) campaign, 75–76, 84, 165, 174
Perot, H. Ross, 124
Peterson, Mark, 97, 105, 109n, 110n, 112n, 177n
Peterson, Paul E., 109n
Petrocik, John, 46n
Petty, Richard E., 68n, 137n
Pfau, Michael, 47n
Pfiffner, James P., 136n, 254
The Phantom President, 15
Pierce, Franklin, 231
Pika, Joseph A., 136n
Pilon, Roger, 135n
Pindyck, Robert S., 161n
Pipkin, Elizabeth, 45n
Poindexter, John, 241
Points of Light Program, 191
Polk, James, 118
Polling, 4–5, 73, 75–77, 78–84, 92, 131
Pomper, Gerald M., 41, 48n, 85n, 252n
Ponder, Daniel E., 74

Poole, Keith, 111n, 146, 159n
Popkin, Samuel, 46n
Postman, Neil, 8, 10n
Powell, Colin, 194, 258, 274
Powell, Lynda W., 134n
Powell, Richard J., 159n
President as pop icon, 11–12, 14, 19–21
The President Vanishes, 15
Presidential acceptance addresses, 7, 12, 31, 35–36
Presidential approval, 49–50, 74, 90–91, 93–94, 102, 106, 125, 141, 153, 209, 216, 228, 243
Presidential communication, 5–6, 9
Presidential films, 4, 15–18
Presidential honeymoon, 245–246
Presidential image, 24
Presidential inaugural, 165, 210, 227, 228
Presidential leadership, 24, 81, 115, 141–143, 154, 157, 167
Presidential legacies, 226, 227, 228–238, 248–249, 256
Presidential leverage, 89–97, 102–107
Presidential libraries, 226, 227, 231
Presidential personality, 24
Presidential Oral History Project (Miller Center, University of Virginia), 259
Presidential public activities, 101, 139, 140, 164, 165, 169–175
Presidential rankings (presidential "greatness"), 230
Presidential Recordings and Materials Preservation Act (PRMPA), 259, 261–264, 271
Presidential Records Act (PRA) of 1978, 257, 259, 262, 264–265, 267, 269, 271, 274
Presidential rhetoric, 78, 80–81, 114, 123, 132, 139, 140, 142, 147, 149, 152, 165, 179, 207–222
Presidential transition, 165
The President's Lady, 19
Press conferences, 166, 210
Primary Colors, 18
Priming, 6, 143, 144–145, 146, 156

PT 109, 16
Public agenda, 89, 98–99, 104, 139, 142, 145, 165, 166
Public Citizen, 272
Public Citizen v. Burke, 263, 269, 271
Public leadership, 122, 128, 131, 132, 139, 140
Public opinion, 4, 9, 73, 78–84, 115, 122, 141–143, 145, 147–148, 151–152, 220, 221
Public Papers of the Presidents of the United States, 168
Pullman, Bill, 13
Purdum, Todd, 87n
Putnam, Robert D., 277n, 278n
Putney Swope, 17

Quirk, Paul J., 137n

Ragsdale, Lyn, 108n, 111n, 126, 137n, 141, 158n, 167, 176n, 177n
Rally events, 53–54, 57, 63
Rally 'round the flag phenomenon, 12, 53, 83
Rapoport, Ronald B., 45n
Ray, Robert, 248
Reagan, Ronald, ix, 4, 17, 20, 21–22, 23, 39, 47n, 83, 94, 113, 115, 120, 127, 128, 132–133, 151, 152, 164, 166, 167, 169, 171, 173, 180–181, 182, 190, 208, 210, 211, 213, 218, 228, 229, 231, 232, 235, 236, 241, 242–244, 249, 258, 259, 262, 264, 265, 266, 270, 273, 274
Redford, Robert, 16
Reeves, Richard, 272
Regan, Donald, 132–133, 138n
Renshon, Stanley, 201n, 202n, 204n, 253n
Republican National Committee, 79
Reynolds, Amy, 47n
Rhetorical presidency, 164, 165
Rice, Condoleezza, 79
Rice, Tom W., 250n
Rich, Marc, 228, 237, 238, 240, 244, 246, 249
The Right Stuff, 16

Rivers, Douglas, 109n, 110n, 112n
Robinson, Michael, 26n, 27n
Rockman, Bert A., 109n, 131, 136n, 137n, 199n, 200n, 252n
Rodham, Hugh, 238, 240
Rodman, Robert, 45n
Romano, Lois, 222n
Roosevelt, Franklin D., 3, 4, 9, 16, 20, 23, 75, 118, 120, 121, 125, 127, 157, 166, 167, 169, 170, 172, 184, 208, 211, 216, 217–219, 230, 232, 233, 260
Roosevelt, Theodore, 164, 232, 237
Rose, Nancy, 109n, 110n, 112n
Rose, Richard, 175n, 181, 199n
Rosen, Corey M., 158n
Rosenblatt, Robert A., 252n
Rosenthal, Howard, 111n, 146, 159n
Rossiter, Clinton, 119, 135n
Rourke, Frances E., 120, 136n
Rove, Karl, 78–79, 82, 84
Rozell, Mark J., 140, 272, 278
Rubenfeld, Daniel L., 161n

Sabato, Larry, 23, 27n, 69n
Saks, Alan M., 46nSchudson, Michael, 30, 42, 44n
Sampson, Arthur F., 260
Samuelson, Robert, 113, 114, 133, 133n, 134n
Sapiro, Virginia, 199n, 205n
Saturday Night Live, 115, 209
Savage, David G., 275n
Saxbe, William, 260
Scavo, Carmine, 200n
Scheele, Henry Z., 47n
Schenker, Alan Evan, 251n
Schier, Steven E., 252n
Schlesinger, Arthur, Jr., 230–231, 234, 250n
Schlesinger, Arthur, Sr., 230, 250n
Schudson, Michael, 30, 42, 44n, 69n
Schwarzenegger, Arnold, 20
Scott, Craig R., 46n
Secret Honor, 16
September 11, 2001, 8, 77, 80, 83, 140, 208, 214, 216, 217–222

Shane, Peter, 272
Shapiro, Catherine R., 50, 51, 68n, 70n, 158n
Shapiro, Robert Y., 76, 80, 85n, 136n, 158n
Shaw, Daron, 47n
Shaw, George Bernard, 25
Sheen, Martin, 18
Sheldon, Winthrop Dudley, 227, 249n
Shenkman, Rick, 222n
Shull, Steven A., 158n, 201n
Sigal, Leon V., 69n
Sigelman, Carol K., 158n
Sigelman, Lee, 158n, 176n
Simendinger, Alexis, 85n
Simon, Dennis M., 108n, 109n, 111n, 141, 159n
Simons, Herbert, 198n
Simonton, Dean Keith, 231, 250n
60 Minutes, 23
Skowronek, Stephen, 91–92, 93, 107n, 108n, 111n, 112n, 199n, 230, 250n
Small, Melvin, 235, 252n
Smith, Carolyn, 176n
Smith, Hedrick, 20–21, 22, 26n
Smith, Richard Norton, 251n, 252n
Smith, Roger A., 201n
Sniderman, Paul M., 69n
Snyder, James M., 110n
Sobel, Joel, 70n
Social Security, 80, 114, 115, 133
Somalia, 24, 57
Sorenson, Georgia J., 202n, 204n, 205n
Sorkin, Aaron, 18
Spangler, Earl, 135n
Spence, A. Michael, 70n
Spitzer, Robert J., 277n, 278n
Stallone, Sylvester, 20
Stanley, Harold W., 205n
State of the Union, 15–16
State of the Union Address, 90, 97, 98–99, 102, 104, 114, 130, 147, 148, 150, 152, 153, 174, 213
Star Wars, 17
St. Clair, Gilbert, 158n
Stein, Robert M., 198n
Stem cell research, 213

Stiff, James B., 137n
Stimson, James A., 47n, 101, 111n, 146, 149, 159n, 160n, 161n
Stockman, David A., 198n
Stokes, Donald E., 46n
Stolberg, Sheryl Gay, 278n
Stone, Oliver, 17
Stone, Walter J., 45n
Stuckey, Mary E., 140, 176n, 198n, 199n, 200n, 202n, 203n, 251n
Sullivan, Louis, 194
Sullivan, Terry, 109n, 110n
Sunrise at Campobello, 16
Suskind, Ron, 222n
Sussman, Glen, 200n
Suzuki, Koichi, 199n
Sweany, Brian D., 252n

Taft, William Howard, 210, 231
Tajfel, Henri, 46n
Talk radio, 24–25
Tarrow, Sydney, 198n
Tax Reform Amendment (1986), 133
Tenpas, Kathryn Dunn, 79, 86n
Term limits, 115–116
Tetlock, Phillip, 48n, 69n
Theiss-Morse, Elizabeth, 108n
Thomas, Dan, 158n
Thomas, Norman C., 136n, 158n
Thompson, Robert J., 200n
Thurber, James A., 45n, 110n
Thurmond, Strom, 197
Tompkins, Phillip K., 46n
Topping, Keith, 26n
Tracy, Spencer, 15
Trent, Judith, 44n, 47n
Truman, Harry S., 121, 125, 127, 166, 167, 170, 172, 229, 233–234
Tuchman, Gaye, 69n
Tulis, Jeffrey, x, 22, 27n, 122, 136n, 176n
Turley, Jonathan, 272
Tuskegee Airmen, 194
Tutwiler, Margaret, 79
Twenty-second amendment, 74, 113–115, 118–122, 127–131, 133
Tyler, John, 231

United Nations, 126, 216
USA Today, 24
U.S. v. Nixon (1974), 260, 261, 267, 268, 271

Van Buren, Martin, 231, 232
van Lohuizen, Jan, 79, 80
Verba, Sidney, 46n
Vietnam War, 6, 13, 14, 15, 16, 17, 23, 100, 180, 234
The Virgin President, 17
Virginia Ratifying Convention, 117
Vrana, Debora, 252n

Wag the Dog, 13, 18
Walch, Timothy, 251n, 252n
Waldman, Michael, 202n, 204n
Wallace, Mike, 23
Wall Street Journal, 231
Walsh, Kenneth T., 27n, 252n
Walster, Elaine, 70n
Washington, George, 166, 211, 230
Washington Post, 248, 259
Waterman, Richard, 112n, 158n
Watergate, 4, 13, 16, 17, 23, 94, 120, 127, 232, 235, 261
Watt, James, 194
Wattenberg, Martin, 31–31, 41, 44n, 45n, 46n, 47n, 48n
Wayne, Stephen J., 136n
Weekly radio addresses, 127, 128, 130, 228
Webster, Scott W., 202n
Wegener, Duane, 137n
Weinberger, Casper, 236, 244
Weinraub, Bernard, 254n

Weinstein, Allen, 273
Welch, Susan, 134n
The West Wing, 18
Whelen, M. Edward III, 270, 272, 278
Whetten, David A., 46n
Whillock, Rita K., 202n
White, John Kenneth, 199n, 202n, 205n
Whitewater, 244, 248
Wild in the Streets, 17
Wildavsky, Aaron, 199n
Will, George F., 135n
Willis, George L., 135n
Willis, Paul G., 135n
Wills, Gary, 27n
Wilson, Graham K., 202n, 204n
Wilson, Woodrow, 221, 230
Winkle, John W., 200n, 202n
Wirthlin, Richard, 79
The Wizard of Oz, 20
Wlezien, Christopher, 160n
Wolff, Michael, 26n
Wood, Dan B., 107n
Wood, Wendy, 68n, 70n
Woodward, Bob, 16, 198n, 251n
World Trade Center, 215, 218
World Trade Organization, 115
Wright Brothers, 194
Wright, Robert, 158n
Wrighton, J. Mark, 110n
Wycliff, Don, 275n, 277n

Young Mr. Lincoln, 15

Zaller, John, 69n, 70n, 159n, 161n
Zarefsky, David, 201n
Zinn, Howard, 198n